T0340232

Economics and Literature

Since the Middle Ages, literature has portrayed the economic world in poetry, drama, stories and novels. The complexity of human realities highlights crucial aspects of the economy. The nexus linking characters to their economic environment is central in a new genre, the "economic novel", that puts forth economic choices and events to narrate social behaviour, individual desires and even non-economic decisions. For many authors, literary narration also offers a means to express critical viewpoints about economic development, for example in regards to its ecological or social ramifications.

Conflicts of economic interest have social, political and moral causes and consequences. This book shows how economic and literary texts deal with similar subjects, and explores the ways in which economic ideas and metaphors shape literary texts, focusing on the analogies between economic theories and narrative structure in literature and drama. This volume also suggests that connecting literature and economics can help us find a common language to voice new, critical perspectives on crises and social change.

Written by an impressive array of experts in their fields, *Economics and Literature* is an important read for those who study history of economic thought, economic theory and philosophy, as well as literary and critical theory.

Çınla Akdere is Lecturer of History of Economic Thought at the Department of Economics, Middle East Technical University, Ankara, Turkey and Associated Member of PHARE (Philosophie, Histoire et Analyse des Représentations Economiques) research center, Université Paris I Panthéon-Sorbonne, Paris, France.

Christine Baron is Professor at the Université de Poitiers, Poitiers, France and Member of the FoReLL (Formes et Représentations en Linguistique et Littérature) research center, Université de Poitiers, Poitiers, France.

Routledge Studies in the History of Economics

For a full list of titles in this series, please visit www.routledge.com/series/SE0341

Economics and Literature

A Comparative and
Interdisciplinary Approach

**Edited by Çınla Akdere
and Christine Baron**

Routledge
Taylor & Francis Group

LONDON AND NEW YORK

First published 2018 by Routledge

2 Park Square, Milton Park, Abingdon, Oxfordshire OX14 4RN

52 Vanderbilt Avenue, New York, NY 10017

Routledge is an imprint of the Taylor & Francis Group, an informa business

First issued in paperback 2019

British Library Cataloguing-in-Publication Data
A catalogue record for this book is available from the British Library

Library of Congress Cataloging-in-Publication Data
Names: Akdere, Cinla, editor. | Baron, Christine, 1960– editor.
Title: Economics and literature : a comparative and interdisciplinary
    approach / edited by Cinla Akdere and Christine Baron.
Description: Abingdon, Oxon ; New York, NY : Routledge, 2018. |
    Includes index.
Identifiers: LCCN 2017027050 | ISBN 9781138294356 (hardback) |
    ISBN 9781315231617 (ebook)
Subjects: LCSH: Economics and literature.
Classification: LCC PN51 .E246 2018 | DDC 809/.933553—dc23
LC record available at https://lccn.loc.gov/2017027050

ISBN: 978-1-138-29435-6 (hbk)
ISBN: 978-0-367-88620-2 (pbk)

Typeset in Times New Roman
by Apex CoVantage, LLC

Contents

PART II

**Economic ideas and metaphors in literature:
An interdisciplinary approach**

PART III

**Facing change: Reflections of economic development
and crises in historical and literary texts**

Illustrations

Figures

Table

Contributors

Çınla Akdere is Lecturer of History of Economic Thought at the Department of Economics, Middle East Technical University, Ankara, Turkey and Associated Member of PHARE (Philosophie, Histoire et Analyse des Représentations Economiques) research center, Université Paris I Panthéon-Sorbonne, Paris, France.

Selin Seçil Akın is Research Assistant at the Ankara University, Ankara, Turkey and PhD candidate at the University of Massachusetts, Amherst, USA.

Christine Baron is Professor at the Université de Poitiers, Poitiers, France and Member of the FoReLL (Formes et Représentations en Linguistique et Littérature) research center, Université de Poitiers, Poitiers, France.

Yves Citton is Professor at the Université Paris 8 Vincennes-Saint Denis, France.

Jean-Joseph Goux is Professor at Rice University, Houston, USA.

Bruna Ingrao is Professor at the Università degli Studi di Roma, La Sapienza, Roma, Italy.

Gilles Jacoud is Professor at the University Jean Monnet, Saint-Etienne, France.

Laura E.B. Key is University Teacher at University of Liverpool, Liverpool, United Kingdom.

Esra Elif Nartok is PhD candidate and graduate teaching assistant at the University of Manchester, Manchester, United Kingdom.

Eyüp Özveren is Professor at the Middle East Technical University, Ankara, Turkey.

Claire Pignol is Associate Professor at the Université Paris I Panthéon-Sorbonne, Paris, France and Member of PHARE (Philosophie, Histoire et Analyse des Représentations Economiques) research center, Université Paris I Panthéon-Sorbonne, Paris, France.

Martial Poirson is Professor at the Université Paris 8-Vincennes-Saint Denis, Saint Denis, France, at New York University, New York, USA and member of "Scènes du monde, création, savoirs critiques" (E.A. 1573).

Alfonso Sanchez is Professor at the Universidad de Zaragoza, Zaragoza, Spain.

Işıl Şirin Selçuk is Research Assistant at the Abant İzzet Baysal Üniversitesi, Bolu, Turkey.

Ali Serdar is Associate Professor at the Özyeğin University, Istanbul, Turkey.

Nathalie Sigot is Professor at the Université Paris I Panthéon-Sorbonne, Paris, France and Member of PHARE (Philosophie, Histoire et Analyse des Représentations Economiques) research center, Université Paris I Panthéon-Sorbonne, Paris, France.

Reyhan Tutumlu Serdar is Lecturer at the Sabancı University, Istanbul, Turkey.

Acknowledgement

Most of the chapters are based on papers originally presented at the international conference "Literary Representations and Economic Theories: Comparative Studies" hosted by the PHARE (Philisophie, Histoire et Analyse des Représentations Economiques) research centre at the Paris 1 Panthéon-Sorbonne University in Paris in May 2013. The conference, organized in collaboration with the Department of Economics of the Middle East Technical University (METU) and the Formes et Représentations en Linguistique et Littérature (FoReLL) research centre at Poitiers University, was financially supported by the Department of Economics of the Middle East Technical University (METU),[1] the Charles Gide Association for the Study of Economic Thought (ACGEPE) and the Regional Council of Île-de-France. We are grateful to all these institutions for supporting this venture, where this book was created.

We thank Claire Heffron for helping with proofreading and Basak Balkan with translation. Claire Pignol, contributor to the field of the interdisciplinarity between economics and literature and one of the initiators of this book project, cooperated in the realization of this work. We thank her for her support and advice. Our special thanks go to Bruna Ingrao, a leading figure who brought economics, literature and art together in her researches. Her work guided us and encouraged us to develop the project. Her contribution to the book cannot be expressed by words because she was, first of all, our inspiration. We would like to thank her with all our hearts for the time she devoted to the careful treatment of all parts of the book. We thank her especially for being with us with patience and affection throughout the process.

Note

1 Scientific projects' codes supported financially by METU are BAP-08-11-2011-124 and BAP-08-11-2011-124.

1 Introduction and overview

*Çinla Akdere, Christine Baron
and Bruna Ingrao*

Money, trade, exchanges; goods, consumption, necessities and luxuries; hard work or rent, investment or speculation, poverty and wealth . . . Since the Middle Ages, literature has portrayed the economic world, in poetry, drama, stories, novels. The diffusion of novels since the 18th century, and their success in the 19th and 20th centuries, offered the opportunity for new plots around economic events, choices or conflicts. Characters could move on new sceneries: polluted manufacturing cities, factories, the obscure financial world or the volatile stock exchange. They could go bankrupt in failed speculations or incurring debt; or they could gain fortunes and status in the market economy, making money by hard work or by investment. They could suffer the conflicts of insatiable desires in the new world of multiplied consumer goods. They could be oppressed by exploitation or unemployment. They had to face the need for money to earn their life. In so many novels, characters meet their destiny in life paths, where they have to face economic choices, and confront the turbulent world of markets.

In his correspondence, Friedrich Engels said that one could learn much more about the economy by reading Balzac than by reading the work of 19th-century economists. He wrote:

> He describes how the last remnants of this, to him, model society gradually succumbed before the intrusion of the vulgar monied upstart, or were corrupted by him; how the grand dame whose conjugal infidelities were but a mode of asserting herself in perfect accordance with the way she had been disposed of in marriage, gave way to the bourgeoise, who horned her husband for cash or cashmere; and around this central picture he groups a complete history of French Society from which, even in economic details (for instance the rearrangement of real and personal property after the Revolution) I have learned more than from all the professed historians, economists, and statisticians of the period together.
>
> (Engels 1888)[1]

In his book, *Le Capital au XXIe Siecle* (*Capital in the Twenty-First Century*), Thomas Piketty effectively took Engels at his word, and discussed how Balzac's novels, or those of other novelists like Jane Austen, Lev Tolstoy or Henry

James, provide trustworthy information on the distribution of wealth and the standards of life for various social ranks. He quoted a few novels to offer his readers a better understanding of economic inequalities in wealth and incomes, transactions on landed property, inheritance, properties and rents (e.g. Piketty 2014: 174 ff. 377 ff., 381, 653 ff., 658). Breaking away from a strictly European focus, Piketty mentioned literary texts by the Egyptian writer Naguib Mahfouz and the Turkish writer Orhan Pamuk, to underline how reference monetary values mould the perception by characters of opportunities and standard of lives, or on the contrary how they become irrelevant in societies deeply affected by monetary instability.

In the more immediate and straightforward reading of the encounter between literature and economics, literary texts provide pictures of economic life, which may be read as testimony, or even evidence, on the historical societies they portray; or, with a more sophisticated eye and in critical distance, they may be deciphered as reflecting the values, opinions and conflicts about economic life which writers perceive in contemporary societies and bring to light in their writings. Feelings and thoughts, as embodied in the stories writers tell, give life to the meditations, conversations or controversies by past or contemporary characters about how the hard world of markets intrudes into the deeper, wider world of human destinies, asking for choices, offering opportunities, or imposing heavy constraints. Money and markets, speculation or bankruptcy, hard work, poverty or wealth, when looked at from a broader, cultural perspective, may be recognized as being part of wider metaphors for human parables and existential conflicts or crises. The literary text offers all of these perspectives to its readers, and literary studies have addressed them all in ample critical reflection dealing with economic life and literature.

It has been suggested that a new literary genre stemmed from writers devoting their attention to economic phenomena, the "economic novel", whose main plot centres on economic events. The nexus linking characters to their economic environment is central in these novels, which put forth economic choices and events to narrate social behaviour and individual desires, exploring even non-economic decisions in the market context. "Economic" novels, which simultaneously stand as literary works and contain references to economic concepts, or even to specialized economic information, have increasingly attracted the attention of scholars in what is now a well-developed subfield of literary criticism explicitly devoted to the economic aspects of literary narration. In the narratives of contemporary societies, economic concepts such as wealth, money, finance, investment, inflation and profits are recurring more and more in literary texts; the way writers portray their characters, and the complexity of human realities, focuses on crucial aspects of the economy.

Since the 19th century, to many authors literary narration offered a way to express critical viewpoints about the social atmosphere in market economies, or the deep social change due to economic development (e.g. as regards negative externalities, or the impact on custom and social structure). The reversal of the balance between the status established by ancestry and the status acquired by fortune, even brutally, by making money in deceitful speculative affairs, is a recurring, disturbing theme in 19th-century literature. The world of the stock exchange, with its speculative business, offers powerful metaphors for the rise and fall of ambitious social climbers, and the parallel decline, or the difficult resilience, of people in social classes whose lives are rooted in agriculture and landed property. Migration, unemployment, the hardness of working conditions, living in poverty and the sufferings during the Great Depression have been the subjects of many literary narrations, side by side with speculation, the banking world, or even competition among multinational firms. Since the beginning of the 21st century, and especially after 2006, in contemporary literature appeared new references to the economic crisis and its financial disasters, or to workers' welfare and the organization of work. New literary movements or single writers protesting against neoliberalism have appeared.[2]

To economists, literary texts provided a variety of suggestions, the most well known of which entered into the history of economic thought with the despising expression of "18th century robinsonades" used by Marx in the pages of his unfinished *Grundrisse* (*Outlines of the Critique of Political Economy*). The novel *Robinson Crusoe* (1719), at the origin of the "robinsonade" literary genre, fascinated economists of various generations. In the 19th century, the lost Robinson, who tried to survive on an island cut off from the rest of the world, provided the paradigm of the *homo oeconomicus* enjoying the virtues of autarchy, and exploring production possibilities, being both producer and consumer. His fictional encounter with Friday offered to Francis Ysidro Edgeworth the metaphor to explore the voluntary barter between two traders in bilateral monopoly, in his book *Mathematical Psychics* published in 1881. In economics, the island metaphor has a long life. It appeared in the unfinished text *Valeurs et monnaie* (*Value and Money*) written by Turgot around 1769, where two savages meet on a desert island and trade fish against furs. In the 1970s, it came back as a metaphor for imperfect information in local economies, in the macro models built by Edmund Phelps and Robert Lucas. In a book published in 1928, Oscar Morgenstern illustrated the chain of conjectures about what a rival will choose by quoting one of the Sherlock Holmes stories, where the detective, pursues his enemy Moriarty, and has to guess what his next moves will be, while in turn the criminal is trying to anticipate what Sherlock will guess and choose. Strategic conjectures about other agents' rational choices are at the core of game theory, to which John von Neumann and Oscar Morgenstern contributed in 1944 their innovative book *Theory of Games and Economic Behavior*, setting up game theory in economics.

Today, captured by the fascination of stories and plots, some professors of economics enrich their academic reading lists with passages from literary classics to exemplify the ways in which writers have been grappling with economic ideas for centuries, or to graphically express by reference to exemplary episodes unpalatable economic ideas which their students have difficulty grasping. The didactic value of literary texts has been argued as a way to achieve better economic literacy, and a whole book was devoted to the use of literary passages to illustrate economic ideas (Watts ed. 2003).

The dialogue is not, however, plain and easy. Since the so-called marginalist revolution in the 1870s, economic theory was mainly focused on the study of maximizing rational choice. Although economic ideas had, and have, their conceptual roots in moral philosophy, history and the humanities at large, authoritative scholars in economics predicated that economic theory should be considered hard science, and as such close to physics or biology. Notably, since the mid-20th century, the theoretical language of economics has been dominated by the imprinting of mathematics and physics, and marked by the use of mathematical models. The discipline evolved being largely divorced from studies in the humanities, not to speak of literature or the arts. In theory and in research practice, the economists aiming at providing comprehensive insights into forward-looking, rational choices relied on mathematical modeling and econometric techniques. On the contrary, the stories told in literature propose another scale of vision of the economic world, approaching economic behaviour within the context of conflictual choices, and thorn paths in life, as experienced by the single, fictional characters. Literary texts provide plenty of opportunities to challenge the simplified representation of rational behaviour proposed in so many economic models. Thus, when looked at from the perspective of economic studies, the conversation with literary masterpieces might offer to professional economists a salutary escape from being trapped in the strict conceptualization of rational behaviour as dictated by prevailing theories in both microeconomics and macroeconomics. The comparisons between economic tales and literary tales, inviting scholars to the trespassing of disciplinary borders, are fruitful and productive, even if the richer, complex reflections they tell cannot be immediately, or precisely, translated into new sets of scientific ideas to understand economic phenomena. Meanwhile, mainstream economics is evolving into a complex research field, and innovative studies in experimental economics go beyond the strict dictates of the rationality assumption. New research currents explore bounded rationality, or even non-rational behaviour, going beyond what H. Simon critically named "Olympian rationality". In forecasting success, economics appears to be less of an exact science than economists would like, as the recent historical experience in the "Great Recession" unfortunately proves.

From the perspective of the history of ideas, the dialogue of economic studies with literature and literary studies helps discover the underlying cultural currents which run parallel in literary works and economic texts. In the various stages of its rather short history (short as compared to the millennial life of literature), political economy, only named economics since the end of the 19th century, was a field of study participating in larger cultural life. From the late 18th to the early 20th century, outstanding scholars in economics were moral philosophers such as Hume and Smith, or accomplished social scientists and political philosophers, such as J.S. Mill, Cournot, Walras and Marshall. In the 20th century, suffice it to mention, among others, Pareto, Hayek, Schumpeter, Keynes, Friedman, or today Sen, all political philosophers who explored economic ideas, building the conceptual language of the discipline. As moral and political philosophers, economists traced the disciplinary borders of their research in dialogue with wide currents in culture, including both the humanities and scientific thought. In this perspective, the encounter of literature and economics offers plenty of suggestions to historians of economic thought for crossing fixed disciplinary borders, to explore the evolution of ideas in our cultural heritage. In turn, studies in the history of economic thought shed critical light on the way writers reacted to controversial ideas about the economy and society at the time they were writing. Since the 18th century, whether they were more or less conscious of it (and most often they were), writers of economic texts and literary authors maintained relationships of reciprocal influence, by sharing controversies, historical environment and cultural roots. Today, as ever in history, conflicts of interest have social, political and moral causes and consequences. Economics cannot escape its birth as a "moral science" back in the 18th century, and it is crucial that it should keep the dialogue with the humanities going on.

The interdisciplinary exchanges between economics and literature are creating a promising new area of research, which is broadening thanks to the joint efforts of scholars in economics, history of economic thought and literary studies (Ingrao 2009). New books on economics and literature have been published, which are relevant for both fields of research, notably so in Victorian studies and in studies on French novels in the 19th century, much as in studies on specific subjects treated by both disciplines.[3] We cannot aim at reviewing the various contributions to this expanding field of research in this introductory presentation. Detailed references on specific subjects will be found in the chapters which follow in this book. Let us just briefly review a few scholars who promoted the opening of studies in economics and literature.

In literary criticism, the specialized body of research that explores characters placed in an economic environment, or sequences of economic events, or economic ideas and controversies as they are narrated in literary texts, emerged as a novel part of literary studies, bringing fresh insight from a new perspective into texts, writers, genres and styles. In the second half of the 20th century, innovative scholars addressed the theoretical relationship between economics and literature from wide, cultural perspectives, exploring a variety of possible exchanges, correspondences and analogies. Swiss linguist Ferdinand de Saussure, who had probably read Pareto's *Manuale di economia politica*, laid the groundwork for comparing linguistics and economics when he proposed the distinction between the diachronic and the synchronic approaches, showing language as a system (Saussure 1916 [1969], McCloskey 1998: 29 ff.). In 1978, in *The Economy of Literature*, Marc Shell discussed the analogies between economic and verbal symbolization (Shell 1978). Other scholars, notably French philosopher Jean-Joseph Goux, argued that economic phenomena lend themselves to literary rendition, while literature, in turn, provides us with stories about the value of art or the fetishization of material goods (Goux 1984).[4] During the 1980s, the study of metaphors, and the link between symbolic forms and economic values, was enlightened both in the literary field and in sociology, notably by French sociologist Pierre Bourdieu, who introduced the idea of "linguistic market", in polemical comparison with the controversial idea of perfectly competitive markets in economics (Bourdieu 1982). Bourdieu's later work on languages again put into contact concepts of symbolic values in linguistics with notions of value in economics (Bourdieu 2001). Economic theories were appropriated by theoretical literary studies to explore concepts such as desire and verbal value, or economic and cultural domination. In 1991, Fredric Jameson characterized postmodernism as the "cultural logic" of a late phase of the capitalist economy (Jameson 1991). Various scholars suggested that studying the connection between economics and literature helps reframe the distinction between exchange value and use value in a linguistic and literary perspective, or to explore the link between economic thought and new ways of shaping subjective identity in the novel (Shell 1978; Kaufman 2011).

At the end of the 20th century, "new economic criticism" emerged as a current in literary studies. The movement began in the United States in the early 1990s. In the introduction to the book *New Economic Criticism: Studies at the Intersection of Literature and Economics*, published in 1999, the editors Mark Osteen and Martha Woodmansee explained that in literary criticism the rise of cultural studies opened the way to the critical reading through economic lenses of many literary works; but they also warned against the risk, by adopting the economic lenses, of easily falling into crude economicism. Notwithstanding common inspiration and interests, the variety of approaches by the contributors doesn't allow us to describe this new current as a unified, coherent field in literary criticism. In its variety, new research in cultural studies contributed to promoting a pluridisciplinary perspective in literary criticism, and in the reading of literary texts, notwithstanding the risks mentioned above. The phenomenon can be explained also by the parallel decline of structuralist approaches to literature and formalism in literary studies.

Simultaneously, some scholars in economics, who were unsatisfied with the neoclassical paradigm, found in literature inspiration for the richer description of behaviour, not reducible to the maximization of profit or utility. In 1985 Deidre McCloskey's *The Rhetoric of Economics* focused on the rhetorical aspects of science in general, and notably of economics (McCloskey 1985 [1998]). By taking into account the rhetorical aspect of each type of discourse, she considered economists as storytellers. Despite the polemical aspect of this thesis, it is a symptom of the revival of interest in classical rhetoric, and of new awareness of the linguistic dimension of knowledge. Language and literature arguably shape the way we think about work, trade or money just as much as professional economic criticism does. The linguistic turn in the social sciences made the link between vocabularies visible. In his book *Das Gespenst des Kapitals*, German scholar Joseph Vogl illustrated this critical, and sometimes polemical perspective by arguing that economic and literary writings both inform knowledge production about economic phenomena (Vogl 2010).

Although theoretical boundaries between academic disciplines appear fixed, most disciplines in the humanities share common ground and influence one another over time. Thanks to research practices and exchanges within common cultural discourse, in the humanities the borders between academic disciplines may fluctuate, allowing combined fields of knowledge to emerge. In the last

30 years, a number of initiatives surfaced with the purpose of creating a joint field of study for economists, historians of economics and literary scholars, in which they could share competences in research and exchange information on themes of joint interest in the interdisciplinary field of economics and literature. Interdisciplinary work generates the conscious production of a new common language in research; it promotes opportunities for each academic discipline to delve into new areas of inquiry that would be impossible to explore without the language and methods of a different field.

Nevertheless, interdisciplinary work as a research practice is still fragile. Academic communities may feel threatened by its potential to rob scholars of their perceived identities, or endanger the leading roles scholars play in their respective fields. Negative reactions concerning interdisciplinarity are often based on the hybrid nature of its academic results, which are initially hard to define. The very vision of interdisciplinarity has been the subject of methodological controversy. According to Dogan and Pahre, the type of knowledge at the core of each discipline determines its potential for specialization or hybridization (Dogan and Pahre 1990). For Stember, hybridization can sometimes result in the evaporation of one or both of the disciplines involved, as they give birth to new inquiries and new fields of scholarship (e.g. cultural studies, black studies, women's studies, media studies, postcolonial studies) (Stember 1991). De Béchillon refers to the emergence of transdisciplinarity as the moment when scholars give up the rhetoric and identity that is specific to their discipline, in order to offer a new discourse in epistemocriticism (De Béchillon 1997). Linking two disciplines is seen as a methodological choice rather than a research theme in and of itself. For Mäki, multidisciplinarity can be defined as the collaboration between disciplines, in which neither the identity nor the content of any of the disciplines involved change, but dialogue occurs (Mäki 2007).

This book is a new, interdisciplinary, or better, transdisciplinary attempt to explore the ways in which economics and literature intersect. For our intents in this book, interdisciplinarity simply refers to the process of sharing ideas, methods and languages from various disciplines and cultural fields. The book aims primarily at promoting a fruitful dialogue among specialists from various backgrounds in the humanities, ranging from economists and historians of economic thought to literary criticism scholars. It outlines how separate fields, such as economics, history of economic thought and literary studies, can mutually benefit from interdisciplinary exchanges and shared subjects. The interdisciplinary or transdisciplinary focus in the book looks at how similar questions were addressed from diverging, or partially converging, perspectives in economic theory and in literary masterpieces, or how these questions were rephrased in different linguistic codes, or for distinct purposes. The chapters in the book seek to capture how the underlying historical environment and cultural currents shaped the common ground on which economists and writers stood, even when in controversial conversation. Simultaneously, the research work here presented shows the complexities of interdisciplinary collaboration between economics, history of economic thought and literary studies. The scholars who contributed to it are conscious of the difficulties of building a common discourse of shared knowledge. They are careful in taking into full account the divergence of purposes, linguistic codes and methods associated with each cultural field, while avoiding disciplinary confinement.

Thanks to the interdisciplinary focus, the editors and authors hope to provide an innovative book, going beyond the exclusively specialist aspects that were put forward in most previously published research on the dialogue between economics and literature. Indeed, each chapter of this collectively authored volume has been conceived and crafted to illustrate the intersections and interactions between economics and literature, making specific references to theories, methods, epistemologies and metaphors covering both fields. In addition to broaching the question of how economic theory was perceived and appreciated by literary writers, the chapters address the evolution of economic theory in comparison with similar themes in literary writings. Looking at the intersections between literature and economics, the contributing authors compare how economic and literary texts dealt with similar subjects, or they explore the ways in which economic ideas and metaphors enter literary texts, or economic texts use, or abuse, literary characters and stories. Some of them focus on the analogies between economic theories and narrative structure in literature and drama. The double look from economics and from literature put forth in the chapters will contribute – we hope – to a better understanding of over-arching themes like wealth, passion, interest, economic agency, money, economic development, economic crisis and social change. Finally, the book suggests that connecting literature and economics can help find a common language to voice critical perspectives on crises and social change. The thought-provoking and challenging role of literature will be addressed in each part of the book in a different way.

The chapters in Part I deal with the concern with passions and interest in economic and literary texts, with references to some French and British authors, novelists or economists in the 18th and 19th centuries. Literary metaphors enter the economic discourse, while economic ideas and events make their way into the plots of novels and plays. Both economists and writers popularize controversies about economic and political ideas.

In chapter 2, "Narratives of passion and finance in the 19th century", Bruna Ingrao addresses in comparative evaluation how speculation is represented in 19th-century novels versus economic writings. The chapter argues that emotions and passions, and their frailties, played a key role in the reading of "commercial crises" by 19th-century economists. British economists such as T. Tooke, J.S. Mill and Lord Overstone described commercial crises, or the "cycle of trade" during speculative bubbles and their aftermath, as going through bursting feelings of optimism and over-confidence later turning into distrust and the collapse of hopes. The later analysis of speculation by W. Bagehot, W.S. Jevons and A. Marshall is also considered. On the literary side, the chapter deals notably with novels by Balzac and Zola that addressed the passions and interests at play in speculative trading. In continuity with studies on how "the speculator" character evolved in Victorian literature, the chapter offers a closer look at novels by Dickens and Trollope. Special interest is paid to some similarities between literary and economic texts in their description of the personalities of professional and non-professional investors involved in stock exchange speculation. While non-professional investors are mostly presented as making myopic forecasts, being victims of psychological "contagion" of optimism and pessimism, powerful financiers and great bankers are typically depicted as self-interested, calculating and "rational". Both economic and literary stories called for welfare judgements, assessing financial behaviour in terms of fairness, moral responsibility, enlightened or myopic self-interest. After the experience of a most severe financial crisis, economists still have to address these issues today.

In chapter 3, "The passions and the interests: The sentimental education of Gustave Flaubert" Alfonso Sanchez takes an unconventional look at the 19th-century masterpiece in French literature, *L'éducation sentimentale* (*Sentimental Education*) by Gustave Flaubert, to show its value as a historical document. Beneath the surface of a romantic plot, Flaubert's *Sentimental Education* offers an overview of the political and economic context for understanding the structural changes French society underwent during the revolutionary period that preceded the Second Republic. The historical background is revolutionary Paris (1848), and *Sentimental Education* is a portrait of economic and political conflicts in France during the revolutionary years. The novel's last part, which takes place between 1848 and 1867, features accounts of the February Revolution as well as Louis Napoleon's coup. Throughout the novel, two main characters, an Orleanist bourgeois and a revolutionary socialist who represent ideological opposites, give specific accounts of the 1848 disaster; they voice scepticism about the possibility for social change. Their changing political views are described with fierce irony, which reveals much of Flaubert's own ideological and political beliefs. The revolution serves Flaubert as a backdrop to show his distrust of progress, of all political action and of the behaviour of the masses.

In chapter 4, "Literature and political economy: Saint-Simon and Jean-Baptiste Say's writings", Gilles Jacoud presents a comparative study of writings by the Count of Saint-Simon and Jean-Baptiste Say, who were both leading figures in French political economy during the first half of the 19th century. Though they met often and shared similar views for a time, their ideas eventually diverged. The chapter argues that both thinkers had a background in literature, were familiar with various literary genres and made similar use of literary writing to put forth their respective ideas regarding political economy. Both Say and Saint-Simon made extensive use of the epistolary genre, though Saint-Simon showed a marked preference for it. Say is known to have deliberately inserted 130 verses of André Chénier's poetry into his *Essai sur le principe de l'utilité*. In the hopes of reaching a wider audience, both thinkers wrote a catechism in brief question-and-answer form. Finally, both Saint-Simon and Say engaged in plentiful editorial work, in pamphlets, essays and books, which allowed them to expound, spread and shape their doctrines of political economy thanks to their experience and skill as writers.

In chapter 5, "Which economic agent does Robinson Crusoe represent?", Claire Pignol deals with the Robinson Crusoe metaphor in economics, looking out for the differences between Defoe's Crusoe and the Crusoe imagined by economists.

Over time, economists used Crusoe as a metaphor to illustrate different theories; they read Defoe's story as an allegory about the beginnings of capitalism in Europe, or used Crusoe's character to illustrate how agents organize scarce resources to maximize their satisfaction. In the novel, Crusoe's character displays not uniform, and even contradictory economic behaviour; he behaves in a more ambivalent manner than the rational agent portrayed by marginalist economic theory since the end of the 19th century. The desert island experience transforms Crusoe: he starts out desiring unlimited riches, but eventually seeks to increase well-being through work. Work, however, is not primarily understood as a means for acquiring goods, but as the best mean to escape his loneliness. Though Crusoe was often identified as a *homo œconomicus*, could he represent an agent like the ones Marx or Keynes had imagined for humanity's future, one who's not bound to serve the productive forces of capitalism? The chapter suggests that focusing the differences between Defoe's Crusoe and the Crusoe imagined by economists may help to focus our own contradictory behaviour as economic agents.

In chapter 6, "Political economy and utilitarianism in Dickens' *Hard Times*", Nathalie Sigot and Çınla Akdere attempt the historical assessment of utilitarian philosophy as compared to Dickens' reading of it. The chapter examines Charles Dickens' understanding of utilitarianism through a study of *Hard Times*. The two authors propose to distinguish what in the novel pertains to Dickens' criticism against political economy, and what pertains to his criticism against utilitarianism. They illustrate their argument by pointing out the dynamics at work throughout the novel. Their comments are in continuity with the recent literature that focused on the joint criticism that Dickens and Bentham made of the administration of their time, but also on the biased presentation by Dickens of Bentham's philosophy, which leads to criticize the exclusive emphasis placed on pain, while the principle of utility emphasizes pleasure as well. The chapter underlines the need to nuance Dickens' position as regards utilitarianism, a philosophy which he knew well, suggesting that for Dickens utilitarianism was open to change, while he was more radical in his criticism of political economy.

The chapters in Part II take a closer look at individuality, and at monetary issues. Based on interdisciplinary analyses, the four chapters in this part of the book explore the analogies between economic theories and narrative structures in a selection of major literary works.

In chapter 7, "Concordances and dissidences between economy and literature", Goux shows some theoretical similarities and differences between the two disciplines. The first convergence can be observed in the 19th century. Writers like Stendhal became aware of a changing social paradigm: the power of money replaces nobility, at the same time romantic poets claim nostalgia of the past, and the divorce between economic calculation and poetry. But during this period Goux observes the rise of the novel and the fact that the novel is invaded by economic themes; this new literary genre emerges in parallel with the new individual emerging in a democratic society, in which all professions are open to everybody. The "enterprising" hero is born. Symmetrically, Goux notices than economists use frequently "micro fictions" when they want to explain their theories. He concludes by showing through M. Friedman and F. Hayek the comparison between signs of communication and economic exchange through the paradigm of circulation.

In chapter 8, "Economics and monetary imagination in André Gide's *The Counterfeiters*", Çınla Akdere and Christine Baron discuss the exploration of André Gide's reading of monetary theory. Money is the link between the characters in the novel, but it represents also metaphorically the difference between use value and exchange value. *Les Faux monnayeurs* deals with a financial scam, and the relationship between characters is determined by money: fraud, theft, debt or refund. This money is not connected with economic activity such as banking, trade or investments. Nevertheless, economic issues are central themes in the novel; they are metaphorically the way in which literary value is represented. Gide, choosing an anti-realistic perspective in the novel, breaks a long tradition in the French novel. In the novel Edouard is a dead ringer of Gide, and Edouard's friends blame him for making a speculative meta-novel more than a presentation of vivid and vibrant characters. But in fact Gide's project includes a meditation about the way the 20th-century novel can renew the genre, arguing that value lies more in the work itself, including the hesitations about the relevant literary forms, than in the final result.

In chapter 9, " 'I always wanted to have earned my first dollar but I never had': Gertrude Stein and money", Laura Key explores the key influences behind Stein's use of money as a metaphor to understand literature as a mutable form of representation, a subject that has been missing from Stein studies until now. The chapter offers a textual analysis of Gertrude Stein's works in relation to money, from *Three Lives* in 1907 to *Wars I Have Seen* in 1945. The author argues that in Stein's writing, money is compared metaphorically to the literary text, both being treated as representative forms of writing with negotiable values. The paper follows the contention that modernist literature should be analyzed in the context of a wider socio-economic framework, rather than being considered part of a distinct aesthetic realm. Key historical moments, as well as Stein's personal experiences and encounters, reignite her continued equation of language with money over the course of her writing. As Stein was pondering the similarities between money and language in *Three Lives*, the United States was suffering under the burden of the financial panic in 1907. In 1936 Stein revisited the theme in her "Money" articles, just after having visited the United States. By underlying the similarity between literary fiction and money as representative forms of writing, Stein's work raises questions about how value is quantified.

In chapter 10, "Georges Perec's *Les Choses* as the privileged domain of contemporary hunter-gatherers", Eyüp Özveren analyzes Georges Perec's novel *Les Choses*, published in 1965, that has been read as a parody of the conflicting emotional universe of human beings who are subject to the vagaries of mass consumption. The story is amenable to an interpretation that compares the behavioural traits of the main characters, Jérôme and Sylvie, with the *homo oeconomicus* postulated by neoclassical economists. As the narrative of the novel presents the reader with issues regarding choice, wealth and consumption, this is a straightforward association. Promising links have been established with Galbraith's *The Affluent Society*, situating the characters and the plot within the context of postwar consumption culture. The chapter draws attention to the connection with Thorstein Veblen's popular classic, *The Theory of the Leisure Class*, interpreting Perec's narrative in light of Veblen's anthropological account of the consumption culture. Finally, the chapter proposes an unusual interpretation of the novel, inspired by institutional and anthropological suggestions, as an adventure of 'primitive hunter-gatherers' in late modernity, amidst an advanced consumption culture.

All chapters in Part III address economic crisis and social change as narrative subjects, but in a variety of perspectives. Three chapters address economic and social change as portrayed by Turkish writers in different times, looking at Turkish literature through the lenses of economic history. The last two chapters advance more provocative connections between the current economic crises and the on-going transformations in theatre and in the media.

In chapter 11, "Transforming economic and social relations: Modern economy in the novels of Uşaklıgil", Reyhan Tutumlu Serdar and Ali Serdar focus on Ottoman Turkish writer Halit Ziya Uşaklıgil (1867–1945), whose three novels *Mai ve Siyah* (*Azure and Black*, 1889), *Ferdi ve Şürekâsı* (*Ferdi and His Accomplices*, 1894) and *Aşk-ı Memnu* (*Forbidden Love*, 1900) provide a valuable account of the changes that occurred in Ottoman society during the 18th and 19th centuries. It deals notably with the consequences of the integration of the previously autonomous empire into the capitalist world economy. The chapter discusses how Uşaklıgil's writings reveal the effects of capitalist relations of production through their impact on the novels' characters, the change of values and the degenerative effects of competition on moral ethics. Finally, it presents Uşaklıgil as an avant-garde author writing in a modern genre, grappling with economic transformations and their effects on social change.

In chapter 12, "Mechanization experience in agriculture in Turkey: *The Pomegranate on the Knoll*", Selin Seçil Akin and Işıl Şirin Selçuk explore the social and economic consequences of mechanization in Turkish agriculture during the 1950s, as seen through Yaşar Kemal's novel *The Pomegranate on the Knoll* (1982). The chapter provides historical background for understanding Turkish agricultural mechanization. As a result of the liberalization of international trade and foreign aid, the number of tractors increased dramatically between 1950 and 1953. Set in this time period, the novel tells the story of five peasants in search of work, emphasizing unemployment in Turkish agriculture after it underwent massive mechanization. Agricultural workers suffered from precarious economic situations, difficult working conditions, and psychological distress from unemployment. Yaşar Kemal used his literary skills to convey how the tractor became a symbol of economic progress and social status for agricultural workers, and engaged critically with this economic symbol, showing the dark side of mechanization.

In chapter 13, "An intertextual analysis of the village novels by Village Institute graduates: Socio-economic scenes of the Turkish village between 1950 and 1980", Esra Elif Nartok analyzes the village novels written between 1950 and 1980 by three Turkish Village Institute graduates (Talip Apaydın, Fakir Baykurt and Mahmut Makal) as representative of what is known as the village novel tradition in Turkish literary history. The chapter illustrates how village novels interacted with Turkey's political and economic realities at the time they were published, looking at their relationship with the Turkish left and at the way these novels succeeded in going beyond classical Kemalist doctrines. The village novels helped the oppressed peasants to bring their experiences and voices to the literary stage where they could be heard by Turkish society at large. Because of the authors' experience of village life and peasant identity, these novels can be read today for the testimony they provide about a phase of Turkish economic history.

In chapter 14, "Theatre in crisis, theatre of crisis: Economics and contemporary dramatic writing and shows", Martial Poirson discusses the influence of Europe's recent economic crisis on contemporary theatre. The chapter deals with recent dramatic writings, while addressing the problems theatre as an institution is confronted with. Theatre, a victim of the crisis, has been confronted with the changing economic environment of the performing arts. The author suggests that recent playwriting gave birth to a new economic genre in dramaturgy, regenerating traditional theatre by using specific techniques like dramatic detour, overflow and backhand. This theatre of crisis is concerned with criticizing economic modeling's *modus operandi* and with bringing to the limelight its hidden realities, taking a close look at the social and cultural constructions of market value. It tackles both economic facts and theories to draw attention to their inherent contradictions, denials and omissions. After being relegated to the margins of the market economy, culture is now at the centre of its very transformation. The author suggests that in France, theatre is foreshadowing a dismantling of the public service infrastructure, but it is also calling for the hope that culture will become an active component of future policies for sustainable growth.

In chapter 15, "Restructuring the attention economy: Literary interpretation as an antidote to mass media distraction", Y. Citton addresses the attention economy. If human attention is our scarcest resource, as we are told by prophets of the attention economy, the capacity to receive cultural goods matters even more than the capacity to produce them. In the age of scarce attention, literature appears simultaneously as a luxury in terms of the time spent to read, as resistance against the alienation of scarce attention operated by market-driven media, and as a source of deeper knowledge about the fundamental mechanisms of valuation. What is valorized except that to which we pay attention? Citton describes four regimes of attention: alert, loyalty to types of contents, projection and immersion. He underlines that the mass media model favours only the first one. As an antidote, literature requests other types of attention. After retracing the course of the attention economy, the chapter shows how psychologists studied human behaviour in order to develop attention, or to prevent attention disorders. The last part of the chapter is devoted to arguing how the attention economy can lead to the attention ecology.

Though all chapters were rewritten to form a cohesive body of work for this publication, the book collects the contributions of scholars in economics or literary studies with different backgrounds, and applying different methodological perspectives on the common subject of economics and literature. The editors appreciated this variety of competences, perspectives and methodologies as enriching the book, and indeed increasing its value as an interdisciplinary effort; they never aimed at unifying under a common line of thought the collected contributions. The reader should be aware of the diverse voices speaking in the pages that follow.

Notes

1 The quoted passage is from a letter Engels wrote to Miss Harkness in April 1888.
2 French writer J.C. Massera narrates the workers' sufferings because of unemployment or relocations; he portrays the language of neoliberalism in business as a kind of Orwellian Newspeak (Massera 2011). The Spanish writer Belén Gopegui, inspired by the political movement of "Los indignados", aims at depicting the negative impact of globalization on workers' welfare (Gopegui 2007).
3 See, among others, Scarpelli 2015 for ample references to both literary masterpieces and critical studies.
4 More recently, in *Frivolité de la valeur*, Goux put into contact pictorial aesthetics and economics; he suggested that impressionism emerged as a technique that allowed artists to represent the world according to their subjective point of view, just at the time mathematical economist Léon Walras explained economic value as the result of individuals' subjective desires for goods (Goux 2011).

Bibliography

Bourdieu, P. (1982), *Ce que parler veut dire: l'économie des échanges linguistiques*, Paris: Fayard.
Bourdieu, P. (2001), *Langage et pouvoir symbolique*, Paris: Seuil.
De Bechillon, D. (1997), "La notion de transdisciplinarité", *La Revue de Mauss*, numéro spécial entitled "Guerre et paix entre les sciences, interdisciplinarité, et transdisciplinarité", no. 10: 185–199.
Dogan, M. and Pahre, R. (1990), *Creative Marginality: Innovation at the Intersections of Social Sciences*, Oxford: Westview Press.
Engels, F. (1888), *Correspondance*, www.marxists.org/archive/marx/works/.../88_04_15.htm.
Gopegui B. (2007), *Il Padre de Biancanieves*, Barcelaona: Editorial Anagrama.
Goux, J.-J. (1984), *Les monnayeurs du langage*, Paris: Galilée.
Goux, J. J. (2011), *Frivolité de la valeur, l'art et l'argent*, Paris: Blusson.
Ingrao, B. (2009), "Economics and Literature", in R. Arena, M. Klaes and S. Dow (eds.), *Open Economics: Economics in Relation to Other Disciplines*, London: Routledge, 30–47.
Jameson, F. (1991), *Postmodernism: The Cultural Logic of Late Capitalism*, Durham, NC: Duke University Press.
Kaufman, V. (2011), "Entretiens : J-J. Goux" in V. Kaufman (2011), *La Faute à Mallarmé. L'aventure de la théorie littéraire,* Paris : Seuil, 241–248.
Mäki, U. (2007), "Varieties of Interdisciplinarity and of Scientific Progress", communication présentée à l'université Paris I Panthéon-Sorbonne, Paris, France, www.univ-paris13.fr/cepn/IMG/pdf/texte_uskali_2_140508.pdf
Massera, J.-C. (2011), *Tunnel of Mondialisation* (livre CD/DVD de 5 chansons et clips vidéo) avec Pascal Sangla (musique), Paris: Éditions Verticales.

McCloskey, D. N. (1998), *The Rhetoric of Economics*, 2nd edition, Madison, WI: The University of Wisconsin Press.

Piketty, T. (2014a), *Capital in the Twenty-First Century*, London: Harvard University Press.

Piketty, T. (2014b), *Le capital au XXIe siècle*, Paris: Seuil.

Saussure De, F. (1916 [1969]), *Cours de linguistique générale*, Paris: Payot.

Scarpelli, G. (2015), *La ricchezza delle emozioni*, Roma: Carocci.

Shell, M. (1978), *The Economy of Literature*, Baltimore, MD and London: The Johns Hopkins University Press.

Stember, M. (1991), "Advancing the Social Sciences Through the Interdisciplinary Experience", *Social Science Journal*, 28 (1): 1–14.

Vogl, J. (2010), *Das Gespenst des Kapitals*, Zürich-Berlin: Diaphanes.

Watts, M. (ed.) (2003), *The Literary Book of Economics: Including Readings From Literature and Drama on Economic Concepts, Issues and Themes*, Wilmington, DE: ISI Books.

Woodmansee, M. and Osteen, M. (1999), "Taking Account of the New Economic Criticism", in M. Woodmansee and M. Osteen (eds.), *New Economic Criticism: Studies at the Intersection of Literature and Economics*, London: Routledge, 2–42.

Part I

Passions and interest

A comparative study of economic
texts and literary masterpieces

2 Narratives of passions and finance in the 19th century

Bruna Ingrao

Emotions in finance in the "overtrading" literature

Along the 19th century, "commercial crises", the sequence of "excitement", "distress" and "panic" in the "cycle of trade", constituted a subject in economics, where human passions and frailties were as relevant as rational choice. In 19th-century literature, both French and British novelists addressed the emotions involved in the speculative game in their stories. After briefly dealing with the overtrading literature on commercial crises, we shall explore the narration of speculation in novels by Balzac, Dickens and Trollope, to go back to the emotional side of economic crises as described by British economists, from Bagehot to Jevons and Marshall. The chapter will close by comparing the description of high finance in Marshall's unpublished notes on speculation and in a famous novel by Zola.

The early literature on financial crises borrowed its terminology from psychology and medicine, with echoes referring to diseases or emotional states of the mind (Besomi 2011). "Panic", "convulsion", "revulsion", "distress", "crises", "excitement" and "depression" lived a parallel life in common parlance as bodily or mental states, and in economic narratives regarding the state of the market.[1] In influential economic writings, which carved the terminology to describe the trade cycle, the echoes of the original meanings were far from being absent, the emphasis being, to various degrees, on the emotions, which simultaneously affect many traders. In the early to mid-19th century, in Great Britain, leading scholars in economics, such as H. Thornton, T. Tooke, J.S. Mill and Lord Overstone, explained financial crises having recourse to the burst of non-rational feelings and the diffusion of imitative expectations during speculative bubbles and their aftermath. This literature is conventionally referred to as the "overtrading" reading of commercial crises, though authors differed in exact interpretation of the phases or ultimate causes of the events culminating in financial crises.

After the full convertibility of the sterling was restored in 1821, it became clear that the gold standard could not protect the economy from the recurrence of commercial crises, a hotly debated issue between the banking school and the currency school. J.S. Mill analyzed commercial crises since 1826 (Mill 1826 [1967]). In his early writings on fluctuations, he distinguished professional traders from rash speculators, who follow in their paths (Forget 1990: 629–630). On Mill's definition speculations are especially risky "mercantile transactions"; but "rash speculations" are "those in which the risk is great, and the prospect of gain not a sufficient equivalent" (Mill 1826 [1967]: 73). They involve the assumption of risk on false expectations, which go beyond reasonable hopes for future gains. Dealers in the trade start speculative investment in stocks on expectations of rising prices grounded in conjectures about a forthcoming disequilibrium. When the low rate of profit of normal times encourages their search for extra profits, they metamorphose into rash speculators, overinvesting in inventories in a game of rivalry to expand their market share, or to anticipate market trends. Rising prices and the dream of quick profits attract investors with scarce information on market fundamentals into the speculative game. People not professionally in the trade look for extraordinary gains by short-term investment strategies. Cumulative investment fuelled by easy access to credit further raises market prices. Speculative expectations are *pro tempore* self-fulfilling, and a general "infatuation" and frenzy prevails in times of "over-trading" (Mill 1826 [1967]: 74–75).

It is a matter of controversy whether Mill maintained the distinction between "speculation" and "rash speculation" in his later analysis of fluctuations. In his later writings, myopic forecasts shared by both professional traders and the public, and the "moods" collectively experienced in the "contagion" of waves of optimism and pessimism, maintain a crucial role in the trade cycle. In 1844, in his review of the controversy between Tooke and Torrens, Mill underlined the psychic aspects in speculative behaviour ("contagious confidence of speculative times", "exaggerated confidence", "a spirit of speculation") (Mill 1844 [1967]: 355, 356). Businessmen who take part in speculative purchases act on "apparent grounds", which justify forecasting the future rise in the price of the goods that are the object of speculative investment; but they "miscalculate" the trend of prices and the prospective gains, due to the intrinsic difficulty to forecast the state of the market, and because of their myopia in not anticipating the reactions of other dealers attracted into the same speculative game.[2] Speculation is fuelled by "the passion of gain" that "over-rides" rational calculus; gambling attitudes lead to exaggerate confidence in prospective profits.[3]

In the *Principles of Political Economy*, Mill again emphasized myopic individual rationality, social passions and imitative behaviour as the mix which fuels the bubble, and then turns distress into panic (Mill, J.S. 1848 [1967]: 527–528). Emotional and cognitive aspects (boldness in pursuing gains beyond what cold evaluation suggests; gambling instinct; cognitive biases in committing fallacies of composition, or in valuing present conditions as reliable predictors of future ones) concur in fuelling the speculation, nurturing the financial collapse that follows.

In booms and bursts, Mill notes the tendency to form expectations looking at our neighbours, becoming prone to herd behaviour. Cognitive biases are magnified by social emotions, which undermine the inductive process of reasoning in the traders' minds. Shared expectations, conceived as "states of the public mind", are formed on frail evidence ("a general impression that the price of some commodity is likely to rise", "a higher price than reasonable calculation justified", "willing to believe that it will continue rising"); the herd behaviour of speculators makes them temporarily self-fulfilling. Social emotions fuel the spreading of bull-ish expectations ("a generally reckless and adventurous feeling prevails", "certain states of the public mind", "the contagion") (Mill, J.S. 1848 [1967]: 527). The "spirit of speculation" that captures hearts and minds obfuscates the forecasting capability grounded on sound evidence. Imitative behaviour is fuelled by social envy, when people believe that their neighbours are pursuing profit opportuni-ties better than themselves. As an effect of "contagion", financial transactions are affected; credit is extended "to persons not entitled to it", beyond the limits set by prudence both on the demand and the supply side. Credit, which offers to specula-tive dealers multiplied means to pursue their apparently sound plans, depends on the reputation of the borrower in his trade. Mill quotes Tooke on the issue (Mill, J.S. 1848 [1967]: 533). It depends on the attribution of status to the borrower, the socially shared recognition that he is a reliable businessman who will hon-our contracts and discharge monetary obligations. In a "commercial revulsion", shared emotions ("a panic as unreasoning as the previous overconfidence") and herd behaviour in the trading community, or in society at large, open a conflict between private rationality ("no one likes to part with ready money, or to postpone his claim to it") and social welfare that is severely damaged by deflation and credit crunch.

Mill saw the episodes of rising and falling prices in commercial crises as tend-ing to level out, prices going back to normal market values (Hicks 1983; Dardi and Gallegati 1992). He trusted the ability of professional dealers to ultimately perceive the long-term trend of prices and lead the adjustment process back to normal equilibrium (Forget 1990: 641). In normative terms, he suggested that young men who were going to work in a merchant's counting house should be trained to learn basic notions on "the circumstances which regulate the price of commodities". He hoped for the development of mental habits of prudence and sober calculation, to protect the community from rash speculation in the future (Forget 1990: 633).

Since 1837 and in well-known writings around the mid-century, Samuel Jones Loyd,[4] later Lord Overstone, described the phases of the "cycle of trade" with a terminology mixing economics with echoes from bodily or psychic states ("qui-escence, improvement, growing confidence, prosperity, excitement, overtrading, convulsion, pressure, stagnation, distress, quiescence"). These phases appeared in a print published in the press and enjoyed some diffusion among the literate public.

In 1867 banker John Mills, a proposer of the periodicity of commercial cri-ses, advanced a theory of the credit cycle rooted in psychic fluctuations in the "social mind" (Mills 1867: 27).[5] Mental "moods" dominate in his narrative that is filled with references to medicine and physiological analogies from the body to the mind. He wrote: ". . . the malady of commercial crises is not, in essence, a matter of the purse but of the mind" (Mills 1867: 17). The ultimate cause is a psychic cycle in collective moods. According to Mills, it is necessary to explore the underlying causes of recurrent "commercial panics", going beyond the super-ficial assertion that "overtrading, in some form or other, is the common forerunner of Panic" (Mills 1867: 11); their periodicity is rooted in fluctuations in credit, defined as "a thing of moral essence". The commercial credit goes through a life cycle from "infancy" to "growth to maturity, diseased over-growth, and death by collapse" (Mills 1867: 17). The "social mind" is periodically subject to "a morbid excess of belief, a *hypertrophy* of belief"; "healthy confidence" degenerates into "the disease of a too facile faith" (Mills 1867: 27). The contagion, after spreading to the commercial classes, infects the "investing class of non-traders". The "crowd of morbid-minded investors" invests funds into joint stock companies "out of proportion to their means" or to rational assessment of prospective gains. In Mills' analysis, the value of money is based on "beliefs", the unconscious mental processes which associate money with "universal acceptance at a certain high rate in exchange" (Mills 1867: 18). On similar, shaky beliefs stand the faith in the monetary value of contracts for deferred monetary payments: "an outlying mass of engagements, chiefly in a documentary form, acknowledgements of debt, with or without specified time of redemption – the substance of which is for the time invisible – and the redemption of which is a matter of more or less certainty, more or less doubt" (Mills 1867: 18). The human mind, especially in the British population "of energetic temperament and a low average of economic training", goes through cycles of optimism and over-confidence turning later into distrust and collapse. "Broadly defined, then, Panics is the destruction, in the mind, of a bundle of beliefs" (Mills 1867: 18).

Balzac on speculation and high finance

In the 19th century in France, many writers addressed the passions and interests arising in speculative trading in plays, novels or short stories built on financial plots (Gomart 2004; Réffait 2007).[6] Balzac published *César Birotteau* and *La Maison Nucingen* in the same year, 1838. He wrote both novels in 1837, and signalled their parallelism and contrast as a key to the understanding of social relations (Balzac 1838 [1977]a: 35, Balzac 1838 [1977]b: 329). In *César Birotteau* as in *La Maison Nucingen* (*The Firm of Nucingen*), human passions and cool calculus mix in complex ways in the behaviour on financial markets by protagonists and antagonists.

The novel *César Birotteau* tells the story of the rise and fall of a middle-class entrepreneur in the perfumery business, who is led to bankruptcy by professional speculators in the banking world. They are the winners, though Birotteau will see his reputation restored just before dying. A narrow-minded self-made man, he nurtures the ambition to reach a status beyond his limited means and capacities; he ventures into a risky speculation that he has no liquidity to sustain till the expected profits materialize. He trusts the ruined notary Roguin, and invests the money saved for the dowry of his daughter in a transaction on land estates, which the dishonest notary proposes to him and other friends. The speculation has good prospects in view of future urban development in the area; but Birotteau ignores that banker Du Tillet, professional speculator and new entrant in banking, secretly manages the capital and manoeuvres to divert the funds. The perfumer is the prey of Du Tillet, who shrewdly pilots his financial distress, forcing him into bankruptcy. The wicked banker will finally succeed in acquiring the land at low prices, having ruined the original investors.

The plot is a story of conflict between enterprise and speculation. In Balzac's novels entrepreneurs gain commercial success, and with it social advancement, thanks to hard work, innovation, marketing strategies and fanciful advertisement (Ingrao 2007). The clue to their success is a mix of tenacious effort, imagination and strong temper. Projectors, bankers and great financiers fight to amass money, buying low and selling high in risky transactions in commodities, estates or stocks; they may lose or win according to their shrewdness or sheer frauds, strategic collusion with other traders, insider trading, manipulation of rumours or political collusion. Speculative manoeuvres are narrated as a dangerous game of appearance and concealment with reciprocal tricks. Agents must guess their chances, and be ready to be flooded even by those they thought were loyal partners. Balzac conceives the speculative manoeuvre par excellence as the fabricated "killing" of a profitable business by an insider, who fuels bullish speculation on some asset by the spread of rumours, just to later cause the precipitous fall of prices, forcing investors to sell at unfavourable terms.[7] Having ruined the original investors, the speculator gains their spoils and the forthcoming profits. The ability to manipulate the market by concealed strategies, devised in secret circles, is at the core of successful speculation, jointly with a touch of crazy, forward-looking imagination.

The financial world includes the dominant banking houses (the Kellers, the *Haute Banque* properly, and the new entrant baron Nucingen) and the mixed group of bankers, brokers and money-lenders, who are stratified in hierarchies according to customers and localization, the funds they place, their straw-men, their alliances with great bankers or their covert association with usurers. Bankers and money-lenders, who deal with traders in the local business community ("le commerce"), filter their contact with the "higher regions" of the *Haute Banque* (Balzac 1838 [1977]a: 207). Balzac's picture of the *Haute Banque* and professional financiers is bleak. The borderline is thin between bankers and usurers, though their distance in lifestyle and connections may be wide. Banker Claparon is a desperate rascal, and the house where he lives and runs his business is a place of moral and material decay (Balzac 1838 [1977]a: 238–239). He is the straw-man of Du Tillet, who ascended to the banking business after having built his fortune in adventurous speculations with his own or other people's money.[8] Du Tillet is revealed to be the associate of Gobseck, the usurer, who is his double in the novel, the dark side of his brilliant facade. At the Stock Exchange, great financiers, bankers of middle status, brokers, money-lenders and usurers meet and exchange opinion (Balzac 1838 [1977]a: 263).

In the Keller Banking House, François Keller, the great liberal banker, meets his guests, cronies and solicitors in a magnificent private office ("le luxe royale de ce cabinet") at the centre of feverish political intrigues and large-scale investment worldwide. His brother Adolphe acts in combination with him[9] in the unadorned office downstairs ("un cabinet froid", "mesquin fauteuils", "rideaux très négligés", "maigre tapis"), where he coolly assesses the guarantees each solicitor is offering, and the profit in each business. Their financial behaviour is a mixture of rational calculus, coolness of temper and gambling instinct; their relational intelligence supports their investment strategies built on financial tricks and quasi-legal frauds (Balzac 1838 [1977]a: 212). François, well-informed, charming, with a distinctive power of persuasion, moves his business on the double scenery of politics and global investment by building alliances and gaining loyalties of partners and affiliates. Politics and social relations are essential part of the scenery in financial games.

"Je n'existe que par le crédit. Nous en sommes tous là" (Balzac 1838 [1977]a: 235).[10] Confidence, as in Bagehot's later description of Lombard Street, is crucial in the Parisian business community. Dealers such as Birotteau gain confidence by reputation and good order in their books, without which their promissory notes would be but scratch paper.[11] In the world of banking and speculative business, reciprocal services, strategic alliances, politics or love affairs buy confidence. Du Tillet's credit is based on his connections in the banking business or high society.[12]

Coolness of mind, hardheartedness and ability in manipulating opinion are the qualities which make the success of financiers in the *Haute Banque*, of which the Keller brothers are the complementary personalities. The high financier, far from being driven by irrational emotions, is a cold *raisonneur*; he is also a gambler, a consummate architect of financial plots, and an actor. Thanks to his coolness of mind, he mounts intrigues to take advantage of emotions and imprudence among the public of investors. However, the driving motive for most financial characters in Balzac's plots is never sheer greediness, but the social ambition to affirm their status, winning power and visibility. It is the need to be recognized by other fellows in society to win, not money *per se*, but a ticket to access the high life of upper classes, manipulating the hearts and lives of other people. In his persecution of Birotteau, Du Tillet is obsessed by vengeance. He ruins his old boss, who had discovered him in the act of stealing, to protect his new status by destroying the man who might unveil his past. The financial game is ultimately a relational game in the human comedy, where social passions take the lead. On the other side of the coin, calculus, strategic rivalry and deception of the public dominate in the minds of dealers, the good as the bad ones, including Birotteu (Guise 1977: 31). Some speculative spirit is inherent in commercial practice, as the ability to exploit profits' opportunities to be reaped by whatever means, including cheating customers, or transferring losses on the back of other fellows.[13] Mrs. Roguin calculates his long-term interest in placing her savings into the hands of Du Tillet to protect her capital from the mismanagement of his husband. Birotteau conjectures how to win over a rival perfumery firm capturing the approval of the famous scientist Vauquelin. Popinot builds his hopes for marriage on his strategy to fascinate new customers by imaginative advertisement and marketing.[14] A degree of charlatanism is part of current business in commercial activity at large.

Calculus is not foreign to love, a selfish passion, according to Balzac.[15] The talent to see the qualities of the beloved person is the selfish side of affective investment in true love by the bourgeois woman, who wishes to form a stable relation in long-term marriage. This emotional calculus nurtures Césarine's love for Anselme, the young clerk, who is lame in one of his legs. Unconsciously, Césarine conceives her happiness as the mimicking of her mother's lifestyle; in forming her attachment, she applies the emotional arithmetic of her rank ("l'arithmétique des sentiments bourgeois"). Nucingen fails in his crazy affair with young Esther; the emotional arithmetic calculated by Césarine and Anselme in their bourgeois love succeeds.[16]

The title originally imagined by Balzac for *La Maison Nucingen* was *La Haute Banque*. This short novel tells the story of the fraudulent bankruptcy that banker Nucingen has shrewdly staged, and that will be the source of large speculative gains to him and his associates, including his wife's lover Rastignac. Malignant speculative moves at the Stock Exchange are described both as swindles and as the result of the ability of Nucingen to systematically beat the gun. By the successful manipulation of rumours, Nucingen gains at the expense of other bankers and gullible investors thanks to his wealth and his insider position. The story is told in a private meeting at a restaurant; the narrator hears the conversation among the guests dining nearby, without being noticed. They are four young "condottieri" navigating the Parisian high society, three of whom are journalists, while the one named Couture is a professional speculator of lower status, with difficulties and the temper of the gambler (Balzac 1838 [1977]b: 330). Through the thin partition wall separating the two rooms (*cabinet particuliers*), their dialogues reveal the trick staged by Nucingen, a metaphor for the uncertain disclosure to public opinion of manipulative speculation. The source of the wealth amassed in speculative business, well known to insiders who have access to the inner circles of the *Haute Banque*, filters to public opinion through fragile walls.

The plot is intertwined with the love story between Godefroid de Beaudenord, a young dandy of noble origin, and Isaure Aldrigger, the daughter of the Alsatian banker Baron Aldrigger, to picture the human costs of the monetary losses which the *Haute Banque* imposes on the losers. Godefroid, Isaure, her sister Malvina and her mother, the wife of deceased Baron Aldrigger, have their wealth devoured in the difficulties of their funds placed in Nucingen's bank, and later in the fall of their stock at the Stock Exchange. As naive investors, they placed their savings in the shares of Claparon's bank; Nucingen will finally sacrifice his associate.[17] Godefroid and family are forced to sell when the price of Claparon's shares is at a minimum due to Nucingen's manoeuvres.[18]

Baron Nucingen, the great banker of the plot, lives the high-pressure life of politicians and high financiers, complacently letting the young lover Rastignac take care of his wife Delphine. A cool gambler and selfish speculator, Nucingen is driven by a powerful social passion, dreaming to emulate the Rothschilds in wealth, prominence and power. His main trait is the ability to conceal plans and manipulate other brokers, professional speculators and bankers;[19] his success is the result of an intelligence for business in whatever trade he is involved.[20] The swindles he carefully plots are speculations as described above: to establish a business managed by a straw-man or associate, collecting funds invested by the wealthy community; to fuel bullish speculation and artfully, by rumours or transactions, make the market turn; to buy the stocks when their price is at a minimum, and wait for their revival, having deprived the naive investors of a substantial quota of their wealth.

Rumours are crucial for the swindles Nucingen is staging at the Stock Exchange and in the Parisian high society, whose money he is placing, and eating, in his speculations. In his previous career, twice he gained large sums in artful liquidity crises. He suspended payments just to liquidate his debts with large discounts, satisfying the worried investors who had their funds placed in his bank. Bixiou, one of the four "condottieri", tells the secret story of Nucingen's third liquidation. Rastignac, the unconscious puppet in the hands of the Baron, gained his own fortune acting as his agent in spreading the rumour of his financial distress, his escape to Bruxelles, his impending bankruptcy (Balzac 1838 [1977]b: 381–382). Nucingen's plans were revealed neither to his wife's lover nor to banker Du Tillet, who was instrumental in mounting the new company formally managed by banker Claparon. On the frightening news spread at the Stock Exchange and in Parisian high society, Nucingen collects letters by investors ordering him to move their funds from his bank into Claparon's new company. Du Tillet, the professional speculator, aims at immediately gaining by bullish speculation on these shares; Nucingen finally gets the spoils with large profits. Insiders play their hard game, each trying to capture information by direct contact or by conjectures on other speculators' moves.[21] Even the Keller brothers, on broker Palma's authoritative opinion, are deceived into selling Nucingen's paper when the panic spreads.[22]

Success in speculation by insiders in the banking business is based on wide-spread losses suffered by upper-class investors with poor financial competence. Upper-class investors are not just ill-informed victims; they are depicted as idle people, dissipating their lives and fortunes. As in Mill's narration, the gambling passion is widespread in the population at large, not just in the financial community. Although an ethical stigma is attached to finance, and financiers must show up theatrically in high society to affirm their status, *Haute Banque* mixes with politics and upper-class nobility. Neither Nucingen nor Keller commits suicide, like the swindlers in Victorian novels. Rastignac, the successful parvenu in contrast to the ruined dandy Godefroid, gains his private fortune and his sisters' dowries thanks to his intelligence and lack of scruples in serving Nucingen in his manoeuvres. Unveiled in its dark side, the speculative business provides effective chances for change of status, and social advancement to ambitious youngsters from lower classes.

Financial plots in Victorian literature

In Victorian literature, financial plots took pride of place both in popular novels and in well-known masterpieces.[23] The wicked speculator is an outstanding character in these stories (Reed 1984; Wagner 2010). Authors who dealt with speculation include notably Thackeray, Dickens, Riddell, Gaskell and Trollope. As Dickens explains in *Martin Chuzzlewit*, a "bold speculator" is an unscrupulous businessman with a genius for commercial frauds.[24] In many novels, the speculator/swindler, since the two characters overlap, is a dangerous intruder into the domestic community, a "bastard" or "foreigner" of dubious origin according to stereotypes or overt racism (mostly anti-Semitism). Even if a national character, by misbehaving the financial swindler breaks bonds of fairness, loyalty and mutual respect. This bleak antagonist is often destined to commit suicide, a metaphor for the final failure of aggressive social climbers who aim at breaking the barriers protecting landed aristocracy or genuine people and custom in the national community. In the narration of speculative business both financiers and their victims fail to adopt strategies of sound risk management. The gambling spirit dominates; altered states of mind prevail in speculative manias with metaphors evoking fever, convulsion or insanity; greedy savers are tempted to invest in fraudulent companies. The exit from speculative investment is destructive for both swindlers and naive investors. Financial scoundrels build their transient success on falsehood, but truth finally will out; as selfish social climbers, they are devoured by the hubris of amassing fortune beyond the limits set by prudent evaluation and social conventions. Their portraits are, however, sketched in chiaroscuro, and they are not deprived of charisma and ambiguous fascination (Wagner 2010: 26).

The opposition between "speculation" and "investment" (a *topos* in Victorian financial fiction) was at the centre of public debate and legal controversies on where to draw the line that divides illegal gambling from legitimate speculative transactions or risky investment (Itzkowitz 2002; Wagner 2010: 71).[25] In Victorian novels, speculation was conceived as the investment of large amounts of money in adventurous projects, with funds amassed thanks to shaky credit, Ponzi schemes or the fraudulent marketing of shares to naive investors. Ideas of speculation do not focus primarily on speculative transactions by brokers at the Stock Exchange; speculation is any placement of funds in financial schemes promising unreasonable profits from future prices, or in fanciful projects advertised to the public or proposed to closed circles of investors. Speculative manoeuvres destroy old fortunes and dissipate life savings, in contrast with sound investment that increases both private and national wealth. They are condemned with harsh judgement and the censure of those promoting them, who induce uninformed savers to risk their wealth. The gullible investors, whose minds are captured by the fanciful schemes, are not spared. In the plots, their crowd includes members of old agrarian aristocracies; high-class women who play the game of being amateur-speculators; young go-getters hoping to make a fortune; unfaithful lower-middle-class clerks. Their greediness or irresponsibility is the object of contempt, and causes their disgrace. Several fictional financiers end their life in bankruptcy and suicide.

Dickens dealt with speculation and financial fraud in his novel *Martin Chuzzlewit*, published in 1843–44. The novel narrates two financial frauds with dire consequences for the people involved. The first one is a real estate speculation in the United States. In the office of the "Eden Land Corporation", Eden, "as it appeared on paper", is the magnificent plan of a new city to be built from scratch, with rich returns for the investors, who buy the plots (Dickens 1843–44 [1997], chap. 21). This fanciful project is recommended as a "speculation" "full of hopes and chances" for people so lucky to invest in it (Dickens 1843–44 [1997]: 339).

Young Martin Chuzzlewit and his friend Mark confidently invest all their savings buying a plot, just to discover that the fabulous Eden is an almost inhabited place in marshy lands. There, they burn their modest wealth and risk dying of malaria. At a deep level, Eden is a metaphor for the delusions of young people who look for quick gains and break bonds with motherland, and the community to which they belong. The second fraud is staged at the "Anglo-Bengalee Disinterested Loan and Life Insurance Company", the pretended international insurance company that manages a Ponzi scheme *avant la lettre*, where early investors were to profit from premiums paid out from the funds of late subscribers (Dickens 1843–44 [1997]: 418 ff.). Tigg Montague, a petty trickster who metamorphosed into a businessman, gaining a reputation of trustworthiness and wealth, manages the company. He induces Mr. Pecksniff to invest his funds in quotas of the company; Pecksniff, one of the great rascals in the story under the respectable façade of a decent teacher and architect, is moved by his sheer greediness. In Dickens' narration, the solitary mind obsessed by the idea of self-interest, far from reaching foresighted, rational choices, is prey to destructive emotions, obfuscating judgement and devouring the soul. Selfishness, a core subject in the novel, is a destructive passion. Speculation fits in as a powerful metaphor for false appearances and cheating, as opposed to authenticity in personal identity, and in relations with other human beings.

Dickens dealt again with frauds in banking and the social costs of bankruptcy in his novel *Little Dorrit*, published in 1857.[26] In Book II of *Little Dorrit*, banker Merdle is apparently a successful financier; but his bank will go bankrupt, and the savers who invested their funds into it will be brought to financial collapse. Merdle, portrayed as a mean, selfish man with no remarkable intellectual qualities, enjoys the reputation of being a banker of fabulous wealth ("his ways being . . . paved with gold"), with connections in politics; he is famed for being devoted to public welfare (Dickens 1857 [1996]: 540). The aura of wealth and power that surrounds his personality in public opinion intoxicates judgement.[27] Dickens compares the blind faith of people investing their savings in his shaky company to an epidemic disease ("a moral infection", spreading "with the malignity and rapidity of the Plague", sparing "no pursuit or condition") (Dickens 1857 [1996]: 539). Speculative expectations spread, with no sound foundation, mouth to mouth, in the contagion of sympathetic emotions. "He's a man of immense resources – enormous capital – government influence. They're the best schemes afloat. They're safe. They're certain" (Dickens 1857 [1996]: 550). Asymmetric information fuels the diffusion of false beliefs. People need to invest their savings, but they know they have poor knowledge and no qualified judgement; they share the opinion of other savers and investors, whom they trust as reliable and better informed. These, in turn, are led astray by the charisma of the high financier.[28] "Bred at first, as many physical diseases are, in the wickedness of men, and then disseminated in their ignorance, these epidemics, after a period, get communicated to many sufferers who are neither ignorant nor wicked" (Dickens 1857 [1996]: 551).

The story underlies the caring, "human liability" decent characters (Amy Dorrit, Arthur Clennam) take as their duty in family life and commercial partnership, versus the manoeuvres of Merdle, who drags other people to ruin (Feltes 1974:

365). It should be read against the background of heated controversies on the mismanagement of funds in unlimited joint-stock banks, before the new legislation on limited liability was extended to banks in 1879. Joint-stock banks' failures were brought to the attention of public opinion for the heavy costs their directors' frauds imposed on savers.[29] Since the mid-1850s, the legislation on limited liability companies was the subject of concern, a concern that was expressed in popular novels (Reed 1984: 185 ff.). In the 1880s and 90s, advertisement of shares in joint-stock companies proliferated in the press, with prospects written in colourful language to attract middle-class investors (Itzkowitz 2002).

Trollope's satirical novel *The Way We Live Now*, published in 1875, is one of the outstanding novels in Victorian financial fiction, though the references to technicalities of speculative transactions are scarce and the gallery of financial characters is simplified in hierarchies and tasks. The plot revolves around a set of financial frauds, with the focus on the fraudulent floating of an international railways company, the fictional emblem for the deceitful prospects eating middle-class savings. Banker Melmotte, the great financier of the plot, commits suicide with prussic acid, as had been the fate of banker John Sadleir (Alborn 1995: 221). In the middle of the story, he enjoys great popularity thanks to the charisma of his wealth, the luxurious parties he offers to his guests, the seats he offers to idle members of the elite in the board of directors of his railways company and his political career. An unpleasant person with "an expression of mental power on a harsh vulgar face", he was "magnificent in his expenditure, powerful in his doings, successful in his business", which is surrounded by an aura of international grandeur (Trollope 1875 [2004]: 67). He buys the magnificent estates of a ruined noble family, the Longestaffe, on a risky leverage scheme, planning to pay the price by mortgaging the land. At the top of his success, the extravagant luxury of the banquet he pays to honour the emperor of China contributes to undermining the shaky foundations of his wealth. Rumours about his dishonesty and forgeries spread. His crazy expenditures and the financial fragility of his schemes force him to forge the signature of his daughter to appropriate her funds. Before the disclosure of this last forgery, trapped in debt and in a liquidity crisis, he kills himself at home, a lonely and desperate man. The plot is intertwined with the scheme for "the grand proposal for a South Central Pacific and Mexican Railways" advanced by Mr. Fisker, the American "projector", who raises the funds to build the line from Salt Lake City to Vera Cruz (Trollope 1875 [2004]: 64). The real plan for "the greatest work of the age" was "to float a company", and advertise it with "brilliantly printed programmes", enjoying the profits from the rising price of its shares on the market (Trollope 1875 [2004]: 65–66). ". . . [F]ortunes were to be made out of the concern before a spadeful of earth had been moved" (Trollope 1875 [2004]: 65). The original investors attribute to themselves fictitious quotas of the stock, to be repaid by selling their shares at a premium on the market. Melmotte leads the new company, gaining further prestige and wealth. "Men were contented to buy their shares and to pay their money, simply on Melmotte's word" (Trollope 1875 [2004]: 264). Finally, the truth is out and the shares fall almost to zero on the market, precipitating Melmotte's fall and suicide.

In the novel Jewish persons are satirically portrayed as outcasts in British society, even when they are "good-natured", as the decent businessman Mr. Brehgert. Melmotte, a foreigner, is possibly a Jew. His "gorgeous mansion" in Grosvenor Square lacks the warmth of ancient roots and family life; it contains "nothing but gold and grandeur, pomatum, powder and pride" (Trollope 1875 [2004]: 241). In Trollope's novel *The Prime Minister*, published in 1876, the swindler Ferdinand Lopez is again a mysterious character, and anti-Jewish prejudice marks his portrait (Trollope 1876 [2011]). An emerging businessman of success of Portuguese origin, he is suspected to be "half foreigner, half Jew". His manners are those of a perfect gentleman ("dressed with perfect care"); but he is not "a man of ancestry" (Jaffe 2002: 47). Ferdinand betrays the hopes of lady Emily (a young British woman of proper ancestry), who falls in love with him and marries him. Though perfectly at ease with the high society lifestyle, he cannot share the values of the community of genuine ancestry. His financial tricks are based on his ability to influence other people's feelings and beliefs. The plot reveals that Lopez's wealth is a bluff, much as his gentleman status; his being a foreign Jew is shown as an inerasable mark (Jaffe 2002: 47 ff.). A forger in business and private life, his attempt at being assimilated into British society is destined to fail. He is disappointed in his political ambitions. Being finally trapped in a liquidity crisis, he commits suicide. The story includes a specific reference to speculation in commodities (coffee and guano); traders buy and sell commodities for speculative purposes without materially having them in stock. Speculative transactions – Lopez argues – imply a game among speculators on conjectures about future trends in commodities prices, with divergence of opinions among buyers and sellers. In the novel, the distinction between investment and speculation defines the dividing line separating reputable wealth, acquired by respecting the values of gentlemanliness, from the frail fortunes amassed at the Stock Exchange by adventurers of dubious origin.

Most financial plots centred on "speculation" deal with specific episodes of financial fraud, artfully built up by a financier, who fuels dreams of incredible gains by selling quotas of a shaky or sham business at home or abroad. Banking frauds and the collapse of speculative business evoke a lethal risk to British society. Selfishness and irresponsibility disrupt the stable bonds of social life, and speculative transactions shake the foundations of the domestic community.

Bubble companies and worthless shares

In 1873, W. Bagehot addressed the explanation of financial crises in his book *Lombard Street*, describing the working of British financial markets, and arguing to defend the role of lender of last resort that the Bank of England should perform in episodes of panics, or to prevent panics during financial crises (Bagehot 1878).[30] It was Bagehot's purpose to demonstrate that panics should be alleviated, or better, stopped at an early stage by the appropriate intervention of the Bank of England offering the required liquidity through credit when everybody in the market was desperately trying to maintain liquidity and meet engagements.[31] According to

Bagehot, financial crises culminating in panics are the final stage of episodes of speculations involving disappointed expectations and excessive borrowing by large groups of market agents at the same time. Bagehot mentioned manias with terminology clearly pointing to mental insanity ("delirium" and "madness"). In the periods of "commercial excitement" and rising prices that precede the drama of panics, the "mercantile community" makes great mistakes. Merchants and producers tend to over-work and over-trade;[32] "saving persons" embark in crazy speculations in "bubble companies and worthless shares".[33] The shared feelings of hope and prosperity in the community offer "a happy opportunity for ingenuous mendacity", a fertile ground for frauds (Bagehot 1878: 158).

Bagehot underlined the state of "confidence" as crucial in the crisis, as later in the recovery. In his description, the role of the money market is to establish confidence among dealers, who otherwise have no reason to trust each other in risky transactions involving large amounts of money.[34] He illustrated the point historically, to emphasize that the rise of credit markets accompanied, and facilitated, the extension of domestic and international trade. The banking system offered relatively safe opportunities to invest savings, and helped to maintain the safe circulation of commercial paper, on which the extended networks of trade depend. According to Bagehot, "opinion" regarding trustworthiness and solvency is essential for financial stability. "Alarm" and "panic" are similarly described in terms of the spreading of "opinion" in the market.[35] "Opinion" is a psychic phenomenon involving shared judgements and evaluations among traders in the market. Expectations are a highly social phenomenon, not at all the solipsistic state of mind of private individuals.

A variety of characters appear in Bagehot's description of manias and financial crises, each of whom with his own strategy of prudent behaviour, his pool of limited information, his specific profession and stock of human capital, his own set of opportunities for gains under different conditions. Bagehot mentions the merchants operating their transactions with promissory notes, the saving public, the professional bill-brokers who belong to "a class of dependent money-dealers", the "minor money dealers" and the main banks, the joint-stock banks with their managers and boards of directors. Each rank responds to a different ethics of prudent behaviour and sound risk management. When panic starts, what appears to be prudent behaviour in terms of individual rationality, spreading simultaneously to all agents and mining confidence and trust, paralyzes trade.[36] The effort of all dealers to protect their business against insolvency by claiming back their money turns into a self-fulfilling prophecy of generalized insolvency. The individual broker, money-dealer or merchant is not necessarily prey to a burst of frenzy; but the result of each trader's prudent behaviour, multiplied by the hundreds or thousands who behave similarly, is an inferior social outcome. Bagehot (much as Mill) signalled that during manias and panics selfish individual rationality clashes with social welfare.

Contrary to Mill and Bagehot, who both saw the origin of fluctuations in speculative bubbles of various origins, including monetary shocks, W.S. Jevons built a theory of the business cycle properly, trying to prove it on sound statistical evidence of periodic recurrence. In his essay "The periodicity of commercial crises and its physical explanation", published in 1878, at the origin of the trade cycle he identified a regular astronomic phenomenon, a natural event instead of conjectures in the traders' minds (Jevons 1878 [2001]a: 187). He connected the estimated decennial variations in harvests in India and other tropical or semitropical regions to the periodic phenomena of sun-spots, conjecturing that they had an impact on the import and export markets in Great Britain (Jevons 1878 [2001]a: 196). Though placing the origin of the trade cycle in the solar period, Jevons had recourse to non-rational feelings and imitative expectations to explain the transmission mechanism in the fluctuations. In his essay, he dealt notably with the South Sea Bubble that he defined a "mania" of "extreme intensity"; he mentioned the regular occurrence of periods of "stock jobbing" even before it, such as "a stock-jobbing mania in the year 1710 or thereabouts" (Jevons 1878 [2001]a: 190–191). After detailed inquiry on the manias and commercial crises he had identified with pretended decennial recurrence, he agreed with the thesis advanced by Mills in the *Transactions of the Manchester Statistical Society* that a commercial panic is "the destruction of belief and hope in the minds of merchants and bankers"; but he rejected the overall psychological interpretation of Mills that "attributes the periodic variations to mental action", since he noted that he could see "no reason why the human mind, in its own spontaneous action, should select a period of just 10.44 years to vary in"(Jevons 1878 [2001]a: 195, 196). In accordance with his theory that pointed out to the origin of recurrence in sun-spots, he looked at the "industrial environment", which influences the state of mind of merchants and bankers "in their dealings", and identified the main influence in the "accounts of the success of harvests, the comparative abundance or scarcity of goods" (Jevons 1878 [2001]a: 196). In the further paper he published in November 1878, he faced the objection that "they who theorise about the relationships of sun-spots, rainfall, famines, and commercial crises are supposed to be jesting, or at the best romancing" (Jevons 1878 [2001]b: 214–215). His "romancing" narrative gave pride of place to the sun as "the great fountain energy" from which "we derive our strength and our weakness, our success and our failure, our elation in commercial mania, and our despondency and ruin in commercial collapse" (Jevons 1878 [2001]b: 214). Jevons underlined the role of speculative conjectures by entrepreneurs in fuelling the phases of the cycle, and his analysis closed on the psychic mood of traders as the amplifying mechanism in the cycle that may explain the severity and width of fluctuations.[37]

In *The Economics of Industry*, published in 1879, A. Marshall and M. Paley Marshall analyzed the trade cycle placing due emphasis on speculative expectations and their disappointment (Marshall and Paley Marshall 1879 [1997]). They dealt with commercial crises in line with Mill's theory, giving considerable weight to the erroneous expectations of entrepreneurs both in fuelling bullish speculation, with the run to expand credit and the consequent inflation, and in aggravating the subsequent fall in prices. In chapter I in Book III, they endorsed an "overtrading" interpretation of the trade cycle, the fall of activity in depression ensuing from the lack of confidence that spreads across the economy. The Marshalls explained the beginning of an expansion with some favourable circumstance, such as a good harvest that encourages expectations of rising profits. On favourable expectations demand and production expand, credit expands and prices rise. Speculators start to build up inventories on expectations of further rises. Thanks to easy credit, the degree of indebtedness increases. The economy finally reaches a state of financial fragility, because of excessive leverage. The turning point happens when some speculators sell their inventories and banks apply more cautious criteria in supplying credit, or stop expanding credit altogether. The perception of increasing risk spreads. Some firms fail to be able to adjust their transactions to price increases. Banks are ever more selective in granting credit, and more speculators sell their inventories to realize the expected gains. The weaker firms go bankrupt with further contagion effects.

In this picture of the trade cycle, Lord Overstone's phases were quoted, and the terminology echoed psychic states: credit is "jubilant"; there is "the desire to buy and the willingness to pay"; speculators are "anxious"; creditors "suspect" debtors; there is "no mood to venture again" (Marshall and Paley Marshall 1879 [1997]: 152,153). In the sequence the Marshalls sketched, psychic phenomena mix with economic dynamics properly. An embryonic multiplier mechanism is at work in their narration. The expansion or contraction of demand in one trade is transmitted to other trades through the increase or decrease of orders firms receive, to which they react by expanding or contracting production with further multiplier effects. Speculation adds further momentum to price movements. "Speculators" are the agents who buy in the rising market with the purpose to profit from further rises in prices, versus the "old" or the "new" firms, which are dealers and producers in the business world. Thus, the Marshalls adopted a loose distinction reminiscent of the one adopted by Mill.[38]

In the transmission mechanism they devised, credit acts as an amplifier of price fluctuations, and is the source of further systemic effects, since "credit supplies a permanent substitute" for the precious metals in the system of payments, a substitute deemed essential to finance the contemporary growth of trade (Marshall and Paley Marshall 1879 [1997]: 151). In the ascending phase, credit provides the means of payment to expand production, but also to finance purely speculative purchases. A boom is fuelled by credit expansion till the economy enters a state of financial fragility for the simultaneous high leverage of too many firms and speculators. In the declining phase, bankruptcies play the role of a perverse multiplier. The credit crunch forces bankruptcy for lack of liquidity even on "sound" firms, whose assets exceed debts in the long term. Speculators are the villains of the piece. A bankrupt speculator transmits bankruptcy to his lenders and other firms.[39] Bankrupt firms suspend their payments and production, disrupting the flows of payments and orders. The language evokes metaphors of collective psychic turmoil ("storm", "dull calm") and the speculative game ends in disaster, as in Victorian financial plots.[40] In the business community dealers form their estimates on the risk of insolvency in interactive processes of learning, charged with intense emotions. Imitative expectations spread on the authority of professional dealers. "General opinion" (the expectations and moods of people not professionally in business) is "much influenced by the authority of manufacturers and merchants" (Marshall and Paley Marshall 1879 [1997]: 155). Professional money dealers, also opinion leaders, spread signals of their evaluations by expanding or contracting loans.

"Confidence" or "distrust" play a crucial role in this narration of the trade cycle. "The chief cause of the evil is a want of confidence" (Marshall and Paley Marshall 1879 [1997]: 154).[41] "Confidence", as Bagehot's "opinion", is not just a private state of mind; it is a collective mood leading to shared estimates on the systemic risk of insolvency. It affects investment in fixed capital, and the entire system of payments and credit. In a "state of commercial disorganization", recovery rests on "a revival of confidence" (Marshall and Paley Marshall 1879 [1997]: 154).

A comparative look at '*la haute finance*'

In later manuscript notes, Marshall ventured into the analysis of speculation, mentioning speculation at the stock exchange betting on equity prices, but also speculation on estates or other assets with variable market prices (Marshall 1899?[1992]).[42] A professional speculator is defined as a cool, rational businessman having a short-term horizon in his speculative investment, aiming at making large profits out of his "earliest and best information", acting promptly on it (Marshall 1899? [1992]: 589). "Professional speculators", conceived as belonging to the community of "real businessmen", play a sophisticated game of rivalry among themselves. Marshall signalled the crude asymmetry of information between professional dealers and the public, and underlined the possibility of manipulative speculation based on forged information by "great financiers". Professional speculators are "shrewd and well informed" in their choices, as compared to the "impulsive and ill informed" amateurs. "Cool" and "shrewd" speculators gain somewhat at the expense of "the investing class"; they systematically gain at the expense of the amateurish public, and they play a game among themselves "for the distribution of his spoil" (Marshall 1899? [1992]: 587–588). Successful speculation is associated to large wealth, for the better opportunities the larger scale of operations affords. "Powerful financiers and great operators" ride "in front of the crest of the tide", by forecasting the trend of market prices before it materializes, thanks to superior access to information and sharp rational analysis (Marshall 1899? [1992]: 590–591). They carefully forge their speculative moves at the stock exchange and may build alliances with other traders ("acting in concert with others"), but they cover their real drift against the risk other professional brokers will discover it. Their success in speculation is based on their ability to anticipate the turns in market prices by anticipating the vagaries of public opinion, which will influence prices. Marshall describes them as cool analysts of market trends and intelligent players, capable of making well-succeeded feints, conscious of their ability to govern by the artful spreading of news the expectations of other brokers or the public, which will influence short-term prices.

Powerful financiers and great operators (whom Marshall calls also *La Haute Finance*, *La Haute Banque*) may be great personalities, whose constructive social role Marshall recognizes. They may be "Schumpeterian" entrepreneurs *avant la lettre*. Marshall reminds "the first Vanderbilt,[43] a man of consummate constructive force" (Marshall 1899? [1992]: 590). Powerful financiers often speculate to collect the funds to promote their entrepreneurial activities; their ultimate psychic motive is not petty monetary gain, but eager ambition. Because of their market power, they may be tempted to manipulate public opinion, fabricating "false news" to support their speculation, or "to prepare the way for a reaction that will support a speculation that they are planning" (Marshall 1899? [1992]: 591). Being opinion leaders, both for their power to spread news and for the signalling value other traders attribute to their moves, they compete with other professional speculators at the stock exchange.

"Professional speculators" of lower rank share neither the power of manipulating opinion nor the freedom of action that wealth and connections guarantee to great financiers and great operators. They are well-informed, professional insiders at the stock exchange, whose purpose is to anticipate "the inferences that half-instructed opinion" of outsiders (the amateur speculators) "will derive from the news and rumours of the day" (Marshall 1899? [1992]: 591). They gain thanks to their ability to bet successfully on the "transient eddies" of stock prices, at the expense of less informed amateur investors. The language referring to "folly", "insanity" or "psychic turmoil" is absent here, as far as professional speculators are concerned. Marshall portrays their speculative game as the sophisticated, rational activity of inferring information from different sources. They rely on the intelligence and connections needed to quickly feel the turns of popular opinion, and to decipher the moves of market leaders. Dardi and Gallegati underlined "Marshall's negative opinion of speculation", his firm condemnation of "gamblers in business", his endorsement of Carnegie's dictum that "the counterfeit of business is speculation" (Dardi and Gallegati 1992: 576). These value judgements converge, even in language, with those expressed in Victorian financial novels.

In *La Maison Nucingen* Balzac spoke of two stages in the speculative business, the pioneering times when only a few strong heads could understand the mysteries of speculative strategies, and the contemporary stage, when stocks of companies are advertised on leaflets ("prospectus") and sold on wide markets.[44] The fictional events in Zola's novel *L'Argent* (*Money*), published in 1891, were placed in the advanced stage of the speculative trade (Zola 1891 [2009]). Transactions at the stock exchange are described with technical detail and reference to specialized agents.[45] Contemporary events offered abundance of sources for the plot (Réffait 2009a: viii ff.).

The novel tells the story of a stock exchange bubble ending in disaster. It is a tale of hubris, a theme of ancient tragedy. Banker Saccard aims at becoming a great financier[46] (such as one of those Marshall described in his notes), a role for which he has somewhat the temper, but not the firm business intelligence. His ambition is mixed with social envy and racist prejudice against the well-established Jewish bankers.[47] The novel narrates the rise of his banking house, the *Universelle*, originally established and advertised on the market as a pretended catholic bank, defying the Jewish "haute banque" that monopolizes the stock exchange. Saccard is driven by his eager ambition to destroy his newly acquired fortune, destroying the fortunes of many crushed by his fall. He is finally flooded by the dominant firm in the Haute Banque. In prosaic, economic terms, the novel stages the destructive conflict between the new entrant and the incumbent in the banking business, and the inherent instability of a non-collusive duopoly in the banking industry and at the stock exchange. Both banking houses are, so to speak, "too big to fail"; finally, Saccard's emerging bank succumbs under the attack of the powerful Jewish banker Gundermann.

In the "Haute Banque", Gundermann is the fictional great operator prominent at the Paris Stock Exchange. It is doubtful whether he has the "constructive force" Marshall attributed to his Vanderbilt type of the "great financier"; but he perfectly fits into the stereotype of the "great operator" practicing malignant speculation. He is portrayed as an exceedingly secret and composed personality of perfectly cool temper, whose force is in patience and logic. His behaviour is never driven by impulsive passions, which might veil his rational judgement or obfuscate his impassibility; but once again the moving force of his character is the obsession for prestige and power.[48] He forges his speculations with shrewd planning of his moves, being able to keep his real aims covered. He makes feints to cheat less informed professional speculators or the crowd of amateur speculators and investors. He builds secret alliances and collects information by allied brokers spying for him. He manoeuvres trade through secret orders to minor dealers, who are his cronies. He manipulates rumours in covert ways, his wealth and connections being instrumental in his manipulative transactions.

Gundermann has the advantage of his large wealth ("la réserve formidable de son milliard") to support a long game of bearish speculation against the shares of the rival bank *Universelle* rising to unreasonable values (Zola 1891 [2009]: 371, 391, 400). As Mill's professional dealers, he understands the fundamentals on which the trend of prices depends; he guesses the abnormal value to which the *Universelle* shares have risen in the bubble.[49] He trusts the economic logic that regulates prices at the stock exchange, when he secretly organizes his attack to force the precipitous fall of Saccard's *Universelle* and bring it to final collapse. He receives crucial information on the fragile financial position of the *Universelle* by Baroness Sandorff, who betrays Saccard, his lover, obsessed by her passion for gambling. Gundermann, impassibly, dismisses her to cover his game.[50]

Saccard, a parvenu, became a successful banker after successes and reverses in various speculations.[51] He is desperately aiming at winning the dominant place that in the end he will not be able to secure for himself. A passionate nature, his dominant passion for a fortune acquired in the speculative gamble will betray him in his ambition, much as it betrays the crowd of amateur speculators.[52] Zola describes his mood in crucial moments with the psychic metaphors mentioned above: fever ("fievre", "fievreux"), anger ("rage"), excitement ("état d'excitation"). A rational gambler and a shrewd professional speculator, he ends by being a "projector", who destroys the lives of the many "amateur speculators" who had invested their money in his banking company. Saccard manipulates public opinion financing a literary journal to capture consensus in favour of his bank, which he publicizes as a project of ethical finance to promote Roman Catholicism all over the world.

The novel portrays a nice collection of fictional "amateur speculators", who press Saccard to get shares in his banking business in the hope of gaining sums which in their ordinary life they would have not dreamed of. They include rich investors in the nobility, high-class women with the gambling passion, lower middle classes looking for the placement of modest savings on which their precarious future depends, and even poor people dreaming of good luck to change their status. At one extreme, Baroness Sandorff, the glamorous lady, is addicted to speculative gambling, her addiction freezing her emotions and dominating her selfish personality. At the other extreme, Dejoie, a poor clerk, invests his scarce savings in the *Universelle* hoping to gain a decent sum for the dowry of his daughter Nathalie. A mixed group of brokers work at the stock exchange, acting on behalf of their customers and on their own behalf with different access to crucial information and diversified strategies of alliances with great operators.[53] As professional speculators, they play their own game to beat the gun, with chances depending on access to covered information, and on the ability to build fruitful alliances or quickly change their strategy. They risk of going bankrupt by engaging in speculations they have not enough funds to sustain. Mazaud, the competent broker who does not speculate on his own money, kills himself after he has been ruined by his loyal alliance with Saccard in bullish speculation on the *Universelle*. Delarocque, another broker, is saved by his prompt change to a bearish position, having been secretly told by another broker that Gundermann is ready to fire all his money to gain his bearish game against the *Universelle* the day after.

The characters of Jewish bankers in the novels we explored call attention to the issue of anti-Semitic stereotypes.[54] In fiction, they are deprived of "sympathy" to other humans, or the emotions and psychic frailties involved in love, friendship, family affections, love for the arts, sense of honour, melancholy, sadness. Their portraits are sketched with emphasis on the cognitive capabilities and instrumental passions, which are deemed essential to their successful financial business, at the loss of more human feelings. Indeed, their traits (greediness, coolness of heart, passion for power, unscrupulous behaviour, secret manoeuvres, lack of pity for the sufferings of common people) compose the stereotype of the wicked Jewish banker in the violent anti-Semitic literature of the late 19th century, and overlap with the older stereotype of the wicked Jew with wide diffusion in European culture.[55]

A glimpse on passions and finance in economics and literature in the 19th century

A crowd of emotional people act in financial markets in the stories told in 19th-century financial fiction as in contemporary economic narratives. Most of the characters portrayed in financial sceneries suffer from cognitive biases and are overwhelmed by socially shared emotions, or the prey to collective moods. The frenzy of gambling in "manias" recurs in economics and fiction alike, as the opposition between "speculation" and "investment" that Keynes brings to new life in depicting the stock exchange in *The General Theory*. In both literary and economic stories, stock markets are notable for asymmetry of information, lack of transparency in transactions, inequality of wealth influencing the demand and the supply sides and the market power of leading operators. "Speculation" and the various characters of "speculators" are charged with emotional resonance and ethical evaluation.

In financial fiction, characters acting in financial markets, be they bankers, brokers, amateur speculators, middle-class savers or rich members of the nobility, participate in social and political networks, which are intertwined with market sceneries. The working of financial markets is affected by the political connections of leading operators, their links to elite circles or their commercial fraternities; even marriage strategies have their role. If the social background is not so rich in economic narratives, 19th-century economists centred their discourse on commercial crises on a variety of players with diverse behaviour and roles, to explain the speculative contagion spreading on the market and ending in systemic financial crises of macro relevance. Market leaders manipulate public opinion. Merchants and money dealers, brokers and bankers, savers and investors may be overwhelmed by the gambling passion, or induced to exceedingly risky behaviour by false imaginations, and by trusting opinion more than well-grounded evidence. In forming expectations and taking financial decisions, they are neither isolated maximizing agents nor perfectly rational forecasters.

Novelists portrayed a gallery of fraudulent financiers and the individual stories of their speculations or final crash in bankruptcy. They took inspiration from financiers of their epoch and notorious collapses of big banks. Their plots reflect the evolving state of financial markets in the 19th century, about legal bans on gambling, bankruptcy law, unlimited or limited liability companies, the marketing of stocks or the transactions at the stock exchange. Speculation and bankruptcy were metaphors to represent the vagaries of human fortunes, the rise and fall of ambitious, and ambiguous, personalities and the social change going on in contemporary societies, where the status acquired by acquiring financial wealth subverted the order of society rooted in local economies, family ties and landed estates. Economists dealt with "commercial crises" or the "trade cycle" to account for historical events in market economies. They dealt with a pressing issue: which mistaken calculus and emotions may drive crowds of professional traders and savers into manias and panics? Which forces lead them back to sound business? In economic narratives, the speculator, far from being a foreign intruder, is the domestic dealer, broker or banker,[56] and the severity of recurring crises with their welfare costs might be mitigated by education, legislation or monetary policy. Though manias and panics impose heavy social costs, recurrence implies the return of the quiet after the tempest; the operation of market forces finally restores market order.

In fiction, a main theme is the costs of bankruptcies, which affect families and community alike, destroy sound business, erase agrarian wealth or force decent people to unemployment and despair. In economics, systemic financial crises, much as the collapse of fraudulent companies in fiction, signal the abrupt failure of the forward-looking plans on which the fortunes of savers and investors depend. In both economic and literary stories, the welfare costs call for an assessment of financial behaviour in terms of fairness, moral responsibility, enlightened or myopic self-interest and the complex balance of emotions and rationality in financial choices. After the experience of a severe financial crisis, economists still must address these issues, though in the language of contemporary theory.

Notes

1 In early use, the word "panic" maintained its usual meaning along with the new one of "widespread apprehension" on the state of markets leading to hasty liquidation (Besomi 2010: 88–89).
2 "A commercial crisis is the recoil of prices, after they have been raised by speculation higher than is warranted by the state of the demand and of the supply. Speculation is almost always set in motion by something which affords apparent grounds for expecting either an extra demand or a deficient supply. But the anticipation may, in the first place, be erroneous; in the second, however rational it may be, the speculation (especially where the prospect of gain is considerable) is very likely to be overdone, each speculator conducting his operations as if he alone knew the circumstances on which the hope of profit is grounded. The rise consequent upon the speculative purchases attracts new speculators, insomuch that, paradoxical as it may appear, the largest purchases are often made at the highest price. But at last it is discovered that the rise has gone beyond the permanent cause for it, and purchases cease, or the holders think it is time to realise their gains. Then the recoil comes; and the price falls to a lower point than that from which it had risen, because the high price has both checked the demand, and, by stimulating production or importation, called forth a larger supply. Besides, many of those who during the high price have contracted engagements, which they trusted to a further rise for giving them the means of fulfilling, are unable to hold on until the crisis is past, but must sell at any sacrifice" (Mill 1844 [1967]: 348).
3 "As long as the seasons vary, as markets fluctuate, and men miscalculate, or the passion of gain (as in gamblers) over-rides their calculations, so long will these alterations of ebb and flow, these 'cycles', as Colonel Torrens calls them, 'of excitement and depression,' continue" (Mill 1844 [1967]: 349).
4 Samuel Jones Loyd (1796–1883) was a renowned banker and politician.
5 On Mills' theory, and the influence Mills had on Jevons, see Peart 1996.
6 Réffait reviewed this profuse literature with accurate coverage and critical intelligence (Réffait 2007, 2009a, 2009b).
7 "La Spéculation? dit le parfumeur, quel est ce commerce? C'est le commerce abstrait, reprit Claparon, un commerce qui restera secret pendant une dizaine d'années encore, au dire du grand Nucingen, le Napoléon de la finance, et par lequel un homme embrasse les totalités des chiffres, écrèmes les revenues avant qu'ils n'existent, une conception gigantesque, une façon de mettre l'espérance en coupes réglées, enfin une nouvelle Cabale! Nous ne sommes encore que dix ou douze têtes fortes initiées aux secrets cabalistiques de ces magnifiques combinaisons" (Balzac 1838 [1977]a: 241–242).
8 He was gambling at the Stock Exchange with his own and other people's money; he profited from his social contacts and love affairs; in contact with politicians and usurers, he earned money and experience travelling abroad, trafficking on debts contracted by the emigrated nobility (Balzac 1838 [1977]a: 88–89).
9 "En bas, Adolphe excusait son frère sur ses préoccupations politiques, et il passait habilement le râteau sur le tapis; il était le frère compromis, l'homme difficile" (Balzac 1838 [1977]a: 212).

10 With these words Du Tillet refuses his support to Birotteau in deep distress.

11 Birotteau had asked his young clerk to cover part of his debt. Anselme initially refused on the advice of his uncle, the judge Popinot, that he should never put his funds at risk issuing fake promissory notes.

12 He fails to write a point on the "i" in his signature to signal to banker Nucingen, to whom his letter is addressed, that Birotteau is not really his protégée (Balzac 1838 [1977]a: 221).

13 See the story of the poor textile worker selling his stock of red caps thanks to a trick told in *La Maison Nucingen* (Balzac 1838 [1977]b: 377).

14 Popinot advertises his oil for the hair under the ridiculous name of "huile céphalique" in a "staggering" advertising leaflet ("a prospectus ébouriffant"), according to Gaudissart, who will act as his marketing agent (Balzac 1838 [1977]a: 153, 156). The oil is a great commercial success.

15 "Si la plupart des hommes ignorent les raisons qui font aimer, toute sympathie physique ou morale n'en est pas moins basée sur des calculs faits par l'esprit, le sentiment ou la brutalité. L'amour est une passion essentiellement égoïste. Qui dit égoïsme, dit profond calcul" (Balzac 1838 [1977]a: 132). See also Guise 1977: 34.

16 In *Splendeurs et misères des courtisanes* Nucingen falls in love with Esther, and his senile love causes her suicide. She kills herself after having spent the night with him to save her beloved Lucien.

17 Banker Claparon is an associate to both Nucingen and Du Tillet and at their command; but Nucingen is portrayed as the banker in ultimate control of the events in the financial world.

18 "La société Claparon fit trop d'affaires, il y eut engorgement, elle cessa de servir les intérêts et de donner des dividendes, quoique ses opérations fussent excellentes. . . . En 1829, Claparon était trop connu pour être l'homme de paille de ce deux colosses, et il roula de son piédestal à terre. De douze cent cinquante francs, les actions tombèrent à quatre cent francs, quoique elles valussent intrinsèquement six cents francs. Nucingen, qui connaissait leur prix intrinsèque, racheta" (Balzac 1838 [1977]b: 389–390).

19 "Le propre de Nucingen est de faire servir les plus habiles gens de la place à ses projets, sans les leur communiquer" (Balzac 1838 [1977]b: 371).

20 In *La Maison Nucingen*, Nucingen is described as a "strong head" ("tête puissante"), able to exploit business opportunities all over the world. His business includes trade in commodities ("les vins, les laines, les indigos"), public procurement, investment in channels, mining in Mexico or Peru, and more (Balzac 1838 [1977]b: 338–339).

21 The money-dealer Gigonnet fuels the panics to gain on minor spreads in discounts, reselling to Werbrust, since he has shrewdly conjectured that the broker is playing a bearish game on Nucingen's paper. Brokers Werbrust and Palma, informed by Du Tillet's occasional remarks, conjecture that Nucingen will not go bankrupt; they purposefully fuel panics to play the bearish speculation, and gain in the later recovery of Nucingen's banking house (Balzac 1838 [1977]b: 386).

22 The details of the plot include fluctuations of shares in silver mining, trade in commodities by Nucingen's bank, early globalization with risky capital investment in Mexico, and so on and so forth.

23 In Victorian studies, scholars spoke of "the entire genre of evil-speculator novels of the period" (Jaffe 2002: 58–59), or "the popularity of the fable of financial ruin" (Herbert 2002: 190). Wagner deeply analyzed the "speculator" in Victorian fiction (Wagner 2010). On finance in Victorian fiction, see also Weiss 1986; Poovey 2002; Malton 2009.

24 "In plainer words he had a most distinguished genius for swindling, and could start a bank, or negotiate a loan, or form a land-jobbing company (entailing ruin, pestilence, and death on hundreds of families), with any gifted creature in the Union" (Dickens 1843–44 [1997]: 262).

25 ". . . the equation of gambling and speculation remained a constant of nineteenth-century discourse . . ." (Itzkowitz 2002: 124). Itzkowitz recalls the change in the legislation

on gambling in Great Britain since 1845, and the debate on speculative transactions, which were common practice at the Stock Exchange. Since the 1860s, they were recognized as regular contracts in courts and official reports (Itzkowitz 2002).

26 Dickens took inspiration from the bankruptcy of the Irish Tipperary Bank, and the suicide of fraudulent financier John Sadleir (Alborn 1995: 213).

27 "But in *Little Dorrit* Merdle stands for more than a mysterious social power; he is the source and the symbol of the disease of speculation which infects the whole society . . ." (Feltes 1974: 363).

28 Popularity and charisma are the mark of other high financiers in 19th-century novels.

29 See the failures of the Royal British Bank in 1855, the Tipperary Bank in 1856 and the City of Glasgow Bank in 1878 (Alborn 1995).

30 The sixth edition was printed in 1875, the year in which Trollope published *The Way We Live Now*.

31 "A panic, in a word, is a species of neuralgia, and according to the rules of science you must not starve it" (Bagehot 1878: 51).

32 "Such a period naturally excites the sanguine and the ardent; they fancy that the prosperity they see will last always, that is only the beginning of a greater prosperity. They altogether over-estimate the demand for the article they deal in, or the work they do" (Bagehot 1878: 156).

33 "They speculate with it [money of "saving persons"] in bubble companies and in worthless shares . . . The mania of 1825 and the mania of 1866 were striking examples of this; in their case to a great extent, as in most similar modern periods to a less extent, the delirium of ancient gambling co-operated with the milder madness of modern overtrading" (Bagehot 1878: 157).

34 "The peculiar essence of our banking system is an unprecedented trust from man to man; and when that trust is much weakened by hidden causes, a small accident may greatly hurt it, and a great accident for a moment may almost destroy it" (Bagehot 1878: 158–159).

35 "An 'alarm' is an opinion that the money of certain persons will not pay their creditors when those creditors want to be paid. . . . it aggravates into a 'panic', which is an opinion that most people, or very many people, will not pay their creditors . . ." (Bagehot 1878: 53).

36 On the panic in 1825, he wrote: "The result was a period of frantic and almost inconceivable violence; scarcely any one knew whom to trust; credit was almost suspended . . ." (Bagehot 1878: 200).

37 "The impulse from abroad is like the match which fires the inflammable spirits of the speculative classes. The history of many bubbles shows that there is no proportion between the stimulating cause and the height of folly to which the inflation of credit and prices may be carried. A mania is, in short, a kind of explosion of commercial folly followed by the natural collapse" (Jevons 1878 [2001]b: 221).

38 "Many speculators seeing the rise, and thinking it will continue buy goods with the expectation of selling them at a profit. . . . Old firms are borrowing in order to extend their business; new firms are borrowing in order to start their business, and speculators are borrowing in order to buy and hold goods: trade is in dangerous condition" (Marshall and Paley Marshall 1879 [1997]: 152). See also Dardi and Gallegati 1992.

39 "Some speculators have to sell goods in order to pay their debts; and by so doing they check the rise of prices. This check makes all other speculators anxious, and many rush in to sell. For a speculator who has borrowed money at interest to buy goods may be ruined if he holds them a long time even when their price remains stationary; he is almost sure to be ruined if he holds them while their price falls. When a large speculator fails, his failure generally causes that of others who have lent their credit to him; and their failure again that of others" (Marshall and Paley Marshall 1879 [1997]: 153).

40 "The commercial storm leaves its path strewn with ruin. When it is over there is a calm, but a dull heavy calm" (Marshall and Paley Marshall 1879 [1997]: 153).

41 "The greater part of it could be removed almost in an instant if confidence could return, touch all industries with her magic wand, and make them continue their production and their demand for the wares of others" (Marshall and Paley Marshall 1879 [1997]: 154).

42 M. Dardi and M. Gallegati, who edited Marshall's manuscript, studied the evolution of Marshall's views from the earlier adherence to "overtrading" theories to the later interpretation of speculation as a persisting component in contemporary business (Dardi and Gallegati 1992: 577).

43 Cornelius Vanderbilt (1794–1877), American tycoon, built his fortune in oceangoing steamship lines and railways.

44 Couture, a speculator, comments on this evolution and the practice to place stocks by advertising (Balzac 1838 [1977]b: 373).

45 For the description of specialized trades and professionals, see Zola 1891 [2009]: chap. X.

46 "Mais il avait toujours été l'homme d'imagination, voyant trop grand, transformant en poèmes ses trafics louches d'aventurier; et, cette fois, avec cette affaire réellement colossale et prospère, il en arrivait a des rêves extravagantes de conquête, à une idée si folle, si énorme, qu'il ne se la formulait lui même pas nettement a lui même. Ah, s'il avait eu des millions, des millions toujours, comme ces sales juifs!" (Zola 1891 [2009]: 393).

47 "La ruine prochaine de la haute banque juive était décrétée, le catholicisme allait avoir l'empire de l'argent, comme il avait celui des âmes" (Zola 1891 [2009]: 392).

48 ". . . car, s'il était, comme il aimait a le répéter, un simple marchand d'argent, et non un jouer, il avait la nette conscience que, pour rester ce marchand, le premier du monde, disposant de la fortune publique, il lui fallait être le maitre absolu du marché; et il se battait non pur le gain immédiat, mais pour sa royauté elle-même, pour sa vie" (Zola 1891 [2009]: 392).

49 "Il ne croyait qu'à la logique. Au-dessus du cours de deux mille francs, la folie commençait pour les actions de l'Universelle; à trois mille c'était la démence pure, elles devaient retomber, comme la pierre lancée en l'air retombe forcément; et il attendait. Irait-il jusqu'au bout de son milliard?" (Zola 1891 [2009]: 392).

50 "Et, quand elle s'en fut allée, hors d'elle, il s'enferma avec ses deux fils et son gendre, distribua les rôles, envoya tout de suite chez Jacoby et chez d'autres agents de change pour préparer le grand coup du lendemain. Son plan était simple: faire ce que la prudence l'avait empêché de risquer jusque-là, dans sono ignorance de la véritable situation de l'Universelle; écraser le marché sous des ventes énormes, maintenant qu'il savait cette dernière à bout de ressources, incapable de soutenir les courses. . . . La logique triompherait, toute action est condamnée qui monte au-delà de la valeur vraie qu'elle représente" (Zola 1891 [2009]: 400).

51 Zola narrated Saccard's reckless speculations on real estates in *La Curée* (1872). See Reffait 2009b: 503 ff.

52 "C'était sa passion qui élevait ainsi Saccard, et sa passion qui devait le perdre" (Zola 1891 [2009]: 322).

53 "Un bon agent était fait de finesse et de prescience, de cervelle prompte et des muscles agiles, car la rapidité assurait souvent le succès; sans compter la nécessité des belles relations dans la haute banque, des renseignements ramassés un peu partout, des dépêches reçues des Bourses françaises et étrangères, avant tout autre. Et il fallait encore une voix solide pour crier fort" (Zola 1891 [2009]: 381).

54 For a shocking comparison, let us remind ourselves of the portraits of his relatives E. de Waal narrated in his book on the Ephrussi family (de Waal 2010). The Ephrussi, a Jewish family, were wholesale dealers in grains; they became a successful dynasty of bankers with banking houses in France, the Austro-Hungarian Empire and Great Britain. Outstanding personalities in the family, who lived in Paris, London or Vienna in the 19th century, were cultivated collectors of arts, supporters of charitable associations and cultural enterprises. Later on, many Ephrussi, who could not fly to Great Britain or the United States, were massacred in the Shoa.

55 This is not to suggest that all novelists nurtured anti-Semitic feelings. Zola was crystal clear in his strong stance during the Dreyfus Affair.
56 In Tooke's story about the 1839 tea bubble, the speculators have no exotic flavour; they are retail grocers and tea dealers (Mill 1844 [1967]: 123).

Bibliography

Alborn, T. L. (1995), "The Moral of the Failed Bank: Professional Plots in the Victorian Money Market", *Victorian Studies*, 38 (2): 199–226.

Bagehot, W. (1878), *Lombard Street: A Description of the Money Market*, 7th edition, London: C. Kegan Paul & Co.

Balzac, H. ([1838] 1977a), *César Birotteau*, Paris: Gallimard.

Balzac, H. ([1838] 1977b), *La Maison Nucingen*, Paris: Gallimard.

Besomi, D. (2010), "The Periodicity of Crises: A Survey of the Literature Before 1850", *Journal of the History of Economic Thought*, 32 (1): 85–132.

Besomi, D. (2011), "Crises as a Disease of the Body Politick: A Metaphor in the History of Nineteenth Century Economics", *Journal of the History of Economic Thought*, 33 (1): 67–118.

Dardi, M. and Gallegati, M. (1992), "Alfred Marshall on Speculation", *History of Political Economy*, 24 (3): 571–594.

Dickens, C. (1843–44 [1997]), *Martin Chuzzlewit*, Hertfordshire: Wordsworth Editions.

Dickens, C. (1857 [1996]), *Little Dorrit*, Hertfordshire: Wordsworth Editions.

Feltes, N. N. (1974), "Community and the Limits of Liability in Two Mid-Victorian Novels", *Victorian Studies*, 17 (4): 355–369.

Forget, E. (1990), "John Stuart Mill's Business Cycle", *History of Political Economy*, 22 (4): 629–642.

Gomart, H. (2004), *Les Opérations financières dans le roman réaliste: Lectures de Balzac et de Zola*, Paris: Honoré Champion.

Guise, R. (1977), "Introduction", in *La Comédie Humaine*, vol. VI, Paris: Gallimard, 3–34.

Herbert, C. (2002), "Filthy Lucre: Victorian Ideas of Money", *Victorian Studies*, 44 (2): 185–213.

Hicks, J. (1983), "From Classical to Post-Classical: The Work of J. S. Mill", in *Collected Essays on Economic Theory*, vol. III, Oxford: Clarendon Press, 60–70.

Ingrao, B. (2007), "La concurrence: Balzac au regard de Cournot", in F. Vatin and N. Edelman (eds.), *Économie et littérature: France et Grande-Bretagne (1815–1848)*, Paris: Manuscrit.com, 195–218.

Itzkowitz, D. C. (2002), "Fair Enterprise or Extravagant Speculation: Investment, Speculation, and Gambling in Victorian England", *Victorian Studies*, 45 (1): 121–147.

Jaffe, A. (2002), "Trollope in the Stock Market: Irrational Exuberance and *the Prime Minister*", *Victorian Studies*, 45 (1): 43–64.

Jevons, W. S. ([1878] 2001a), "The Periodicity of Commercial Crises and Its Physical Explanation", in *The Palgrave Archive Edition of the Writings of Economics of W. S. Jevons*, New York: Palgrave, 187–200.

Jevons, W. S. ([1878] 2001b), "Commercial Crises and Sun-Spots", in *The Palgrave Archive Edition of the Writings of Economics of W.S. Jevons*, New York: Palgrave, 201–221.

Malton, S. (2009), *Forgery in Nineteenth-Century Literature and Culture: Fictions of Finance From Dickens to Wilde*, New York: Palgrave MacMillan.

Marshall, A. ([1899?] 1992), "The Folly of Amateur Speculators Makes the Fortunes of Professionals: The Wiles of Some Professionals", Appendix in Dardi, M. and Gallegati,

M. (1992), "Alfred Marshall on Speculation", *History of Political Economy*, 24 (3): 571–594.

Marshall, A. P. and Marshall, M. ([1879] 1997), *The Economics of Industry*, London: Macmillan 1879, reprinted in *Collected Works of Alfred Marshall*, Bristol: Overstone Press.

Michie, E. B. (2001), "Buying Brains: Trollope, Oliphant, and Vulgar Victorian Commerce", *Victorian Studies*, 44 (1): 77–97.

Mill, J. S. ([1826] 1967), "Paper Currency and Commercial Distress", in J. M. Robson (ed.), *The Collected Works of John Stuart Mill*, vol. IV, London: Routledge and Kegan Paul, 71–123.

Mill, J. S. ([1844] 1967), "The Currency Question", *Westminster Review*, XLI: 579–598 reprinted in Robson, J. M. (ed.), *The Collected Works of John Stuart Mill*, vol. IV, London: Routledge and Kegan Paul, 341–362.

Mill, J. S. ([1848] 1967), "Principles of Political Economy", in Robson, J. M. (ed.), *The Collected Works of John Stuart Mill*, vol. III, London: Routledge and Kegan Paul.

Mills, J. (1867), "On Credit Cycles and the Origin of Commercial Panics", *Transactions of the Manchester Statistical Society*, Session 1867–1868, Manchester, 11–40.

Peart, S. (1996), "*Ignorant* Speculation and *Immoral* Risks: Macheaths, Turpins and the Commercial Classes in Nineteenth-Century Theories of Economic Fluctuations", *The Manchester School*, LXIV (2): 135–152.

Poovey, M. (2002), "Writing About Finance in Victorian England: Disclosure and Secrecy in the Culture of Investment", *Victorian Studies*, 45 (1): 17–41.

Reed, J. R. (1984), "A Friend to Mammon: Speculation in Victorian Literature", *Victorian Studies*, 27 (2): 179–202.

Reffait, C. ([1891] 2009a), "Presentation", in E. Zola (ed.), *L'argent*, Paris: Editions Flammarion.

Reffait, C. ([1891] 2009b), "Dossier", in E. Zola (ed.), *L'argent*, Paris: Editions Flammarion.

Réffait, C. (2007), *La Bourse dans le roman du second XIXe siècle*, Paris: Honoré Champion.

Trollope, A. ([1875] 2004), *The Ways We Live Now*, Hertfordshire: Wordsworth Editions.

Trollope, A. ([1876] 2011), *The Prime Minister*, Oxford: Oxford University Press.

Waal de, E. (2010), *The Hare With Amber Eyes: A Hidden Inheritance*, New York: Farrar, Straus and Giroux.

Wagner, T. (2008), "Speculators at Home in the Victorian Novel: Making Stock-Market Villains and New 'Paper Fictions'", *Victorian Literature and Culture*, 36 (1): 43–62.

Wagner, T. (2010), *Financial Speculation in Victorian Fiction*, Columbus, OH: The Ohio State University Press.

Weiss, B. (1986), *The Hell of the English: Bankruptcy and the Victorian Novel*, Lewisburg: Bucknell University Press.

Zola, E. ([1891] 2009), *L'argent*, Paris: Garnier-Flammarion.

3   The passions and the interests

The Sentimental Education
of Gustave Flaubert

*Alfonso Sanchez**

"The masses, the numbers are always idiotic. I have few convictions, but I have that one strongly. But the masses must be respected, however inept they may be, because they contain the germs of an incalculable fecundity. Give it liberty, but not power."

Gustave Flaubert[1]

Written between 1864 and 1869[2] and published that year, Gustave Flaubert in *Sentimental Education* intended to make the moral chronicle of the men of his generation.[3] A lost generation, if considering the conclusions reached by the main character of the novel and one of his life-adventure fellows at the end of it, in one of the most shocking sequences to the critics at the time of its appearance. It was the generation born in the decade of the 20s of the 19th century, who were very young when the revolution extolling Louis-Philippe occurred, who also lived through the collapse of the Orleanist system, witnessing the revolution of '48, the short life of the Second Republic and the coup of Louis Napoleon. Even in old age, they could still witness the disaster of Sedan, the Commune and the advent of the Third Republic.

Therefore, still very young, they attended to what D. Pinkney called "The Decisive Years in France 1840–1847", which later will be referred to in the following pages, and during which France – and Europe – experienced a series of changes and crucial transformations in the political, cultural and economic realms that were to outline the future of the country (Pinkney 1986). It is precisely during these years, lengthening the period until 1851 and, after a jump in time, closing the account in 1867, when the action takes place, allowing Flaubert to locate a sentimental story – transcript of his own – in a historical background describing the changes experienced by the French society, especially during the revolutionary period.

In his story, Flaubert describes with a psychological insight the slips in attitudes, behaviour and rhetoric of characters who, in the words of his friend Maxime Du Camp, were a faithful reflection – like the accounts narrated – of the real characters Flaubert met at that time, even though in some cases mingled together and serving as the basis for a model – archetypal in part – of the society of his time. He himself, together with his friend Du Camp, somehow served as support for the creation of the main character of the novel: Frédéric Moreau.

Sentimental Education begins with the description of the boat trip that Frédéric Moreau, young student who will go to Paris in that year 1840 to continue his studies in law, makes the previous summer to visit his mother in the village of Nogent. On that trip, he falls for a married woman, much older than him, wife of an industrial adventurer, and starts a love story never consummated – a dormant passion, says Flaubert – sliding on the background of the novel.[4] The protagonist, arrived in Paris, plunges into a college life marked by the bohemian and meets several students and youngsters, most of them republicans, who live with passion and concern during the last years of the Orleanist monarchy: occasional republicans, authoritarian socialists, "pure" socialists and misplaced loyalists, mixed with artists, journalists and, with them, the enterprising adventurer, Mr. Arnoux. He is the owner of a property, *L'Art Industriel*, devoted to the sale of works and objects of art, and husband of the woman who, from the beginning of the novel, captures the heart of young Frédéric.

In constructing the historical framework constituting *Sentimental Education*, Flaubert describes the behaviour and ideas of some characters whose dramatic changes reflect the forces that led to the explosion of '48 and the failure, first of the socialists and democrats and, later, of the republicans themselves, together with the failure of their political and economic proposals. Carrying out such a task took him five years of heavy reading and visits to scenarios he would subsequently describe in a meticulous way.

On the pages that follow, it is intended to address the analysis of economic and political ideas interspersed in the novel, as Flaubert put them into the mouths of characters who lived in the complex economic environment of change produced by the beginnings of the industrial revolution in mid-19th-century France, and to analyze to what extent those ideas were a reflection of the thought and feeling of the writer who also lived at that time.

The decisive years: 1840–47

The economy

The economic progress made by France between the years 1835 and 1837, experienced soon after – between 1839 and 1841 – a decline accompanied by an aggravation of the political situation (Goujon 2012: 333).

France remained a heavily agrarian society in which the new Orleanist structure coexisted with the Old Regime, and was dominated by *Grands Notables*, aristocrats, landowners, bankers, industrialists and large-scale traders, who were favored by a highly restrictive census suffrage. However, from the mid-40s of the century on, the French economy began to experience slow progress based on the development and modernization of the textile industry and, subsequently, of the metallurgical industry. The first steps were also taken regarding the financial system (the *Caisse General du Commerce*, anticipating a new banking model, was founded by Jacques Laffite in 1837) along with some first, though timid, achievements in the field of transportation and railroad, that served as elements for the take-off to be experienced over the next decade.

Nevertheless, between 1838 and 1840 a series of poor harvests, coupled with adverse weather conditions and heavy flooding during the fall of that last year, led to a sharp rise in foodstuff prices that brought about a wave of violence, along with a strong fiscal response on the part of the population. There was as well a revival of a spontaneous-like labor movement, resulting in numerous strikes, that opposed to purchasing power loss (Todd 2008: 369).[5] All this was accompanied by a set of publications, truly overwhelming in number, of Republican and Socialist writings strongly criticizing the July Monarchy, alleging non-fulfilment of promises and the deterioration of the situation of the working class.

From the beginning of the fifth decade, according to David Pinkney, a new and decisive period began:

> the most exciting and most significant years of the regime (the July Monarchy) where the neglected years of the Soult-Guizot ministry, 1840–1848. Contrary to the common perception of them as dull and reactionary, characterized by Louis-Philippe's and Guizot's unyielding resistance to change, they were filled with change, change that in almost all areas of national life turned France in new directions and shaped its long future.
>
> (Pinkney 1986: XI–XII)

However, after a particularly dry summer in the year 1846, the resulting poor cereal harvests led to a rise in the price of bread, still the main food product for the masses, aggravated by hoarding practices. Bad harvests of other basic commodities such as potatoes, and a cattle crisis, brought about famines accompanied by strong popular responses sought to confront such practices, preventing the movement of grain for other markets through looting or coerced sale. Some of these responses led to riots and life-taking altercations like the one in Buzançais in 1847, in which a wealthy owner was lynched by peasants, causing strong repression followed by some executions (Jardin and Tudesq 1973: 234).

Along with the agrarian crisis and the industrial crisis – the textile industry being the most affected by the decline in textile sales – the financial crisis, falling share prices and numerous banking bankruptcies entered into the equation. The difficult situation, coupled with the growing demand for expansion of electoral roll induced a campaign of *banquettes Républicaines* that began in Paris – the first of them on July 9, 1847 – and culminated at the dawn of the February Revolution the following year. The fact of the banquet scheduled in Paris on the 22nd of that month being suppressed and banned by the authorities, together with the excessive repression against citizen protests – the executions of *Boulevard des Capucines* – triggered the uprising that ended with the Orleanist regime.

The social question

The economic growth experienced during the Restoration had a clear counterpart in exacerbating social inequalities and the spread of the problem of pauperism that inevitably accompanied the changing process before industrialization. The deterioration was particularly evident during periods of crisis (Goujon 2012: 203).

It was in the years immediately preceding the Orleanist period when the writings of the so-called utopian socialists like Saint-Simon, Fourier and subsequently, Blanc and Cabet, emerged in France. Later, other writers of religious orientation such as B. of Lamennais, who denounced the increasing poverty of the working class, joined the group. Around the same time, secret organizations of various types began to appear. They fought against the authorities and sometimes gathered both Republicans and Bonapartists, even Liberals, in the period prior to the coming to power of Louis-Philippe d'Orléans.[6]

In 1834, the most powerful of all, *la Société des Familles*, was constituted. It was socialist-oriented, and Barbès and Blanqui were the men behind it (Alexandrian 1979).

The year 1840 saw a real publication explosion on social issues (Pinkney 1986: 93) (Harvey 2006). That year saw the birth of, among others, the work of Louis Blanc, *Organisation du travail*; *Voyage en Icarie* by Étienne Cabet; *Qu'est-ce que la proprieté* by J. Proudhon; *De l'Humanité* by Pierre Leroux and some editions of Pierre Buchez's newspaper, *L'Atelier*. At that time, the situation was really critical (Pinkney 1986: 94).

In the years following the crisis, and until the outbreak in February 1848, there would be multiple publications of books and pamphlets that, along with the contributions of a press in full swing, would echo the claims described. The ideas of the early utopians, collected quite critically by Flaubert in *Sentimental Education*, will be in full agitation – at that time, Paris was the real intellectual hotbed of Europe – by the time Marx goes to Paris in 1843 – after his exile in London, he came back in March 1848 – and learns about the ideas of all these thinkers (Blanc, Proudhon, Leroux). All of them will make a more or less intense impression on his thinking during his training period, before processing together with F. Engels *The Communist Manifesto*. It is precisely this period of political and intellectual swing that reflects and starts the novel by Gustave Flaubert.

The sentimental education

After publishing *Madame Bovary* (1856) and *Salambó* (1862), Flaubert started to write *Sentimental Education* in 1864. In the years to follow, the so-called "hermit of Croisset" alternates seclusion with his visits to Paris, where he maintains regular contact with his writer friends: Gautier, Turgenev, the Goncourt brothers and George Sand, among others (Winock 2013: 244–248).

He also visits some members of the imperial family, among whom he had special relationship with Prince Jerôme Napoleon and especially with the one who was his friend, confidant and maybe something else, Princess Mathilde, cousin of the Emperor (Lotman 1989). His friends and even his own editor, Levy, suggested more suitable titles for the story and more commercially appealing ones as well, (*La vie et les femmes; Les illusions perdues*, etc.), but Flaubert wanted one that would invoke the story of a defeated generation like his (Thibaudet 1935: 150).

In *Sentimental Education* (hereinafter: SE), Flaubert tells a love story inspired by his own.[7] At the age 14, on a vacation in Trouville, he fell in love with a married woman, 11 years his senior, called Elisa Schlessinger –Mme Arnoux in the novel – to whom he was to worship for a lifetime without ever consummating his passion. With this passion as the backdrop of the story, the events occurring in France principally between 1840 and 1851 are narrated, with a final scene taking place between the years 1867 and 1869, at the time he completed the writing. The common thread will be the character of Frédéric Moreau who, like Flaubert himself, and around the same time, would be continuing his studies in law at the University of Paris. The first two parts of the three in the novel take place between 1840 and 1848, the last part allotted to the narrative of the life of Frédéric during the February Revolution and the days that followed, until the coup of Louis Napoleon.

In recounting such avatars, Flaubert draws a collective portrait of the years of decay of the Orleanist society where characters of various ideologies intermingle: Loyalists, Liberals, Republicans, Socialists, Democrats and Orleanists of a different nature. If we believe the words of his friend Maxime Du Camp, who shared his life with him, in those years all the characters were inspired – and properly interspersed, as would Marcel Proust do subsequently in a masterful way – on real people he knew personally in most cases.[8]

The characters

Arnoux's friends

Once Frédéric arrives in Paris in the autumn of 1840, he arranges to see the woman who had won his heart shortly before. To do so, he gets closer to her husband, Mr. Arnoux, a young and prosperous industrialist who had driven his business by speculation during the early years of the Orleanist monarchy. Arnoux owned *L'Art Industriel*, an establishment comprising a painting magazine and a painting store. As the business declined he would progressively devote himself to land trading, kaolin exploitation, ceramics trading and other various speculative activities, to finally end up running a religious items store. Bankrupted and persecuted, he had to flee Paris: "his intelligence was not high enough to attain to Art, nor commonplace enough to look merely to profit, so that, without satisfying anyone, he was ruining himself" (SE: 686). Selfish, sassy, yet generous, he was swarmed with artists, journalists, middling businessmen and some damsels (lorettes), who provided favors in exchange for his generous gifts.

Pellerin was a painter – whose model could have well been the famous photographer Nadar – who "read every work on aesthetics in order to find out the true theory of the Beautiful, convinced that when he had discovered it, he would produce masterpieces" (SE: 563).[9] Minion of Arnoux, however, he felt cheated by the industrialist and, therefore, had his artistic pride hurt. Actually, he hated trading: "Pellerin launched into a harangue against shopkeepers; he saw no difference between them, whether they were sellers of candles or of money"

(SE: 599). As reported in the novel, he ended up his life in a very different way: "after having turned his hand to Fourierism, homeopathy, table-turning, Gothic art and humanitarian painting, he had become a photographer; and he was to be seen on every wall in Paris, where he was represented in a black coat with a tiny body and a big head" (SE: 865).

Other of Arnoux's acolytes was Régimbart, "the citizen", an idle and idiotic disbeliever, to whom Arnoux, however, attributed high intellectual conditions and intelligence. He used to spend his time wandering the city streets, drinking absinthe and ritual vermouth while reading *The National* and expressing his opinions aloud: "It was not his fondness for drinking that attracted citizen Régimbart to these places, but the inveterate habit of talking about politics there. His ardour had fallen with age; he had no more than melancholy in his head. Seeing him with such a serious face, it looked as if the world was spinning around his head. Nothing came of it, and no one, not even his friends knew about his occupations, even though he boasted about running a business agency" (SE: 565).

During the Orleanist monarchy, Régimbart looked forward to revolution and actively conspired with the clubists; when it finally occurred, he thought it had nothing to do with that and, eventually, his only concern was to preserve the national borders. Along with the followers of Arnoux, Frédéric – who was then on the side of those defending the regime change – met different characters who, considering their attitudes towards the events of 1848, constitute a genuine taxonomy of the revolutionaries of that time. Thibaudet believes these are of three kinds: the self-interested revolutionary, the authoritarian socialist and the "true revolutionary" (Thibaudet 1935: 170).

The revolutionaries

Deslauriers, the sidekick character of Frédéric – perhaps created in the image of his friend Du Camp and his own – is the self-interested revolutionary. Ambitious as he is, he wants to make money, thrive in politics, run a newspaper and share the fortune Frédéric has inherited.[10] Deslauriers will encourage Frédéric to stand as candidate for Congress twice, in the 1848 and 1850 elections. Luck had not been on his side, his having failed the competitive examinations to Chair due to his equally advanced and absurd thesis on the right to test. He would fail as well in his project of running a newspaper because of lack of support on the part of his friend Frédéric.

The most ruthless portrait is the one of Sénécal, the authoritarian socialist whose favorite activity was to rant against the bourgeois and predict the revolution. Born in Lyon, son of a foreman, he had inherited a taste for authority and command, and defended the revolution in terms of a need for dominance and a passion for justice (Thibaudet 1935: 171). He was a math teacher, among his numerous and failed activities – intelligent and of republican convictions, the future Saint-Just, according to Deslauriers. He relished reading Louis Blanc and believed that art's only concern should be motivating the masses. He hated Cousin and Eclecticism as he considered them to develop selfishness and obstruct solidarity. He denounced as well the political and financial scandals and criticized Louis-Philippe incessantly, whom he called "a vulgar national guard, the most tacky, sad and boring".[11]

Banned as a college professor after beating the son of an aristocrat, he tries repeatedly to influence Frédéric so as obtain different jobs, a fact that does not stop him from complaining about the salary, abhorring his employers and, while working as a foreman with Arnoux, evidencing a despotic authoritarianism towards the workers under his supervision (always in line of duty). He had quite a revolutionary record; he had entered in the revolutionary club *la Société des Familles*, and had participated in the mutiny of 1839. Since then, he had been guarded by police.

Deslauriers and Frédéric, at the time, admired him as a man willing to sacrifice for an idea. However, towards the end of the novel, Flaubert turns Sénécal into a reactionary policeman at the service of the coup of Louis Napoleon, who, in the presence of the astonished Frédéric, will take the life of his old revolutionary fellow Dussardier with his sword.[12]

As a counterpoint to the character of Sénécal and as the third version of the revolutionary of the time, Flaubert introduces the character of Dussardier, the pure revolutionary. He is an orphan who works as a delivery man for a laces and novelties store, and who is arrested for defending a young man facing aggression from the police in a street altercation.[13] He is a man of the people, of few readings – *The Mysteries of Paris* and a biography of Napoleon – who outrages at the spectacle of injustice:

> he slightly confused the police with murderers; for him, a police informer was like a parricide. He naively attributed all evil on earth to Power, and he hated it with such an essential, permanent hatred, which had completely possessed his heart and refined his sensitivity.
>
> (SE: 716)

He would support the revolution in February 1848 and afterwards, in the month of June of the same year, he would defend the Republic against the workers, convinced it was for the best. Later, after witnessing the repression carried out by Cavaignac, he would not stand the enormous guilt:

> he should have maybe been on the other side, with the people in overalls, because they had been promised a lot of things that were not finally accomplished. Their overcomers hated the Republic, and had also been tough in the confrontation. No doubt they were wrong but not quite, and the brave boy was tortured by the idea that he could have fought justice.
>
> (SE: 797)

As it has been mentioned, three years later, while defending the Republic at the time of the coup of Louis Bonaparte, he would be killed, as a trick of fate, by his former comrade, the authoritarian Sénécal, who was now at the service of power.

The Orleanist bourgeoisie

Along with Jacques Arnoux, his acolytes and lovers, and the friends of Frédéric, the Orleanist entrepreneur Monsieur Dambreuse appears among the characters. He was actually the Earl of Ambreuse, who in 1825 left his nobility and his party – the loyalists – to engage in industry and "by pricking up ears in every office, getting involved in all companies on the lookout for good opportunities, subtle as a Greek and laborious as an Auvergner, had he amassed an estimated quite considerable fortune . . . and in his brushes with power, he favoured the center-left" (SE: 549–550). And quite cunningly, in order to appease their former coreligionists of Faubourg Saint-Germain, he sent his haughty lady to socialize with the duchesses and preside over charity meetings. In this way, "she made them believe that Mr. Dambreuse could still repent and serve again" (ibid.). In his office, there were outstanding portraits of Louis-Philippe and General Foy and only half a dozen straw chairs, unlike his sumptuous private residence; "it was like those dark kitchens where great feasts are prepared" (SE: 655).

He argued, however, that luxury consumption stimulated trade, and defended mergers of large companies, such as in the coal industry, because even if they seemed to be monopolies, they were necessary; but what he stood for above all was sacred protectionism.[14] Like his industrial and political Orleanist friends – some of them being former Carbonari[15] – he was concerned about the new ideas on the organization of work, as they came from "the kind of man who wants to change the world . . . To bring what? The Republic? As if a Republic were possible in France" (SE: 657). His friends, like him, believed the problem of pauperism was being exaggerated. Poverty existed, but its solution did not depend on science or power; it was purely an individual matter. When the lower classes abandon their vices they would be released on their needs and when the people become more moral, they would become less poor. According Dambreuse, no good would be achieved out of capital development. Therefore, the only possible way was to trust, as the Saint-Simonians wanted "Goodness me, they were to some extent right, let us be fair to everyone", the cause of progress to the ones able to increase public wealth (SE: 719).

He was thus a man of great flair for business and, as shown in the February events, great adaptive capacity in politics; not for nothing could the following be seen in his coat of arms: "on a background of sable, a sinister golden arm with a tight fist, silver gauntlets, and this motto: B*y all means*". In his story, Flaubert focuses on his character his hatred for the Orleanist bourgeois: the careerist, classless in his own interest, fortune hunter and person of no scruples "had acclaimed Napoleon, the Cossacks, Louis XVIII, 1830, the workers, all regimes. He loved Power with such fervor that would have paid for selling himself" (SE: 829).

1848: The revolution

On February 22, the riot causing the fall of Louis-Philippe broke out. The events occurred in this period of time are those covering most of the pages of the third part of *Sentimental Education*, a fact that shows to what extent was Flaubert interested in describing the ideological slippages of his characters in response to the revolution, just at that time of confusion. He devotes only 20 pages to the rest of the period (1849–1850), with few time references. The latter were mainly devoted to recounting the ideological shift from the more conservative sectors that would result in the so-called party of order, which would eventually end up supporting the emperor-to-be. That would be the time, as we shall see later, to round off the portrait of former Orleanist businessman and banker, Monsieur Dambreuse.

The revolution in the sentimental education

Flaubert was in Croisset when he learned of the outbreak of the revolution and prepared, as it has been already mentioned, to move to Paris with his friends Du Camp and Bouilhet to experience the events firsthand. The scenes he contemplated are recounted in detail in the third part of the novel, in which the events are vividly described through the vicissitudes suffered by Frédéric and his companions.

As the coup took place, everybody got excited and hurried for the revolution: from Republican and Socialist friends as Deslauriers, Sénecal and Dussardier, to the industrial Arnoux and, of course, Frédéric himself. The chaos generated in the days that followed the revolutionary outbreak was described by Flaubert with such pungency that raises the tone of the story:

> Property, at the time, rose in their regard to the level of Religion and was confounded with God. The attacks it received seemed sacrilege, almost a form of cannibalism. In spite of the most humane legislation that ever existed, the spectre of the '93 reappeared, and the blade of the guillotine vibrated in every syllable of the word "Republic" – which did not prevent the institution to be despised for its weakness. France, missing a master, began to cry with terror, like a blind man without his stick or an infant who has lost his nurse.
>
> (SE: 765)

The one who scared the most, and had reasons for it, was Dambreuse, the Orleanist industrialist who feared the people would avenge him by snatching his properties in the Champagne. Therefore, he changed his attitude and language, as he had done 20 years before, but now trying to adapt himself to the new situation. He welcomed unreservedly the insignia *Liberty, Equality, Fraternity*, commented that he had always been a Republican on the inside, that Guizot had gotten him in trouble and that he felt sympathy for the workers: "more or less, we are all working men". As the elections of April to the National Assembly were approaching, he proposed Frédéric become a candidate; with his support, "he would get the votes of the Extremists owing to his opinions, the votes of the conservatives on account of his family. And, perhaps, also, added the banker with a smile, thanks to my influence, in some measure" (SE: 766).

Against this background, a dazed Frédéric "let himself be conquered by the universal madness". He immediately prepared a speech for the consideration of

Dambreuse wherein, in an exalted tone, he considered the defence of pecuniary interests shameful, and called for free trade, claimed income tax, progressive taxation and people training. The speech ended: "Do not save a thing, you rich! Give away, give away". Dambreuse, shocked and stunned, tried to temporize with the exalted youth but, from that moment on, he decided that he should himself stand for election, and he did successfully.

The Club of Intelligence

> Frédéric's attempt to stand for election and, to this end, his visits to the revolutionary clubs to win votes, allowed Flaubert to make an unusual description of the ideological magma in which revolutionaries of all kinds of those organizations were immersed.[16]
>
> (SE: 769)

Frédéric did not dare to risk; his friend, the revolutionary Dussardier, sought the proper forum for him, the Club of Intelligence; "such a name augured well". In describing the vicissitudes experienced by his character in a visit to the Club, Flaubert launched all possible diatribes towards revolutionaries and socialists whom, with the exception of the "pure socialist", he belittled in the novel as much as he hated in real life.[16]

The master of ceremonies in the Club of Intelligence was his friend Sénecal, who opened the session with the *Declaration of the Rights of Man and of the Citizen*, after which they sang a hymn by poet Béranger, and a series of unusual interventions happened.

Amid the din Frédéric attempted to assert his candidacy but his vindictive and authoritarian friend, now presiding over the assembly, did not let him speak, for he was not able to prove having participated in the uprising from the start. He was expelled from the room at the shout of "Aristo!" He left offended, reproaching himself for his devotion, without reflecting that the accusations brought against him were just: "What a fatal idea was his candidature! But what asses, what cretins! He drew comparisons between himself and these men, and soothed his wounded their pride with the thought of their stupidity" (SE: 775).

Finally, after his dismal failure, Frédéric did not run for election. The one who did, getting his seat, was Dambreuse, who had been hooraying "Long live the Republic!" three months before to end up stating that he "particularly loathed Lamartine (for having supported Ledru-Rollin) and Pierre Leroux, Proudhon, Considérant, Lamennais, all the hotheads, all the socialists" (SE: 783).

Revolutionary backlash

In June, the National Workshops that had given work to many unemployed workers closed; this was a sign of impending tragedy. Notwithstanding, Frédéric (who was always more attentive to love affairs than to revolutionary ones in decisive moments)[17] was about to consummate a love rendezvous on the outskirts of Paris, where he received the news about his friend Dussardier having been wounded during the days in that month that witnessed new revolutionary events. Flaubert crudely related these:

> There was an explosion of fear. They avenged themselves on everything at once, on the newspapers, the clubs, the gatherings, the doctrines, on everything that had exasperated them over three months; and in spite of the victory that had been gained, equality (as if to punish its defenders and expose its enemies to ridicule) manifested itself in a triumphal fashion, as an equality of brute beasts, a dead level of bloody turpitude; for the fanaticism of self-interests balanced the madness of need, aristocracy was as rabid as the mob, and the cotton nightcap showed itself as no less hideous than the red cap. The public mind was disturbed as it is after great convulsions of nature. Men of wit and imagination were turned into idiots for the rest of their lives.
>
> (SE: 797)

It was at that time when his friend – injured as he tried to defend the Republic, this time against the workers – confessed, as it was mentioned before, that he was tortured by the idea of having fought against justice. Perhaps this confession made Flaubert feel greater sympathy for this kind of non-authoritarian and honest socialist (Barbés-style) compared to those others he hated.

Flaubert's description of the events that followed the defeat of the progressive Republican alternative was due to describe the other revenge: the one of the industrial and financial bourgeoisie that, after the ill times, had readapted to the new and advancing order, but in another direction; discourse changed, returning to the values that had always advocated: property, country, family and religion. They advocated an "iron hand" to save France from stagnation and anarchy; everyone was relocated in the new scenario, like Pellerin, the Fourierist friend of Frédéric, who now believed that the most favorable regime for the arts was "an enlightened monarchy". As for the nonetheless naive industrialist Arnoux, he tried to explain to the other industrial friend of Dambreuse that there were two types of socialism, one being good and one being evil, to which the latter replied with a defence of property. For him, it was a written law in nature: "the lion even, if he could speak, would declare himself a property-owner!" (SE: 804). No doubt the situation was still as new as ambiguous, and thus did Dambreuse continue to defend General Cavaignac, who, after the events of June, had come to power.

A year later, and after the new revolutionary wave of June 1849 – not reported in *Sentimental Education* – the turn had been accomplished. Dambreuse, who "like a barometer, constantly reflected its latest variations", now detested Cavaignac for being just a traitor and showed his fervor for General Changarnier. Dambreuse Palace, as it appears in the novel, had become an intimate subsidiary of Poitiers Street, a strong conservative committee. Symbolically, the banker dies of a haemorrhage after the dismissal of Changarnier. As it was previously reported, at the time, his friends had concluded that socialism and sleeplessness as a result of anarchy had killed him.

Frédéric and his friend Deslauriers also doubted and changed their minds in the course of events. The latter did now detest workers, for he had had to fight them the previous year in his attempts to hold a position within the interim government: "I have had enough of these characters [workers], in turn grovelling before the scaffold of Robespierre, the boots of the Emperor, and the umbrella of Louis-Philippe, just scum, always ready to serve whoever flings bread into their gobs!" (SE: 822). Frédéric, never committed, confessed to his friend that the Republic had certainly aged, and that "Progress can be realised only through an aristocracy or through one single man? The initiative always comes from the top! The people have the status of a minor, whatever they say!" (SE: 823).

In the novel, Flaubert, skipping the events that occurred between 1849 and 1850, or quoting them implicitly, refers directly to the coup of Louis Napoleon – without quoting him – to reflect the ultimate act of violence and meanness involved in the already reported murder of his friend Dussardier.

The house of the Turkish woman

To finish the novel Flaubert takes a leap of 16 years in time through a resource that Marcel Proust called the "Flaubert's blancs", consisting in passing, by means of an improvised change of narrative rhythm, from one sequence to another temporarily distant, being both unrelated (Proust: 1927). In the last two chapters that close the book, Frédéric receives the unexpected visit of Arnoux's wife, who, years later, offered herself to him – or so did he believe – being, once more, his life-long love (his dormant passion) unconsummated this very last time.[18]

In the winter of 1868 Frédéric and Deslauriers would again be reunited by "the fatality of their nature, which made them always reunite and be friends again". Deslauriers had married Miss Roque, Frédéric's former fiancée who had later eloped with a singer. He had been a prefect, head of colonization in Algeria, secretary of a pasha, newspaper manager, advertising agent, and finally, he had been employed as a lawyer for an industrial company. Meanwhile, Frédéric lived like a bourgeois and had already squandered two-thirds of his fortune. They reviewed the list of their friends: one had become a senator, another one managed the theatres of the city, the Fourierist Pellerin had become a photographer and Cisy, the loyalist friend, had devoted himself to religion, was father of eight children and lived in a castle. They had no news of Sénécal the traitor; Arnoux had died the previous year and his lovers, inevitably, had gained weight. Only the "citizen" Regimbart was still crawling, as a spectre, through the boulevards in search of absinthe.

Both Frédéric and Deslauriers had failed. What was the reason?

> It was perhaps for not having followed a straight line, said Frédéric. In your case that may be so. I, on the contrary, sinned through excess of rectitude, without taking into account a thousand secondary things more important than anything else. I had too much logic, and you too much sentiment.
>
> (SE: 866)

Then they decided to blame the old times. They recalled their school days and how, while still teenagers, they had escaped with a bunch of flowers picked from the garden to go to the house of the Turkish woman, a place of perdition locally known as "the place you know" or "a certain street below the Bridges". They got so frightened they could not go on with the adventure, but after recalling the incident, the two old friends agreed to something that shocked the critics and certain sectors of society at the time the work was published: " 'That was the best time of our lives!" said Frédéric. "Yes, maybe it was. The best time of our lives!" said Deslauriers" (SE: 868).

The passions and the interests

The rhetoric of intransigence

Flaubert, like his characters, experienced the political and economic transition that witnessed the industrial revolution feeling completely out of place. Born in 1821, he had seen the advent of the Orleanist monarchy, the revolution of 1848, the launch of the industrialization of the country and the birth of the social question. Having witnessed such drastic mutations, however, or perhaps due to it, he did not believe in progress, or industry, or social change. He observed, with great distrust, the role of the masses, which, he being an individualist, horrified him. As Michel Winock stresses, his behaviour is as such the "homo duplex's", especially in the field of politics" (Winock 2013: 460).

It is indeed a difficult task to recall the ideas about politics, economy or society from such a contradictory person, of extreme and sometimes changeable opinions, but, on occasion, they were revealed in the mouths of his characters, especially in *Sentimental Education* and in his posthumous novel *Bouvard et Pécuchet*. The latter incorporates a second part containing several incomplete texts, including the *Dictionary of Received Ideas*, in which many references on the suggested topics are to be found.

Perhaps, as suggested by Julian Barnes, there are some tracks to be found in order to reconstruct a biography, not as a linear thread, but through the "collection of holes tied together with a string" defining the net of life (Barnes 1984). In order to do so, we suggest the re-reading of the extensive correspondence Flaubert maintained with his lover Louise Colet in the 50s and with his great friend George Sand in the decades of the 60s and 70s. It is in them, and in the *Dictionary of Received Ideas*, where Flaubert more than anywhere else reveals, often vehemently, his views on society, progress, industry, electoral suffrage, politics, religion, socialism and the bourgeoisie.

Once such ideas have been herein shown as contained in the pages devoted to *Sentimental Education*, we would further explain how Flaubert, consistent with his low opinion of political activity, shared them. He focused, in a subtle yet devastating way, on some of his characters to show their convenient slides along the main part of the story in the novel (1840–51). And to do so, two very different characters are both portrayed as the main target and the ones who summarized the disaster of '48 and the impossibility of social change: the Orleanist bourgeois and the revolutionary socialist. Their adaptive rhetoric and changing political views, on which we think Flaubert projects his ideological and political ghosts, are penetratingly and highly ironically described.

The rhetoric of Dambreuse, the Orleanist industrialist and financial bourgeoisie, corresponds to the one Albert Hirschman called in his *The Rhetoric of Reaction* the "perversity thesis". According to it, "the attempt to push society in a certain direction will result, indeed, in a movement, but in the opposite direction" (Hirschman 1991). Dambreuse, who had prospered and built his vast fortune in the heat of the Orleanist monarchy, certainly regarded with awe how weakness, or lack of strategic direction of the rulers of Louise Philippe, was leading to a cataclysm, (the year '48). He would adapt to the new situation, naturally changing attitudes, and redefine his political stance to defend his interests.

Nevertheless, he would always consider that any attempt to widen the electorate, tackle the social question from more egalitarian positions, conferring power to a centralized state, give "so much freedom to newspapers" or secularize society "in excess" while endangering the principle of property may only lead to a misguided path that would eventually bring about the deterioration of the economic situation and lead to social anarchy, severely harming his interests. After the revolution, he hides, changes his life by changing external signs, uses misleading rhetoric ("more or less, we are all working men", "there was some merit in the views of temperate socialists like Saint-Simon") and seeks allies such as Frédéric, to have a person of trust in parliament, even though his proposals (free trade, inheritance reform) horrified him. In short, it was all about winning time while the social adventure of revolution corroded and melted itself. The banker, as J. De Maistre, believed that the "cruelty of divine providence" would put things back in their proper place (Hirschman 1991).

Revolution, progress and socialism

Indifference, if not distrust, to progress as well as hatred of socialism in its most authoritarian form were constants in Flaubert's life, which radicalized with the passing of time. Back in March 1848, he already wrote to his lover at the time, Louise Colet, about his impressions of the revolution:

> You ask my opinion concerning what has just taken place. Well, it is all very funny. The expressions on the faces of the discomfited are a joy to see. I take the greatest delight in observing all crushed ambitions. I don't know whether the new form of government and the resulting social order will be favorable to Art. That is a question. It cannot be more bourgeois or more worthless than the old. As for being more stupid, is it possible?
>
> (Flaubert 1998)

Four years later, in April 1852, he returned to writing, commenting that "his hairs fell down as if they were political convictions" and lashed back against the Socialists:

> The ideal form of the State, according to the Socialists, is not a kind of huge monster absorbing into itself all individual action, all personality, all thought,

managing everything, doing everything. A priesty tyranny . . . Thus, since 1830, France rants around an idiotic realism; the infallibility of universal suffrage is about to become a dogma that would eventually succeed the infallibility of the Pope.

(Flaubert 1998)

In his letters, he acknowledged he had not the slightest patriotic feeling –years later, at the time of the war against Prussia, he would change his mind; nor did he believe in progress: "the more humanity advances, the more it is degraded".[19] The Republicans seemed to him the wildest pedagogues in the world who hated the crowds "always led by ringleaders and instigators". It is true that he did not leave the bourgeoisie standing either, which now, after the coup of Louis Napoleon, led the destiny of the country:

God help the ones who believed in the apotheosis or in paradise! Now people are more positive, and so on. But still, how long can the stick of the dangling carrot be for this good bourgeois of our time! What an idiot! What a fool! For vulgarity does not prevent cretinism.

(Flaubert 1998)

He was not interested in the economy;[20] besides, he experienced financial difficulties his whole life.[21] He did not have any faith in the development of society based on industry either, as evidenced by the peculiar, either direct or indirect, impression he had when reading Adam Smith's *The Wealth of Nations*, as he explained to Louise Colet in August 1853:

What a ruckus does industry cause in the world! What an outrageous thing the machine is! Speaking of industry, have you ever thought about the quantity of stupid professions industry creates, and about the mass of stupidity that must come from it in the long run? That would be a frightening statistic to compile! What can one expect from a population like that of Manchester, which spends its lives making pins? And the making of a pin requires five or six different specialties! When subdividing work, it appears, along with the machines, hundreds of machine-men. What a role the one of the railway conductor or the printing fitter! Etc., Etc. Yes, humanity bends towards stupidity.

(Flaubert 1998)

Years later, he maintained correspondence with his close friend George Sand, who had completely different political views to his own. He still expressed the same views on politics, electoral suffrage, socialism and the bourgeoisie. However, this fact did not prevent their friendship from being sincere and lasting for almost two decades.

The correspondence between them was especially intensified after 1866, being those the years in which Flaubert was writing *Sentimental Education*. At that time, Flaubert was immersed in reading the socialist writers of the 30s and 40s: Louis Blanc, Cabet, Proudhon, Lamennais, Saint Simon and the Saint-Simonians, among others, and was documenting himself on the events referred to in his novel. It was, perhaps, due to this fact that he commented about those readings to his address, keeping an extremely critical opinion of the Socialists, despite her attempts to soften that view since she had been or still was friends with some of those Socialists – for instance, Armand Barbés. Such criticism did not involve an alternative defence of the party of Order or the Napoleonic regime; Flaubert, deep inside, thought that modern democracy and constitutional monarchy did not differ too much (Flaubert 2010: 167).

He thought about portraying all the mistakes made, whether they were made by one side or the other, "The patriots will not forgive me for this book, nor the reactionaries either!" He criticized Louis Blanc because he dreaded every reference of Christianity in his doctrine "and from that divine source hatred, war, the collision of all interests cannot result"; in his view, democracy was based on the morals of the Gospel. Over the years, Flaubert would become increasingly more individualistic and would feel a great contempt for the masses, yet he tried to respect the human element in them. Speaking of universal suffrage, he wrote to Sand:

> The masses, the numbers are always idiotic. I have few convictions, but I have that one strongly. But the masses must be respected, however inept they may be, because they contain the germs of an incalculable fecundity. Give it liberty, but not power.
>
> (Letter of October 7, 1871)

As he did not believe in universal suffrage he expressed the same indifference towards democracy and towards constitutional monarchy (Winock 2013: 462), whom he considered to be benevolent tyrants. Ultimately, he opted for a government of elites: "What we need most of all, is a natural, that is to say, a legitimate aristocracy. For that, I understand a majority that consists of everything but figures" (Flaubert 1998).

In his *The Rhetoric of Reaction*, Albert Hirschman points to Flaubert, together with Jacob Burckhardt,[22] as examples of the *perversity thesis* in addressing their considerations on the participation of the masses in politics:

> Universal suffrage, one of Flaubert's favorite bêtes noires, a frequent butt of his passionate hatred of human stupidity. With heavy irony, universal suffrage (suffrage universel) figures in his Dictionnaire des idées reçues, as the "last word of political science". In his letters, he pronounced it "the shame of the human spirit" and the equal of (or worse than) other absurd notions, such as the divine right of kings or the infallibility of the Pope.
>
> (Hirschman 1991)

Flaubert, influenced by the ideas of Spencer, ended up hating everything related to politics. He advocated abstention and when the plebiscite promoted by Louis Napoleon was held in 1870, he did not vote. In regarding various political issues different from suffrage – as, for instance, the consideration of progress, or education – he rather stood in what Hirschman called the *futility thesis*, according to which, and unlike the *perversity thesis*, "any attempt at change is abortive, that in one way or another any alleged change is, was, or will be largely surface, facade, cosmetic, hence illusory, as the "deep" structures of society remain wholly untouched" (Hirschman 1991).

It is a significant fact, as Hirschman asserts, that such thesis was coined in the aftermath of the revolution in January 1849, by the journalist Alphonse Karr: "plus ça change plus c'est la même chose". Another example cited by Hirschman, which we believe to be closer to the ideas of Flaubert, is the Baron of Lampedusa, who makes a character of his novel *The Leopard* say the following: "If we want things to stay as they are, things will have to change". Now, instead of being a law of change, it is a law of immobility to which we thought Flaubert subscribed due to his complete lack of confidence in progress.[23]

This solitary leopard, the "Bear of Croisset" as he liked to call himself, isolated from the world, had become unsociable – except with his people – and believed in nothing more than a timeless art and style. He had seen too many passions and interests fighting each other frantically in the years he had had to live. He felt defeated as a member of a generation that, according to him, had tried everything – even a revolution – and had accomplished nothing. There was only one thing for him to do: portray it.

Notes

* I want to thank Professor Salvador Almenar Palau and Professor Andrea Ginzburg for his helpful comments and suggestions for the writing of this work, provided during the long conversations we shared on Gustave Flaubert's narrative and the work of Albert Hirschman.

1 Letter of October 7, 1871 to Louise Colet.

2 In 1845, Flaubert wrote a very different first version of *Sentimental Education*, which he never published in his lifetime (Flaubert 1966).

3 In a letter written to his acquaintance Marie-Sophie de Chantepie, he said: "I want to write the moral history of the men of my generation; "sentimental" would be more accurate (Lotman 1989: 250).

4 Flaubert depicts the studies in law and the love affair of his character in the same years in which he had gone through the same adventures.

5 Tensions increased in June with the so-called Humann Act, enacted on February 25, 1841, that sought to update inventories so as to update the tax on doors and windows, which resulted in a tax burden increase for the population.

6 The most active secret societies were the ones of the Carbonari, inspired by the secret sects that had fought in Italy during the Neapolitan revolution and were brought to France by the exiled. It commenced its activities in 1821. The first one was Les Amis de la Verité, where a young Ph. Buchez participated. Later on, he was to play an important role in similar movements. Its aim was to "return to the people their sovereignty" (Alexandrian 1979).

7 "Il faut s'entendre, quand on dit que Frédéric c'est Flaubert. Flaubert moins la littérature, comme Salammbô c'était la littérature moins Flaubert. On peut dire: Frédéric c'est lui dans la mesure à peu près où il dit: Mme. Bovary, c'est moi . . . Flaubert a exprimé dans ce faible qu'est Frédéric la somme de se faiblesses" (Thibaudet 1935: 153).

8 "Il n'est pas un des acteurs que je ne puisse nommer, je les ai tous connus ou côtoyés, depuis Frédéric, qui n'est autre que Gustave Flaubert, jusqu'à Mme. Arnoux, qui est l'inconnue de Trouville transportée dans un autre milieu" (Thibaudet 1935: 151).

9 "An old woman in tatters attended on him, he dined in cheap restaurants and lived without a mistress. His learning, picked up in the most irregular fashion, rendered his paradoxes amusing. His hatred of the vulgar and the 'bourgeois' overflowed in sarcasms, marked by a superb lyricism, and he had such religious reverence for the masters that it raised him almost to their level" (SE: 564).

10 In his youth, Deslauriers "dreamed of formulating a vast system of philosophy, which might have the most far-reaching applications" (SE: 546). Besides, he "longed for riches, as a means for gaining power over men. He would have liked to possess an influence over a vast number of people, to make a great noise, to have three secretaries under his command and to give a big political dinner once a week" (SE: 576).

11 "[T]here was a certain hard, cold look in his grey eyes; and his long black coat, his entire costume, savoured of the pedagogue and the ecclesiastic . . . Sénécal – whose skull came to a point – fixed his attention merely on the systems" (SE: 574 and 580).

12 According to Flaubert's biographer, Jacques Suffel, "there may be some of the double agent at the police service Lucien de la Hodde in Sénécal" (Suffel 1958: 104). Over the years of the writing of *Sentimental Education*, Flaubert profusely documented himself on the facts of '48, on Republicans and Socialist writers of the time and on the secret societies as well. His double moral standard cruelly fits with the view Flaubert had about socialism, especially in its most authoritarian side, to which we will refer later.

13 "Le vrai révolutionnaire de 1848, c´est Dussardier. Il nous donne peut-être la seule figure fraîche et franche, belle et sympathique, qu´on rencontré dans L´Education (parmi les hommes du moins). Il est révolutionnaire par enthousiasme, par besoin de protéger le faibles et les battus" (Thibaudet 1935: 171).

14 Dambreuse, being one of the main promoters of *The General Union of French Coal Mines,* defended it by stating: "Thus we heat, we light, we penetrate to the very hearth of the humblest homes. But how, you will say to me, can we be sure of selling? By the aid of protective laws, dear Monsieur, and we shall get them; that will be our concern! For my part, anyhow, I am a downright prohibitionist! The Country before anything!" (SE: 682).

15 "Most of the men assembled there [at Dambreuse's place] had served at least four governments; and they would have sold France or the human race in order to preserve their own incomes, to save themselves from any discomfort or embarrassment, or even though sheer baseness, through instinctive worship of force" (SE: 721).

16 His criticism of socialism was one of the topics covered in the intense correspondence with George Sand from the 60s until her death. Flaubert hated, above all, the authoritarian socialism (Sénécal model in the novel) and, as he related to Sand, believed it was tainted with the influence of religion. On the other hand, he respected pure "socialists", as his character Dussardier, who would offer their entire lives for an idea. He admired Barbés and, whilst writing *Sentimental Education*, Sand got Flaubert an interview with him so that he could relate the details of one of his fierce imprisonments. It is true that Flaubert, even aware of being a bourgeois, hated the bourgeoisie as well.

17 "Such indifference to the misfortunes of the nation had in it something shabby and bourgeois. His love suddenly weighed on him as if it were a crime" (SE: 793).

18 Many scholars of Flaubert have considered these the most intense and round chapters of the work which, compared with his notebook 19, constitute, partly, a faithful representation of his real affair with Elisa Schlessinger.

19 Flaubert hated the railway: "But he didn't just hate the railway as such; he hated the way it flattered people with the illusion of progress" (Barnes 1984).

20 In a letter to George Sand from October 7, 1871, he mentioned the economist Frédéric Bastiat, for reasons unknown to us, as an example: "imagine, on the other hand, that in each community there was one bourgeois, only one, who had read Bastiat, and that this bourgeois was respected: things would change!" (Flaubert 2010: 171). What is certain is that he was against protectionism, a stance reflected in emphatic fashion in the character of Mr. Dambreuse.

21 Flaubert was bankrupted in the last years of his life because of the bankruptcy of the company run by his niece's husband, Ernest Commanville, who was his administrator and banker.
22 In 1845, Burckhardt had written: "I know too much history to expect anything from the despotism of the masses, but a future tyranny, which will mean the end of history". Vid. The letters or Jacob Burckhardt, quoted in (Hirschman 1991).
23 In his *Dictionary of Received Ideas*, it can be read: "Progress: always misunderstood and too hasty". In one of the first letters to Louise Colet in the summer of 1846, he wrote as an introduction: "In all of politics, there is only one thing that I understand: the riot. I am as fatalistic as a Turk, and I believe that whether we do everything we can for the progress of humanity, or nothing at all, makes no whit of difference" (Flaubert 1998).

Bibliography

Agulhon, M. (1992), *1848 ou l'apprentissage de la République*, Paris: Éditions du Seuil.

Alexandrian, S. (1979), *Le socialisme romantique*, Paris: Éditions du Seuil.

Barnes, J. (1984), *Flaubert's Parrot*, London: Jonathan Cape Ltd.

Flaubert, G. (1881), *Bouvard et Pécuchet*, Paris: Alphonse Lemerre, Éditeur. Krailsheimer, A. J. (trans.) (1976), *Bouvard and Pécuchet (with the Dictionary of Received Ideas)*, London: Penguin Classics.

Flaubert, G. (1966), *L'Éducation sentimentale suivie de La Première Éducation sentimentale*, Paris: Le club français du livre.

Flaubert, G. (1972), *L'Éducation sentimentale*, Paris: Michel Lévy Frères.

Flaubert, G. (1998), "Lettres à Louise Colet", in *Correspondance*, Paris: Gallimard.

Flaubert, G. (2013), *Sentimental Education*, A. Tooke (trans.), Hertfordshire: Wordsworth Editions Ltd.

Flaubert, G. and Sand, G. (2010), *Correspondencia (1866–1876)*, Barcelona: Mabot.

Goujon, B. (2012), *Monarchies postrévolutionnaires 1814–1848*, París: Éditions du Seuil.

Harvey, D. (2006), *Paris, Capital of Modernity*, New York: Routledge, Taylor & Francis Group.

Hirschman, A. (1977), *The Passions and the Interests: Political Arguments for Capitalism Before Its Triumph*, Princeton, NJ: Princeton University Press.

Hirschman, A. (1991), *The Rhetoric of Reaction: Perversity, Futility, Jeopardy*, Cambridge, MA and London: Belknap Press of Harvard University Press.

Jardin, A. and Tudesq, A. J. (1973), *La France des notables: L'évolution générale, 1815–1848*, Paris: Éditions du Seuil.

Lotman, H. (1989), *Gustave Flaubert: A Biography*, Boston, MA: Little, Brown.

Pinkney, D. (1986), *Decisive Years in France 1840–1847*, Princeton, NJ: Princeton University Press.

Proust, M. (1927), "A propos du 'style' de Flaubert", in *Chroniques*, Paris.

Suffel, J. (1958), *Gustave Flaubert*, Paris: Editions Universitaires.

Thibaudet, A. (1935), *Gustave Flaubert*, Paris: Gallimard.

Todd, D. (2008), *L'identité Économique de la France. Libre-Échange et protectionnisme. 1814–1851*, Paris: Bernard Grasset.

Winock, M. (2013), *Flaubert*, Paris: Gallimard.

4 Literature and political economy

Saint-Simon and Jean-Baptiste Say's writings

Gilles Jacoud

Claude Henri de Rouvroy (1760–1825), Count of Saint-Simon (1760–1825), and Jean-Baptiste Say (1767–1832) dedicated themselves to political economy in the first decades of the 19th century. Though they met often and developed a closeness of thought for a time, they eventually saw their ideas diverge and became the leaders of two different conceptions of political economy: industrialism organized by planning for Saint-Simon and liberalism for Say. Saint-Simon took from Say the fundamental concepts of industry, production and utility but he did not follow Say in the distinction he made between political economy and politics; he developed a conception of well-being which is not reduced to wealth and he distanced himself from the liberalism advocated by Say.

Saint-Simon and Say wrote at a time when political economy was becoming an autonomous discipline. Certainly, the existence of economic thought was not recent and the long mercantilist period gave rise to the publishing of a *Traicté de l'œconomie politique* (*Treatise on Political Economy*) as early as 1615 penned by Antoine de Montchrétien. The physiocrats caused it to advance in the middle of the 18th century and Say acknowledged that François Quesnay had the merit of having been "the first to treat scientifically political economy" (Say 1826a: 293). But Say nevertheless considered that "there was no such thing as political economy before Smith" (Say [1803] 2006, vol. 1: 33). This did not stop Say from being critical towards him: "he lacked clarity in some places, and method just about everywhere else" (Say [1803] 2006, vol. 1: 36) and he has been criticized "with reason for his long digressions" (Say [1803] 2006, vol. 1: 40). Smith's book is "a vast chaos of correct ideas, with a hotchpotch of positive knowledge" (Say [1803] 2006, vol. 1: 40).

Say considered that he was the first to have written a treatise on political economy worthy of that title and Saint-Simon acknowledged his contribution, while not agreeing with his decision to place political economy outside the scope of politics. Say reminded the reader on numerous occasions that political economy belongs to the moral and political sciences, and his predecessors or even his contemporaries could hardly be designated as economists as far as they continued to explore other scientific areas, notably philosophy. It is, therefore, not at all surprising that the authors who were interested in political economy, including Say himself, adopted literary forms utilized by authors from other disciplines to spread their ideas.

Both Saint-Simon and Say had an approach which led them to put forward their ideas regarding political economy by borrowing much from literature. Such an approach is all the more understandable as Saint-Simon's education was initially based on the teachings of Rousseau whereas Say ventured into literature by writing plays. And although both were scholars in political economy, their skills cannot be reduced to a single field. Saint-Simon is also recognized as philosopher. As for Say, his participation in the *Décade philosophique, littéraire et politique* was the one of "a promising young man of letters" (Schoorl 2013: 15): his contributions concerned literature and politics in wide sense and before the publication of his *Traité d'économie politique* (*A Treatise on Political Economy*) he was "at the crossroads of literature, politics, and economics" (Schoorl 2013: 15).

The aim of this article is to show the extent to which the recourse to various literary genres allowed Saint-Simon and Say to expound and spread their ideas. Saint-Simon had a marked preference for the epistolary genre, and Say did not rule it out, as the first section will show. Saint-Simon and Say also both had recourse to writing a catechism in the form of brief questions and answers to try to reach a wide public, and they drafted certain papers in the form of dialogues, which will be the object of the second section. Besides this, both authors engaged in plentiful editorial work, which consisted of pamphlets, essays and books as the third section will show.

Letters: from correspondence to published texts

Many of Saint-Simon's papers are in the form of letters. In fact, he had been perfecting this means of persuasion over a long period. If we leave aside some brief private correspondence, the first known text by Saint-Simon is a letter; the stakes of this letter were high as the author was writing to attempt to save his own life. The context was that of the Revolution. Under the decree of September 17, 1793 concerning suspects, he had been arrested on November 19 and imprisoned in the Sainte-Pélagie prison. Transferred on May 3, 1794 to the prison of Luxemburg, the usual stage before the guillotine, he put pen to paper and drafted a letter to the Committees of Public Safety and General Security, in which he argued for his defence. Evidently, he managed to be convincing because he was still alive at the end of the period of Terror and was set free on October 9.

The first known printed text by Saint-Simon is a collection of three letters which he sent to the administrators of the Lycée. This private institution of higher education became the Athenaeum, where Say taught in 1802. Saint-Simon, who was one of the founding members on the governing board of the Lycée, questioned its members at a meeting on January 26, 1802. His aim was obviously to propose reorganizing knowledge within the general framework of the vision he intended to promote. His proposition having fallen on deaf ears, he drafted a first letter for the administrators of the Lycée three days later and a second on the ninth of February. Boasting of a "new conception" (Saint-Simon [February 9, 1802] 2012, vol. 1: 83), he wished to teach during the courses in the Lycée and on "general metaphysics" (Saint-Simon [January 29, 1802] 2012, vol. 1: 82), but this request remained without response. He drafted the third letter, which he printed with both previous ones within a 10-page brochure, thus inaugurating an approach which consisted in presenting several of his texts in the form of letters sent to various addressees.

Shortly after his initiative with the administrators of the Lycée, Saint-Simon stayed in Geneva where, having divorced Sophie de Champgrand, he seems to have wanted to ask for the recently widowed Madame de Staël's hand. From there he published his *Lettres d'un habitant de Genève à l'humanité* (*Letters from an Inhabitant of Geneva to Mankind*) anonymously in 1802, quickly completed and republished in the form of a 50-page pamphlet entitled *Lettres d'un habitant de Genève à ses contemporains* (*Letters from an Inhabitant of Geneva to his Contemporaries*).

In proceeding in this manner, Saint-Simon returned to a mode of expression that many had used before him to disseminate his ideas. Epistolary novels already existed in Antiquity and experienced a renewal in Europe in the Renaissance. In France, Montesquieu subsequently turned to *Letters persanes* (*Persian Letters*) to criticize society (Montesquieu 1721). Jean-Jacques Rousseau used the same method of letters on several occasions. The epistolary genre remained popular at the end of the 18th century: Pierre Choderlos de Laclos' *Liaisons dangereuses* (*Dangerous Liaisons*) brought together a total of 175 letters in this way in 1782. Abroad, the genre was met with success, particularly in Samuel Richardson's novels, *Pamela* in 1740 and *Clarissa* several years later. Saint-Simon utilized this literary genre to spread his ideas.

At the time when he published the *Lettres d'un habitant de Genève à ses contemporains*, Saint-Simon also drafted a *Lettre aux Européens* (*A Letter to the Europeans*), which remained in the form of manuscript. Another manuscript, *Lettres de deux philanthropes* (*Letters from Two Philanthropists*), which seems to date from 1804, presents Saint-Simon's plan regarding social organization and is composed of eight letters.

In 1807 and 1808, Saint-Simon published an *Introduction aux travaux scientifiques du XIXe siècle* (*Introduction to Scientific Discoveries of the nineteenth Century*) and, desirous to make the work known to the scientific community, sent the two volumes to the Longitude Office. He decided not to pursue his work by publishing the following volumes but by turning to the writing of letters. He explained his process in this way:

> Convinced by the experience that I was not ready to draft the work I had conceived, I decided to publish *Letters*, where I deal separately with the questions the partial solutions to which are the principles I shall use to reorganize scientific system. The *Letters* I printed did not spark off, as I had hoped, a general discussion, but this work was very useful for me, first of all because it was an opportunity for me to develop my ideas, then because it attracted the attention of several people who were kind enough to communicate their observations.
>
> (Saint-Simon 2012, vol. 1: 225–226)

These *Lettres au Bureau des longitudes* (*Letters to the Longitude Office*), published in three parts, 100 pages in total, are the implementation of a method which Saint-Simon was determined to reproduce.

This closeness between correspondence and publishing goes beyond the strictly scientific realm. Confronted with financial difficulties which endangered his scientific projects, Saint-Simon engaged in a debate with the Count of Redern, a rich Prussian with whom he had associated to speculate on the sale of national properties during the Revolution. The 1807 correspondence relative to the case which brought both men into conflict is assembled in a volume which Saint-Simon had printed. The debate came to the fore again in 1811 and 1812 and the letters exchanged on this occasion were once more printed.

The *Mémoire sur la science de l'homme* (*Notes on the Study of Man*), which Saint-Simon drafted in 1813, employed an already proven method. He incorporated a letter to Doctor Bougon from Alençon into the foreword. In 1814, the article he published in *Le Censeur* (*The Censor*) is a "Letter on the setting up of the opposition party" (Saint-Simon 2012, vol. 2: 1303). In 1816, several printed papers also took the form of letters. This is also the case with *Quelques idées soumises par M. de Saint-Simon à l'assemblée générale de la Société d'instruction primaire* (*Some Ideas Submitted by Mr. Saint-Simon to the General Assembly of the Society for Primary Instruction*) and the letter *A MM. Les électeurs de 1816* (*To Messrs the Electors of 1816*). The same year, he began to publish *L'Industrie* (*Industry*). The publication of the second volume in 1817 was followed by diverse circulars, which systematically accompanied the journals of the third volume. They are leaflets, drafted in the form of mail, that despite their resemblance to advertising, give a good insight into the contents. The second volume is essentially made up of "Political and Philosophical Correspondence", which presents 10 "Letters from Henri Saint-Simon to an American" successively.

In 1819 *Le Politique* (*Politics*) was published in the form of a series of issues, the continuation of the title of which indicates that it was written by a company of men of letters. Saint-Simon contributed to the writing of numerous articles contained in these issues. The epistolary style can be found on several occasions and the unpublished manuscripts also contain three letters which constitute a "Call to scholars to raise politics to the rank of observation sciences and for the admission of political writers to the scientific body" (Saint-Simon 2012, vol. 3: 2002). The same year, Saint-Simon also published a letter tantamount to a *Pétition à Messieurs les membres de la Chambre des députés pour demander un article à la loi de finances* (*A Petition to the Gentlemen Members of the Chamber of Deputies to Request a Section to the Law of Finances*).

L'Organisateur (*The Organizer*), which succeeded *Le Politique*, took the shape of 14 letters, which were published at the end of 1819 and the beginning of 1820, the first one of which contained what Rodrigues, follower of Saint-Simon, would indicate as the parable. After the third edition of the text, Saint-Simon was sued and sentenced to a fine and a prison sentence for insulting the royal family. The murder of the Duke of Berry, son of future Charles X and heir of the throne, a few days later led to his being charged with moral complicity. Disputing the penalty and the charge, he organized his defense in front of the court by publishing the *Lettres de Henri Saint-Simon à Messieurs les jurés qui doivent se prononcer sur l'accusation intentée contre lui* (*Letters from Henri Saint-Simon to the Honourable Gentlemen of the Jury Who Must Decide upon the Charges Brought Against Him*) in March 1820. The 42-page brochure contained four letters. He pleaded his cause with such efficiency that he obtained a nolle prosequi.

The writing of letters having proven its efficiency, Saint-Simon turned again to it a few months later. He published a paper *Sur la loi des élections. Circulaire de douze industriels du département de la Seine à tous les Français entrepreneurs de travaux industriels* (*On the Law of Elections. A Circular from Twelve Industrialists in the Seine Department to All French Industrial Entrepreneurs*) composed of a series of five letters.

It is with the publication of *Du système industriel* that the epistolary technique of Saint-Simon expresses itself most completely. The first volume of the work corresponds to a compilation of 20 letters. The second volume contains seven and the third four letters. These letters were the objects of preliminary publications before their incorporation into the three volumes. The editors of the work summarized Saint-Simon's methodology in this fashion: "practically speaking, he invents a mode of unprecedented public communication for his own purpose: *free circular political letters, financed by subscription, and sent almost weekly* to various segmented groups of people" (Saint-Simon 2012, vol. 3: 2325).

Both the brochures *Des Bourbons et des Stuarts* (*On the Bourbons and the Stuarts*) and *Suite à la brochure* (*The Continuation of the Brochure*), published in January 1822, between the letters of the second volume of *Du système industriel* (*On the Industrial System*) and those of the third volume, also have recourse to the epistolary style. The first one ends with a letter to the French people. The second begins with a letter to the king followed by several letters to the French people.

Whilst Saint-Simon abundantly used the technique of open letters in his publications and transformed letters sent to addressees into publications, Say also used both methods. He used the first one in his contributions in the *Décade philosophique, littéraire et politique*, the newspaper he managed for almost six years during the Revolution. This newspaper which, as its name indicates, was published every 10 days, following the periodicity of the revolutionary calendar which divided the month into three decades, contains 64 pages dealing with diverse subjects. The introductory text indicates that it "is mainly dedicated to the Arts, to Agriculture, to the Sciences, to Morality and to Literature". Most of Say's papers in the *Décade* did not deal with political economy. He approached social issues, which he sometimes presented in the form of letters to the newspaper. It is the form he resumed in what is doubtless his first text on political economy, his letter of May 9, 1795 regarding the price of foodstuffs (Say 1795).

Having been recognized as an economist, Say had less recourse to the publication of open letters. On the other hand, he found an interest in editing elements of his correspondence on political economy. This is what he did when publishing his *Lettres à M. Malthus* (*Letters to Mr. Malthus*, Say 1820). Indeed, Say had the opportunity to meet Thomas Robert Malthus and established correspondence with him to discuss points on which they disagreed. Considering that the arguments he developed in his letters presented an interest for readers other than their direct addressee, he decided to publish these. Five long letters were assembled in a 184-page work.

Say also intended to publish a work assembling his criticism of McCulloch's *Discourse* published in 1825 in the *Revue encyclopédique* (*Encyclopaedic Review*); his letter of May 1821 to Robert Prinsep, the translator of the English version of the *Traité d'économie politique* (whom he blamed for not having translated either the "Preliminary speech", which is of use as introduction to the work or the *Epitomé*, which concludes it and whose criticism expressed in note form he contested); and finally his correspondence with David Ricardo. He ended up abandoning this idea, explaining in a letter to Francis Place that he wondered whether it was not too late to take McCulloch to task over *Discourse* and in which he asks himself how Ricardo's family would react over two years after his death.

Say may also have intended to publish his correspondence with Pierre Samuel Dupont de Nemours. Say did indeed exchange letters with the last great representative of physiocracy. These letters bring to light their differences on the conception of political economy. Their correspondence was not published during the life of Say but was partially published in the *Œuvres diverses de J.-B. Say* (*Various Works by J.-B. Say*, [1848] 1966: 361–397). In this posthumous edition, the contents of a letter dated November 15, 1815 drafted by Say differs from the original received by Dupont de Nemours after his exile to the United States, preserved in the Eleutherian Mills Historical Library. Say doubtless has, as Steiner states (1997: 39), changed the letter himself to clarify his ideas with a view to publication, even if it meant taking some liberties with the contents of the text sent.

For Saint-Simon and Say, the putting into writing of scientific discourse in the form of letters, therefore, was a means of communication which had its place among the other means of the dissemination of knowledge. It was a means which could be all the less disregarded as the authors were targeting a broad audience, since, as Say stated, knowledge of political economy must not be reserved for an elite but is "everyone's business" (Say [1803] 2006, vol. 1: 58). The desire on the part of both authors for an extensive proliferation of their thought also led them to resort to the writing of catechisms and dialogues.

Catechisms and dialogues

Say, who had attained celebrity thanks to his *Traité d'économie politique* in 1803, the second edition of which he published in 1814, was concerned to reach a wider public than the readers of this work. So, he published in 1815 a *Catéchisme d'économie politique* (*Catechism of Political Economy*) aiming to give "accessible instruction intended to familiarize people with the main truths of political economy" (Say [1826] 1966: 3).

Say was not the first one to publish a catechism with no religious instruction, even if the meaning of the word in a non-religious sense was then relatively recent.

In an issue of the *Cahiers de l'Institut d'histoire de la Révolution française* (*Journal of the Institute of the History of the French Revolution*) entirely dedicated to republican catechisms, Jean-Charles Buttier notes that

> the entry 'catechism' in the *Dictionnaire de l'Académie française* (*Dictionary of the French Academy*) published in 1795 – year III still only mentions the religious meaning of the word. Only in the sixth edition, dated 1832–1835, do we find the following: 'title given to certain works which expound a field of science briefly, and which are set out in the form of question and answer. *Catéchisme d'économie politique.*'
>
> (Buttier 2009: 1)

It is however during the period that preceded the Revolution that non-religious catechisms began to be written. And with the Revolution, they benefited from a real boost.

The reason for the *Catéchisme d'économie politique* (hereafter *Catéchisme*) drafted by Say is explained by his conviction that political economy should not be reserved for an elite, but was the business of everyone.

> We cannot hope, nevertheless, that every citizen be versed in this science. Not everyone can know everything; but it is highly possible and desirable that we acquire a general understanding of this discipline, and that we have no false ideas about anything, particularly concerning those things which we are interested in knowing in depth.
>
> (Say [1826] 1966: 3)

It is a book for the uninitiated that aims to be easy to understand, for readers who may not have the opportunity to go beyond this.

The first edition of the *Catéchisme* was published in 1815. It is a 160-page book organized into 25 chapters with a few pages in each. Every chapter is composed of a series of questions, every question being followed by a limited answer of a few sentences, even a few words, and sometimes even to only one in case of acquiescence or denial. Some rare footnotes elucidate an answer from time to time. An index containing 118 words or expressions concludes the book.

The following year, the *Catéchisme* was translated into several languages, but Say was not completely satisfied by this first edition, as he admitted himself.

> I was not satisfied with this short guide, and I truly regretted seeing it translated into English, German, Spanish and Italian before I could make it less unworthy of this honour; I managed to prevent it from being printed in French when the first edition was exhausted and I waited, before publishing it again, to have entirely reworked it, made it much clearer, taken advantage of some sensible criticisms, and introduced some principles which were only firmly established after its first publication.
>
> (Say 1821: vj)

The second edition was thicker as it reached 264 pages. The number of chapters went from 25 to 30; some disappeared and were replaced with new ones. Regarding the notes Say specified that "they are not intended for novices" (Say 1821: 201) but "for more advanced people" (Say 1821: 201), numbered 54 and were put at the end of the chapters where they took up 50 pages. As for the index, it went from 118 to 192 entries. Although intended for the readers who had no basic knowledge of political economy, the *Catéchisme* nevertheless took on a new dimension and became a source to which a public desirous of more rigorous explanations could also refer.

The third edition of the *Catéchisme* was published in 1826. The book reached 300 pages, with 60 notes on 65 pages, and benefited from an improved index detailing, for every entry, explanations of the contents of the passages to which the entry referred. Say did not stop there, even if this third edition was the last in his lifetime, and he planned updates which were introduced in posthumous editions.

Saint-Simon had most probably heard of the Say's *Catéchisme* when in 1823 he started publishing his *Catéchisme des industriels* (*The Catechism of the Industrialists*). Like that of Say, it is written in the form of questions and answers to bring basic knowledge to non-specialist readers. Unlike that of Say, it did not take the form of a complete book straightaway but, as for Saint-Simon's previous papers, that of a semi-periodical giving rise to successive editions. Contrary to Say, and here too as for other papers, Saint-Simon shared the writing with other authors. He tried to finance a series of issues through a subscription to the whole scheme.

The first 66-page issue of the *Catéchisme des industriels* was published in December 1823. The back page proposed a subscription for six issues to be published before the end of 1824 and which were to form two volumes. The subscription for six issues included a volume added to the third issue; on page 46 Saint-Simon asserted that he had laid the foundation for the work and confided its execution to his follower Auguste Comte. The second 120-page issue was published in March 1824. As for the third issue, it caused a rupture between Saint-Simon and Comte. While Saint-Simon was the exclusive author of the first two issues, Comte was the only author of the third issue, published in April 1824, but it was Saint-Simon's name and not his which appeared on the front cover. Saint-Simon declared in the foreword that the issue was written by Auguste Comte, whom he continued to present as his follower, but he presented the issue has having been mandated by him and criticized Comte who, allegedly, presented only a partial version of the system conceived by Saint-Simon and in so doing fell well short of expectations. Having emancipated himself from Saint-Simon's supervision, Comte had the issue reprinted the same year under his own name with the title *Système de politique positive* (*System of Positive Polity*, Comte 1824). The fourth issue of the *Catéchisme* was published in June and contained only 46 pages. The promised continuation was not published.

The catechism is based on the principle of a dialogue between the person who raises the questions and the one who answers. The dialogue was a long-established method utilized in the sciences by illustrious thinkers. Galileo defended heliocentric theory in publishing his *Dialogo sopra i due massimi sistemi del mondo*

(*Dialogue Concerning the Two Chief World Systems*) in 1632. The arrangement of his book in the form of a discussion between several people allowed him to confront different conceptions all the while causing the one that he wanted to defend to emerge. The dialogue proved to be equally appropriate for the presentation of political economy: Ferdinando Galiani used it in his *Dialogues sur le commerce des bleds* (*Dialogues on the Commerce in Wheat*, Galiani 1770) half a century before Say and Saint-Simon did. It was a vehicle adapted for philosophical critique, which allowed the writer to avoid the unwieldiness of a treatise and to rely on the rapid exchanges between a few protagonists rendering the argumentation readily accessible to the reader. Diderot used it as well in several of his works in the eighteenth century. In Say and Saint-Simon's time, dialogue was still a means of written expression used by philosophers or representatives of other disciplines. Giacomo Leopardi was still writing a series of dialogues in the *Operette morali* (*Small Moral Works*) commenced in 1824 (Leopardi 1982).

The dialogue is a process that Saint-Simon used in papers other than the *Caté-chisme des industriels*. It is present in an embryonic way in several texts but it is more systematized in some. In the "Second correspondence with Messrs. the industrialists" integrated into the first volume of *Du système industriel*, he presented three letters "to Messrs. the farmers, manufacturers, traders, bankers, and other industrialists" (Saint-Simon 2012, vol. 3: 2402–2434) in which an observer formulated objections, which were all addressed. In the third volume, he established a "Dialogue between a producer of the department of the Seine and the author of the *Système industriel*" (Saint-Simon 2012, vol. 4: 2784–2791). In the *Opinions littéraires, philosophiques et industrielles* (*Literary, Philosophical and Industrial Opinions*), published in 1825, a "Dialogue" (Saint-Simon 2012, vol. 4: 3116) is established between three people who occupy central functions in the Saint-Simonian vision of society: "the artist, the scholar, and the industrialist" (Saint-Simon 2012, vol. 4: 3116–3144). The *Nouveau christianisme* (*New Christianity*), Saint-Simon's last work, was subtitled *Dialogues entre un conservateur et un novateur* (*Dialogues between a Conservative and an Innovator*). The work was published in April 1825, a few weeks before Saint-Simon's death, and can be considered as being a part of an unfinished work because it contains, as a complement to the subtitle, *Premier dialogue* (*First Dialogue*), while the text announces a "second interview" (Saint-Simon 2012, vol. 4: 3222) and a "third dialogue" (Saint-Simon 2012, vol. 4: 3223).

Say chose too to integrate dialogues into articles, which he drafted for the *Décade philosophique, littéraire et politique* (Say 1966: 615–659). This technique was suited to him considering his experience of writing plays. But while Saint-Simon had recourse to this widely at the end of his work, Say followed the inverse approach. It is a form of writing which he seemed to give up from the moment he specialized in political economy. He however entitled "Dialogue" two extracts of his *Petit volume contenant quelques aperçus des hommes et de la société* (*A Small Volume, Containing Some Views of Men and Society*), which he published in 1817 and the work, constituted by a series of short extracts, contains some other passages with very brief dialogues. But Say probably judged this form of writing ill-suited to the presentation of scientific demonstrations. His advocacy of political economy's scientific dimension was perhaps unsuited to resorting to this type of expression, despite having been used by his illustrious predecessors to disseminate scientific discourse. From then on catechism would be considered suitable only for basic presentations aimed at beginners. Say tried hard to reinforce the content of these in the new editions of the catechism. In his other papers on political economy, he restricted himself to the questionings of readers, which sometimes allowed him to ask a question on his own behalf and so to express his thought by answering.

Pamphlets, essays, books and other writings

After his first literary papers and his articles in the *Décade*, Say came to write on political economy by using various kinds of writing. In 1800 he took part in a competition launched by the moral and political sciences class of the Institute on the question as to which are the proper institutions to found morality in a people. The thesis he wrote on this occasion was published under the title of *Olbie*, the name he gave to an imaginary society which has succeeded in freeing itself from vice and in practicing virtue. It was the opportunity for him to show that political economy can bring enlightenment to people and change society.

His membership of *Tribunat* led him to draft several reports, in particular on the finances, and in 1803 he published his *Traité d'économie politique*, which made him famous. During the Restoration, on his return from a mission to England carried out for the new government, he wrote his report in the form of a text intended for a wide public by publishing *De l'Angleterre et des Anglais* (*England, and the English People*) in 1815. Two years later, he published his *Petit volume*. Next year, he distinguished himself with two brochures: *De l'importance du port de la Villette* (*On the Importance of the Port of La Villette*) and *Des canaux de navigation dans l'état actuel de la France* (*On Navigation Channels in the Present State of France*). Extending the methodology employed in the *Décade*, he drafted reviews of books and articles for *The Censeur européen* (*The European Censor*), the *Revue encyclopédique* and the *Encyclopédie progressive* (*Progressive Encyclopaedia*). He also added notes to the French translation of the *Principles of Political Economy and Taxation* by David Ricardo in 1819 and to the second edition of the *Cours d'économie politique* (*Course on Political Economy*) by Henri Storch in 1823. Whist a professor at the Athenaeum then at the Conservatory of Arts and Trades, he transformed the contents of his lessons entitled *Cours complet d'économie politique pratique* (*Complete Course in Practical Political Economy*) into an impressive book in 1828–29.

All these papers are in literary form, without recourse to the slightest mathematical formalism. Say even inserted poetry into his *Essai sur le principe de l'utilité* (*Essay on the Principle of Utility*), which contains 130 verses of André Chénier. Say gave some explanation for this:

> I do not feel the need to apologise for these long quotations. When poetry adds to its own charms that of the most robust reason, there is enough to satisfy even the gravest of spirits, and it deserves to be welcomed by people

whose conjectures have for object the happiness of people and the true honor of nations.

(Say 1966: 739)

The literary dimension of Say's work even incited him to try to enter the French Academy. It seemed a "logical consequence for someone with his reputation and network" (Schoorl 2013: 139) and "the literary merits of this writings were such that a membership" (Schoorl 2013: 139) was possible. Say sought institutional recognition but the sciences class of the Institute had been abandoned in 1803 and it had not been reinstated at the time of the reopening of academies during the Restoration. It was thus incumbent upon him to convince the Academy that his writings were literature. He began a kind of lobbying with the Institute from 1814, and after the reopening of the Academy he tried to be admitted. To this purpose, he sought the support of a member, Baron Cuvier, in a letter attached to a copy of the fifth edition of the *Traité*, which he sent him in 1826. Count Daru, an academician with whom he sat in *Tribunat*, noted that Say's lack of closeness with the political powers constituted a handicap. Nevertheless, François Andrieux, one of his former collaborators on the *Décade* and also a member of the Academy, declared to Say that he was willing to welcome him as colleague, as his admission would give an additional dimension to literature by showing that it could be an instrument in the service of a useful purpose. Say pursued his attempts to convince with the academicians notably by sending them his *Cours complet*. The attached letter to the copy of the fifth volume, which he sent to François Just Marie Raynouard at the end of 1829, clearly expounded his desire to benefit from the recognition of the defenders of literature (Schoorl 2013: 141). Say did not however obtain the support which would have enabled him to gain entry to the Academy. The Revolution of 1830 however brushed aside obstacles and he obtained institutional recognition with the creation of a chair of political economy at the *Collège de France*. On October 26, 1832, the class of moral and political sciences at the Institute was restored and established as an Academy. For Say, it was, however, too late: he died less than three weeks later.

Contrary to Say, who wrote alone, Saint-Simon relied heavily on his secretaries who were involved in the writing process. Augustin Thierry, from 1814 to 1817, then Auguste Comte from 1817 to 1824 and Léon Halévy in 1824 and 1825 were real co-authors. Other collaborators also participated in the publication of the writings instigated by Saint-Simon. So, these writings have a collective dimension which the texts by Say do not. They also have the peculiarity, in comparison with those by Say, of being published in the form of semi-periodicals, the edition of which remained unfinished.

Saint-Simon produced diverse writings before recruiting the young Augustin Thierry as a secretary, but it was only with *De la réorganisation de la société européenne* (*On the reorganisation of European society*), signed jointly in 1814, that he met with success. With his help, he launched *L'Industrie*, published from 1816 to 1818 in the form of volumes divided into issues published with irregularity. Elected or future politicians such as Jean-Antoine Chaptal, Casimir Perier or

Jacques Laffitte signed certain contributions. But out of six intended volumes, only three were entirely published and the fourth was limited to a first issue of 19 pages.

Le Politique was launched in 1819 *by a company of men of letters*, as its complete title indicated. The company in question was made up of Saint-Simon, Comte and two other members. While 36 issues were planned, the publication stopped with the 12th. Six months after this interruption, the first issue of *L'Organisateur* on which Comte collaborated was published. The third issue, promised in March 1820, was not published. At that time Saint-Simon, had just disentangled himself from the judicial disputes in which the content of the first issue had involved him. Indeed, this issue contained his famous parable, in which he cited the Duke of Berry as among those people whose disappearance would cause no regret; when the latter was murdered this inevitably attracted problems for Saint-Simon.

That same year Saint-Simon launched *Du système industriel*, again with the help of Comte. The issues continued until 1822, at the rate of 12 for the first volume, six for the second and four for the third, which remained unfinished. The collaboration between Saint-Simon and Comte continued until the conflict which accompanied the publication of the third issue of the *Catéchisme des industriels* ended this. And with the fourth unfinished issue the *Catéchisme* underwent the same fate as the previous publications.

With Léon Halévy as his new secretary, Saint-Simon collaborated with a team of authors to launch the *Opinions littéraires, philosophiques et industrielles*, which aspired to become a periodical but which was the object of a publication in a single issue. The *Nouveau christianisme*, Saint-Simon's last work, was obviously planned to be a part of the second volume of the *Opinions*. It was limited to the first dialogue out of the three intended, also making it an unfinished work.

Unlike Say, who after the *Décade* did not try to create new editorial media, Saint-Simon thus embarked indefatigably on projects he had difficulty in seeing through, even if the numerous published brochures constitute volumes which have a certain unity. He hardly published in the existing reviews, contrary to Say, who showed a certain academicism in this sense, at least during the last years of his life. But it is true that Say survived Saint-Simon by about eight years and it is in the last decade of his existence that he contributed to the *Revue encyclopédique* and the *Encyclopédie progressive*.

The difference between Saint-Simon and Say in the form of the expression of thought undoubtedly lies in the fact that Say, more than Saint-Simon, wanted to make of political economy a science and selected the medium which did this best. It is because he deemed that all the previous writings, no matter their form, did not allow one to have a clear and complete view of political economy and its laws that he decided to write a treatise on this new science. The intention was to make a systematic presentation of it. This desire explains the transformation occurring in the second edition in 1814 where the presentation of the science of the production, the distribution and the consumption of wealth becomes more theoretical and is no longer organized into five parts but three, each devoted to one of these three dimensions. It is a desire which can more generally explain "*the endless revision of the* Traité" (Steiner 1998: 231).

Conclusion

Saint-Simon and Say both dedicated their existence to political economy, but they did not have the same conception of this. For Saint-Simon, it remains attached to philosophy and to politics, while for Say the discipline had to free itself. Thus, the writings of the former belong to several disciplines and it would be difficult to try to isolate the specifically economic texts from the others. Those of the second are much more widely centred on political economy. They use various literary genres, which allowed both authors to expound and to spread the ideas which are at the heart of their doctrine. Saint-Simon aimed to be a philosopher and the modes of expression that he used were those of philosophers, means of expression which, for that matter, they did not have the monopoly of, as the ways of disseminating written expression were already so varied in the arts and sciences. Say also embraced a vast field of knowledge, all the while specializing in political economy within the moral and political sciences. He was all the closer to the means of expression which Saint-Simon used as he defended a conception of political economy which rejects recourse to mathematics. The publishing of letters was for him a means of conveying knowledge of political economy and Saint-Simon also had recourse to this process widely. The determination common to both authors to reach a wide public also led them to publish a catechism. They also developed their thought in diverse articles and books.

Both authors, however, differed in their editorial practices. Say was the only signatory of his writings and his major works form a homogeneous set, even if it is true that the *Cours complet* is constituted by six volumes with the publications being spread out from April 1828 to December 1829. Saint-Simon conceived his most important writings as elements of irregular periodicals, but had difficulty in delivering the initially planned volumes and he shared the writing with collaborators. The result is more the fruit of teamwork, even if he treated Thierry or Comte with condescension by presenting them as his followers when their name was mentioned on the cover. This writing by several hands sometimes does not allow the contribution of each author to be identified. In that respect, Saint-Simon's writings prefigure the method which would follow his disciples when they expounded his *Doctrine* (Bazard et al. 1830a, 1830b). The putting together of the *Doctrine de Saint-Simon* (*Doctrine of Saint-Simon*) was a collaborative effort which could hardly be allotted to just one person. Henri Fournel could claim, "Where is the author? It's everybody and nobody" (Fournel 1833: 69).

If Saint-Simon and Say differed in the collective or individual nature of the writing of their work, both authors did nonetheless have in common resorting to a diversity of means of expression to disseminate their ideas. Both authors' fields of study were vast, as were those of the authors examining economics for at least the next two generations, but Say wanted to favour political economy within the moral and political sciences, and his publications evolved towards a more visible academicism. Having become the reference in political economy, he wrote, after Saint-Simon's death, several articles on the subject in the *Revue encyclopédique*, of which the subheading, *Analyse raisonnée des productions les plus remarquables dans la littérature, les sciences et les arts* (*A Reasoned Analysis of the Most Remarkable Productions in Literature, the Sciences, and the Arts*), highlights both the quality and the diversity of their content.

Bibliography

Bazard, S.-A., et al. (1830a), *Doctrine de Saint-Simon. Première année. Exposition, 1829*, Paris: Mesnier.

Bazard, S.-A., et al. (1830b), *Doctrine de Saint-Simon. Deuxième année. Exposition, 1829–1830*, Paris: Everat.

Buttier, J.-C. (2009), "De l'éducation civique à la formation politique. Les catéchismes politiques dans la France du long XIXe siècle", *La Révolution française. Cahiers de l'Institut d'histoire de la Révolution française*, 1, *Les catéchismes républicains*, http://lrf.revues.org/115 (accessed July 15, 2014).

Comte, A. (1824), *Système de politique positive*, Paris: Imprimerie de Setier.

Fournel, H. (1833), *Bibliographie saint-simonienne*, Paris: Alexandre Johanneau.

Galiani, F. (1770), *Dialogues sur le commerce des bleds*, Londres.

Galileo, G. (1632), *Dialogo [. . .] sopra i due massimi sistemi del mondo*, Fiorenza: Batista Landini.

Jacoud, G. (2010), *Political Economy and Industrialism: Banks in Saint-Simonian Economic Thought*, Abingdon and New York: Routledge.

Jacoud, G. (2012, Winter), "Why Does Jean-Baptiste Say Think Economics Is Worth Studying?", *History of Economics Review*, 55: 29–46.

Jacoud, G. (2013), *Money and Banking in Jean-Baptiste Say's Economic Thought*, Abingdon and New York: Routledge.

Leopardi, G. ([1824–1832] 1982), *Operette Morali: Essays and Dialogues*, Berkeley, Los Angeles, CA and London: University of California Press.

Saint-Simon, H. (2012), *Œuvres complètes*, Paris: Presses universitaires de France, 4 vols.

Magnan de Bornier, J. and Tosi, G. (2003), "La méthode de Jean-Baptiste Say: au service d'une discipline autonome", in J.-P. Potier and A. Tiran (eds.), *Jean-Baptiste Say: Nouveaux regards sur son œuvre*, Paris: Economica, 19–39.

Montchrétien, A. de ([1615]), *Traicté de l'œconomie politique*.

Montesquieu, C. L. de (1721), *Lettres persanes*, Amsterdam: Pierre Bunel; Cologne: Pierre Marteau, 2 vols.

Potier, J.-P. and Tiran, A. (eds.) (2003), *Jean-Baptiste Say: Nouveaux regards sur son œuvre*, Paris: Economica.

Say, J.-B. (1795), "Economie politique: Lettre aux Auteurs de la Décade, Sur le Prix des Denrées", *La Décade philosophique, littéraire et politique*, 5 (38): 277–280.

Say, J.-B. ([1803, 1814, 1817, 1819, 1826, 1841] 2006), *Traité d'économie politique*, Paris: Economica, 2 vols.

Say, J.-B. (1815), *Catéchisme d'économie politique*, Paris: Crapelet.

Say, J.-B. (1820), *Lettres à M. Malthus*, Paris and Londres: Bossange.

Say, J.-B. (1821), *Catéchisme d'économie politique*, 2nd edition, Paris and Londres: Bossange.

Say, J.-B. (1826a), "Economie politique . . .", *Encyclopédie progressive*, 1: 217–304.

Say, J.-B. (1826b), *Catéchisme d'économie politique*, 3rd edition, Paris: Aimé-André.

Say, J.-B. (1828), "De l'influence des futurs progrès des connaissances économiques sur le sort des nations", *Revue encyclopédique*, 37: 14–34.

Say, J.-B. ([1828–1829] 2010), *Cours complet d'économie politique pratique*, Paris: Economica, 2 vols.

Say, J.-B. ([1848] 1966), *Œuvres diverses de J.-B. Say*, Osnabrück: Otto Zeller.

Say, J.-B. (1996), *Cours d'économie politique et autres essais*, Paris: Flammarion.

Say, J.-B. (2003a), *Leçons d'économie politique*, Paris: Economica.

Say, J.-B. (2003b), *Œuvres morales et politiques*, Paris: Economica.

Schoorl, E. (2013), *Jean-Baptiste Say: Revolutionary, Entrepreneur, Economist*, Abingdon and New York: Routledge.

Steiner, P. (1990), "L'économie politique pratique contre les systèmes: quelques remarques sur la méthode de J.-B. Say", *Revue d'économie politique*, 5: 664–687.

Steiner, P. (1997), "Politique et économie politique chez Jean-Baptiste Say", *Revue française d'histoire des idées politiques*, 100 (5): 23–58.

Steiner, P. (1998), "The Structure of Say's Economic Writings", *The European Journal of the History of Economic Thought*, 5 (2): 227–249.

Tiran, A. (ed.) (2010), *Jean-Baptiste Say: Influences, critiques et postérité*, Paris: Editions Classiques Garnier.

5 Which economic agent does Robinson Crusoe represent?

Claire Pignol[1]

To cite Jean-Paul Engélibert, Daniel Defoe's novel *Robinson Crusoe* is a "literary myth of modernity". The instant success of the novel, Rousseau's praise in *Émile*, homages from Stevenson or Conrad, the many and various rewritings – collective desert island adventures (or "robinsonades") from the 17th century onwards, inverted robinsonades from the 19th century – make Crusoe a character that both builds on and reflects modern man's representation of himself.

Economists have appropriated this myth to denounce it, or otherwise to see in it a confirmation of their approaches. Crusoe is without a doubt one of the rare literary characters to have impregnated, even superficially, political economy: the *New Palgrave*, the reference dictionary for economists, has an entry for "Robinson Crusoe" where the novel is introduced and discussed. It is certainly the only novel that, in economics, enjoys such a reputation.

There appears to be a certain ambiguity in the way that economists use the novel, one that reflects and reinforces the character's own ambiguity. In the novel, as in the commentaries written on it, in economics as much as in literature, for an economist it is striking to remark that several types of economic agents are mixed together in the same character – not only different, but even contradictory. We will discuss here the patterns and issues that this jumble of characters presents, based on the hypothesis that such a mixture is perhaps what best expresses the fact that we ourselves are a contradiction of economic agents.

After an overview of the way the novel has been interpreted and used in economics and in literature, we will see how the desert island experience transforms Crusoe. From an agent subject to a desire for unlimited riches, he becomes a *homo œconomicus* (in the sense used by economic theory since the 19th century), seeking to increase his well-being through work. It also becomes clear, however, that Crusoe paradoxically heralds an anti-*homo œconomicus*, characterized by going beyond the limits of an economy given over solely to subsistence.

Overview: the ambiguity of a myth

There appears to be as much ambiguity in the way economists have used the Crusoe character as there is in literary interpretations.

Robinson's posterity in economics: robinsonades or Robinson?

Firstly, in economics, the Crusoe character must be distinguished from the robinsonades invented by classical economists from the end of the 18th to the beginning of the 19th century. Little interested in Defoe's character, they portrayed lone agents – similar, though only in that sense, to Crusoe – who meet each other by chance. These robinsonades demonstrate the theory of value: their purpose is to establish conditions of exchange, without taking account of historical circumstances. As Karagöz underlines, neither a model of isolated agent nor the name of Robinson Crusoe can be found in the major work of the classical school (Karagöz 2014: 78).

As we know, Marx condemned these castaway adventures[2] and insisted on the essential difference between Crusoe's work, of immediate social value, and the private work of a merchant agent, whose social nature is perhaps problematic. He thus began a tradition critical of naturalism in political economy, a tradition where calling a theory a robinsonade was equivalent to discrediting it. This is firstly because Crusoe's adventure is the story of an isolated individual portrayed as a 'natural' man, while all economic realities are actually historical. Secondly, essential questions about economics are less about an individual and their actions, than about the coordination of their behaviour through collective acts. Thus, reducing economic questions to those posed by Crusoe is equivalent to refusing to correctly state economic questions.[3]

While Marx treats this enthusiasm for robinsonades in classical political economy with some irony, early neoclassical authors from the end of the 19th century, on the contrary, discovered the Crusoe character as an example of the psychological verity of their approach. Not all marginalist authors used Robinson Crusoe. As it is detailed in White (1982), Karagöz (2014) and Soellner (2016), those who did followed several goals. Jevons (1871) and Wicksteed (1888) invoked Defoe's *Robinson Crusoe* to explain the principle of diminishing marginal utility; Menger (1871), to illustrate the idea that the relative value of corn and water depends on the available quantity. Wicksell (1893) or Knight (1960) went beyond these ideas and use Robinson's story to illustrate utility maximization. Wicksell refers to Robinson's utility maximization by assuming a given amount of labor time that Robinson has to divide between digging roots and gathering rushes, but Wicksell or Brown explain this as the trade-off between leisure and goods (Soellner 2016: 41). Böhm-Bawerk (1889), Clark (1899), Jevons (1871) and Fisher (1930) imagine a Robinson who optimizes inter-temporally and thus saves and invests according to his rate of time preference and the rates of return of possible investments (Soellner 2016: 41–43). Edgeworth (1881) uses the arrival of Friday on the island to illustrate bilateral exchange (see White 1982: 118).

For those economists, Robinson Crusoe is used to embody the immutable individual element that expresses the human nature at the root of any economy. White (2008) emphasizes it:

> The role of a Crusoe economy [for late 19th-century authors] was not simply to illustrate various components of supply and demand theory. It was also

utilized to support the claim that the principles of rational behaviour, and above the laws of economics as defined by that theory, *could be applied to any type of economy – from the isolated individual to 'modern civilization'.* It appears obviously in Clark's following citation:

> The general laws of the wealth-creating and the consuming process are the same in all economies; . . . It is not because the life of a Crusoe is of much importance that it has been introduced in economic discussion. It is because the principles by which the economy of an isolated man are directed still guide the economy of a modern state.
>
> (Clark 1899: 52)

Similarly, Marshall explained in the fifth edition of the *Principles* that the decisions of investments are "the same . . . in all phases of civilization, and not peculiar to its modern, or so called 'capitalist' phase. Our illustration will be equally applicable to Robinson Crusoe a to an enterprising builder of today" (*Marshall date II, 368*).[4] Later, in the Walrasian tradition, Robinson is met to express the case of an immediate combination of consumption and production decisions, without the help of prices (Koopmans 1957: 17). In modern textbooks in microeconomics, Robinson has left his mark on even the most recent and elaborate of economic theories (Varian 1992: 349–351; Varian 2010: 609–630; Mas-Colell et al. 1995: 526).

Robinson's posterity in literature: an "economic interpretation" from a literary viewpoint

If the Crusoe character and the concept of the economy that he represents for economists is ambiguous, traditional literary interpretations of the novel are traditionally no less so. Two interpretations prevail: the first, economic and realist; the second, allegorical and religious (Engélibert 1997; White 1982). According to the religious interpretation, based on a symbolic reading of the text, Crusoe's adventure is an allegory based on puritanical tradition. The story of a conversion, and the stay on the island, can be read as the spiritual trial of a hero in search of salvation.

We will concentrate in particular on the economic interpretation portrayed especially by Ian Watt. Literary critic and historian of the 20th century, Watt has worked on the rise of the novel in the 18th century. According to him, Robinson Crusoe, like Faust, Don Juan or Don Quixote, reveals the problems of individualism in the modern period, and Defoe's character is especially emblematic of the "characteristic aspirations of Western man" (Watt 1951: 95). The Crusoe character then embodies the modern *homo œconomicus* in search of economic and social success, and his insular seclusion, is a metaphor for the isolation of man at the start of the Enlightenment. From a more contextual perspective, this interpretation sees Defoe's novel as expressing the development of the middle classes after the 1688 revolution; the novel thus appears to portray the emergence of the bourgeoisie.

This interpretation is based on three themes developed in the novel:

i) The first is the back-to-nature theme, which sets the Crusoe economy in the nature of things. For Ian Watt this reading of the novel as a return to an agricultural life without society is above all Rousseau's reading: Crusoe, says Rousseau, would develop Émile's imagination about material work and train him to make judgements not on others, but on the utility of things. It is worth noting that this is also, paradoxically, the reading made by the first neoclassical economists, who defined the agent, even before exchange, in their relationship with nature: non-socialised production.

ii) The second economic theme of the novel, doubtlessly the most important one, is the exaltation of the dignity of work, credo of capitalism, which gives an ideological sense to the division of labor. Crusoe relives the happy tale of the economic development of humanity, mastering highly diverse skills and gaining, through this labor, a multitude of objects that have improved its well-being. The role of labor in forming the agent, the individual, is comparable to the place that it begins to take up in society.

iii) The third and final economic theme is Crusoe's isolation, which becomes a metaphor for the isolation of the modern individual after the dissolution of traditional social ties. In other words, according to Watt, a metaphor for the atomization of *homo œconomicus*. But it is also a metaphor for the isolation of the 17th-century English bourgeoisie, living like Crusoe in a political no-man's-land. Thus Crusoe transfers a rudimentary economy onto the island, which both resembles and absolves England's burgeoning capitalism.

Nature, work and isolation: three themes transpose a nascent capitalism onto an economy that defines *homo œconomicus* as outside of history, in direct contact with himself and with nature, mediated purely by his own work. This first economic reading of the novel, making each person's relationship with the economy appear to be a given, is nevertheless closely intertwined with historical and social themes. The homage to isolation can also be read as the expression of a specific historical situation, that of the rising bourgeoisie, with Crusoe as its hero. There are therefore two accounts of the novel: the story of an economy outside of history, that claims to be true to all economic agents in all societies; or concurrently, the story of a moment in humanity's economic development: capitalism and the rise of the bourgeoisie.

A psychoanalytic interpretation of Robinson's economy

Finally, it is worth citing Marthe Robert, a literary critic of the 20th century known for her psychoanalytic reading of modern literature; using Freud's "family romance of the neurotics", she suggests an interpretation that is partly economic, but characteristically different from those mentioned previously. In the family romance, when a child sees that their parents' social position is not the one they had imagined, they make up a more satisfying story of their origins. Freud thus identifies two stories: that of the foundling, according to Marthe Robert embodied in narrative literature by Don Quixote, and that of the bastard, tenaciously making his way, embodied by Crusoe. More precisely, Crusoe's is the tale of the path from foundling to bastard: Crusoe, disappointed by his father's low position in life, casts aside his parents by running away. If running away is patricide, shipwreck is the punishment. This is in keeping with the myth of the foundling. But the ship-wreck is also a baptism that allows Crusoe to begin a new life where he painstak-ingly reclaims a place and a power in society: here then is the bastard story.

This is an economic interpretation, firstly because of the role of work in the story: it is by work that Crusoe substitutes the foundling myth with that of the bas-tard. But it is also an economic interpretation in that Marthe Robert makes a paral-lel between a child's desire to escape a background without glory, and the fact that bourgeois civilization, a society of class and not of caste, is precisely one where it is possible to pass from one class to another. Politically or economically, it is the bourgeoisie that allows this childhood desire to be expressed and made a reality, to escape one's situation at birth. Crusoe thus embodies a desire – the desire to escape one's background – that might exist outside of the bourgeoisie, but that can also find its legitimacy and the right political conditions in a bourgeois society.

> Robinson Crusoe . . . can only be described in a society in movement, where the man with neither birthright nor quality can have some hope to raise him-self up by his own means, even if it means a hard fight against the legacy that prevented him from climbing. It is the genius of Daniel Defoe that foresaw just how much the narrative genre owes its existence to the ideologies of the free enterprise.
>
> (Robert 2000: 140)

Once again a point of articulation can be found between a specific desire out-side of history, imaginable in any society, and the possibility of making the desire come true in specific historical conditions. But whether this is about a desire or its coming true, in Marthe Robert's interpretation work is not what ties the economic agent to nature, what allows them to interact with things unsullied by others. It is firstly a social interaction, a method for resolving status rivalries, and for moving up the social hierarchy. This is the official ideology of a burgeoning capitalism: any man can change his life through his work. This ideology is based on a denial of the individual's motivations, motivations that are not only a desire for the well-being of an agent that was soon to be called *homo œconomicus*, but a desire for glory and social power.

There are several varied economic concepts present here. It is not enough to present Crusoe as a *homo œconomicus*, because he possesses a mix of traits that recall several kinds of economic agents: a merchant in that he seeks enrichment, a bourgeois in that he is worried about his social position, a capitalist in that he hoards, and on the island an agent in that he wishes only for the improvement of his well-being. And yet, all of these characters do not define a *homo œconomi-cus* expressing all of these dispositions or aspirations. It is not enough that these dispositions are all elements of economics for them to define an economic agent. On the contrary, *homo œconomicus* has been built up in economics as a very particular kind of agent, opposed to all other kinds of economic agents. And Crusoe embodies these diverse types of contradictory agents one after the other, but also sometimes simultaneously.

In part, Crusoe's capacity to represent contradictory types of agents is the result of the fact that staying on the island is a transformative experience. This transformation is especially visible in his attitude towards money. But beyond the transformation story, there remains a certain amount of confusion regarding how far this transformation goes. Some factors make its extent seem mitigated, or at least suggest the permanence of old character traits beneath the changes brought about by an island reclusion. This means that even if Crusoe is defined for the most part by the economy, he is not necessarily a clearly defined economic character. For the economist, this is what makes him interesting.

The desert island experience and the creation of a *homo œconomicus*

How does the insular experience turn Crusoe into the *homo œconomicus* as defined in economics? By the transformation of the character's attitude towards two economic objects: money and work.

Money and the desire for enrichment

The insular experience brings about a change in the character's attitude towards money. He starts out with a merchant's attitude, seeking a speedy path to enrichment, and ends with a *homo œconomicus*' attitude, only concerned with his well-being, for whom money means nothing because it has no intrinsic use. Amongst the factors that emphasize this transformation, the most notable are those that suggest that the Crusoe before his shipwreck wanted to become rich (thus his father's warnings against a too hasty desire for enrichment, the sale of his servant and companion of misfortune, despite the man having helped him to escape slavery and remained faithful), and those that express his transformation after the shipwreck, where he notices the lack of utility of money. Thus, when finding gold and silver on his wrecked boat, he exclaims: "Oh drug! What art thou good for? Thou art not worth to me – no, not the taking off the ground" (Defoe 1913: 41). The same scene occurs when he finds gold on another wreck. He also regrets having sold his slave, not for moral reasons, but for selfish and material reasons. He thinks how useful his slave would have been for farming on the island, whereas money is of no use to him. To summarize, the Crusoe from before the shipwreck wants to make his fortune; the Crusoe of the island no longer cares about anything but his well-being, his production, and curses the desire for enrichment that was the cause of his travels and thus of his being shipwrecked. From an economic perspective, this transformation is from a desire for monetary enrichment to a desire for well-being.

However, it is a characteristic of political economy, from the 18th century up to today, to maintain that money lacks intrinsic value, that money is never desired for itself,[5] that it is needed 'only to be got rid of', an intermediary imposed by the difficulties of bartering. This discourse on money allowed political economy to take form in the 18th century, in physiocracy and early political economy. Even in mercantilism, in which the search for money is seen as an essential objective of economic policy, money is desired not for its intrinsic value but an increase in the quantity amount could be a condition of economic growth. From both viewpoints (mercantilist and liberal), it is through this discourse on the lack of money's intrinsic value that political economy proved its harmlessness, and thus broke with the Aristotelian idea that there was a possible danger in an economy as soon as a good economy was replaced by bad chrematistics: the desire for unlimited enrichment. Lastly, this discourse on money naturalized economics, by separating it from politics. Money was the domain of the prince, while political economy, which aims to go beyond any monetary appearance, dealt not only with money but also with work, one of the most mutual of human experiences.

From this perspective, Crusoe from before the shipwreck embodies a mercantilist vision of the economy. This means that, for the individual as for a country, enrichment is synonymous with accumulating precious metals. Crusoe from after the shipwreck, transformed by an insular experience, heralds the agent in physiocracy, in classical economics, and even beyond in neoclassical theory from the late 19th century up to today.

The contrast between the two Crusoes is not, however, so clear. This is firstly because it is hard to be sure if the Crusoe from before the island really does unambiguously embody the merchant seeking enrichment: it is his father who attributes to him a desire to make his fortune while talking about his taste for travelling: "[he] designed me for the law; but I would be satisfied with nothing but going to sea" (Defoe 1913: 12). Secondly, because the disdain he shows on the island for money does not deter him from keeping it, or from forgetting it when he has the chance to leave. His apparent disdain for money does not go so far as for him to refuse it completely. Finding a load of merchandise on a wreck he visits at the end of his stay, he takes a precise inventory: rum, cordial, shirts, handkerchiefs, neckcloths and also gold and silver, which he describes in detail: "three great bags of pieces of eight, which held about eleven hundred pieces in all . . . wrapped up in a paper, six dubloons of gold, and some small bars or wedges of gold; I suppose they might all weigh near a pound" (Defoe 1913: 259). The precision of his description seems to belie the assurance that follows: "as to the money, I had no manner of occasion for it: it was to me as the dirt under my feet". Crusoe is in fact so little indifferent to this money that he finds even more – "I found in this seaman's chest about fifty pieces of eight, in reals, but no gold" – keeps it – "I lugged this money home to my cave, and laid it up, as I had done that before which I had brought from our own ship" – and regrets being unable to retrieve more:

> it was a great pity, as I said, that the other part of this ship had not come to my share; for I am satisfied I might have loaded my canoe several times over

with money; which, if I had ever escaped to England, would have lain here safe enough till I might have come again and fetched it.

(Defoe 1913: 260)

Crusoe knows well that the uselessness of money only carries weight on the island, for him both a prison and a refuge. Of course, being restricted to confinement strips money of any use and thus gives him an escape from the corruption of money. But neither Crusoe nor the reader ever forget, either that outside of the island this money would have value again, or that he wants himself to escape the island. The ambiguity of his desires is most striking in the opposition between the feeling of being a prisoner of the island: "for though I was indeed at large in the place, yet the island was certainly a prison to me" (Defoe 1013 p. 136), and the understanding that this imprisonment protects him: "It was now that I began sensibly to feel how much more happy the life I now led was, with all its miserable circumstances, than the wicked, cursed, abominable life I led all the past part of my days" (Defoe 1913: 156).

This attitude towards money means that at least two economic aspirations cohabit within this character, both in his actions, but also in his understanding of economics inherent in his actions: the desire for monetary riches versus a desire for real riches, made of useful things. If all of political economy, from the 18th century up to today, is built upon the idea of a richness composed of useful things and not of money, Crusoe's ambivalence, feeling despite this the uselessness of money in his reclusion, shows the permanence of a more mercantilist perception of riches.

Though not the same as money, one of Crusoe's well-known traits is his penchant for inventories, for accounts and calculations.[6] He counts the things he retrieves from wrecks as much as the things he makes. He imagines with pride the surprise of someone visiting his cave like a shop. In the same breath that he uses to reject money, he evaluates in money that which he desires:

I had . . . a parcel of Money . . . about thirty-six pounds sterling. Alas! there the nasty, sorry, useless stuff lay! I had no manner of business for it; and I often thought with myself that I would have given a handful of it for a gross of tobacco-pipes . . . nay, I would have given it all for sixpenny-worth of turnip and carrot seed out of England, or for . . . a bottle of ink.

(Defoe 1913: 178)

Such equivalences remind one of the marginalist result of utility maximization, such that the rate of exchange between two commodities is in relation to their relative scarcity. Here, the relative scarcity of tobacco (seeds or ink) versus the relative plenty of gold coins with marginal utility close to zero determines their marginal rate of substitution. As Jevons noticed, even Robinson Crusoe can "look upon each of his possessions with varying esteem and desire for more, although he [is] incapable of exchanging with any other person" (Jevons 1871: 80). It is however a bit odd that the commodity used as a numeraire here is gold, in spite of its uselessness on the island, according to Robinson himself.

When he does not calculate, as when he builds a canoe that he claims to have cost him "infinite labour", "a prodigious deal of pains" and is useless because it is far too heavy to carry to the shore, he scolds himself: "now I saw, though too late, the folly of beginning a work before we count the cost, and before we judge rightly of our own strength to go through with it" (Defoe 1913: 175–176).

White, in his article on Robinson Crusoe in the *New Palgrave* (2008), considers that the character of Defoe's novel, in contrast to marginalists' *homo œconomicus*, calculates poorly. We will see how it is true concerning especially the calculation of utility of goods versus disutility of labor. But up to this point, what is most clearly and more importantly obvious is not whether Crusoe can count well, but that he thinks about it often, that he displays an interest in these questions, and that he is not silent on them.

Work, subsistence and sufficiency

The second element that makes Crusoe a *homo œconomicus* is his relation to needs and to work, the way in which he worries about his subsistence. Marthe Robert points out that no other hero that precedes him, Ulysses or Don Quixote, is preoccupied in this manner. They feed themselves, of course, but without working like ordinary men to ensure their subsistence. Instead, they vanquish it in glorious combat. Crusoe, on the contrary, worries about the means for earning his subsistence without being heroic, counting not on his courage, but on his industry and on the tools and merchandise he retrieved from the wreck. "It was in vain to sit still and wish for what was not to be had", he writes only as soon his second day on the island; "this extremity roused my application" (Defoe 1913: 75). No glorious combat there to ensure his subsistence; anyone can identify with this unheroic hero.

He appears to be even less heroic when, very soon after, his survival ceases to be an issue. He manages to extract from the ship beached on the shore tools and materials which make it clear to him that his subsistence is not in danger.

> Then it occurred to me again, how well I was furnished for my subsistence . . . What would have been my case, if I had been forced to have lived in the condition in which I at first came on shore, without necessaries of life, or any means to supply and procure them? . . . I had a tolerable view of subsisting without any want as long as I lived.
>
> (Defoe 1913: 92–93)

From this moment on, Crusoe does not fear want, and congratulates himself regularly. Having "stated . . . very impartially, like debtor and creditor, the comfort I enjoyed, against the miseries I suffered", he contrasts the hardship of his isolation: "I am divided from mankind, a solitary; one banished from human society", with the happiness of lacking nothing for his subsistence: "But I am not starved and perishing on a barren place, affording no sustenance" (Defoe 1913: 96).

Sure of his subsistence, needs are replaced with well-being. He does not work in order to subsist, whatever he does, he aims towards improving his well-being.

Crusoe rejoices in having no battle to take part in, no wild beasts to tame. His exploits consist only of very ordinary tasks, requiring a long, monotone and fastidious amount of time, while previous heroes do glorious battle, or use subtle cunning, with immediate results. Marthe Robert seems right in remarking to what point Crusoe:

> breaks the conventions of a purely theoretical Utopia, where life sustains itself miraculously without taking issue with concrete problems. For the first time in narrative literature, reality could not be vanquished with only the strength of desire, one needed tools, calculations, all the experience and patience of a workman. Up to this point the novel was a notoriously idle genre . . . the name suggests that one never works in one. Crusoe put an end to that imposed idleness . . . With him, work, exertion, and need took their place at the heart of the utopia. It was no longer a case of denying the empirical world in order to take revenge on or lament how disappointingly bereft one was, but instead to transform it at any moment into a vast workshop where the mind and the hands were equally active.
>
> (Robert 2000: 141)

Robinson, anti-*homo œconomicus*: consumption and work

The trade-off between consumption and leisure

This tendency to work to satisfy one's needs or better one's well-being unambiguously expresses the actions of the ordinary man, the *homo œconomicus*, who uses rare resources (that is, natural resources) and working time to satisfy possibly infinite needs or desires. He appears to clearly illustrate the trade-off that happens between consumption and leisure, between the usefulness procured from goods and the uselessness implied by work, as microeconomics would put it. It is easier to understand that late 19th-century marginalist economists claimed that Defoe's character proved the truth of their analyses: Crusoe, more even than he expresses the aspirations of a bourgeois to climb the social hierarchy, heralds the calculating *homo œconomicus*, the atemporal agent living in touch with himself and detached from historical contingencies.

However, the very conditions in which Crusoe trades-off between leisure and consumption are, for at least two reasons, very different to those of the agent maximizing his usefulness, as portrayed by neoclassical theory. The first of these differences comes from his relation to needs, the second from his relation to work.

The moderation of needs

Let us begin by saying that *homo œconomicus* is defined by the desire to always consume more: it's a constant of economic thought since the 18th century, more or less explicitly, more or less adamantly, to assume that there is a rarity of resources compared to need. From the "desire of bettering our condition, a desire which, though generally calm and dispassionate, comes with us from the womb, and never leaves us till we go into the grave" described by Smith in the *Wealth of Nations* (1776 p. 415), to the non-satiation hypothesis of the modern general equilibrium theory, the agent is faced with desires exceeding their resources, and in economic theory an abundance of means relative to need is never put forward. We should bring qualifications to this statement concerning both the economists and philosophers of the 18th century and the first marginalist authors. Mandeville, Hume and Smith have taken their part in the debates on luxury goods and their frivolity or, on the contrary, their social function. Later, Walras (1988 [1889]: 107).) and Pareto (1909: 199 et p. 667) assumed the existence of a satiation point. However, the marginalist authors who used Robinson as an illustration of economic man didn't follow their predecessors of the 18th century and, when they accepted the existence of a satiation point, assumed a local non-satiation, the satiation being a characteristic of a society which escapes the economic problem. Geanakoplos' comment about the non-satiation hypothesis in the general equilibrium model is suggestive: "The non-satiation hypothesis seems entirely in accordance with human nature" (Geanakoplos 2008). From that viewpoint, as Sollner emphasizes (Soellner 2016: 50), Robinson is characterized, at the opposite, by the moderation of his needs. Rousseau has been aware of it and it is in opposition to the burgeoning political economy, and promoting the moderation of needs, that he made Crusoe an example for Émile (Rousseau 1969: 455). Crusoe's moderation in needs is not due to the fact that Crusoe is reasonable, although this is the case for Émile's education. It is due to the situation of a man deprived of socialization, whose needs are consequently extremely limited.

It is therefore the island that imposes on Crusoe a moderation of needs that so inspires Rousseau, and makes Crusoe, in this sense, an anti-*homo œconomicus*. This moderation changes considerably the economic issues he needs to resolve, compared to those of the *homo œconomicus* described by economists. Crusoe only needs to produce enough for his consumption, a quantity that cannot be infinite:

> My stock of corn increasing, I really wanted to build my barns bigger . . .
> I found that the forty bushels of barley and rice were much more than I could
> consume in a year; so I resolved to sow just the same quantity every year that
> I sowed the last, in hopes that such a quantity would fully provide me with
> bread.
>
> (Defoe 1913: 170–171)

Only when Friday arrives is the cultivation allowed expand, measured in terms of what he will need: "I began now to consider that having two mouths to feed instead of one, I must provide more ground for my harvest, and plant a larger quantity of corn than I used to do" (Defoe 1913: 285).

He expresses himself the distinction between the desert island and the English economy he has left:

> In the first place I was removed from all the wickedness of the world here;
> I had neither the lust of the flesh, the lust of the eye, nor the pride of life. I had

nothing to covet, for I had all I was now capable of enjoying . . . There were no rivals; I had no competitor, none to dispute sovereignty or command with me. I might have raised ship-ladings of corn, but I had no use for it; so I let as little grow as I thought enough for my occasion . . . But all I could make use of was all that was valuable: I had enough to eat and to supply my wants, and what was all the rest to me? . . . if I sowed more corn than I could eat, it must be spoiled . . . In a word, the nature and experience of things dictated to me, upon just reflection, that all the good things of this world are no further good to us than they are for our use; and that, whatever we may heap up indeed to give others we may enjoy as much as we can use and no more . . . I possessed infinitely more than I knew what to do with. I had no room for desire, except it was of things which I had not, and they were but trifles, though, indeed, of great use to me.

(Defoe 1913: 176–178)

This moderation of needs through forced isolation makes Crusoe an economic agent whose problem is less a rarity of resources, than the permanence of desire. Richard Steele wrote of Alexander Selkirk (the man believed to be the real-life Crusoe) that: "When those Appetites were satisfied, the Desire of Society was as strong a Call upon him, and he appeared to himself least necessitous when he [was wanting in] everything" (cited in Barthes 2002: 55).

Today, the agent of neoclassical analysis carries Crusoe's name; an agent with desires that are a given of nature, previous to any socialization, and whose objective is to satisfy these desires. The novel, however, sees the desires and needs of a man given over to isolation as a problem. Crusoe survives only through a semblance of socialization: he writes a journal, prays to God, tames a parrot in order to speak, and lives only in the hopes of a return to social life. If he is interesting to economists because they can use his character, it is a very superficial interest. Economics remembers less the character of Crusoe and the difficulties he faces existing outside of human society than the situation which he has been artificially placed in. This is despite the fact that Defoe's Crusoe, especially before meeting Friday, comes up less against the problem of efficiently using nature to satisfy his needs, than against a longing for human society.

The attitude towards work and working time

The second major difference between Defoe's Crusoe and the *homo œco-nomicus* is his relationship to work. While the *homo œconomicus* wishes to limit as much as possible their working time, Crusoe, who has an unlimited amount of time, does not seek to mitigate his exertion. To say it in marginalist terms, he doesn't determine his labor time by equalizing the marginal productivity of his labor with his subjective evaluation of the relative value of good in leisure (i.e. the quotient of marginal utility of goods on marginal utility of leisure). That has been detailed by White (1982), Karagöz (2014) and Soellner (2016).

His time on the island is entirely taken up by work, and this long working time is in contrast with the speed of enrichment through trade. He often mentions that, to produce the smallest object, his work is "infinite", and requires "an inconceivable deal" of pains. When he makes furniture, without which "I was not able to enjoy the few comforts I had in the world", it takes him a "prodigious deal of time" and "infinite labor". "This will testify for me that I was not idle, and that I spared no pains to bring to pass whatever appeared necessary for my comfortable support" (Defoe 1913: 99).

Similarly, when he manages to make his own bread, he does little to hide the lengthiness and difficulty of the affair. He lists the tools that he did not have: plough, spade and shovel. He makes them, but they are so flawed that they wear down quickly, and he describes with minute detail the work of planting, harvesting and storing the wheat.

> However, this I bore with too, and was content to work it out with patience, and bear with the badness of the performance . . . and all these things I did without, as shall be observed; and yet the corn was an inestimable comfort and advantage to me too. But this, as I said, made everything laborious and tedious to me; but that there was no help for.
>
> (Defoe 1913: 163)

Of course he works this much, like *homo œconomicus*, to increase his well-being. But this is neither the only, nor the first reason that he does so. Firstly, it is important to note that he feels as much satisfaction surveying his finished work, as he feels satisfaction in consuming. On imagining a visitor discovering his cave:

> so that had my cave been to be seen, it looked like a general magazine of all necessary things; and I had everything so ready at my hand, that it was a great pleasure to me to see all my goods in such order, and especially to find my stock of all necessaries so great.
>
> (Defoe 1913: 99)

This pleasure from surveying his work is doubled with the pleasure of possession: "my country-seat . . . my bower . . . my tent . . . my cattle" (Defoe 1913: 206).

Above all, however, work in itself is a pleasure for Crusoe, a source of satisfaction. He expresses amazement at being able to carry out, by force of effort, any craft, though he is only an ordinary man without any special talent. Having arrived on the island on the 30th of September 1659, he writes about his day in his journal, on the 4th of November of the same year:

> The working part of this day and the next were wholly employed in making this table, for I was yet but a very sorry workman, though time and necessity made me a complete natural mechanic soon after, as I believe they would do any one else.
>
> (102–103)

When he manages to make bread, he is amazed at being able to do alone what is usually accomplished through a complex division of labor:

> It might be truly said that now I worked for my bread. It is a little wonderful, and what I believe few people have thought much upon, viz., the strange multitude of little things necessary in providing, producing, curing, dressing, making, and finishing this one article of bread.
>
> (Defoe 1913: 162)

This amazement, as Ian Watt remarks, shared by Rousseau, who wants himself to pass it on to Émile, is only really a surprise for an individual who is part of a complex division of labor. Crusoe appears to express nostalgia for a self-sufficiency that perhaps never existed, but which, with the development of a merchant and capitalist society, is no longer at its most extreme. This nostalgia is anti-economical because economics promotes division of labor, which increases productivity.

This kind of relationship towards work makes Crusoe part of a paradoxical utopia. A utopia, because when on the island Crusoe is happy. This happiness comes from a good relationship with his work. Paradoxical, because a utopia generally excludes or at least limits working time. The utopia of economic science would be to reduce working time while at the same time enjoying potentially infinite consumption. However Crusoe's utopia – and Rousseau is aware of this – is one that relishes not consumption, but infinite work.

Not only are natural resources abundant on the island, but working time is even more so, and Crusoe does not seek to reduce it: "but what need I have been concerned at the tediousness of anything I had to do, seeing I had time enough to do it in? nor had I any other employment, if that had been over, at least that I could foresee, except the ranging the island to seek for food" (Defoe 1913: 95–96). Again, when he makes his furniture, he has to cut a whole tree to make just one plank: "but this I had no remedy for but patience, any more than I had for the prodigious deal of time and labor which it took me to make a plank or board; but my time and labor was little worth, and so it was as well employed one way as another" (Defoe 1913: 99).

Crusoe seems a far cry from the figure of the rational economic agent: instead of a *homo œconomicus* confronting the rarity of nature and wanting to save his work and exertion, he is more like two economic agents, or more precisely, post-economic.

He seems similar, first of all, to the unestranged worker described by Marx in his *Manuscripts of 1844*, distinguishing man from animal by the "free, conscious activity" he exerts in work, since "[animals] build themselves nests, dwellings, like the bees, beavers, ants, etc. . . . It produces only under the dominion of immediate physical need, whilst man produces even when he is free from physical need and only truly produces in freedom therefrom" (Marx 1844: 31–32).

For Marx "in creating a world of objects by his personal activity . . . man proves himself a conscious species-being" (Marx 1844: 31), and this praise for work underlies and explains the estrangement from work: if the production of the world's objects was not what brought man in contact with himself and with others, then the estrangement from work, the dispossession of the worker, would not have brought about the "estranged life", the "estranged man" that characterizes the condition of the worker under capitalism (Marx 1844: 33). *Critique of the Gotha Program* also reveals that the highest point of communist society will be reached when work will have become "not only a means of life but life's prime want" (1875). Work is done, not to satisfy need, but as the expression of each person's humanity, and this is precisely what Crusoe experiences, without this work ever ceasing to be work or being seen as pure leisure. Work, when it becomes a primary need, remains an experience of exertion and difficulty, in expectation of results.

The economic agent described by Keynes in "Economic Possibilities for our Grandchildren" also comes to mind: an agent freed from the needs of subsistence. In this text written in 1930, Keynes declares that the economic problem of humanity, defined by the struggle for subsistence, will soon disappear, and so, "for the first time since his creation man will be faced with his real, his permanent problem – how to use his freedom from pressing economic cares, how to occupy the leisure, which science and compound interest will have won for him, to live wisely and agreeably and well" (Keynes 1963: 367).

This situation, Keynes predicts, will be that much more difficult to resolve, because man, forced since the beginning of humanity to employ his time for the purpose of satisfying his needs, will find himself lacking in such a justification for his activity.

Conclusion

Defoe's hero is supposed to be symbolic of the beginnings of capitalism in Europe, repeatedly used by economists to illustrate an analysis of an agent's behaviour faced with a miserly nature. It is doubtlessly a paradox that Crusoe, identified with *homo œconomicus*, represents an agent like the one imagined by Marx or Keynes for humanity's future, beyond the development of the productive forces of capitalism, "into the lap of economic abundance" (Keynes 1963: 368). Defoe's Crusoe, though he is undeniably a character plagued by economic questions, is nevertheless essentially different from the Crusoe imagined by economists. More than the question of a miserly nature and man's infinite need, his behaviour towards work and desire shows that the economic problems he faces are about the construction, or rather the permanence, of a desire to live. But just because Crusoe represents an agent freed from the necessities of subsistence, or because the economic problem that defines him is less about scarcity than about the use of time and resources, does not mean that there is no economy. It remains present firstly through work, in the Marxian sense of the first of human needs. It also remains present in that the desire to live is linked to material acts that aim to maintain a life and build a world of objects. In terms that do not explain but rather express surprise, this work of literature states that which escapes scientific argument: to what point the economy, in the largest sense, forms our individual modern-day lives.

Notes

1 I thank Bruna Ingrao, Fritz Söllner and the editors for their helpful comments on a previous version.
2 "The individual and isolated hunter and fisherman, with whom Smith and Ricardo begin, belongs among the unimaginative conceits of the eighteenth-century Robinsonades, which in no way express merely a reaction against over-sophistication and a return to a misunderstood natural life, as cultural historians imagine" (Marx 1957).
3 "Since Robinson Crusoe's experiences are a favourite theme with political economists, let us take a look at him on his island. . . . All the relations between Robinson and the objects that form this wealth of his own creation, are here so simple and clear as to be intelligible without exertion. . . . Let us now transport ourselves from Robinson's island bathed in light to the European middle ages shrouded in darkness. Here, instead of the independent man, we find everyone dependent. . . . Let us now picture to ourselves . . . a community of free individuals, carrying on their work with the means of production in common. . . . *All the characteristics of Robinson's labour are here repeated, but with this difference, that they are social, instead of individual*" (Marx 1967, our italics).
4 Cited by White 1982: 118.
5 Even commodity money is demanded not for its use value but as a means of exchange, for its purchasing power.
6 Such a calculation recalls Max Weber's idea of capitalism, which can also be recalled by the importance of religion in Crusoe's narration. As White emphasizes, Defoe's novel can be read as a "moral tale or fable of redemption through a nonconformist Christian salvation" (White 1982: 119).

Bibliography

Barthes, R. (2002), *Comment vivre ensemble: Cours et séminaires au collège de France*, 1976–77, Paris: Seuil.
Böhm-Bawerk, E. (1889), *Kapital und Kapitalzins: Positive Theorie des Kapitales*, Innsbruck: Wagner.
Brown, H. G. (1926), *Economic Science and the Common Welfare*, 3rd edition, Columbia: Lucas Bros.
Clark, J. B. (1899), *The Distribution of Wealth: A Theory of Wages, Interest, and Profits*, New York: Macmillan.
Defoe, D. (1719 [1913]), *Robinson Crusoe*, Philadelphia: G.W. Jacobs and Co.
Edgeworth, F. Y. (1881), *Mathematical Psychics: An Essay on the Application of Mathematics to the Moral Sciences*, London: Kegan Paul & Co.
Engélibert, J.-P. (1997), *La postérité de Robinson Crusoé: un mythe littéraire de la modernité*, Geneva: Droz.
Fisher, I. (1930), *The Theory of Interest, as Determined by Impatience to Spend Income and Opportunity to Invest It*, New York: Macmillan.
Geanakoplos, J. (2008), "Arrow – Debreu model of general equilibrium", in S. N. Durlauf and L. E. Blume (eds.), *The New Palgrave Dictionary of Economics*, 2nd edition, New York: Palgrave Macmillan.
Jevons, W. S. (1871), *The Theory of Political Economy*, London: Macmillan.
Karagöz, U. (2014), "The Neoclassical Robinson: Antecedents and Implications", *History of Economic Ideas*, 22 (2): 75–100.
Keynes, J. M. (1963), "Economic Possibilities for Our Grandchildren", in J. M. Keynes (ed.), *Essays in Persuasion*, New York: W. W. Norton & Co., 358–374.

Knight, F. (1960), *Intelligence and Democratic Action*, Cambridge, MA: Harvard University Press.

Koopmans, T. (1957), *Three Essays on the State of Economic Science*, New York: McGraw Hill.

Marshall, A. (1907), *Principles of Economics*, 5th edition, London: Macmillan.

Marx, K. (1857), "Grundrisse: Foundations of the Critique of Political Economy", www.marxists.org/archive/marx/works/1857/grundrisse/ch01.htm

Marx, K. ([1932] 2000), *Economic & Philosophic Manuscripts of 1844*, M. Mulligan (trans.), *Marx/Engels Internet Archive*, www.marxists.org/archive/marx/works/download/pdf/Economic-Philosophic-Manuscripts-1844.pdf

Marx, K. (1967), "Capital: A Critique of Political Economy", www.marxists.org/archive/marx/works/1867-c1/ch01.htm

Marx, K. ([1972] 1875), *Critique of the Gotha Programme*, Peking: Foreign Languages Press, www.marxists.org/archive/marx/works/1875/gotha/ch01.htm

Mas-Colell, A., Whinston, M. and Green, J. (1995), *Microeconomic Theory*, Oxford: Oxford University Press.

Menger, C. (1871), *Grundsätze der Volkswirthschaftslehre*, Vienna: Braumüller.

Pareto, V. (1909), *Manuel d'économie politique*, Paris: V. Giard and E. Brière, http://gallica.bnf.fr/ark:/12148/bpt6k5518153f/f7.item.r=sati%C3%A9t%C3%A9.zoom

Robert, M. (2000), *Roman des origines et origines du roman*, Paris: Gallimard.

Rousseau, J.-J. (1969), *Emile, Œuvres Complètes*, Tome IV, Bibliothèque de la Pléïade, Paris: Gallimard.

Smith, A. (1776), *An Inquiry Into the Nature and Causes of the Wealth of Nations*, vol. 1, London: Strahan and Cadell.

Soellner, F. (2016), "The Use (and Abuse) of Robinson Crusoe in Neoclassical Economics", *History of Political Economy*, 48 (1): 35–64.

Varian, H. R. (1992), *Microeconomic Analysis*, 3rd edition, New York: Norton.

Varian, H. R. (2010), *Intermediate Microeconomics*, 8th edition, New York: Norton.

Walras, L. (1889), *Eléments d'économie politique pure ou Théorie de la richesse sociale*, 2nd edition, Lausanne: F. Rouge; Paris: Guillaumin; Leipzig: Duncker & Humblot.

Walras, L. (1988), *Eléments d'économie politique pure ou Théorie de la richesse sociale*, Œuvres complètes, Tome 8, Paris: Economica.

Watt, I. (1951, April), "Robinson Crusoe as a Myth", *Essays in Criticism*, 1 (2): 95–119.

Watt, I. (1957), *The Rise of the Novel: Studies in Defoe, Richardson and Fielding*, London: Chatto and Windus.

Watt, I. (1996), *Myths of Modern Individualism: Faust, Don Quixote, Don Juan, Robinson Crusoe*, Cambridge: Cambridge University Press.

White, M. V. (1982), "Reading and Rewriting: the Production of an Economic", *Southern Review*, 15: 115–142 reprinted in Grapard, U. and Hewitson, G. (eds.) (2011), *Robinson Crusoe's Economic Man*, London: Routledge.

White, M. V. (2008), "Robinson Crusoe", in S. N. Durlauf and L. E. Blume (eds.), *The New Palgrave Dictionary of Economics*, 2nd edition, New York: Palgrave Macmillan, www.dictionaryofeconomics.com/article?id=pde2008_R000163

Wicksell, K. (1893), *Über Wert, Kapital und Rente nach den neueren nationalökonomischen Theorien*, Jena: Fischer.

Wicksteed, P. H. (1888), *The Alphabet of Economic Science*, New York: Kelley & Millman.

6 Political economy and utilitarianism in Dickens' *Hard Times*

Nathalie Sigot[1] and Çinla Akdere[2]

Charles Dickens' 10th novel, *Hard Times* (1854), is generally presented as a critique of Benthamian utilitarianism (Gilmour 1967; Holloway 1962; Klingel 1986; Law 1996), which Davis (1999: 171) qualifies as a "systematic" assessment and others (Arneson 1978; Fielding and Smith 1970) as a satirical one. However, this view of the novel should not lead to the neglect of a second subject of criticism which is just as present: Dickens' analysis of political economy. Historically, this is the critique that has received the most attention. English-language studies of the novel have predominantly debated this aspect, as is illustrated for example by the controversy between the author and Harriet Martineau.[3] While the latter had been a regular contributor to the weekly created by Dickens in 1850 (*Household Words*), she stopped these contributions after the publication of *Hard Times* because of her disagreement with its satirization of political economy (cf. Fielding and Smith 1970).

As Law indicates (1996: 1), one of the reasons which explains *Hard Times'* current success is "the novel's direct engagement with the key early Victorian problem of the physical, moral and social condition of England after several decades of rapid industrialization, and appropriate private and public responses to it". Thomas Carlyle initiated what he called the "Condition-of-England question" in *Chartism* (1839) and here Dickens resumes the debate (Law 1996: 1). Carlyle denounces both the living conditions of the population and the development of a materialistic or utilitarian mind-set (cf. Welch 2006). It is this double critique that Dickens takes up, but while doing so, he adds to the confusion between utilitarianism and political economy, both in literary discussions and among critics of this discipline. This problem was already endemic in his time,[4] and remains so even now, as is revealed by Arneson (1978: 64) when he states

> in responding with sensitivity to the diffusion of the Benthamite spirit in early Victorian popular culture, Dickens creates a philosophical satire that is broad and rough but also generally accurate. The satire is aimed at the classical political economists' model of human psychology (which for present purposes we may take to be substantially the same as Bentham's).

And yet it is a mix-up that deserves to be discussed, for at least two reasons. To start with, Dickens indulges in this confusion only once in *Hard Times*, when he mentions the "utilitarian economists" (192). And then, there is the issue of how the novel differentiates between economics and utilitarianism. On one hand, since the effects of economic activity are negative and irreversible, all that falls under the domain of the economy is marked by permanence. On the other hand, it seems that it is possible to challenge utilitarian philosophy, which Dickens considers as underpinning Victorian morality – that is, it is possible to call into question a specific interpretation of utilitarianism; namely, the one the author associates with the society he describes. In other words, while *Hard Times* may be interpreted as a critique, it is not one of utilitarianism as such, but of the way this philosophy was being interpreted at that particular time (see Fielding, K. J. 1956).

Our article will re-examine Dickens' understanding of utilitarianism through a study of *Hard Times*. In agreement with what the current literature has recently done,[5] we will demonstrate the need to nuance Dickens' position as regards utilitarianism, a philosophy which he knew well (see Goldberg 1972; Stone 1985). To do so we need to distinguish what, in this work, pertains to his criticism against political economy and what pertains to his criticism against utilitarianism (I). We will illustrate our arguments by pointing out the dynamics at work throughout the novel and we will prove that for Dickens, utilitarianism was open to change, while the effects of the economy remain inalterable and admit no solutions (II).

A double critique

Dickens, in *Hard Times*, is one of the rare novelists to have referred directly to the economists of his epoch. However, it remains difficult to distinguish where he criticizes political economy and where utilitarianism, and this for at least two reasons.

The first reason is related to the author's sketchy description of economic activity. Neither economic activity, nor its aim – profit, development, progress – are truly clarified: Dickens limits himself to describing their effects, as when he portrays Coketown, the city where the action takes place. Similarly, Bounderby is defined as a "banker, merchant, manufacturer, and *what not*" (18 – our emphasis). Unlike his other novels, such as *Oliver Twist* – where the accent is placed on the devastating effects of economic institutions (the workhouses), *A Christmas Carol*, which condemns the exploitation of child labor, and also *Our Mutual Friend*, which presents a society divided into social classes and denounces greed and self-interest – here, Dickens chooses to describe economic matters mainly through the personality traits of his characters, or to be more exact, through the lack of certain traits in *some* of his characters. The world he denounces is one where the capacity to reason – his main characters are excessively imbued with this capacity – reigns to the detriment of all capacity for imagination. And yet the faculty to reason is at the heart of the utilitarianism satirized by Dickens (cf. below).[6]

The second reason which explains the difficulty in distinguishing between the two critiques has to do with the association Dickens sometimes – but rarely – makes between the two terms. At a first level, this association may be identified in Louisa and Bounderby's marriage, which, according to Winch (2009: 370), "can be taken as an emblem of the union between utilitarianism and industrial employers"; moreover, Dickens refers to utilitarian economics. Lastly, this confusion reappears during the confrontation between Gradgrind, whose philosophy is inspired by utilitarianism, and one of his ex-pupils, Bitzer, now working at the Bank and thus a creature of the world of economics. This latter states:

> It was a fundamental principle of the Gradgrind philosophy that everything was to be paid for. Nobody was ever on any account to give anybody anything, or render anybody help without purchase. Gratitude was to be abolished, and the virtues springing from it were not to be. Every inch of the existence of mankind, from birth to death, was to be a bargain across a counter. And if we didn't get to Heaven that way, it was not a politico-economical place, and we had no business there.
>
> (340)

Nevertheless, it seems that beyond a few explicit elements, such as the use of the word "utilitarian", economics make an appearance essentially in acts and speeches, while utilitarianism describes values. The majority of characters symbolize these two aspects of reality condemned by Dickens. This is the case especially of Gradgrind and Bounderby. But the former is dominated by his values, meaning utilitarianism, while the latter is characterized first and foremost by the economy, as is demonstrated by how Dickens embarks on his description, saying he is "a rich man" (18). Therefore each of these characters is mainly a symbol – and they are not the only ones – one of economics, (Bounderby), the other of utilitarianism (Gradgrind).

The critique of political economy

Hard Times undertakes the critique of political economy in mainly two ways. The first involves facts, and the other, speech.

When it comes to facts, the effects of economics are explained through two big groups of elements. The first concerns social stratification in the little town where the story is set. While poverty is symbolized by the two worker's characters, Stephen Blackpool and Rachel, wealth is principally (but not only) represented by Bounderby. He is the one who is "rattling his money" (39) to flaunt his wealth to the poor acrobats he is speaking to; he has also acquired a "snug little estate", with "elegant furniture", and many paintings (198).

This opposition between poverty and wealth leads the author to stress four themes: social conflict, the dominant importance of work, the cult of success, and lastly, the inability of the wealthy to understand the poor.

Social conflict is mainly described in the chapter entitled "Men and Brothers" (163–172), which covers a union meeting. This description has provoked much criticism, because the author satirizes a union member named Slackbridge, who is an intolerant demagogue. He was probably inspired by a real person, Mortimer Grimshaw, whom Dickens had observed at Preston, in January 1854, during a long strike in the textile industry that lasted more than eight months (cf. Dutton and King 1981).[7] In the novel, Slackbridge convinces the workers of Cokeville to shun Stephen Blackpool, who rejects his call to strike. Dickens underlines the lack of solidarity between workers and the negative consequences of strikes, which he calls "an honest mistake" (quoted by Balkaya 2015: 60); in other words, he does not consider strikes to be a useful tool to change workers' conditions. Balkaya (2015: 60) notes that the union leader's name reflects this view:

> Through the word-combination 'slack' and 'bridge', Dickens, in a way, implies that the orator is not a trustworthy person since the word 'slack' means 'not pulled tight; not firm in keeping control; not active; not taking proper care or effort' (Longman Dictionary 1267). That is to say, Slackbridge, is not a tight 'bridge' between the workers and banker and manufacturer Bounderby; Slackbridge does not 'take proper care of effort' for the welfare of the workers. . . .

The absence of solidarity within the working class is emphasized when Slackbridge accuses Stephen Blackpool, in absentia, of having robbed the Bounderby bank. Thus siding with the banker, the symbol of capitalism, he proposes that the worker's union adopt a resolution to shun Blackpool.

The universe of Cokeville is dominated by the idea of work: "You saw nothing in Coketown but what was severely workful", writes Dickens (27). The workers are described as an indistinct mass which moves around at fixed hours, following the rhythm of the factory bell: in the morning one hears "a clattering of clogs upon the pavement" (81); at noon, "more clattering upon the pavements" (82); and in the evening, "the Hands, men and women, boy and girl, were clattering home" (76). The roads serve only to lead the workers to and from work. Furthermore, the town is where the workers live, while Gradgrind lives "a mile or two" (12) and Bounderby "about fifteen miles" (198) away from town. The account of Louisa's limited knowledge of the workers echoes the portrayal of the town as an immense factory:

> She knew of their existence by hundreds and by thousands. She knew what results in work a given number of them would produce in a given space of time. She knew them in crowds passing to and from their nests, like ants or beetles. But she knew from her reading infinitely more of the ways of toiling insects than of these toiling men and women.
>
> (186)

The cult of success makes its appearance again with Bounderby, who enjoys speaking of his past poverty and is described as a "Bully of humility" (18), ever ready to repeat that he owes nothing to no one. Paradoxically, he is also present in Dickens' ironic remark on bankruptcy: Bounderby acquired his country house following the bankruptcy of "one of the Coketown magnates, who, in his determination to make a shorter cut than usual to an enormous fortune, overspeculated himself by about two hundred thousand pounds" (198). Dickens accentuates this magnate's recklessness when he draws a parallel with the poor workers: "the bankrupts had no connexion whatever with the improvident classes" (*ibid.*). And yet the cult of success insists on individual responsibility, such that poverty is deemed to be the consequence of the poor person's faulty behaviour.

The lack of understanding of the rich towards the poor is brought out by a theory which Bounderby repeats several times throughout the novel and which is met with widespread acceptance (83). It is about the supposed "ambition" of the poor, who aim "to be fed on turtle soup and venison with a gold spoon" (83; 90; 150; 286). Bounderby also declares that the work done by the workers in the factories is "the pleasantest work there is, and it's the lightest work there is, and it's the best paid work there is" (150). The lack of understanding is revealed again when Stephen, invited by Bounderby to explain how he was shunned by the members of the union, addresses Louisa, now Bounderby's wife, and not the man himself (175), as if knowing intuitively that he would be incapable of understanding the workman's world.

The second major factual element concerns the consequences of economic activity. Industrialization defaces the town. Cokeville is described as a polluted, insalubrious town (at least in the poor neighbourhoods). Pollution is such that the sun can only rarely penetrate through, suffocating all in "a blur of soot and smoke" (131). "It was a town of red brick, or of brick that would have been red if the smoke and ashes had allowed it; but, as matters stood it was a town of unnatural red" (26). Everything is black, but "black like the painted face of a savage" (*ibid.*), which creates an air of anonymity: the streets all resemble one another, as do the people. The town is presented as "the opposite of nature" (Carré 1973: 73); to use a single word, it is inhumane.

As already indicated, Dickens describes the consequences of economic activity at great length but ignores the activity itself. The main characters are, or used to be, manufacturers: Gradgrind is retired, while Bounderby is a "banker, merchant, manufacturer, and what not" (18). The bank is mentioned several times, but only because this is where the plot takes place: one of Gradgrind's sons is revealed to be a crook, who, after having robbed the bank, implicates Stephen Blackpool as the culprit. Lastly, although the names of Adam Smith and Malthus appear in the novel, this is only because two of Gradgrind's sons are so named, but in fact, neither plays a role in the story, while his three other children all contribute to the plot in some way. Louisa is the one who leads Gradgrind to question his values; Thomas illustrates the dangerous consequences of his education, since he commits theft and intentionally lets someone else bear the blame, and lastly, Jane is hastily mentioned at the end of the novel, because she was raised under Cecilia Jupe, aka Sissy's, influence. Sissy is a child of another world, that of the circus; taken in by the Gradgrinds, she opens Louisa's eyes to the positive effects of an alternative education.

The second level of the critique is situated in the speeches made by the characters. Thus economic science is described only as a theory of wealth, which forgets man and does not concern itself with his well-being. Interested in "the most complicated social questions", Gradgrind observes them from his office, described by Dickens as a kind of "observatory . . . without any windows", since he has "no need to cast an eye upon the teeming myriads of human beings around him, but could settle all their destinies on a slate, and wipe out all their tears with one dirty little bit of sponge" (112).

The lack of interest in the repartition of wealth is highlighted in an anecdote Sissy tells Louisa about how she replied to a question asked by Mr. M'Chaokumchild, the school teacher:[8] let us assume, he said, that " '[t]his schoolroom is an immense town, and in it there are a million of inhabitants, and only five-and-twenty are starved to death in the streets, in the course of a year. What is your remark on that proportion?'". Upset by this question, Sissy tells Louisa that she did not find "a better" answer than "I thought it must be just as hard upon those who were starved, whether the others were a million, or a million million". But she concludes that "that was wrong" (68). It is thus impossible for any person who comes from outside the capitalist system, such as Sissy, the daughter of an acrobat, to understand economic theory. Sissy tells Louisa about the difficulties she faces "after eight weeks of induction into the elements of Political Economy" (66). More generally speaking, the neglect of social justice creates a gap between economics and morality.

The critique of utilitarianism

The author's second critique concerns utilitarianism and is conducted in three ways.

First, the physical features of the main character of the novel, Gradgrind, are shaped by utilitarianism. He is portrayed as having a "utilitarian . . . face" (117). Although the meaning of this adjective is never explained, it is sufficient to portray this character: the reader understands that Gradgrind's face reflects the utilitarian values which he defends. He is therefore the symbol of this philosophy, even more so since he has "virtually retired from the wholesale hardware trade" (12) and no longer plays a part in any economic activity. He is deeply involved in education and the novel begins by showing him in "his school" (11), a "model school" (15), delivering a speech on facts and maths to a group of attentive children. The same characteristics serve also to describe the environment in which he lives: his house, Stone Lodge, has no charm, but is "a calculated, cast up, balanced, and proved house" (13); it is most importantly a utilitarian, or, to quote its owner, an "eminently practical" house (14).

Next, it is possible that Gradgrind's retirement and the opportunities it provides to help him to shift towards a new, political career are linked to benthamian utilitarianism. This philosophy is first and foremost a reformative one, and the reforms it proposes are supposed to rest on parliamentary power. We know that Dickens had faith in utilitarianism and shared Bentham's aim to reform society. But *Hard Times* expresses some disappointment about the possibility of promoting happiness through parliament. First, writing of Gradgrind's ambition to gain a seat in the House of Commons, Dickens says that, having realized this ambition, he became "one of the respected members for ounce weights and measures, one of the representatives of the multiplication table, one of the deaf honorable gentlemen, dumb honorable gentlemen, blind honorable gentlemen, lame honorable gentlemen, dead honorable gentlemen, to every other consideration" (109). Second, James Harthouse, who plays an essential role in Gradgrind's transformation through the feelings he stirs up in Louisa, is an aristocrat, whose brother presides over the House of Commons. This brother is rapidly sketched out and seems inaccessible to human suffering: faced with a train accident which leaves five people dead, he reacts with humour and rules out any serious investigation of the event "and brought the railway off with Cheers and Laughter" (149).

Lastly, utilitarianism shares the same values as Victorian society. Calculations lie at the centre of this philosophy: they are founded on facts and observations only and leave no place for introspection. Gradgrind is thus a member of what Dickens qualifies several times as the school of "Hard Fact fellows" (149; 196). These calculations put aside all feeling: both Gradgrind and Bounderby are "devoid of sentiment" (17). One student of the school that they have created explains that the heart serves only to circulate blood and is open only to reason and not to feelings, such as compassion (338): "educating the reason without stooping to the cultivation of the sentiments and affections" (58). This is, in fact, typical of the utilitarian system. Sentiments are opposed to rationalism, which privileges personal interest: "the whole social system is a question of self-interest", says one of Gradgrind's students (339). Lastly, and most surprisingly, utilitarianism is described as rejecting all pleasure. This aspect is developed at several occasions. It is linked to the wealthy classes' lack of understanding, as already mentioned, which leads them to refuse the poor classes' needs for entertainment.[9] The rejection of pleasure is also associated with the rejection of all feeling. When her father asks her if she is happy, Louisa replies " 'I am as cheerful, father, as I usually am, or usually have been'" (110).

The dynamics

Dickens constructs his plot in such a way that he is led to describe the future of different characters in the novel's final chapter, titled simply "Final" (346–352). This dynamic demonstrates an asymmetrical treatment between utilitarianism and political economy. *Hard Times* illustrates that economic activity and its effects are immutable. The author underlines this by pointing out the total lack of change in Bounderby's and Rachel's characters, in Rachel's life and also in Coketown. Conversely, two characters undergo radical change. First, Gradgrind, the main utilitarian character, realizes how erroneous was the philosophy which guided him throughout his life when Louisa reveals to him that her education condemned her to unhappiness. Second, Gradgrind's son, Tom, repents of his immoral behaviour, which caused him to flee from his family and above all, to push Louisa away. Tom and Louisa thus both question the values with which they have been brought up, even if Tom's death does not allow him to go beyond this repentance. However, Louisa is

> grown learned in childish lore; thinking no innocent and pretty fancy ever to be despised; trying hard to know her humbler fellow-creatures, and to

beautify their lives of machinery and reality with those imaginative graces and delights, without which the heart of infancy will wither up.

(352)

The immutability of political economy

Bounderby's behaviour could have changed under the influence of many factors. But just as this character is immutable, so is political economy.

One of the occasions which could have transformed Bounderby takes place when Gradgrind asks him to be understanding of Louisa's depressive state of mind and allow her to remain in the family home for a while. Bounderby refuses and exclaims he could not "be surprised by anything Tom Gradgrind did, after his making himself a party to sentimental humbug" (290). He remains inflexible and sets an ultimatum for Louisa to return home. When she does not obey, he sends her things back, thus implying that their marriage is over. Next, he is revealed to have lied about his childhood. Before being confronted with his mother, Mrs. Pegler, he had always done his best to create an image of the "self-made man", describing his miserable childhood, his past poverty, his life as a vagabond: "I passed the day in a ditch, and the night in a pigsty" (18). The appearance of Mrs. Pegler, who is offended that anyone should have believed that she had abandoned her child (308–310), proves that Bounderby's earlier years were nothing like what he had presented and that his success relied, in fact, on the sacrifices his modest family of tradesmen had made for him (309) when they financed his apprenticeship. In both cases, Dickens puts forward Bounderby's hypocrisy. For example, when Stephen Blackpool asks him to understand the torments he suffers because of his wife, "A creature so foul to look at, in her tatters, stains and splashes, but so much fouler than that in her moral infamy, that it was a shameful thing even to see her" (80), and asks him about the possibility of a legal separation, Bounderby insists on the "sanctity" of marriage (88), before admitting that there is a law allowing for divorce, but that this is reserved only for the rich. He then concludes, saying about Stephen's wife, "If she has turned out worse – why, all we have got to say is, she might have turned out better" (89). When Gradgrind tells him about Louisa's difficulties and begs him to allow her to remain alone in her family home for a while, Dickens alludes to the speech he had made to Stephen Blackpool: "Mr. Bounderby", he writes, "may have been annoyed by the repetition of his own words to Stephen Blackpool, but he cut the quotation short with an angry start" (288).

But Bounderby does not care in the least about being coherent with his moral discourse on marriage. His behaviour, characterized by hypocrisy, stays unchanged, but his discourse changes, not only because at that time, the law was applied differently to the rich and the poor, but mostly because Bounderby is guided by his conceit: "'I am pretty well known to be rather an uncommon man, I believe; and most people will understand fast enough that it must be a woman rather out of the common, also, who, in the long run, would come up to my mark'" (289). It's also this conceit that leads him to draw up a "vain-glorious will" (349) with which he aims to pursue and amplify his activities, to multiply himself through the arrival of "five-and-twenty Humbugs, past five and fifty years of age, each taking upon himself the name, Josiah Bounderby of Coketown"; and these

> should for ever dine in Bounderby Hall, for ever lodge in Bounderby Build-
> ings, for ever attend a Bounderby chapel, for ever go to sleep under a Bound-
> erby chaplain, for ever be supported out of a Bounderby estate, and for ever
> nauseate all healthy stomachs with a vast amount of Bounderby balderdash
> and bluster.
>
> (350)

As Bounderbys multiply, so do the nefarious effects of his will, which will lead to a "long career of quibble, plunder, false pretences, vile example, little services and much law" (*ibid.*). Even after his death, he continues to inflict pain, through his will.

The immutability of political economy is also invoked through Rachel. Throughout the novel, she is consistently described as a sincere, honest and generous symbol of poverty and the working class. At the end of the novel, she is portrayed as "a woman working, ever working, but content to do it, and preferring to do it as her natural lot, until she should be too old to labour any more" (351). Stephen Blackpool shares these same qualities, and even if his death does not allow Dickens to return to him in his final chapter, a previous chapter states that his tragic destiny never led him to anger or a desire for revenge (321–324).

Finally, Rachel's description, which emphasizes work, repeats one of Coke-town's main characteristics, which is that life is lived in rhythm with "the ringing of the Factory bell" (351).

The evolution of utilitarianism

Two of the novel's characters demonstrate utilitarianism's capacity for change: Gradgrind and his son Tom.

The manner in which Gradgrind changes is explained in some detail. A first crack in his behaviour appears on page 108, regarding his attitude towards Sissy. Although she is unable to adopt the values which he defends, "he really liked Sissy too well to have a contempt for her; otherwise he held her calculating powers in such very slight estimation that he must have fallen upon that conclusion". We also note the introduction of feelings in Gradgrind's universe; he himself will realize this only later, at the same time as he admits the failure of what he calls his "system":

> "Louisa, I have a misgiving that some change may have been slowly working
> about me in this house, by mere love and gratitude; that what the Head had
> left undone and could not do, the Heart may have been doing silently".
>
> (265)

However, the transformation of Gradgrind is above all the product of a double rupture: he first becomes aware of the negative effects of his "system" when his daughter takes refuge in his home after Harthouse declares her his love. She reproaches her father for not having taught her how to tell the difference between good and evil, or how to face her feelings: "your philosophy and your teaching will not save me. Now, father, you have brought me to this. Save me by some other means!" (258). Then it is Tom's turn to prove his father that his education was harmful. As mentioned before, he robs a bank and sets Stephen Blackpool up so it is the latter who stands accused. Once his duplicity is discovered, and explanations are sought, Tom replies:

> "So many people are employed in situations of trust; so many people, out of so many, will be dishonest. I have heard you talk, a hundred times, of its being a law. How can I help laws? You have comforted others with such things, father. Comfort yourself!"
>
> (335)

Gradgrind's evolution is also physical: gone, the "utilitarian face" – he becomes "a white-haired decrepit man" (350). The day after Louisa's revelation, he loses all assurance, which had rested on his faith in facts:

> He had a jaded anxious look upon him, and his hand, usually steady, trembled in hers. He sat down at the side of the bed, tenderly asking how she was, and dwelling on the necessity of her keeping very quiet after her agitation and exposure to the weather last night. He spoke in a subdued and troubled voice, very different from his usual dictatorial manner; and was often at a loss for words.
>
> (262)

More fundamentally still, the values which he once defended are completely transformed. Despite being held in contempt by his former relations, he is now "making his facts and figures subservient to Faith, Hope, and Charity" (350); from now on, he will use his role as a member of parliament to defend the interests of the people. Dickens reengages with one of his old convictions – that the situation of the poorest can be improved through parliamentary reform.

Gradgrind's evolution has yet another specificity which we need to underline: it takes place under the effect of a dawning of awareness. However, this awareness does not lead to a questioning of utilitarianism as such, but of its ill interpretation. Utilitarianism is a philosophy of happiness. It is when Gradgrind realizes that the educational principles that he applied to his daughter did not bring her this intended happiness that he wavers in his faith: "I know you have intended to make me happy", says Louisa (263).

The second character who evolves is Tom, Gradgrind's son. Often referred to as a "whelp" (157), he receives an education which leaves very negative effects with little hope for change:

> It was very remarkable that a young gentleman who had been brought up under one continuous system of unnatural restraint, should be a hypocrite;

but it was certainly the case with Tom. It was very strange that a young gentleman who had never been left to his own guidance for five consecutive minutes, should be incapable at last of governing himself; but so it was with Tom. It was altogether unaccountable that a young gentleman whose imagination had been strangled in his cradle, should be still inconvenienced by its ghost in the form of grovelling sensualities; but such a monster, beyond all doubt, was Tom.

(157)

Both his behaviour, especially as regards the bank robbery and the fact that he allows an innocent man to be accused in his stead, and his reaction once his responsibility is discovered, are in conformance with the qualities inculcated in him by his education. Thus, at the moment he is to escape the country with the help of his family and the workers of the circus where Sissy had lived before being taken in by the Gradgrinds, Tom refuses to recognize his mistakes and accuses his sister, Louisa, of having denounced him: "You have regularly given me up", he says, as he pushes her aside (337). Yet, the final chapter shows him, "A lonely brother, many thousands of miles away, writing, on paper blotted with tears, that her words had too soon come true, and that all the treasures in the world would be cheaply bartered for a sight of her dear face" (351). The change in values here is treated in a cursory way, as Tom dies "in penitence" (*ibid.*), while travelling to Coketown "with hope of seeing" his sister (*ibid.*). This strikes a marked contrast with Bounderby, whose violent death – he "die[s] of a fit in the Coketown street" (350) – takes place five years later, and whose will provokes the series of above-mentioned dreadful consequences.

Conclusion

While *Hard Times* confirms the critiques of utilitarianism which were already present in *Oliver Twist* (1837–1839),[10] it addresses the additional matter of political economy even more urgently. To be sure, Dickens has distanced himself from utilitarianism, under the influence, it seems, of Carlyle, to whom he dedicates the novel, but he also demonstrates optimism towards this philosophy: the characters who believe in it follow a positive evolution and slowly drift away from the caricatural figure who has faith in reason alone – to the detriment of all feeling – and in abstract calculations based on facts. Dickens' break with utilitarianism, which literature often dates back to the beginning of the 1850s, and of which *Hard Times* bears the marks, is perhaps less violent than it seems. Here and in *Oliver Twist*, Dickens criticizes the effects of this philosophy as interpreted by Victorian society (doubtlessly under the influence of political economy). The critique has simply changed shape: while before, in many of his works, Dickens observed the negative effects of institutions, here he looks at the core of utilitarian philosophy, at how it has led to a calculation which leaves no space for feelings.

Notes

1 PHARE, University Paris 1 Panthéon-Sorbonne, Maison des Sciences Economiques, 106–112 Boulevard de l'Hôpital, 75647 Paris France Cedex 13. E-mail: nsigot@univ-paris1.fr
2 Middle East Technical University, Department of Economics, Office A-202 Universiteler Mah. Dumlupinar Bulv. No:1 06800 Cankaya Ankara Turkey. E-mail: cakdere @metu.edu.tr
3 Some of these writings have been reproduced (partially) in Collins (1986). See also Hodgson (1854: 299–301).
4 As Williams (1970: 90) highlights, "When Dickens was writing, the utilitarian emphasis was a compound of rationalism and *laissez-faire* economics, in spite of the substantial contradiction between an appeal to general utility and a recommendation of non-interference".
5 Contemporary literature focuses either on the joint criticism that Dickens and Bentham made of the administration of the time, or on the biased presentation made by the former of the philosophy of the latter, which leads to criticism that emphasis is placed on pain alone, while the principle of utility emphasizes pleasure *as well* (Blake 2009).
6 On this theme, Arneson (1978: 61) stresses "the similarity between Dickens' complaint against a vaguely discerned spirit of the times and the much more focused criticism urged by J.S. Mill against Bentham in his 1838 essay in London and Westminster Review: Bentham, says Mill, lacked himself, and failed to appreciate, a certain sort of imagination [. . .] Mill concludes that Bentham, lacking imagination and an historical sense, saw accordingly in man little but what the vulgarest eye can see".
7 As underlined by Carré (1973: 71), Dickens' work is more concerned with artisans and employees rather than with the world of industrial England.
8 Henderson (2000: 142) believes that Mr. M'Choakumchild represents the economist McCulloch, whose *Principles of Political Economy* (1825) was very popular.
9 The privation of the working class of any entertainment is also linked to religion, which imposes moral values on the poor without ever taking their needs into account; certainly Dickens tells us that the workers do not belong to "the eighteen denominations" which inhabit Coketown, but religion serves as a basis to explain their reprehensible behaviour, such that the members of "a native organisation in Coketown itself . . . indignantly [were] petitioning for acts of parliament that should make these people religious by main force" (28). Let us stress that neither Gradgrind, nor Bounderby practice any religion.
10 The novel describes the miserable life of a child of the workhouse, an innocent victim of reactionary capitalism and of The Poor Law Amendment Act of 1834. passed under the influence of these philosophers "putting entirely out of sight any considerations of heart, or generous impulse and feeling" (Dickens 1837–1839: 123). Dickens is an early critic of these laws on the poor, an issue studied by Stone (1985: 380).

Bibliography

Arneson, R. J. (1978), "Benthamite Utilitarianism and *Hard Times*", *Philosophy and Literature*, 2 (1): 60–75.

Balkaya, M. A. (2015), *The Industrial Novels: Charlotte Brontë's Shirley, Charles Dickens' Hard Times and Elisabeth Gaskell's North and South*, Cambridge: Cambridge Scholar Publishing.

Blake, K. (2009), *Pleasures of Benthamism: Victorian Literature, Utility, Political Economy*, Oxford: Oxford University Press.

Carré, J. (1973), "Le proletariat industriel de *Hard Times* de Dickens", in *Hommage à Georges Fournier*, Paris: Les Belles Lettres, 71–86.

Collins, P. (1986), *Charles Dickens: The Critical Heritage*, London and New York: Routledge.

Davis, P. (1999), *Charles Dickens A to Z: The Essential Reference to His Life and Work*, New Yok: Checkmark Books.

Dickens, C. ([1837–1839] 1846), *The Adventures of Oliver Twist; or, the Parish Boy's Progress*, London: Bradbury & Evans.

Dickens, C. (1854), *Hard Times: For These Times*, London: Bradbury & Evans.

Dutton, H. I. and King, J. E. (1981), *Ten Per Cent and No Surrender: The Preston Strike, 1853–1854*, Cambridge: Cambridge University Press.

Fielding, K. J. (1956), "Mill and Gradgrind", *Nineteenth-Century Fiction*, 11 (2): 148–151.

Fielding, K. J. and Smith, A. (1970), "Hard Times and the Factory Controversy: Dickens vs Harriet Martineau", *Nineteenth-Century Fiction*, 24 (4): 404–427.

Gilmour, R. (1967), "The Gradgrind School: Political Economy in the Classroom", *Victorian Studies*, 11: 207–224.

Goldberg, M. (1972), *Carlyle and Dickens*, Athens, GA: University of Georgia Press.

Henderson, J. P. (2000), " 'Political Economy Is a Mere Skeleton Unless. . . ': What Can Social Economists Learn From Charles Dickens?", *Review of Social Economy*, 58 (2): 141–151.

Hodgson, W. B. (1854), "On the Importance of the Study of Economic Science as a Branch of Education for All Classes", in *Lectures on Education*, London: John W. Parker, 263–316.

Holloway, J. (1962), "Hard Times: A History and a Criticism", in J. G. Dickens and G. Pearson (eds.), *Dickens and the Twentieth Century*, London: Routledge & Kegan Paul, 159–174.

Klingel, J. E. (1986), "Dickens's First Epistle to the Utilitarians", *Dickens Quarterly*, 3: 124–128.

Law, G. (1996), "Industrial Relations: Carlyle's influence on *Hard Times*", *Humanitas*, 34, Waseda University. www.f.waseda.- jp/glaw/arts/IndRels.pdf.

Stone, M. (1985), "Dickens, Bentham and the Fictions of the Law: A Victorian Controversy and its Consequences", *Victorian Studies*, 29, reprinted in Parekh, B. (1993), *Jeremy Bentham Critical Assessments*, vol. 3, London and New York: Routledge, 371–399.

Welch, P. J. (2006), "Thomas Carlyle on Utilitarianism", *History of Political Economy*, 38 (2): 372–389.

Williams, R. (1970), "Dickens and Social Ideas", in M. Slater (ed.), *Dickens 1970: Centenary Essays*, New York: Stein & Day, 77–98.

Winch, D. (2009), *Wealth and Life*, Cambridge: Cambridge University Press.

Part II

Economic ideas and metaphors in literature

An interdisciplinary approach

7 Concordances and dissidences between economy and literature

Jean-Joseph Goux

A few figures who have a relation to money or to economic life emerge very early in literature. Still, it is only in the first decades of the 19th century that literature and economy truly meet. Certainly, there is the famous usurer Shylock in W. Shakespeare's *Merchant of Venice*; certainly there is the old Harpagon, in the *Miser of Moliere*; certainly also there is, as soon as the start of the 18th century, Robinson Crusoe, with whom we might think was born a new figure of the individual, prior to the emergence of *homo oeconomicus*; certainly there is "The Man of Forty Crowns" by Voltaire, to cite only the most salient characters, invented by famous authors. Still, these literary figures, if they typify attitudes to money, or wealth, or individual labor, are far from confronting a society that makes money the centre of its preoccupations, of its values, and even less a discipline still in formation whose aim is to study production, exchange and the consumption of wealth.

Only in the first decades of the 19th century does something change in the relation between economy and literature. From then on become visible the multiple relations that literary fiction can have to economic life, and beyond economic life, to the concepts of economic theory. From this meeting several types of relations become clear: relations of what might be called concordance, or correspondence, but also more conflictual relations of antagonism, opposition, defiance or dissidence.

Beginning in the 1830s, with the reign of Louis-Philippe, the "bourgeois king", it becomes evident to contemporaries that a deep upheaval in economic practices and mores tipped French society into a new era, where money was becoming the new power. If this movement began earlier, it begins at this date, corresponding to the visible foisting of what Polanyi has called the "self-regulating market", when a sharper consciousness of economic realities emerges, and it becomes clear that the values of the nobility are collapsing in the face of a new feudalism, that of money, of the bank, of the bourgeois merchant. Writers, whether they be novelists or playwrights, echo the mental and moral upheaval accompanying this pivotal moment in French society: Vigny, Balzac, Stendhal, to cite only the most salient, saw with lucidity this "great transformation" to borrow Polanyi's expression. They put into fictional representation, through theatre and novel, this changeover of mores, values and ideas towards a new world, which was effacing more and more the moral heritage of the Ancient Regime.

This is a civilization which has "replaced the principle of Honour with the principle of Money" (Balzac 1989: 70), Balzac writes in 1835. In addition, Stendhal, in *Lucien Leuwen* (a novel written between 1830 and 1836) enounces directly: "Since July the bank is at the head of the State. The bourgeoisie has replaced the faubourg Saint-Germain, and the bank is the nobility of the bourgeois class" (Stendhal 2007: 734). Thus, it is a radical displacement of political and social domination, giving financial, banking, stock-trading operations and a prominent position. Literature represents this upheaval, this fracture, which soon replaced, as was often written at the time, the old feudality of the time with a feudalism of money or factory.

At this moment also the interest of certain novelists for not only economic life, but the still young science of political economy, asserts itself. Balzac and Stendhal are among them. Stendhal had acquired (as has been shown by numerous and often recent work) a solid economic culture (Lallemand 2010). He was a reader of Adam Smith, of Jean-Baptiste Say, of Étienne Bonnot de Condillac, of Jeremy Bentham, of Sismondi, of David Ricardo, of Thomas Malthus, and these authors fed his reflections on wealth and poverty, on the importance of finance in political life, the reflection of which we find explicit echoes in *Lucien Leuwen*, about both the workers revolt of 1830 and the accession of Lucien's father, a high financier, to the rank of ministry of finance.

The knowledge Balzac had of economists is less well established, but it surfaces in certain passages of his novel, such as the long reference to Jeremy Bentham in *Eugénie Grandet* (written in 1834), when one of the characters, the president of Bonfons, explains to the Grandet father, that usury is legal because money is a commodity like any other and that the great English public figure has shown that the moral reprobation against the usurers is mere silliness. More generally, meditations on the motivation of pecuniary gain as the tendency summarizing all human sentiments, and which makes the miser such a fascinating character, a meditation which we find a few pages earlier and that recurs in Gobseck and other novels of Balzac, that seems to come straight from economists or philosophers who have preceded them.

However, this irruption of economic preoccupations among writers is not self-evident. Is there not between economics, as reality and as science, and literature, an unbridgeable chasm? Cold, calculating, quantified, denuded of sentiments and poetry – is not the world of economics, as practice and theory, opposite to what the novelist tries to express about the human condition? Thus, is there not a radical divorce between literature and economics?

At the same moment when Balzac and Stendhal make the world of business and pecuniary interest a new material, promising intrigue, twists and drama, Alfred de Vigny, more sombre, sees in the coming world the death of the poet, purely and simply. His play *Chatterton*, of 1834, announces with precocity more than a century of opposition between artists – rejected, ignored, damned – and a bourgeois society centred exclusively on pecuniary interests. The suicide of Chatterton, a poor soul misunderstood by almost all, exemplifies in an extreme, melodramatic way the incompatibility between the finalities of poetry and those of the capitalist world embodied by the horrible John Bell, "absolute baron of his feudal manufacture", (Vigny 2001: 63) glued to his account book, unjust and contemptuous towards his own wife, his workers and even the venerable pastor.

The décor and all the characters are set for several generations. The new society, dominated by money, turns poetry into a commodity like any other, and in so doing, it kills the poet, who becomes a "book publishing worker". Language and words are reduced to having only a mercantile value. "We are talking about ideas, good God!" cries Chatterton, "What sells are words. Some words can even go for up to one shilling; thoughts no longer have currency" (Vigny 2001: 101). There is not just a parallel here between language and money (to which I will return), but language is money; language has a selling price. Thus, the poet, "spirit defeated by number", sells his soul, his words, and finally, in an ultimate gesture before his suicide, even his body to the surgery school, in order to pay his post-mortem debts.

Vigny has painted the darkest tableau of this divorce between economic calculation and poetry, the highest form of linguistic art. From then on, the struggle has begun: Do literature and poetry not become by necessity a critique of political economy in the face of a society dominated by money?

Beyond Vigny's romantic and theatrical complaint, is there not in fact and radically within economic practice, and within the concepts that rendered it too, a principle and an effect of dehumanization, which places economic science and literature on two radically heterogeneous planes, strangers and potentially in conflict?

This suspicion has been expressed often, in different terms. There may be, at the very foundation of economics, as both practice and theory, a principle of abstraction and reduction, which would oppose it to the aims of life. There may be an alienation of life, or what Michel Henry, a few decades ago, called an "an inversion of the teleology of life", in the principles of the economic (Henry 1976).

Gilles-Gaston Grangier had already highlighted before, in his work on economic methodology, the neutralization underlying economic reasoning. Marginalist economics, for example in Jevons, by making economics, in the lineage of Bentham "a calculus of pleasures and pain", does not relate the satisfactions or "dissatisfactions" to the activity which engendered them, but only keeps traces; "all that subsists of the act is the calculation" (Grangier 1968). There is here an objectification and a reduction of human action, which evacuates the intuitive content of economic activity. It is, says Grangier, a "neutralization of action". We are not dealing with behaviours, with their tentative nature, their seeking, the field of situations and actions within move real actors, but results subsumed into the concept of equilibrium. To put it simply, if we define the selling price in free competition using supply and demand curves, we put forward objectified results, taking it at the instant when it is determined, ignoring bargaining and its own time scale, where is expressed the living action of subjectivities.

We could say that the enterprise of the novelist, who does not pretend to science, is all the opposite. They must grasp the behaviour in its fullness. This is why the apparent divorce between economics and literature did not keep the novelists of the "century where all is money", as Stendhal says, to make from economic things the rich and living material of tales featuring the whole range of human drama.

If economy is the world of value that can be numbered, measured, quantified, it is also that of some of the great stakes of life: opulence or indigence, success or bankruptcy, and it is the site of interminable intrigues, combinations with which to play, to speculate, undertake, win and sometimes trick. Continuing the preceding illustration, we could say that the economist works only on the price, fixed, neutralized, objectified, quantified results of a whole series of mercantile behaviours, underlying intrigues, which they ignore by principle or by method, but which, on the other hand, interest the novelist to the upmost.

Romanesque fiction allows itself to be invaded by themes, intrigues, characters belonging to the world of money (usury, banking, stock-trading, marketing, accounting, the bill of exchange) or that concern singular financial situations (such as dowry, income, pension, inheritance, bankruptcy), but this is also a mode of representation and a way of writing which is being transformed to match these prosaic, dry, selfish realities now dominating social life. All these things without poetry, which up to then interested only merchants, bankers and notaries, characters as gray as their costumes and as denuded of freshness and life as a series of numbers on an account book, are becoming the surprising substrate for the novelist. A whole part of reality which literature seemed to want to avoid until then, holding it low, without nobility, without grandeur, without sentiment, of a heavy and prosaic tone, is now entering the field of narration, even if often in a voluntarily ironic and dark way.

For Balzac, money is not only omnipotent and "omniconvenient", but it is also, more surprisingly, omniscient, as says one of the characters of La maison Nucingen. By taking the point of view of money, the novelists can have on all being, like the usurer Gobsek, the point of view of God. The omniscience of money opens the era of the omniscient narrator, who dominated the modern novel[1] – until the innovations attempted by a few novelists such as Gide, and then the severe objections of the Nouveau Roman during the 60s of the last century.

The decisive fact is that it is the same social reality, the same practice, the same type of relation between individuals which would come to determine at the same time the rise of a certain literary genre, the novel, and the accelerated development of a still-young science, political economy. The rise of the modern novel has as precondition a more and more egalitarian society where the autonomous, free individual flourishes, constructs himself. The novel is first a biography or a combined multiplicity of biographies, the story of one or several individuals following their personal path through a complex society where their initial social conditions do not fully determine the course of their lives, but where their own efforts as well as chance, encounters and initiatives end up tracing a destiny for them, an unexpected destiny.

In this description of the essential nature of the modern novel, we recognize right away a certain notion of the individual and of individualism, which is also that of economic liberalism.

The author who has best described, without intending it, the common histori-cal and social grounds for the novel genre and the liberal economy is, without doubt, Alexis de Tocqueville, even if about America rather than France, and even if Tocqueville was not concerned with the 19th-century literary representation of the world. Meditating on the new individual emerging from democratic societies, Tocqueville writes this:

> When all the prerogatives of birth and fortune are destroyed, all the profes-sions are open to all, and one can reach the summit of each by one's own means, an immense and easy career seems to open to the ambition of men, and they gladly imagine that they are called to great destinies. Yet immense obstacles that they had not perceived confront them. They have destroyed the bothersome privileges of a few; they meet the competition of all.
>
> (Tocqueville 1840)

Within a few lines, Tocqueville gives a remarkable description of the individual in post-revolutionary society, a description of which we see the economic back-ground (freedom of enterprise, legitimate quest for individual profit, fierce com-petition on the market in the wide or narrow sense), but the description also gives, at the same time, an immediate key for the comprehension of the most typical characters of 19th-century literature.

Each individual becomes, within certain limits, the entrepreneur of his own existence. In a society which wants itself to be more equalitarian, his ambition is not slowed or determined in advance by his "condition", rank or birth, and he thinks himself called to a grand destiny, to exceptional success. Nonetheless life choices are numerous, uncertain, and it is difficult to choose. More still, success is difficult, for all are competing against all. In addition, much disillusion lies ahead.

In this description, do we not recognize just as much the enterprising heroes of the novels of Balzac, the steadfast ones of Stendhal or of Flaubert, as well as, in the same authors, the deeply hesitating and disillusioned, who stand by and miss the infinite possibilities offered to them (often because of an impossible and interminable love, as is the case of Lucien Leuven, or like Frederic Moreau in *Education Sentimentale*?

Inversely, we have the Comte de Monte Cristo, ideal fantasy, absolute myth, of an individual without name, without notable heritage, but son of adventure and chance, who inherits an immense fortune giving him a place among the most important.

If there is a visible affinity at that time, between the novel and political econ-omy, it is not just because novelists, in front of the importance taken by money in human affairs, borrow from economic life a new décor, a theatre where pecuniary interest, profit, rent, lending, debt, etc. play out; but it is also because this affinity has a deeper dimension and that beyond this necessary and striking scenography, there exists a narrow concordance between the new individual presupposed by political economy and the new individual animating and founding the new genre of the novel itself.

This new individual is at the same time the active agent of a liberal, enterprising economy, which the economists have begun to theorize, and the typical character of the realist novel. This new individual, who seeks to selfishly maximize his satisfaction, his wealth, this individual in whom economists could see, in his idealized and pure form, the model for a *homo oeconomicus*, is indeed the practical, social and institutional reality of a new representation, at the same time theoretical and fictional.

The allusion to the famous *homo oeconomicus* only underlines the unexpected correspondence between economy and literature, this time at the level of method itself, which obliges us to return for a moment to this method.

If economics can claim to be a science, it is indeed not an experimental science, unlike physics and chemistry. The chemist, the physicist and even the biologist can place a phenomenon under study within certain artificially determined conditions, made to vary at will. They isolate the phenomenon and methodically modify certain parameters. It is in this sense that Bachelard could say that the phenomena studied by physical sciences are not given, but rather constructed. The economist, meanwhile, cannot construct phenomena, except at a scale trivial to the completely complex whole of society. As Charles Gide writes quite truly: unlike the physicist or the chemist, the economist, "even doubled by a legislator or an all-powerful despot", lacks the ability to artificially vary the conditions of social phenomena (Gide 1913: 16).

Economics is thus condemned to use a deductive method, starting from a few simple principles, taken as axiomatic, theoretical fictions from which we abstractly draw consequences. As a science, economics finds itself in a difficult and always contested position, even today. It has neither the possibilities of an experimental science, nor the status of a true hypothetico-deductive science, such as mathematics or Newtonian mechanics, even if Walras harboured the Newtonian dream, and if economics still tries, in spite of numerous failures, to give itself the appearance of a Newtonian science.

In fact, the economic method begins with concrete situations, phenomena which cannot be fully stripped of their very tangled empirical reality, but from which are deduced supposed consequences. The first economists proceeded in this way.

This explains the short fictions, fables, little novels often found at the beginning of their arguments, and explains the famous and venerable *homo oeconomicus*.

"Let us suppose", writes Condillac, "a small settlement just established, which has made its first harvest . . . and let us suppose moreover that after having allocated the wheat necessary to sow the earth, there remains one-hundred tonnes", etc. With this little novel, Condillac begins his 1776 treatise *Commerce and Government Considered in Their Mutual Relationship*. At exactly the same date, Adam Smith transports us to a perhaps ancient and savage society, a period before the accumulation of surplus and the appropriation of the land. He imagines a people of hunters, where the cost of labor to kill a beaver is two times higher than for killing an elk. Imagine how many elk one will trade, then, for a beaver? The answer is two, and you have just discovered one of the most important laws of political economy!

The same kind of fable is found in Ricardo, where the bow and arrows of the hunter are compared to the canoe of the fisherman. Marx contests, with good reason, the demonstrative value of these fictions where the economist is only projecting the categories of his own society onto a completely different society. It would be an anachronism, he explains, to believe that the primitive fisherman and hunter exchange their goods in accordance with the bourgeois law of value, in proportion to labor-time, as if the bourgeois form of labor was the eternal, natural form of social labor. In addition, Marx adds with humour that Ricardo "commits the anachronism consisting of making the primitive fisherman and hunter refer, to value their instruments of labor, to the 1817 annuities table of the London Stock Exchange" (Marx 1957: 37).

Nonetheless, the unstable, misunderstood, composite methodological status of economics as science obliges the economist to inventions permitting him to dream this discipline as deductive (if not logico-deductive) when the inductive and historical element cannot be ignored.

A fiction of the same order, but even more central and fundamental, and which economic science could not do without, was the *homo oeconomicus*. His profile begins to appear as soon as the notion of purely economic individual interest, and rational maximization, become prevalent, before Pareto baptized him thus.[2]

It is no exaggeration to suppose that this way of thinking, clearing a type and sketching a narration, brings surprisingly close together economics and literature.

The creation of human types by the novelist, based on a necessarily limited observation (such as the miser, the usurer, the grand speculator, the prodigal, the ambitious, etc.), and the creation of the hypothesis or postulate of a *homo oeconomicus*, might be considered as the same order of reality, or rather of fiction. At hand is a human type, made clear through imagination and abstraction, about which it is difficult to establish the degree of generality but which is supposed to be representative of a certain common behaviour of human beings. Thus there would be, at base, a common approach: bringing to light types of behaviours – a common, but also competing, approach.

As far as the *homo oeconomicus* is concerned, let us note that literature at the same time comforts and undermines this economic fiction. Notice that some of Balzac's characters behave strictly like *homo oeconomicus* (at least in the simplified sense of this complex notion): father Grandet and his nephew Charles Grandet, the usurer Gobsek, the banker Nucingen that "Napoleon of Finance", are motivated exclusively by financial interest, and this even before the notion of *homo oeconomicus* had been more clearly cornered and identified by named by economists like Pareto. But what makes the eminent interest of the literary gaze is that we cannot miss that many other characters, in Balzac, Stendhal, Flaubert, Zola (to say nothing of novels where the economic is not central), are not *homo oeconomicus*.

Of the unfortunate Eugenia Grandet, Balzac writes: "for her, wealth was neither a power nor a consolation: she could exist only by love, by religion, by her faith in the future. To her, love explained eternity" (Balzac 1972: 194). We have here, by anticipation, an almost frontal critique of the abusive generalization of the notion of *homo oeconomicus*. In the face of her father, who is a dark caricature of a man preoccupied only with financial gain, in the face of her beloved cousin Charles who, during the course of his distant voyages, loses all notion of justice and injustice and becomes a monster, making commerce and investment of everything, including men and children, Eugenie embodies the anti–*homo oeconomicus*. She entertains values, existential finalities, which are not financial interest, or the maximization of pecuniary profit. Besides, the coexistence and opposition of the two within the same plot often makes the dramatic strength and the critical dimension of many literary works; Chatterton is exemplary: on the one side John Bell, the unfeeling and calculating capitalist, the "absolute baron of his feudal manufacture", and on the other his devoted wife Kitty and Chatterton himself, the poet, his eyes turned towards the heavens.

In addition, it is not by accident that, in these literary works, women are in a position to contest the economic logic (one could certainly develop this point at length).

Literary fiction here sets itself in opposition with what is also a fiction, but a fiction constructed and sustained by economic science, by implicitly contesting the universality of the assumptions on which the *homo oeconomicus* is based.

There are even extreme examples, such as the main character of François Mauriac's *Nest of Vipers*, written in 1932, where a kind of conversion following the death of kin transforms a rich, miserly, greedy, selfish, hard character into a very different man whose whole life becomes an effort to get rid of his wealth. A situation, to be sure, about which the novelist has grasped the strangeness and the exceptional paradox in our time, by revealing towards the end of the novel, following his death, that many of his friends thought he had gone mad.

So we have in these novels a kind of game, a scenography confronting the model of economic man against what contests its universality, whether it be love, generosity, faith (aesthetic, religious), or sometimes the quest for power, etc. And we could argue that since the beginning of the 19th century, literary fiction has not ceased, under varied forms and more or less indirect, to oppose the whole variety of human behaviours and ends against the model of economic man, without, it is true, allowing us to measure the degree of pragmatic truth contained in this contestation.

Whatever the dissidence between economy and literature, still there is a strong solidarity, perhaps homology even, to be established between language and money. Literature, as a language and reflective work on language, cannot escape the implicit or explicit parallel making it inseparably tied to economics. The comparison between language and money is at the same time very ancient, since we find it already in Antiquity, and very modern, since contemporary economists such as Friedrich August von Hayek and Milton Friedman still have recourse to it. Writers, poets, as well as economists and linguists, have taken advantage of this comparison, under highly varied angles, and with often quite different theoretical and political intentions. From Rabelais to Gide, through Hugo or Mallarmé, from Turgot or Diderot to Saussure, Bergson or Valery, whether it is source of poetic metaphor or the object of a more rigorous structural logic, the homology between language and money has not ceased to feed a fruitful parallel between exchange of signs in communication and economic exchange on the market. This durable and justified parallel can only directly or indirectly implicate, or compromise, literary writing and its themes. We could go so far as to argue that a society's concept of language at a certain moment is homologous to its concept of money, which drags literature into the same vicissitudes, the same stakes as economics. Gold standard or fiat money, inconvertible money, dematerialized electronic money, each of these monetary regimes lead us into certitudes and suspicions, expectation or interrogations of where the notion of real, of representation, of truth are at stake. In each case, the relation between language and the world is in play.[3] For example, we see to what extent the notion of the gold standard can mark a time, as much in literary representation as in philosophical thought. We see, too, to what extent the notion of monetary signs convertible to gold, or especially today, inconvertible, can upend thinking. A whole relation to reality, to truth, to representation is affected, indexed to the status of money, in its homology to language.

I want to close on this point, simply recalling a comparison made by Henri Bergson in 1911, and that the following century has since rendered of an interesting but also troubling anachronism:

> I do not deny the usefulness of abstract and general ideas – not more that I contest the value of banknotes. Yet in the same way that the bank note is merely a promise of gold, a concept is only worth by virtue of the perceptions it eventually represents.
>
> (Bergson 1938: 145)

Through this comparison, we see to what point, to what depth, the definitive suspension of all "promise of gold", by disappearance of the gold standard and convertibility of paper money, could modify our relation to representation and to truth. The Bergsonian image of the gold standard has become impossible and anachronistic. What can replace it? Must we today think without promise, without the assurance of a treasure, without knowing what may guarantee value and meaning in the absolute? Has not the promise of gold today become the indefinite circulation of a debt, referring "promises to pay" to other "promises to pay", in an interminable game of reference, a kind of madness of which contemporary art and literature have sometimes given us the presentiment by its bookkeeping games, whose direct relation to a stable referent seems to be absent?

Notes

1 I developed this point in Goux (2000: 87), and more recently in Goux (2014).
2 On the notion of *homo oeconomicus*, see M. Foucault (2004: 275). Foucault shows that the appearance of the *homo oeconomicus* corresponds to the conception of an "interested subject", but a purified interest, who has become calculating, rationalized. More recently, P. Demeulenaere (1996) has analyzed in a detailed way all the ambiguities of this paradigm.
3 In several essays, I have tried to demonstrate these correspondences, and particularly in *Les monnayeurs du langage* (1984), and in *Frivolité de la valeur* (2000).

Bibliography

Balzac, H. de (1972), *Eugénie Grandet*, Paris: Gallimard.

Balzac, H. de (1989), *La Maison Nucingen, Melmoth réconcilié*, Paris: Gallimard.

Bergson, H. (1938), *La pensée et le mouvant*, Paris: PUF.

Demeulenaere, P. (1996), *Homo oeconomicus, Enquête sur la constitution d'un paradigme*, Paris: PUF.

Foucault, M. ([1979] 2004), *Naissance de la biopolitique*, Paris: Gallimard/Seuil.

Gide, C. (1913), *Cours d'économie politique*, Paris: Recueil Sirey.

Goux, J.-J. (1984), *Les monnayeurs du langage*, Paris: Galilée.

Goux, J.-J. (2000), *Frivolité de la valeur*, Paris: Blusson.

Goux, J.-J. (2014), "Monnaie, échange, spéculation, la mise en représentation de l'économie dans le roman français du XIXéme siécle", in F. Spandri (ed.), *La littérature au prisme l'économie: Argent et roman en France au XIXe*, Paris: Classiques Garnier.

Grangier, G.-G. (1968), *Essai d'une philosophie du style*, Paris: Armand Colin.

Henry, M. (1976), *Marx II, une philosophie de l'économie*, Paris: Gallimard.

Lallemand, J. (2010), "Pauvreté et économie au XIXe Siècle", *Cahiers d'économie politique/Papers in Political Economy*, 59: 119–140.

Marx, K. (1957), *Contribution à la critique de l'économie politique*, Paris: Editions sociales.

Stendhal (2007), *Lucien Leuwen*, Paris: Les classiques de poche.

Tocqueville, A. de (1840), *De la démocratie en Amérique*, Tome II, Paris: Flammarion.

Vigny, A. de (2001), *Chatterton*, Paris: Gallimard.

8 Economics and monetary imagination in André Gide's *The Counterfeiters*

Çınla Akdere and Christine Baron[1]

Introduction

André Gide (1869–1947) has written a novel which "disrupts the laws of genre" (Sageart 1925). *Les Faux-monnayeurs*,[2] first published in 1925, is an utterly decontextualized text which sets the challenge of representing reality as it is. Its very subject is this challenge itself. Reality shows us not only a group of counterfeiters but also their falseness,[3] jointly with the artificiality and the hypocrisy in human relations such as those of family, friendship or love. Yet it would be a mistake to categorize Gide's novel as a psychological one (Moutote 1990: 19–20). For the author, to represent reality is to make a choice between certain aesthetics in literary language. His aesthetic is marked by a crisis of representation. While refusing to subscribe to the 19th century's model of the realistic novel, he remains aware of the impasse of anti-representational,[4] symbolist aesthetics. What constantly underlies all relations between the characters is money relations.

J.-J. Goux (1984) focuses on the epistemological nature of the encounter between economic science and literature by pointing to the homology between what relates to "economics" and what relates to "aesthetics" in Gide's work. He underlines the similarities between "aesthetic representation" and "the status which fiction grants to money". He states that it is possible to understand the problems inherent to the aesthetics of representation by observing how Gide represents money. According to Goux (2000), language and money share the same role: that of exchange. Forest summarizes this aspect of Goux's work by sketching out what happens in the domains of literature and economy in order to achieve the question of exchange. Exchange takes place in the literary domain when "literary texts [are] restored to their meaning", while in the economic domain exchange is the act of a voluntary transaction between two traders where two goods are exchanged one against the other, or one against money. Forest (2000: 20) finds this homology also in Balzac and Zola:

> In certain cases, writers such as Balzac, Zola, Gide or Ramuz don't make this homology explicit, but we notice that there is a surprising homology between the idea of money, which is at work in these novels, and their world of aesthetic representation, as if the status they grant money in fiction acted as

a sort of *mise en abyme* of linguistic problems and the apparatus of representation. This harmony creates an unexpected, yet extremely revealing, bridge between economics and aesthetics.

Narratives that describe monetary transactions – in other words, different roles that money plays in the economy – constitute a link between the characters. It represents a metaphor that the novel does not state explicitly, because even the writer is not aware of it: "For some time past a certain number of counterfeit coins have been put into circulation. So far as I am informed" (Gide 1973: 339).

The aim of this article is to understand the nature of monetary exchange in order to decipher the nature of what, in *The Counterfeiters*, relates to the economic relations. First of all, what is at stake in the novel is the problem of value, literary value, but also the authenticity of human relationships – in other words, what is not representable in literature.[5] False money seems to be an allegory. Through money, Gide explores the interest, passions and faith of his characters in *The Counterfeiters*. Money is also an interconnection between stories; then, we will focus on circulating money itself, which, changing hands also changes status. In the last part of this contribution, we will describe a few contextual elements of the novel, especially what concerns currency and convertibility. Even if Gide doesn't have a direct dialogue with economics, the context alights many aspects in his novel.

The question of value

In the 1960s and 1970s, literary studies on *The Counterfeiters* reinforced the idea that the novel had broken away from realistic aesthetics, and Gide's own comments on his work seem to accept this decontextualized point of view. The writer declared in his journal that his own life had lacked financial constraints, and he seemed to express a sharp regret about this condition of ease, which allowed him to dedicate himself freely to his work. However, to make this observation means recognizing, through discursive argument, just how deeply the economic theme and the question of literature are strangely interlinked in *The Counterfeiters*. Indeed, even if the intrigue of the young counterfeiters is relatively marginal, the question of money is reintroduced in the text in the form of theory of value and through the use of different methods, be it by creating metaphors about interpersonal relationships with reference to the flow of money, or by reflecting on economic value and literary value.

Gide describes his aim in writing this novel in his *Journal of The Counterfeiters*: "To group in a single novel all that was presented to me and taught to me by life"[6] (Gide 1927: 13). He wrote: "To write this book well, I need to convince myself that it's the only and last book I will ever write. I want to pour everything in it, without reserve" (Gide 1927: 35). He confesses that this is not possible: "As dense as I would like this book to be, I can't possibly put everything into it" (Gide 1927: 13). He does not want to unveil events in one go. It's more important to hide them:

I would prefer for events to never be told directly by the author, but rather exposed by the actors whom these events will have affected in whatever way.

I would like these events to appear slightly deformed in the telling; the read-er's curiosity will be piqued by the sole fact that he will have to reconstruct [the event]. The story needs his collaboration to be told well.

(Gide 1927: 32–33)

Here, the story of the counterfeiters is discovered "bit by bit, through conversa-tions where, at the same time, all the characters are fleshed out" (Gide 1927: 33). He has no fear that this attitude should discourage the reader because "bad luck for the lazy reader: I don't want them" (Gide 1927: 96).

To start with, we go through an unusual kind of *mise en abyme* because we consider that the novel which Edouard is writing is the same as Gide's one. The subject of this novel is difficult to describe. We could even say that it is a book without a precise subject, just like Gide's novel. We follow the questioning on the subject of Gide's novel through the dialogues about the subject of Edouard's novel: "And . . . the subject of this novel?" asks Sophroniska in the second part, to which Edouard replies brusquely, "It hasn't got one. And perhaps that's the most astonishing thing about it. My novel hasn't got a subject" (Gide 1925: 187). The most concrete definition given about the novel's subject is the follow-ing: "I invent the character of a novelist, whom I make my central figure; and the subject of the book, if you must have one, is just that very struggle between what reality offers him and what he himself desires to make of it" (Gide 1925: 187–188).

Yet, both books are called *The Counterfeiters*. But the title is deceptive: "May I? . . . *The Counterfeiters*", said Bernard. "But now you tell us – who are these Counterfeiters?" Edouard responds: "Oh dear! I don't know", (Gide 1973: 191). Then we learn that "in reality, Edouard had in the first place been thinking of cer-tain of his fellow novelists when he began to think of *The Counterfeiters*, and in particular of the Count of Passavant" (Gide 1973: 191). Why did Gide choose this title for his novel? According to Moutote (1990: 37), Gide had maybe read *The Case of Wagner* by Friedrich Nietzsche, where Schopenhauer is said to be "an old, pessimistic counterfeiter" and had then used this term twice, for *The Immoralist* and *The Counterfeiters*. He used the first title for his account on Nietzsche's *The Will to Power: An Essay on the Transvaluation of all Values*; the third part of the book carries this title. Gide may have read this title in Henri Albert's translation of *The Twilight of the Idols*.

And again, the term "false coiner" is applied to Saint Paul in *The Antichrist* (Moutote 1990: 240). The term appears in its plural form only in *Ecce Homo*, where it is applied to German philosophers, called "unconscious false-coiners". It is doubtful whether Gide needs this reference. In 1913, in *The Vatican Cellars*, he announces he is working on "The False Coiner". For that matter, there is continu-ity between the characters and the preoccupations between the two works, despite certain obvious differences. Steel explains that

amongst the numerous affinities we notice for example that a financial decep-tion serves as a pretext for the intrigue of both novels; in the first, some con artists' ruse, in the second, issuing counterfeit money, and in both cases, the crooks and counterfeiters turn out to be very intelligent and even cultivated young people.

(Steel 1975: 62)

What makes it difficult to interpret the appearance of money is Gide's aim to define or describe events "without ever having the events told directly" (Gide 1927: 32–33). This implicitness hides certain of the functions that money plays in the story's organization. However, the novel contains no mention of the process whereby wealth is produced by economic actors offering their workers, their capital or their property for use. Economic interests are not unveiled. Here is how Steel describes the monetary reality in *The Counterfeiters*:

André Gide's fictional world does not gravitate around the monetary system that was in vigour under the Third Republic. It would have been unthinkable for this young spirit, nurtured in the bosom of symbolism and still vibrating with an internal moral conflict which opposed a puritan exaltation to a forbidden sexuality, to imitate Balzac by demonstrating the economic mechanisms of a society, or even the social theatre staged by the economy . . . The economic relations which link people among each other become important considerations. In two works, *The Cellars of the Vatican* and *The Counterfeiters*, monetary questions take on a significant importance, both in the episodic structure and in the novel's symbolic framework. The title of *The Counterfeiters* itself is enough to explain the dual role played by money: true and fake, real and symbolic.

(Steel 1975: 61–62)

Here, it is a question of deconstructing human relations – family, friendship, love – into monetary relations. However, what is exchanged against money is the relation itself. A relationship based on trade takes the place of a well-defined human relationship such as family affections, and demotes the latter to just an element in the chain of economic relations. If money is the symbol of material value, it is traded in the name of emotional values, which engender relations of family, friendship and love. Money unites people only while it is exchanged, while it passes from one hand to the next. In the novel, money does not remunerate an economic activity, but it serves as an intermediary between friends, lovers and family members. The monetary exchanges interest Gide because they are indeed fake human relationships – not that they interest him as economic phenomena of development or trade. When Madame Sophroniska reproaches Edouard for writing a novel not of living beings but of ideas, he defends this abstract and intellectual reality (the ideal) while rejecting the *roman à thèse*, and explains his view: "Up till now we have been given nothing but novels with purpose parading as novels of ideas. Ideas . . . ideas, I must confess, interest me more than men, interest me more than anything. They live, they fight, they perish like men" (Gide 1973: 190).

This abstraction of human relations through monetary relations also presents a solution to Gide's difficulties in constructing a social environment in this and in all of his novels: "The annoyance, you see, is the obligation to portray one's characters . . . I know how they think, how they speak . . . but as soon as I have to dress them, give them a social status, a career, wages, neigbours, relatives, family, friend, I give up" (Gide 1927: 58–59). This difficulty is explained in Steel's analysis of *Prometheus Illbound* (1979):

> It is true that a certain five hundred franc note plays a leading role in *Prometheus Illbound*, but it seems that this was a simple idiosyncrasy. And it seems that to him is generally superfluous to even situate his characters in relation to money. For them, as for their author, to be rich is a foregone conclusion.
>
> (Steel 1975: 62)

It is easy to notice that Gide's characters are either rich or poor and that their belonging to one group or the other determines their behaviour as to money, and motivates them to steal or to borrow. Be that as it may, in the novel, the nature of money is to circulate. Gide writes in his *Journal of The Counterfeiters*: "I would like a devil to wander incognito throughout the book and the less we believed in him, the more his reality would assert itself. Therein lies the nature of the devil whose opening motif is 'Why should you fear me? You know perfectly well that I don't exist'" (Gide 1927: 37). Money is this devil which roams throughout the book and helps to reveal more reality "the less we believe in him".

Edouard slowly burdens himself with economic notions: "Ideas of exchange, of depreciation, of inflation, etc., gradually invaded his book (like the theory of clothes in Carlyle's *Sartor Resartus*) and usurped the place of the characters" (Gide 1973: 192). Goux interprets this by suggesting that we reflect on the correspondence between literature and economic science, and asks the following question: "Does a novelist remain a novelist if, instead of promising characters and a story, he begins to expose ideas – and above all, an economic theory?" (Goux 1984: 14). In *The Counterfeiters* some type of phantasmal economic exchange takes place between the characters. Money is a "system of symbols", such as language (Goux 1984; Polanyi 1957). What is the underlying signification behind the monetary discourse in *The Counterfeiters*? What is the imagination of money in the novel?

The imagination of money

Money is first and foremost the concrete coins and bills that circulate among the characters in the novel. It creates a link between disparate stories. Secondly, it is a metaphor of kinship; but most of all, it is the symbolic *medium* through which the poetics of the modern novel are analogically constructed, or rather, it is the instrument which allows us to conceive of these poetics. The economic paradigm is indeed less one of the themes of the novel than what contributes to conceive the laws of its genesis between outmoded figuration and impossible symbolism. Lastly, if there is in Gide's work an economic crypto-thought, this seems to us to be caught up in a permanent contradiction between a refusal of certain economic notions (the accumulation of capital) and the acceptance of other values, but also the reclaiming of aesthetics by economics.

Some of the stories are constructed around money matters, bringing together two mediums of exchange: what is exchanged against money is the relation itself. The first group includes material mediums such as notes, checks, inheritances, debts, loans, entries in bank accounts; the second comprises the imaginary mediums such as child allowance (Mère Profitendieu's), the need for money (Vincent's); or the lack of money (Bernard Profitendieu's), as the failure to have a medium, the absence to have access to a medium of exchange. The Vedel-Azaïs and La Pérouse families are in straitened circumstances. Passavant has money but he continuously wants more. Judge Molinier has a hard time keeping up with his status, while Profitendieu has inherited wealth. Vincent's mother helped him to obtain 5000 francs, which he loses while gambling. Later on, he will win 10 times more. Laura is rescued by Edouard. Bernard borrows money from Edouard. Georges steals 100 francs from his family. It would seem that Gide's devil is hiding among the relationships, which the circulation of money has established between the characters. Bernard steals Edouard's pocketbook from the train station's left-luggage office and the coin found in his pocket makes the watchman look at him with respect. Georges steals a book from a bookshop because he lacks a few francs to buy it and the narrator catches his previously unknown nephew thieving at his sister's; Vincent is goaded to the gambling table where he will lose all his family's savings. Money re-establishes a lost link between characters also throughout the many intrigues; lost, gambled, stolen or returned, money reunites them. If, according to Gide's oft-repeated saying, "bad money drives out good", it's because it is limited to public exchange, where it circulates a lot, while we keep the "good" money at home.

"Crude" money circulates more freely, but, in the novel, when it changes hands, it also changes status. Thus, as Goux writes in *Les monnayeurs du langage* (1984), Vincent's adventure follows a monetary logic. His mother saved 5,000 francs for him: 1. He should have helped Laura during her pregnancy; 2. He loses the entirety of the sum while gambling; 3. Passavant lends him money; 4. He wins back 50,000 francs though sheer luck; 5. Lady Griffith falls in love with him; 6. He gives a portion to Laura in order to leave her; 7. Whether it is hoarded or abandoned to fate, whether it is a gift of love freely given or a compensation payment to an unwanted lover, money determines the distance between the characters.

Money circulates among the characters in such a way that it creates a precarious relationship, limited to the moment when the trade is made. Whatever the nature of this relationship – family, friendship or love – money neutralizes the link and legitimizes the distance. Vincent's case, the fact that he wants to give the 5,000 francs which his mother gave him, to Laura, to exonerate himself from having impregnated her, illustrates how Gide depsychologizes relationships:

> He was obliged to confess to himself that he had no very violent passion for her; but he knew she was in Paris without means of subsistence; he was the

cause of her distress; at the very least he owed her that first precarious aid which he felt himself less and less able to give her – less today than yesterday.

(Gide 1973: 37–38)

This circulation has nothing to do with the economy because although money exchanges hands, nothing is purchased and no economic production is financed. To clarify further, the universe of *The Counterfeiters* is one where the accumulation is not transformed into production, just like Edouard's sterile literary work while he meditates on his novel.

Each monetary transaction represents a social link which will last a certain amount of time. Each monetary exchange hides a relational exchange. In an economy based on exchange, money plays three roles: to be the means of payment; a unit of account (in cash, a means of payment); and a store of value (Phillon 2004: 3) The usage of money is a sign of confidence because it is "accepted by all to serve to connect individuals among each other" (Guerrien 2002: 357). In a certain way, asserts Guerrien (*ibid:* 357), this "presupposes confidence among individuals, but also toward the institution which issues the money (hence the expression 'fiduciary money' from *fiducia* – confidence – in Latin)". Money, as a medium of exchange, allows us to avoid the difficulty of the mutual coincidence of wants induced by the barter system. In trade, "money has the quality of being accepted universally and without cost, at least in a certain geographic zone (generally a country)" (*ibid:* 356). *The Counterfeiters* contains no real reference to any of the three roles of money. There is no mention of money in bank accounts, or in economic or financial transactions, or in investment. There is no notion of trade, of production, distribution, exchange, credit, bank, actions, taxes or accumulation. The text contains no reference to economic history, and it does not involve any specific economic link or activity. In other terms, even as money circulates and is exchanged, economic reality is by no means represented in the background. Money is transformed into a simple currency of exchange, which is totally disconnected from its economic roles.

In the aesthetic chosen by Gide, money, intrinsically lacking in value, is responsible for the intrinsic lack of value in human relations. We first hear of falsity as that concerning money, expressing a fake or fictional value, during a dialogue between Edouard and Bernard:

"Well, imagine a false ten-franc gold piece. In reality it's not worth two sous. But it will be worth ten francs as long as no one recognizes it to be false. So if I start from the idea that . . ." "But why start from an idea?" interrupted Bernard impatiently. "If you were to start from a fact and make a good exposition of it, the idea would come of its own accord to inhabit it. If I were writing *The Counterfeiters* I should begin by showing a counterfeit coin – the little ten-franc piece you were speaking of just now."

(Gide 1973: 192)

This dialogue establishes two conceptions of money: money may be of silver/ gold, or it may be just a worthless piece of paper but stores the value. But it also presents two understandings of the novel: on the one hand, there is the realist novel of the 19th century, where meaning is immediately convertible into a reality shared by the author and the reader, and on the other hand, there is abstraction and the consequent wavering; the novel as an idea of a novel, where value depends on the credit the reader grants to the author.

A few contextual elements: currency and convertibility

The era in which Gide wrote was marked by a complex and perturbed monetary reality. The novel was written during a very specific economic period in history, which we call the interwar years. He hesitates about the exact dates during which his novel takes place. He notes in his *Journal of The Counterfeiters* that he "can pretend to be both precise and vague. If my story leaves any doubt whether it takes place before or after the war, it will be that I have remained too abstract" (Gide 1927: 27). The matter of fake coins is a problem specific to the period: "The whole story of the counterfeit gold pieces can occur only before the war, since at present gold pieces are outlawed. Similarly, we no longer share the same thoughts and preoccupations, and if I aim for the general interest, I risk being out of my depth" (Gide 1927: 27).

This complete and total upheaval of the capitalist economies, in particular as concerned monetary matters, affected all the countries which, from the beginning of the war onwards, had switched to a fiat currency. The gold standard let the standard unit of a currency have the value of a fixed weight of gold. Each unit of the currency that was issued had to have a fixed external value, and it was guaranteed to be freely convertible into gold. Under this monetary system, the currencies of different countries were fixed to a certain weight of gold, and their values in gold defined the bilateral exchange rates. Gold was an internationally valid currency, recognized by each country in the system. This created a stable monetary system, where gold was kept by each national bank as a store of value. But the stability of the monetary system was a highly debated question in historical studies. Such a system was especially useful with regard to the control of credit expansion and thus of national debt of each country's legislation and historical evolution, and also because it prohibited the issuance of money without a corresponding amount of gold in the state reserves. The aim was to build confidence in the system to avoid inflation caused by devaluation. The gold standard became dominant in Europe only at the end of the 19th century; legislation in Great Britain changed along the years.

Abandoning convertibility to gold created the illusion of instituting good money as a measure of value. It was also thought that this would help to avoid the risk of inconvertibility. In cases of panic, crisis or negative forecasts for the general economic situation, if the demand for notes and the value of circulating notes is superior to the banks' gold reserves, the issuing institution can declare bankruptcy. In such cases, the institution can suspend the conversion of notes into gold or in metallic currencies. The government can also intervene to unblock the crisis and may declare gold to be a currency protected by a law which fixes the equivalence of notes in gold (Phillon 2004: 9).

In the novel, gold has an archetypical value but it never appears in the form of an intrinsic value. The idea that Gide evokes, of issuing notes, was the subject of a great debate in Great Britain in the 19th century. Two schools of thought, the British Currency School, led by David Ricardo and his disciples, and the British Banking School, founded by Thomas Tooke (1774–1858) and Henry Thornton (1760–1815), developed opposing arguments concerning how notes should be issued. The former claimed that "the amount of banknotes in circulation must be determined by the issuing institution according to the amount of gold held as a reserve" (*ibid.*, p. 9). A non-regulated issuance of banknotes would create inflation. The second school, on the other hand, defends the "freedom of currency issue" as long as there is a need, but under condition of convertibility (*ibid.*, p. 9). The opposition between Passavant, the prolific writer of bad books which circulate abundantly, and Edouard, the writer who prefers rarity and quality, reflects this debate metaphorically.

Fake money is the symbol of fake relations. Furthermore, in the novel, money is also a symbol for paternity; the first forgery is that of the child's origins. There are two illegitimate children whose situations are mirrored: Laura's and Bernard Profitendieu's. On the first page, Bernard discovers that he is an illegitimate child and gives the name he now refuses to bear back to Profitendieu and wonders about the possibility of substituting a legal paternity to biological paternity. But the latter is defined in monetary terms as a refusal of indebtedness. Bernard ends his farewell note: "I sign this letter with that ridiculous name of yours, which I should like to fling back in your face, and which I am longing and hoping soon to dishonour". And, as very often in Gide's novel, it is the epigraphs which express a link with the economic metaphor: as a king mints money, the father stamps the child with his effigy. Chapter VI's opening epigraph, borrowed from Shakespeare is revealing: "We are all bastards;/And that most venerable man which I/Did call my father, was I know not where/When I was stamped" (Gide 1973: 56).

The adopted father undergoes devaluation, and the noble father soon follows suit: Passavant. Gontran tries to force himself to feel something when faced with his father's remains but finds nothing in his heart. When it comes to Father Vedel, he is pauperized by his faith. Faced with Armand, who suspects his loss, he cannot admit to it, at the price of placing his whole family in danger, since it is as a pastor that he earns his living. The man of law, the nobleman and the man of faith all fall from grace. As Goux writes, the three functions denied the fathers are the three function of money: measure, trade, payment. Profitendieu is not real, Father Passavant can't be a measure because even if he is their biological father, no affection binds him to his children, and lastly, the language spoken by Pastor Vedel, who has lost his faith, has the value of funny money.

Bernard is also beset with a lack of self-esteem. But in the end, returning to the adoptive home, he re-evaluates the biologically fake paternity as a chosen paternity:

> I think that my supposed father, who stood in my father's place, never said or did anything that could let it be suspected that I was not his real son; that

in writing to him as I did, that I had always felt the difference, I was lying; that, on the contrary, he showed a kind of predilection for me, which I felt perfectly, so that my ingratitude towards him was all the more abominable; and that I behaved very ill to him.

(Gide 1973: 200)

This is no longer about biology but about transmission and love. Bernard then settles his relationship with the state; before, he felt like an outlaw. Now, he realizes that the state is a convention and this makes it worth his respect. If he rehabilitates the convention, it's because he is haunted by the nostalgia of a true coinage: "To be worth exactly what one seems to be worth – not to try to seem to be worth more" (Gide 1973: 201). He promotes integrity to a primary value, in accordance with the banal idea that appearance is opposed to inner worth. He tells Laura, "I am afraid that when I no longer feel you near me, I shall be worth nothing at all – or hardly anything " (Gide 1973: 201).

Conclusion

An author who addresses monetary matters could be expected to present his characters from a realistic perspective. But it seems that Gide sees the economic theme differently, through the angle of a structural homology, which allows him to ponder the *bête noire* of literary theory: the question of value. But this byway holds another interest – it offers the possibility of recusing the direct representation of reality and unites the asceticism of abstraction (which is a feature of the narrator-novelist's aesthetics) and the concrete preoccupation with the characters' economic destiny. The capitalist system is boiled down to the concept of convertibility of money into gold, and it is presented as the basis of a society where relationships are not converted into a value of human ties. *The Counterfeiters* treats the matter of value without mentioning value, just as the character of Lucien Bercail would like to tell a story without speaking of the story – to give an impression of death, without speaking of death. We find here a debate on the modern novel which creates nothing but itself: "The sun of truth, we are assured, bathes in its rays the modern novel, banishing for ever the lies spread by the old novels" (Pavel 2003: 11). In *The Counterfeiters*, money serves as an element symbolic of a world where there is no convertibility: gold is no longer the store of value for money; feelings are no longer the store of value for relationships.

Notes

1 The authors wish to thank Bruna Ingrao, whose recommendations enriched this chapter.
2 Translated as *The Counterfeiters* in English.
3 See H. Halmstad (2008).
4 See J.-M Houpert and P. Petitier (2001).
5 *L'irreprésentable en littérature* (2001) by J.-M. Houpert & P. Petitier.
6 All quotes from *Journal of The Counterfeiters* are translated from French by Başak Balkan.

Bibliography

Forest, P. (2000), "Entretien avec Jean-Joseph Goux", in *Money Sings*.

Gide, A. (1925), *Les Faux-Monnayeurs*, Paris: Gallimard.

Gide, A. (1927), *Le Journal des faux-monnayeurs*, Paris: Gallimard.

Gide, A. (1973), *The Counterfeiters*, New York: Vintage Books.

Goux, J.-J. (1984), *Les monnayeurs du langage*, Paris: Galilée.

Goux, J.-J. (2000), *Frivolité de la valeur*, Paris: Blusson.

Guerrien, B. (2002), *Dictionnaire d'analyse économique*, Paris: Éd. de la Découverte.

Halmstad, H. (2008), "Les différents sens du faux dans Les Faux-Monnayeurs d'André Gide", hh.diva-portal.org/smash/get/diva2:239249/FULLTEXT01

Houpert, J.-M. and Petitier, P. (2001), *L'irreprésentable en littérature*, Paris: Harmattan.

Moutote, D. (1990), *Réflexions sur les faux-monnayeurs*, Paris: H. Champion.

Pavel, T. (2003), *La pensée du Roman*, Paris: Galllimard.

Phillon, D. (2004), *La monnaie et ses mécanismes*, Paris: Éd. de la Découverte.

Polanyi, K. (1957 [2002]), *The Great Transformation*, Boston, MA: Beacon Press.

Sageart, M. (1925), "Préface", in A. Gide (ed.), *Les Faux-Monnayeurs*, Paris: Gallimard.

Steel, D. (1975), "Lettres et l'argent: l'économie des faux-monnayeurs", *La revue des lettres modernes*, 4: 439–444.

9 "I always wanted to have earned my first dollar but I never had"

Gertrude Stein and money

Laura E.B. Key

In 1907, the New York Stock Exchange suffered dramatic losses, causing panic throughout the US as citizens lost confidence in the stock market and the banking system. Suddenly, people rushed to withdraw their savings, leading to the bankruptcy of many financial institutions. This was nothing new. The Panic of 1907 was one in a long line of panics that occurred roughly every 20 years during the 19th century (Gordon 2008).[1] What was different about this panic, however, was that it occurred soon after the money debates of the late 1890s, when, during the 1896 presidential election, money became the chief symbol for the fluctuating economy, and the nation became divided over the question of whether money should be backed by gold, silver or no metal at all. After pro-gold Republican candidate William McKinley won the election, the Gold Standard Act of 1900 supposedly brought questions surrounding monetary instability to an end, as the gold standard was re-established as the legal source of monetary value (Ritter 1997: 28–61). Stock market fluctuations showed, however, that backing by precious metals did not ensure stability in investments, the jobs market or commodity prices, all of which became uncertain in a time of panic. Demand for withdrawal of hard cash from banks increased as trust in a seemingly precarious banking system was lost. As R.F. Bruner and S.D. Carr argue, "the nation had lost its confidence. It would take leadership and courage to bring it back" (Bruner and Carr 2009: xiii). Bruner and Carr explain that the interconnection between different elements of the economy, such as stocks, debt, currency and gold, led to a domino effect that sent shocks throughout the US economy (Bruner and Carr 2009: 3–4). There was no central bank in this pre–Federal Reserve era, which meant that a system of free banking existed. Many banks were small and local, and when they failed, people's money disappeared; even if citizens kept their money at home in banknotes, the paper on which the money was written became worthless when the issuing bank collapsed (see Rothbard 2002). As such, the Panic of 1907 made a mockery of the idea that the gold standard acted as a safe form of backing for money that helped to prevent losses, destabilizing the illusion of the concrete nature of monetary value once more. People were forced to face the discrepancy between specie and paper money, the sudden worthlessness of paper notes revealing paper money, a representation of value, to be completely unstable.

At this same time, young American writer Gertrude Stein was beginning to experiment with novelistic form and content. Stein began writing her first published novel, *Three Lives* (Stein 1909), in 1907, which she deemed to be "the first definite step away from the nineteenth century and into the twentieth century in literature" (Stein 1960: 54). Stein was inspired to begin manipulating form and content in ways that mirrored monetary instability, altering syntax and accepted textual structures to show that language does not have a fixed value, and foregrounding the materiality of the text, which, like paper money, is only a fusion of paper and words that stands in for another concept: the outside world. An analysis of Stein's work alongside discourses of money has remained peculiarly absent from Stein studies until now, despite its recurrence as a theme in her oeuvre and the fact that she wrote five articles specifically about money in the 1930s.[2] Stein returns persistently to money as a theme, which serves as a point of comparison with language as a mutable representative form, subject to rules imposed upon its function by the society in which it is used. By recognizing the similarity between literary fiction and money both as representative forms of writing, Stein's work raises questions about how value is quantified. The undoing of accepted textual value is rendered intelligible by the thematic metaphor of money as an unstable value form.

The connection between money and literary value has been examined in relation to 18th-century British fiction and *fin-de-siècle* American naturalism.[3] The rise of literary modernism in the early 20th century, however, has been examined little in this regard. In the context of a fluctuating American marketplace in 1907, Stein's focus on money in *Three Lives* taps into social concerns about the instability of values, examining the fluidity of money in thematic terms while the malleability of language is exposed.

In this chapter, close textual analysis is combined with a consideration of external social factors on the development of Stein's unique writing style. The paper follows the contention of modernist scholars such as Michael Soto and Walter Kalaidjian, who argue that literature should be analyzed in the context of a wider social framework rather than being considered part of a distinct aesthetic realm, quite apart from the historical events of the day.[4]

Stein studies

Since the late 1970s, scholars in Stein studies have striven to unite the autobiographical and philosophical readings of her work, which, previously, were often treated separately. Such work emphasizes philosophical and psychological questions about gender, race and sexuality in Stein's writing, whilst also analyzing the mechanics of Stein's nonstandard language use. Many of these studies evaluate Stein's modernism only in terms of the relation between textual structure and her personal biography, without much interest in the wider socio-historical context of her writing.[5] This historical void has been addressed by B. Conrad's analysis of Stein in the context of the American economy and M. North's study of contemporaneous racial discourses in relation to Stein's writing (Conrad 1995; North 1994).

Such studies demonstrate the significance of contemporaneous socio-political concerns in understanding Stein's oeuvre.

A large body of Stein scholarship is concerned with her treatment of language as a material object. The current study interprets Stein's experiments with the materiality of language through the lens of money, a representative form that embodies the conflict between materialism and abstraction, with which many argue that modernism was connected. Paper money is a type of fiction, given value only by the words inscribed upon it; the associated value is a social construct.[6] Stein's focus on money in *Three Lives* can be understood a manifestation of her concerns about the void between representation and reality, which are also seen in the challenges to accepted forms of money posed by upheavals in the economic system. Literature becomes another representational category, like money, whose stability cannot be maintained as its accepted norms are revealed to be socially constructed. Stein's focus on materiality breaks down the one-to-one correspondence with the world beyond and renders the relationship between life and text abstract. Her preoccupation with representation provides a structural basis from which Stein could conduct her textual experiments, allowing her to develop an original, modernist style in the early 20th century that was deeply influenced by her socio-economic context.

Representations of money in *Three Lives*

Stein's work in the 1900s and 1910s is seen retrospectively as groundbreaking, but it was unrecognized within the American literary scene at this time, being commercially unsuccessful. It took two years and many rejections before her first text, *Three Lives*, was published, an enterprise that Stein eventually decided to fund via her own means (Wagner-Martin: 87). *Three Lives* is a tripartite tale telling the stories of three working-class women named Anna, Melanctha and Lena, who live in the fictional American town of Bridgepoint. Although the three women's lives never intersect, certain overarching themes unite the three sections of the text. For example, there is much evidence in all three sections to indicate that money-related issues are of importance in Stein's writings. Given the raised demand for cash and scepticism surrounding US banks when *Three Lives* was written in 1907, the recurrent themes of saving and spending, where money is portrayed as ephemeral and difficult to maintain, cannot be ignored. For example, in part one, "The Good Anna" is poor because she gives her earnings away:

> But Anna always found new people to befriend, people who, in the kindly fashion of the poor, used up her savings and then gave promises in place of payments. Anna never really thought that these people would be good, but when they did not do the way they should, and when they did not pay her back the money she had loaned, and never seemed the better for her care, then Anna would grow bitter with the world.
>
> No, none of them had any sense of what was the right way for them to do. So, Anna would repeat in her despair.

The poor are generous with their things. They give always what they have, but with them to give or to receive brings with it no feeling that they owe the giver for the gift.

Even a thrifty German Anna was ready to give all that she had saved, and so not be sure that she would have enough to take care of herself if she fell sick or for old age, when she could not work. Save and you will have the money you have saved was true only for the day of saving, even for a thrifty German Anna. There was no certain way to have it for old age, for taking care of what is saved can never be relied on, for it must always be in strangers' hands in a bank or in investments by a friend.

(Stein 1985: 59–60)

Here, Anna's interaction with money comes to characterize her whole outlook on life, suggesting that lack of confidence about money has a wider significance on an individual's life. When Anna's friends do not pay her back, she "grow[s] bitter with the world". Money, a representative form, is depicted as all-powerful, having comprehensive effects on her entire existence. The "promises" that Anna's friends give in place of payments echo paper banknotes, which have worth beyond their material value only as far as a bank promises to pay a certain sum of gold to the bearer upon receipt of the note. Given the collapse of so many US banks in 1907, this depiction of the bitterness that Anna feels towards these unfaithful borrowers indicates Stein's interest in using literature to examine the idea that money is intangible and difficult to preserve. If anecdotal evidence is to be believed, Stein read American newspapers regularly and, despite living in Paris, she would have been exposed to the financial situation in her native country and its direct effects on her potential readership, which goes some way to account for her character's wariness about money (Stein 1960: 23).

The instability of money is paralleled by the malleability of language, which *Three Lives* exposes through formal play. The word "really", for instance, recurs throughout the text to the point where the word's meaning seems arbitrary and the reader focuses upon its material attributes: "Anna never really thought that these people would be good"; "Perhaps we all be dead by then, the good Anna would repeat, but even that did not really happen"; "The things that Anna really needed were to rest sometimes and eat more" (Stein 1985: 59; 69; 74). Just as Anna fears the instability of the intangible "promises" her friends offer her instead of money, the meaning of words is also rendered questionable; the more "really" is repeated, the less it seems to hold a tangible meaning. This linguistic repetition removes realist meaning from the word – and it is fitting that the word "really" is chosen for this task of challenging the link between text and reality.[7] Repetition continues until only the material qualities of the word's sound and shape remain, the illusory quality of its value becoming foregrounded. This breakdown of the relationship between material word and external concept is even more pronounced as the word "really" could be removed from all these sentences and they would still be understandable. Using such rhetoric, *Three Lives* shows how easily language can become devalued, losing the meaning with which it is associated. This focus on words as objects with a negotiable value is echoed symbolically by the mention of banks in the passage, which are portrayed as places of instability: "taking care of what is saved can never be relied on, for it must always be in strangers' hands in a bank". Money, like language, is depicted as slippery and unstable because the individual has no control over the larger system.

The connection forged between money and language develops further in the third part of *Three Lives*, "The Gentle Lena". Here, Lena's entire being is characterized by her linguistic compliance and monetary ignorance:

> Lena always saved all her wages. She never thought of any way to spend it. The German cook, the good woman who always scolded Lena, helped her put it in the bank each month, as soon as she got it. Sometimes before it got into the bank to be taken care of, somebody would ask Lena for it. The little Haydon boy sometimes asked and would get it, and sometimes some of the girls, the ones Lena always sat with, needed some more money; but the German cook, who always scolded Lena, saw to it that this did not happen very often. When it did happen, she would scold Lena very sharply, and for the next few months she would not let Lena touch her wages, but put it in the bank for her on the same day that Lena got it.
>
> So, Lena always saved her wages, for she never thought to spend them, and she always went to her aunt's house for her Sundays because she did not know that she could do anything different.
>
> (Stein 1985: 226–227)

Lena's inability to vocalize her everyday wishes is mirrored by her lack of control over pecuniary matters. Thusly, money handling becomes a metaphor for existence as others rule both her money and life. Just as in "The Good Anna", the bank appears as a mysterious site where money is "taken care of" but no explanation is provided regarding how or why. Money, when it is placed in the bank, becomes invisible; once it is an ephemeral concept, divorced from the physicality of the wages that Lena receives, her colleagues and relatives no longer have a method by which to obtain it for themselves and even Lena, to whom the money belongs, cannot physically "touch" it. Money as a representation thus is unstable because it is too easily transferable, whereas, ironically, once it becomes figurative, untouchable money in a bank, it is re-stabilized because the gap between reality and the representation of reality is no longer visible. Paper money, therefore, performs the same role as the literary text, masking its status as a representation through its marking with letters and numbers that reflect outside concepts, to which society attaches a value. The materiality of both types of text, however, becomes the downfall of realist representation because both money and text are physical objects in themselves, and this tangible physicality prevents society from forgetting the difference between representation and reality, calling their ability to function as representations into question. Therefore, money provides such an effective metaphor for the literary text for Stein; both paper money and literature can never become the things that they represent, yet both act to maintain the illusion of a mirror between fiction and reality. In this way, Stein invites the reader to question the function of literary narration.

By refusing to participate in the economy by spending money, Lena protects herself from the fear embodied in the void between representation and reality that Anna experiences when she gives away physical money and receives nothing in return, negating the value of the money. The moments when spending interrupts the economy of saving can be compared metaphorically to the interruptions to an otherwise predominantly linear and ostensibly realist storyline caused by the use of seemingly meaningless repetition and a lack of standard punctuation and formatting – for example, the use of speech without a line break or speech marks, which occurs frequently in the story. Such devices emphasize the material qualities of the text – its physical existence as paper and ink – thus reinforcing the gap between the written word and reality. Language here can facilitate understanding but it can also be a hindrance to the discovery of meaning.

It is notable that in the middle section of the text, "Melanctha", which many critics have seen as the most "modernist" section because it provides the greatest challenge to accepted literary conventions, the theme of money is less prominent. There *are* still references to money, particularly at the beginning and the end of Melanctha's story, where the characters' financial situations are mentioned: "Jane Harden always had a little money and she had a room in the lower part of town"; "Sometimes Jem Richards would be betting and would be good and lucky, and be making lots of money" (Stein 1985: 95, 198). In the middle section that concentrates on Melanctha's relationship with Jeff Campbell, however (which consists mainly of dialogue written in a pseudo-black vernacular with little punctuation and excessive repetition, and in which the storyline loses its linearity), the monetary theme is sidelined. Here, I contend, the absence of the money plot symbolizes an attempt to escape representation, which is reiterated by the difficulty for the reader in maintaining a sense of the storyline against the challenge posed by its nonstandard presentation. The incessant repetition of ideas with subtle semantic changes renders words meaningless to the reader because the repetition adds no new information to Jeff and Melanctha's narrative: "Jeff was at last beginning to know what it was to have deep feeling"; "now at last he had learned what it was to have deep feeling"; "Always now Jeff felt now in himself, deep feeling" (Stein 1985: 131, 132, 150). The lack of narrative progress encourages the reader to focus on the linguistic devices employed in textual construction rather than accepting the text as a depiction of reality.

The idea that words as material objects can behave both as a method of communication and as a hindrance to understanding evokes C. Stimpson's thesis that Stein uses linguistic devices deliberately to veil textual meaning. For Stimpson, this ambiguity allows Stein more freedom of expression within the boundaries of social convention: "The texts [were] often coded rather than open; sublimated rather than straightforward; hazy with metaphors and silence rather than lucid" (Stimpson 1977: 505). Such language, Stimpson argues, allowed Stein to allude to controversial social issues such as homosexuality and the social role of women. Although wider social issues are significant in *Three Lives*, I posit that, rather than functioning as a site to explore controversial issues, "Melanctha" becomes a space for the deeper study of words as created objects themselves. Melanctha is portrayed as being aware that words are only a representation, unable to function as a mirror to reality: "You see, Jeff, it ain't much use to *talk* about what a woman is really feeling in her. You *see* all that, Jeff, better, by and by, when you get to really feeling" (Stein 1985: 123, my italics). Ironically, despite Melanctha's apparent distaste for speech above inner feeling, this section consists largely of dialogue and thus the storyline becomes even more meaningless; Jeff and Melanctha's "inner beings" become lost in the sea of words. Through the high usage of dialogue and the third-person narrator, the reader is given a surface portrait of the couple, which functions only to accentuate the materials of language – the ways in which society constructs it, rather than being a natural, innate manner of expression. Stimpson concludes that Stein's focus on language as material object was a result of her being unable, rather than unwilling, in the context of a socially restrictive American society, to express herself in a straightforward manner. On the contrary, the lack of detailed characterization in *Three Lives* is a deliberate attempt to free writing from the constraints of its socially imposed role as a window to the outside world. Rather than being restricted by social protocol, Stein's work begins to undo the terms by which literature is understood, widening its purpose to focus on social issues. As such, social allegory (the thematic handling of questions about money) is combined with the scrutiny of language as a socially manipulated form of communication. In this way, Stein's text is ensconced deeply in its historical moment, raising questions about the value of representative modes in society. The literary text becomes a site for rewriting the social function of representation. Instead of mirroring reality in a realist fashion, the material attributes of the text are manipulated to divorce the written word from the world beyond. The text thus mimics the structure of money in challenging the relationship between reality and representation, uniting social anxieties about the monetary and artistic form in the early-20th century.

Stein's wider interest in money and economies of exchange

Despite her absence from the US, Stein would have been aware from the media of the US political and financial situation in 1907 and, in her later writings, the continued references to money and its abstract intangible form indicate that she remained preoccupied with the economy of her homeland throughout her career. Given Stein's thematic and structural conflation of money and language, it is conceivable that Stein's perception of the loss of correspondence in the US between words and objects, or between the written word on the banknote and real gold, was rooted in her direct experience of 1890s America, a time when representation in the form of money was challenged by the notion that value was not fixed.

By considering Stein's personal biography in relation to the wider socio-economy, her writings are an attempt to reconcile her position within a larger structure from which she was separated physically, being an expatriate, but with which she remained involved. From her position in France, Stein did not have direct experience of the socio-economic effects of the Panic of 1907. The handling of money in *Three Lives* is somewhat anachronistic; the female characters prioritize saving, rather than spending, for example, an idea which did not correspond with changes to America's economy, where consumption was triumphing over production and the public was required to spend to strengthen the nation's economic position. The central characters of *Three Lives* all die, suggesting that they are outmoded; no alternative is offered, however. Even Jeff Campbell prioritizes the saving of money, despite being the most professional character and presumably having one of the best incomes.[8] Jeff states:

> Instead of just working hard and caring about their working and living regular with their families and saving up all their money, so they will have some to bring up their children better, instead of living regular and doing like that and getting all their new ways from just decent living, the coloured people just keep running around and perhaps drinking and doing everything bad they can ever think of, and not just because they like all those bad things that they are always doing, but only just because they want to get excited.
>
> (Stein 1985: 110)

Although it is notable that Jeff refers to "the coloured people" in the third person, thus suggesting that, personally, he may not need to subscribe to the economy he proposes, the greater significance of this speech is that it corroborates a larger theme in *Three Lives*. The text champions an economy which is irrelevant to most American citizens, for whom a growing economy meant increased employment and, concomitantly, a greater availability of money; the economy of saving would merely restrict the economy and limit its growth. This economic imperative was encouraged by an expanding advertising industry (including the literary magazines in which Stein strove to be published), which was convincing the public to spend in order to help prevent the panics associated with restrictions to cash flow.[9] In contrast, Stein, who self-confessedly never made her own money until the publication of *The Autobiography of Alice B. Toklas*, lived on an allowance that was part of her parents' legacy, making a savings-based economy crucial to her survival: "I always wanted to have earned my first dollar but I never had" (Stein 1938: 28). It is notable, too, that Stein never managed her own money; the household expenses were taken care of by her brother, Leo, with whom she lived in Paris initially and, later, by her long-term partner, Alice Toklas.[10] Stein's lack of control over her own finances, then, coupled with her absence from the US, removed her from the advancing capitalist economy. Indeed, she is an example of the "rentier class" of American writers discussed by P. Delany, whose "inherited incomes absolved them from active struggle in the marketplace" (Delany 1999: 337). Delany argues that the rentier lifestyle made much modernist experimentation possible due to the lack of financial pressure upon several writers.

In her private life, Stein, like her characters in *Three Lives*, avoided all involvement with money-related issues, which, ironically, was perhaps the reason for her fascination with money and its functions. Her work can be viewed, therefore, as a space in which the complexity of an economy that seemed beyond the control of its participants could be considered. Comparing Stein's attitude towards money in *Three Lives* with her discussion of the topic in her much later works of fiction and nonfiction exposes Stein as a writer with an unrelenting preoccupation with monetary instability. Stein wrote five short articles specifically about money for the *Saturday Evening Post*, published between June and October 1936, no doubt inspired by her one-and-only return visit to a Depression-affected US for a lecture tour in 1934–35, only a year after Roosevelt imposed an unprecedented four-day banking holiday in an attempt to halt economic decline, after which he also ratified the printing of enough Federal Reserve notes to support the struggling banks.[11] These articles, all related in theme and content, consider the same kinds of questions about materiality that her exploration of money and language raised in her early work, such as money's intangibility and the difficulty of retaining it or defining its value. Again, Stein also uses nonstandard linguistic devices such as repetition and a lack of punctuation, re-emphasizing the connection between money and language which is present in *Three Lives* but in reverse, so that here, by breaking down accepted textual norms, Stein attempts to come to an understanding of the structure of money.

> Everybody now just must make up their mind. Is money money or isn't money money. Everybody who earns it and spends it every day to live knows that money is money, anybody who votes it to be gathered in as taxes knows money is not money. That is what makes everybody go crazy. . . .
>   That is what everybody must think about a lot or everybody is going to be unhappy, because the time does come when the money voted comes suddenly to be money just like the money everybody earns every day and spends every day to live and when that time comes it makes everybody very unhappy. I do wish everybody would make up their mind about money being money.
>
> (Stein 1971: 331–332)

Writing after the American economic boom of the 1920s from the post–Wall Street Crash perspective of the Depression-ridden 1930s, Stein remains interested in questions of monetary form. Grappling with the problem of whether money is quantifiable and tangible or not and whether it has some intrinsic quality that renders it money, this article explores similar concerns raised by the Greenbackers' contention in the 1890s that money did not have to be backed by gold in order for it to function as money; instead, a social agreement could be made to give non-backed money an exchange value – an idea that was brought back into prominence in the 1930s by Keynesian economics.[12] This realization brought to the fore concerns over whether gold really did give intrinsic worth to money or whether this was merely a social construct; money might be backed by gold but, nonetheless, gold was not money per se because it was a separate object all in itself. Stein's "Money" articles reiterate such concerns by asking "Is money money or isn't money money", indicating the two sides to the debate and suggesting that it is down to members of the public to "make up their mind[s]". This persistent concern about the mutability of money becomes a responsibility of the public as Stein asserts, "the time does come when the money voted comes suddenly to be money", indicating the power of the people in determining monetary form in a democratic nation.

Here, the wide-reaching economic problems caused by the Wall Street Crash and subsequent Depression are projected entirely onto money as an ultimate symbol of value, and it is the instability of this money which is fearsome; it makes everybody "go crazy". Indeed, the US government now realized the importance of ensuring that the public remained confident in money; when the decision was taken to print extra notes in 1933, Treasury Secretary William Woodin stated of the plan, "It won't frighten the people. It won't look like stage money. It'll be money that looks like real money" (Federal Reserve Bank of Boston 1999). Echoing this political acknowledgment of the void between paper money and specie, Stein continued to question the link between money and value in an article entitled "All About Money":

> When you see a big store, and see so many of each kind of anything that is in it, and on the counters, it is hard to believe that one makes any difference to anyone. When you see a cashier in a bank with drawers filled with money, it is hard to realize that one makes any difference. But it does, if you buy it, or if you take it away, or if you sell it, or if you make a mistake in giving it out. Of course, it does. But a government, well a government does just that, it does not really believe that when there is such a lot that one does make any difference.
>
> (Stein 1971: 334)

Here, Stein discusses the difficulty of conceptualizing the real value of money when it is represented in paper form. She recognizes that money has a crucial role in social relations but, apart from its physical, paper form, the value of which relies on a social agreement, its functions are invisible, making it a baffling medium. By referencing the actions of governments here, a link is made with events occurring in US politics and banking at the time, indicating once more that Stein was interested in contemporary discourses of money, which she compared metaphorically with the malleability of the written word.

Moreover, the two-sided nature of money alluded to by Stein also evokes Georg Simmel's (1990) theory of money, first published in German in 1900, not long before Stein arrived in France, in which money allows human beings to understand life but is also alienating. Given Stein's interest in money from her first publication in 1907 onwards, these musings about money indicate that, from her position in Europe, Stein was influenced by an intellectual climate that was trying to make sense of the connections between money and society.[13] Moreover, it was in 1936, when the "Money" articles were published, that British economist John Maynard Keynes' *The General Theory of Employment, Interest and Money* was released, opposing the concept of a return to the gold standard and positing the idea that paper money was the key to solving failing economies in times like the Depression because it would facilitate economic growth, challenging many existing economic theories and changing the intellectual battlefield in relation to money (Keynes 1965). During the same decade, Irving Fisher's theory of debt deflation suggested that markets were harmed by a loss of confidence when profits fell, leading to the hoarding, rather than spending, of money, which could be reversed through spending (Fisher 1993). Such challenges to the traditional economic theories of scholars like Adam Smith and David Ricardo were viewed with suspicion by many, and such controversial potential solutions to the financial crisis of the 1930s circulated in the media.[14] Although we cannot be certain of the extent to which Stein followed contemporary economic debates, such discourses circulated in 1930s society – we can return here to the point that Stein claimed to read American newspapers, despite her absence from the country.[15] Just as the participation or otherwise of the characters of *Three Lives* in the economy is measured by their transactions with money, Stein in 1936 turns both to writing and money, and the similarities between the two media, to raise questions about money, its form and value. Again, despite, or perhaps because of, her lack of understanding of American money due to her absence from the country and non-participation in the economy, Stein seeks to understand it imaginatively through linguistic metaphor.

Bryce Conrad (1995), in his discussion of Stein's "Money" articles, suggests that Stein's absence from the US rendered her perception of American money antiquated:

> Stein could come by no strict accounting of how value was generated in America – she realized that there was a distinction between 'money' – currency in its nineteenth-century pre-Gold Standard sense – and 'not money' – speculative capital of the sort wielded by the corporate interests that had defined market economics during the period of her thirty-year absence.
>
> (Conrad 1995: 229)

Conrad interprets Stein's puzzlement about money as bound with her commodification as a celebrity after the success of *The Autobiography of Alice B. Toklas*, contending that, as an expatriate, she was unable to understand an increasingly consumerist US society in which value was not born of production but was created by the selling of images and ideals. Although Stein's long absence from the US may have had some bearing on her perception of American money, the concerns she raises in her "Money" articles can in fact be understood as a literary rendering of wider social concerns about the instability of money post-1929. Rendering Stein's view antiquated is, therefore, a simplistic interpretation of her understanding of money. Instead, Stein's writings are deeply interconnected with social fears created by social change both in relation to money and to culture. Money thus offers Stein a metaphorical springboard for her modernist experimentation, rendering inadequate studies that understand modernism as a backlash against capitalism; here, the capitalist economy provides the inspiration in itself.[16] Though Stein's characters in *Three Lives* might be anachronistic in economic terms (mirroring her own economically unproductive existence for most of her life), her comparisons of monetary and literary form offer an intellectual appraisal of the instability of representation, which was very relevant to Depression-era financial uncertainty. Reality versus representation can thus be a persistent theme in Stein's oeuvre, uniting her different writing styles, from ostensible fact to fiction and from her early to her late work. In this light, Stein's experiences as a well-known writer in her later career do not provide the germ of her interest in money and form as Conrad suggests; rather, they serve to reignite a fascination that was present from her early days as an expatriate writer.

Stein reflects upon her "Money" articles in *Everybody's Autobiography* (1938), revisiting the idea of money as an ephemeral object, 29 years after she first explored this matter in *Three Lives*:

> I have been writing a lot about money lately [*sic*], it is a fascinating subject, it is really the difference between men and animals, most of the things men feel animals feel and vice versa, but animals do not know about money, money is purely a human conception and that is very important to know very very important. About every once in so often there is a movement to do away with money. Roosevelt tries to spend so much that perhaps money will not exist, communists try to live without money but it never lasts because if you live without money you have to do as the animals do live on what you find each day to eat and that is just the difference the minute you do not do that you have to have money and so everybody has to make up their mind if money is money or if money isn't money and sooner or later they always do decide that money is money.
>
> (Stein 1938: 28–29)

Her question "Is money money or isn't money money" is reformulated subtly in this extract and this linguistic connection between the two texts, using similar, but not identical, forms of language, is reminiscent of the use of quasi-repetition in *Three Lives*. Stein's thesis that money is the difference between men and animals once more puts money on a par with language because, firstly, speech and literacy, like money, separate human beings from the animal kingdom and, secondly, because the creation of money relies upon literacy.

As M. Shell contends, the writing inscribed upon the coin or note gives money a value; writing thus has a transformative power, being able to alter the worth of paper or metal.[17] Money, then, by virtue of its use of writing (itself a man-made mode of representation) becomes a form of representation in itself and operates only through society's acceptance that the written word gives money an economic value. This is reiterated by Stein in the passage above as she discusses social attempts to "do away with money . . . but it never lasts". There is a tension here; despite money being a man-made concept that ostensibly could be abolished, its use has become naturalized in society to the point where it seems indispensable, just as in the "Money" articles, or in *Three Lives*, where the characters are preoccupied with saving money even though they struggle to understand its functions.

Significantly, however, Stein stresses that "money is purely a human conception", demonstrating her understanding of money as a free-floating concept without essential qualities (Stein 1938: 28). This definite statement, compared with the way in which money is portrayed as an active force in the "Money" articles (where money, of itself, "suddenly comes to be money") indicates that Stein came to a more stable interpretation of the meaning of money as her career progressed (Stein 1971: 332).

Stein's view of money as lacking intrinsic value reinforces the distance between reality and representation that I have argued is key to an understanding of the relationship between money and language in her texts. Just like her literature, which challenges the relationship between the written word and the real world, Stein's writings about money in her later career reiterate her preoccupation with the disconnection between representation and reality, where the written text can only ever approximate the world beyond.

Stein continued to be preoccupied with the homologous qualities of money and language from the beginning until the end of her career. *Wars I Have Seen*, an autobiographical volume published the year before her death, following her experience of World War II, indicates Stein's enduring interest in money as a representative form. Here, Stein recounts an event that epitomizes the emblematic correspondence between money and language; now a literary success in the US following the publication of *The Autobiography of Alice B. Toklas*, she describes an encounter with a group of American troops in France at the end of the war:

> they told me where they had been and what they thought of the people they had seen and then they wanted autographs and they gave me pieces of money to write on, and one Pole who was the most extravagant gave me a hundred franc bill to sign for him, funny that a Pole should have been the most wasteful of his money, perhaps he was only going to spend it anyway, and one of them told me that they knew about me because they study my poems along with other American poetry in the public schools.
>
> (Stein 1945: 165)

Not only does this quotation symbolize the coming together of writing and money in Stein's account of signing the banknote, it also demonstrates the ability of words to reinvest a devalued note with an economic value, given the war's detrimental effect on currency values as well as the uselessness of French money to American troops who were due to return home. As Stein, had achieved literary fame in the US at last, the autographed banknote would have commanded a price beyond that of its monetary face value, thanks to the written inscription. By writing upon a banknote that already has a printed face value, then, Stein modifies the value of the paper and this symbol of money and writing thus reiterates questions raised in her other writings about whether the value of money can ever be fixed. Further, the note is also given artistic worth by association with Stein and so the note's value is manifold; words, in the form of Stein's name, invest the note with a new monetary value but its artistic association also adds value, so it is transformed into a collectible object, which the owner may refuse to sell for any price. Writing becomes the key to bestowing more than one type of value upon the paper object as Stein literally rewrites the terms under which the note is received in society, indicating the transformative power of language.

The text suggests, furthermore, that Stein came to sign money regularly: "I had already given him my autograph on a piece of French paper money, it is hard to write on French paper money but I finally did get the habit" (Stein 1945: 163). This idea strengthens further the contention that the signing of banknotes is used wilfully in this text to symbolize a crossover between literary and monetary worlds. By allying money with language explicitly, Stein figuratively unites her persistent concerns about representation but also, through the format of autobiography, takes a direct role in manipulating the conditions by which representation and value are understood. Writing as herself this time, rather than veiling her story with characterization as in *Three Lives*, Stein takes control of this persistent anxiety and uses it to create a new piece of writing, utilizing history to push towards the literary future.

Conclusion

Throughout her career, Gertrude Stein combined the theme of unstable representative forms with linguistic fragmentation, drawing an analogy between monetary instability and the malleability of the literary text. Stein thus renegotiates the terms by which the role of American literature is understood, helping to render literary production a freer practice, less constrained by the socially constructed limits of accepted linguistic and literary form. By recognizing the structural similarity of money and literature, Stein produced work that encouraged a less rigid view of what could constitute literature. After earning her "first dollar", her conflation of money with writing, both as representative media, did not abate, but it did evolve; as she became more confident in the manipulation of literary value, she began to write more frequently in her own voice, rather than as a fictional narrator. Stein continued to use the written word to examine the functions of money, writing and value, developing a literary style that led to her becoming one of the most enduringly important figures of American modernism.

Notes

1 Indeed, as Gordon notes, in the US, financial panics have continued to occur roughly every two decades to the present day.
2 Bill Brown's popular online magazine, *NOT BORED!*, tackles the connection between Stein and money in an edition dedicated to money and literature, contending that Stein recognised the structural similarity between paper money and other types of writing, whose value is negotiable. The only academic article to tackle Stein's relationship with money, however, is by Bryce Conrad. Conrad discusses Stein's money articles within a larger discussion about Stein's position in the American marketplace but his article deals with wider economic concerns rather than with money as a representative object.

Conrad notes the timeliness of the "Money" articles in relation to Stein's pecuniary success and celebrity, both of which she achieved only in the 1930s, but does not address the importance of money within Stein's wider oeuvre (Brown 2005; Conrad 1995; Stein 1971: 331–337).

3 D. Zimmerman contends that a sub-genre of naturalism, which he dubs "panic fiction", provided a forum for writers to untangle the complex socio-economic structures of modern life (Zimmerman 2006).

4 Soto (2004) contends that early 20th-century American literary texts provided readers with a framework through which to interpret social concerns. Kalaidjian (1993) seeks to understand American modernist literature as part of a larger cultural moment in which literature participated. The present study also follows the "new economic criticism" – an area of literary studies that has argued that the schism between economics and culture, which is generally assumed to exist in modern Western societies, is a man-made construct that obscures the structural similarities that unite the two realms (Woodmansee, Osteen 1999).

5 For example, L. Gilmore and C. Stimpson situate Stein's work in relation to her identity in terms of class, gender, sexuality and race but the wider relationship of the texts to the society in which they were produced is largely overlooked (Gilmore 1991; Stimpson 1977). See also Bernstein 1992; Brodzki and Schenk 1998.

6 On Stein and materiality, see DeKoven 1981; Stimpson 1985; Stimpson 1977.

7 I use the term "realism" in the sense of a text which seeks to depict the world as closely to reality as possible; as a transparent window on to the world. "Modernism", then, is the movement away from the belief in a one-to-one correspondence between text and reality.

8 Although an African-American doctor would have earned less than his white counterpart in 1907, he remains the only major character with a professional job.

9 D.D. Hill discusses how American advertising grew in the early 20th century as a way to increase demand for goods (Hill 2002). M. Friedman and A.J. Schwartz (1971) examine how public withdrawal of money from banks and refusal to participate in the economy due to lack of trust intensified the 1907 panic, and that once the public regained trust in the economy, the nation began to recover (Friedman and Schwartz 1971: 157–167).

10 In his biography of Stein, Richard Bridgman (1970) explains how "Gertrude Stein had never been more than selectively independent. From childhood on, she had always left the practical responsibilities to others", detailing how first Leo, and then Alice, ran the household. Linda Wagner-Martin (1995) also details how the Steins' eldest brother, Michael, became the financial head of the family after their parents' deaths, investing their parents' legacy in real estate and controlling the allowances given to family members.

11 For more on the US government's economic decisions in 1933, see Fuller 2012.

12 For more information on the Greenbackers, see Ritter 1997). See also Keynes 1965.

13 Whilst there is no evidence to suggest that Stein was aware of Simmel's work and the text did not appear in a complete English translation until 1978, the similarity between contemporary economic theories and Stein's concerns about money indicates her influence by the European intellectual climate of the early 20th century.

14 For more information on the treatment of the Depression and the American economy in the 1930s press, see Welky 2008.

15 Stein writes that she read American newspapers regularly in *The Autobiography of Alice B. Toklas* (Stein 1960: 23).

16 On modernism as anti-capitalist, see Antliff 2007; Moglen 2007.

17 For Shell, this connection between money and writing as symbolized by the words inscribed upon money is what allows a comparison between money and literature to be tenable (Shell 1978: 88).

Bibliography

Antliff, A. (2007), *Anarchist Modernism: Art, Politics, and the First American Avant-Garde*, Chicago: University of Chicago Press.

Bernstein, C. (1992), *A Poetics*, Cambridge, MA: Harvard University Press.

Bridgman, R. (1970), *Gertrude Stein in Pieces*, New York and London: Oxford University Press.

Brodzki, B. and Schenk, C. (1998), *Life/Lines: Theorizing Women's Autobiography*, Ithaca, NY: Cornell University Press.

Brown, B. (2005), "Gertrude Stein's Difficult Paper", www.notbored.org/gertrude-stein. html (accessed February 2, 2010).

Bruner, R. F. and Carr, S. D. (2009), *The Panic of 1907: Lessons Learned From the Market's Perfect Storm*, Hoboken, NJ: John Wiley and Sons.

Conrad, B. (1995), "Gertrude Stein in the American Marketplace", *Journal of Modern Literature*, 19 (2): 215–233.

DeKoven, M. (1981), "Gertrude Stein and Modern Painting: Beyond Literary Cubism", *Contemporary Literature*, 22 (1): 81–95.

Delany, P. (1999), "Who Paid for Modernism?", in M. Woodmansee and M. Osteen (eds.), *The New Economic Criticism: Studies at the Intersection of Economics and Literature*, London: Routledge, 335–351.

Federal Reserve Bank of Boston (1999), "Closed for the Holiday: The Bank Holiday of 1933", www.bos.frb.org/about/pubs/closed.pdf (accessed February 2, 2012).

Fisher, I. (1993), "The Debt-Deflation Theory of Great Depressions", *Econometrica*, 1 (4): 337–357.

Friedman, M. and Schwartz, A. J. (1971), *A Monetary History of the United States, 1867–1960: A Study by the National Bureau of Economic Research, New York*, Princeton, NJ: Princeton University Press.

Fuller, R. L. (2012), *"Phantom of Fear": The Banking Panic of 1933*, Jefferson, NC: McFarland and Company.

Gilmore, L. (1991), "A Signature of Lesbian Autobiography: 'Gertrice/Altrude'", *Prose Studies*, 14 (2): 56–75.

Gordon, J. S. (2008), "A Short Banking History of the United States", *Wall Stree Journal*, www.wsj.com/articles/SB122360636585322023 (accessed February 2, 2014).

Hill, D. D. (2002), *Advertising to the American Woman, 1900–1999*, Columbus, OH: Ohio State University Press.

Kalaidjian, W. (1993), *American Culture Between the Wars: Revisionary Modernism and Postmodern Critique*, New York: Columbia University Press.

Keynes, J. M. (1965), *The General Theory of Employment, Interest and Money*, New York: Harcourt, Brace and World.

Moglen, S. (2007), *Mourning Modernity: Literary Modernism and the Injuries of American Capitalism*, Stanford, CA: Stanford University Press.

North, M. (1994), *The Dialect of Modernism: Race, Language, and Twentieth-Century Literature*, New York: Oxford University Press.

Pizer, D. (ed.) (1995), *American Realism and Naturalism: Howells to London*, Cambridge: Cambridge University Press.

Ritchie, A. C. (1951), *Abstract Painting and Sculpture in America*, New York: Museum of Modern Art.

Ritter, G. (1997), *Goldbugs and Greenbacks: The Antimonopoly Tradition and the Politics of Finance in America, 1865–1896*, Cambridge: Cambridge University Press.

Rothbard, M. N. (2002), *A History of Money and Banking in the United States: The Colonial Era to World War II*, Auburn: Ludwig von Mises Institute.

Shell, M. (1978), *The Economy of Literature*, Baltimore, MD and London: Johns Hopkins University Press.

Simmel, G. (1990), *The Philosophy of Money*, London: Routledge and Kegan Paul.

Soto, M. (2004), *The Modernist Nation: Generation, Renaissance, and Twentieth-Century American Literature*, Tuscaloosa, AL: University of Alabama Press.

Stein, G. (1938), *Everybody's Autobiography*, London and Toronto: William Heinemann Ltd.

Stein, G. (1945), *Wars I Have Seen*, London: B.T. Batsford Ltd.

Stein, G. (1960), *The Autobiography of Alice B. Toklas*, New York: Vintage.

Stein, G. (1971), *Look at Me Now and Here I Am: Writings and Lectures 1909–45*, London: Penguin.

Stein, G. (1985), *Three Lives*, Harmondsworth: Penguin.

Stimpson, C. R. (1977), "The Mind, the Body, and Gertrude Stein", *Critical Inquiry*, 3 (3): 489–506.

Stimpson, C. R. (1985), "The Somagrams of Gertrude Stein", *Poetics Today*, 6 (1/2): 67–80.

Wagner-Martin, L. (1995), *Favored Strangers: Gertrude Stein and Her Family*, New Brunswick, NJ: Rutgers University Press.

Welky, D. (2008), *Everything Was Better in America: Print Culture in the Great Depression*, Urbana and Chicago, IL: University of Illinois Press.

Woodmansee, M. and Osteen, M. (eds.) (1999), *The New Economic Criticism: Studies at the Intersection of Economics and Literature*, London: Routledge.

Zimmerman, D. A. (2006), *Panic! Markets, Crises, and Crowds in American Fiction*, Chapel Hill, NC: University of North Carolina Press.

10 Georges Perec's *Les Choses* as the privileged domain of contemporary hunter-gatherers

Eyüp Özveren

Georges Perec's popular novel *Les Choses* (*Things: A Story of the Sixties*), published in 1965, has been often read as an account and parody of the conflicting emotional universe of human beings who are subject to the vagaries of mass consumption. As such, the story is amenable to an interpretation that compares the behavioural traits of the main characters of the novel, Jérôme and Sylvie, with that of *homo oeconomicus* postulated by economists, as the narrative of the novel presents the reader with issues regarding choice, wealth and consumption. There is no surprise in this straightforward association. Much more interestingly, promising links have already been established with John Kenneth Galbraith's *The Affluent Society*. This step situates the main characters and plot of the novel within the matrix of postwar consumption culture. A parallel association can be pursued with respect to Jean Baudrillard's *La société de consommation*, which enters into a dialogue with the work of Galbraith. Baudrillard himself is known for his unorthodox engagements with political economy in relation to signs and symbolic exchange (Poster 1988: 57–97). In this paper, we want to move further in this direction. We would like to draw attention to the institutionalist background of Galbraith's work that leads us inevitably to the predecessor of his *The Affluent Society*, that is Thorstein Veblen's once equally popular classic, *Theory of the Leisure Class*. What Veblen accomplished in his book was to read fin-de-siecle America with anthropological glasses. We argue that Perec's narrative can also be interpreted in light of Veblen's anthropological critique of the consumption culture. Moreover, economic lessons of anthropology have since Veblen been much elaborated by Karl Polanyi and his followers. Last but not least, Marshall Sahlin's *Stone Age Economics* provides us with an effective instrument for re-reading *Les Choses* as an adventure of 'primitive hunter-gatherers' in late modernity amidst an advanced consumption culture.

Perec (1936–1982) was a French novelist, but he was also a filmmaker and essayist as well as documentarist (an information specialist) with a deep interest in cataloguing and classification that manifests itself in his novels. He was a member of the Oulipo (*Ouvroir de littérature potentielle*) group as of 1967. This is an international group of literary figures (the more famous other two being Raymond Queneau and Italo Calvino) and mathematicians. Perec is known for his "constrained writing", his preference *pace* Flaubert for "*froideur passionnée*" (passionate coldness), as he puts it (Perec 2011: 14), formulaic constructions and classifications that abound in his works and mark his style. Perec's novel, *Les Choses: une histoire des années soixante* (*Things: A Story of the Sixties*), first published in 1965 and awarded the Prix Renaudot, has attracted much attention, not only because it reflects the aura of the 60s, but also because it provides valuable material for social scientists in general, and economists in particular. The book has been quickly recognized as a faithful representation of the consumption culture of the 1960s, and, as Roland Barthes noted, for its Brechtian "realism of situations" rather than a conventional "realism of the details" (Perec 2011: 11, 16). This explains why it was a success in terms of the record numbers it sold. It is obviously better known to a wider segment of the intelligentsia than his other novels, say *La Vie mode d'emploi* (*Life: A User's Manual*; 1978), which was awarded the Prix Médicis and considered as more significant, in fact, by some literary critics as a forerunner of postmodern fiction.

Perec admitted in an interview that his first published book, *Les Choses*, was autobiographical in a restricted sense. It contained details from his own life such as his apartment, the jobs he once worked at, as well as reminiscences of a trip he had made to Tunisia (Perec 2011: 21). Nevertheless, this was of secondary importance compared with what he considered as his main task, that is, to put into writing the society of his time. To achieve this end, he claimed, he first had to 'describe' the environment or the setting. He saw *Les Choses* as preface to another book where true 'characters' would finally appear on this very stage (Perec 2011: 27). He characterized *Les Choses* as a study of setting (*étude de milieu*), or as a record of what he observed around him (Perec 2011: 58). Moreover, as someone who lived in Paris and who deliberately set his stories in Paris, in places he knew best (Perec 2011: 150), it was but natural that the descriptive representations of this setting would overweigh other elements of the book. He felt obliged to distance himself from *Le Nouveau Roman* of Alain Robbe-Grillet, where descriptions also predominated, by emphasizing that the writers he admired most and took up as a model, from Rabelais to Joyce, passing by way of Stendhal and Flaubert, were storytellers (Perec 2011: 163). Given the range of writers he named, it is obvious that the weight of storytelling fluctuated significantly from one to the other, and hence, while not being fully excluded, it was also almost incidental to Perec's narrative. The combined effect of all these admissions is to reinforce the contextually representative capacity of Perec's time/space-specific *Les Choses* from the viewpoint of the economist.

Economists have time and again turned to literature for a variety of reasons. First and foremost, among these are to identify allegedly truthful 'representations of the economic', such as money, wealth, consumption and conditions of the working class in novels. This is to search for evidence, when possible, data, to support certain economic arguments. This becomes more attractive when the realist or naturalist 19th-century novels are concerned.[1] Another important reason is to cast a different light on the novel by reading it with the eyes of an economist. This paper will proceed by identifying first, the less-than-perfect fit between *Les Choses* and a neoclassical economic interpretation. In the following section, *Les*

Choses will be linked to a select institutional economic literature on consumption to lay the foundation for the third section. In the third section, an alternative unorthodox interpretation of *Les Choses* that benefits from the lessons of anthropology will be elaborated. The light this unorthodox interpretation casts on *Les Choses* is far more promising – for seeing certain aspects of the novel that would otherwise go unnoticed – than a mainstream economic interpretation which ultimately succumbs to the pressure of testing the internal consistency of mainstream economic theory rather than helping understand the novel and its true worth.

The neoclassical approach to Perec's *Les Choses* and its limitations

With the abundant material it contains that is of relevance to consumption analysis, *Les Choses* is immensely attractive to any novice involved in mainstream economic analysis. Fiction though it is, *Les Choses* is the least formulaic and puzzling of Perec's novels. It is simple and straightforward. It is the story of a couple fascinated by the world of consumption who wish to escape the necessity to work and jump instead directly into the enjoyment of the riches (Perec 2011: 57). The novel hosts hardly any ambiguity except for the ending, and the plot is matched with a simple linear narrative line. As is evident from its subtitle, it purports to serve as something else than fiction, that is, a 'documentary' history of the 60s. The matter-of-fact narrative style combined with an enlisted inventory of consumption goods leave little to be desired. All this serves to cultivate a sense of the novel as a mirror image of the 1960s par excellence. This reflection-function of the novel makes it attractive for one-to-one matching with, if not testing of, the assumptions of the textbook version of neoclassical economic theory[2] concerning omniscient, rational, self-interested, consistent and utility-maximizing agent behaviour faced with a budget constraint. Moreover, as if deliberately arranged as such to make the task of the economist easier, there exists an unusual economy of characters; they are only two, Jérôme (24 years old) and Sylvie (22). It is true that there exists a circle of friends around them, but they remain indistinguishable, anonymous and provide only some sort of background music and a reality-effect. Because Jérôme and Sylvie also constitute a family, that is, a household, the task of the economist, who wishes to interpret their behaviour (and thereby the novel) is enormously simplified. After all, the two can conveniently be treated as one, that is, the household can be approximated to an individual agent, as is usually done in economic analysis on the consumption side, while matched with firms that are also symmetrically treated as if they were individuals on the opposite production side.[3]

Neoclassical economics is committed to the idea of an equilibrium. While the roots of this heritage extend back to classical political economy, the status and concomitant virtues of equilibrium have been reinforced during time. The study of the properties of this equilibrium has attracted much attention. The equilibrium is bestowed with superior attributes. It is all-beneficial in terms of optimizing general welfare as well as making every individual as better off as s/he could be without making anyone else worse off. All resources are most efficiently allocated among alternative uses. The economy attains the best of its potential performance. This all sounds like mere utopia rather than stark reality to the uninitiated stranger to textbook economics. Neoclassical economists are fortunate enough to have two pieces of evidence that supports the likelihood of such an equilibrium. First, there seem to be times when the market economy functions in a state approximating to this ideal state. Second, the argument goes, a market economy functions better than any other alternative in terms of its performance in resource allocation, hence the equilibrium-characteristic of it can be taken seriously. The combined effect of the two arguments is that equilibrium is likely and superior. If the belief in equilibrium can be maintained, the study of equilibrium properties overshadows the study of how the market economy arrives at it. Methodologically speaking, it is somewhat legitimate from the viewpoint of mainstream economists to assume how individual economic agents get there, if we know that they get there, that is, the equilibrium is secured. But what if the equilibrium does not exist? What if we move out of the domain of economic analysis and market-based economic life? What if we venture into the domain of literature and turn our attention to *Les Choses*?

The search for an equilibrium in *Les Choses* is bound to end in vain. If anything, we are faced with a linear narrative, the linearity of which starts before the narrative, as by the time we are introduced to the characters they have already been launched on their very path for quite some time, and by "the happy and yet the imaginable saddest possible" end of the story, it is hinted (Perec 2011: 13) that they will continue along their path, this time by succumbing to the "rules of the game" (Perec 2011: 23), once we part ways with them. The storyline is divided into three phases, Jérôme and Sylvie's life in Paris, their life in Sfax, Tunisia and their future life in Bordeaux that remains beyond the scope of the novel. But there is no reason to assume that, either any, or all, of these phases correspond to equilibrium states. If all did, we would be progressing from one equilibrium to another. If only one or two did, we would observe a sense of stability and a subsequent disinclination of characters to move away from it. Neither is true. If we forced ourselves hard, we could at best interpret the progress of characters through the novel as movement from one state of disequilibrium to another and then to still another, and so on and so forth.[4]

The word 'equilibrium' makes a unique appearance in *Les Choses*. In juxtaposition to the above discussion of the real phases of narrative time associated with specific spatial coordinates, it belongs to the subjective domain of expectations and dreams that nevertheless go unrealized. It is the utopian alternative that has no place in the 'real' world of this novel. It is introduced at the end of the very first chapter and the characters move further and further away from it as the narrative progresses:

> For their means and their desires would always match in all ways. They would call this balance [*équlibre* in the original, (Perec 1965: 16)] happiness and, with their freedom, with their wisdom and their culture, they would know how to retain and to reveal it in every moment of their living, together.
>
> (Perec 2011: 25–26, 16)

This equilibrium, unrealized as it will be as the storyline advances, has hardly anything to do with equilibrium in the economic definition of the term. The reference to wants and means (*moyens et désirs*) should not mislead us. It has more to do with a permanent state of harmony and bliss, and a psychological 'balance' than with anything else. Once we admit that there exists no equilibrium in *Les Choses*, comparable to that of neoclassical economic analysis even metaphorically, we are left in a void. As of this point, we cannot simulate the recommended approach of neoclassical methodologists and make wide-of-the-mark (of reality) assumptions concerning the way the agents behave. Had we been able to identify at least one state of equilibrium in the novel, it would have legitimized our making behavioural assumptions concerning Jérôme-cum-Sylvie *pace* the conventions of mainstream economists.[5]

Before we square off this discussion, there remains one last issue that we need to address. Even without equilibrium existing in the novel, we could be faced with actual descriptions of agents making choices, given a budget constraint. One plausible inference would be that the evidence in the novel confirms that characters behave like neoclassical economic agents, but their behaviour as such does not automatically generate an equilibrium. This would mean we find supporting evidence for the existence of the neoclassical agent, not for equilibrium, in the novel. This would at first sight support the 'realism' of economic agents. Most discouragingly for a mainstream economics–minded reader, however, *Les Choses*, a 'descriptive' novel about consumption and commodities, does not contain a single depiction of characters jointly or individually making a choice among two or more consumer goods given their budget constraint. Nor do we see them regretting a choice they have made in the past, when later faced with a choice they would have wished to make but deprived of the chances to do so because of the now-regretted choice they had made previously, given their limited budget. This peculiar omission in the novel gives a final blow to any neoclassical economics–inspired reading and interpretation of the novel in question. If the agents in question do not come to the point of making actual, economically feasible choices, this is because they have already been blocked in the pre-decision-making phase: "they thought only in terms of all or nothing. The bookcase would be light oak or it would not be. It was not" (Perec, 201: 30). Jérôme and Sylvie are paralyzed by their convictions before they can make any such simple economic choice.

There are choices and choices. Some choices are qualitatively different from, and more important than, other choices. Perec makes it clear that he has a sense of these meta-choices which then pave the way for the consistent making of lesser 'economic' choices.[6] However as far as the subset of more important choices are concerned, not all choices are equally weighted. Which of the two open paths are taken is all-important and launches one on a path dependence. There is a telling example. Whereas one option is to postpone real plans until one makes enough money first, the other is to see life as freedom, and experience the riches of the world right away to satisfy their wants without further delay, as our two characters prefer. According to Perec, those who choose the first are not necessarily wrong while those who choose the second are bound to be unhappy (Perec 1965: 71).[7]

Beyond the above types of choices, there exists another. If anything, it is history that makes the most important choices on behalf of our characters and cripples them more. When it comes to choosing a profession, like many of their colleagues, our two characters are forced to become market researchers. As such, history chooses for them, just as it is again the case, when they contemplate moving to the countryside to escape from Paris, they are led by a series of events to find themselves in Tunisia (Perec 1965: 29–30, 121–122). When they see an advertisement in *Le Monde* for recruiting teachers to work in Tunisia, they find it difficult to make up their mind, as Tunisia does not measure up to their dreams of the West Indies, United States or Mexico. Nevertheless, circumstantial conveniences oblige them to take up this less-than 'opportunity' to make their suboptimal escape (Perec 1965: 121–122). At the end of the novel, in the Epilogue, in another critical crossroads in the storyline, in fact a bifurcation point in their life trajectory, they move from Tunisia abruptly back to France: "*Mais il ne leur sera pas si facile d'échapper à leur histoire. Le temps, encore une fois, travaillera à leur place*" (But it will not be so easy for them to escape their destiny. Time, once again, would take the matter to its hands on their behalf) (Perec 1965: 149). The role of destiny, if not accident, in determining the course of life of these two characters is thus no less than that of all-important fate in ancient Greek tragedies. No matter what they do, they are bound to remain a toy in the hand of greater forces at work. They are so much accustomed to obeying their fate as the determinant of their major choices that they hurry to seek safe anchor by taking sides politically without being genuinely committed, even in rare circumstances when a choice was not forced upon them, as was the case during the Algerian War (Perec 1965: 85–86). This underlying philosophy of Perec's work reflects the structuralism and determinism of the 1960s and 1970s much more than either the then-fashionable existentialist voluntarist following of Jean-Paul Sartre or Albert Camus, or the individualism associated with rational agents since the 18th century that has come into vogue again during the recent past.

An institutional economic groundwork for rereading *Les Choses*

We have seen above how Oulipo, the literary group to which Perec belonged, described how they saw themselves as "*rats qui construisent eux-mêmes le labyrinth dont ils se proposent de sortir*" (rats who themselves build the labyrinth out of which they then struggle to get out). This had, above all, to do with the mathematical and/or formulaic literary structures the members constructed, which then held their minds and literary work captive. The domination of form over the content was thus expressed by this comparison. Not surprisingly, Perec described the state of mind of his characters, Jérôme and Sylvie in much the same way: "*Ils se sentaient enfermés, pris au piège, faits comme des rats*" (They felt enclosed, caught in a trap as if they were rats) (Perec 1965: 69). The same sense of entrapment is suggested, this time not by recourse to a rat but to a squirrel by John Kenneth Galbraith, the heterodox economist who authored the then–very influential, now-classic *The Affluent Society*. In the "The Dependence Effect" section taking up the addiction characteristic of the consumption culture, Galbraith makes his analogy:

> Consumer wants can have bizarre, frivolous, or even immoral origins, and an admirable case can still be made for a society that seeks to satisfy them. But the case cannot stand if it is the process of satisfying wants that creates the wants. For then the individual who urges the importance of production to satisfy these wants is precisely in the position of the onlooker who applauds the efforts of the squirrel to keep abreast of the wheel that is propelled by his own efforts.

> (Galbraith 1958/2000: 230)

The convergent senses of entrapment and captivity manifest in these three quotations encourage a rereading of Perec with Galbraith in mind. This implies starting with consumption culture as cultivated by the stronger elements that dominate the production leg of the economic system. Galbraith's book is based on the experience of the 1950s in the US, a historical period which in many ways was a forerunner of the France's experience in the 1960s. The consumer society experience of this period provided the starting point of Perec's *Les Choses* as well as the formative context of Jean Baudrillard's *La société de consommation*. To the then-contemporary observers, the so-called Golden Age of Capitalism or *Les Trente Glorieuses* associated with the unprecedented postwar economic performance of the advanced capitalist countries was also the high time of welfare state and consumer society.

Consumption is one of the most ancient habits of human beings, if not the most ancient. Mankind first started consuming the gifts of nature as hunters and gatherers, long before they engaged in the making of utensils as well as settled agriculture, even on an occasional basis. Not only is consumption ancient, but also it has experienced an exponential growth over the course of history, but more so, over the last two centuries. Attempts to reduce consumption on part of either authorities or the consumers themselves have largely failed. Let us just remind ourselves of the dramatic failure of once communist regimes or slow or 'small is beautiful'–type consumer movements. In fact, the only consumer movements that have proven popular are those that have sought to expand consumer rights and enhance the quality of consumption. In an originally unintended way, the concept of 'consumer sovereignty' holds true. Yet this is the truth, but not the whole truth. It seems that the driving force of the economic dynamics of the last two centuries has originated from the supply side precisely because "[i]t is, however, the producer who as a rule initiates economic change, and consumers are educated by him if necessary" (Schumpeter 1983: 65). He also foresaw that we would be introduced to an "*embarrass de richesse*" in the postwar era (Schumpeter 1942: 116). As of the mid-20th century, far from fostering 'affluent societies' increasingly everywhere, consumption entered the phase of unsustainable obesity. It is about this phase that Galbraith wrote extensively. Big business that plans, creates and manipulates consumer demand to its own advantage is a major concern of his.

Perec's novel takes place during the French version of this transition to consumer society. Jérôme and Sylvie's demand is not so much for consumer durables or mass-produced consumer goods as typical. It is much more subtle and sophisticated. It is brand-, quality- and origin-conscious particularly in relation to imported clothing and accessories (Perec 1965: 35–36). Our two protagonists consciously reproduce their difference, this 'distinction', to differentiate themselves from the mass of consumer populace and to belong to a small group of about 10 members with similar tastes, who constitute a consumer elite. Irrespectively of this major difference, however, they are just as passive recipients of magnetic attractions and manipulations that originate from the opposite side. A magic spell is thus cast over them; they are seduced. With its exquisite shopping districts and display windows, Paris became a perpetual temptation (Perec 1965: 18). They do not resist the temptation. On the contrary, they yield wholeheartedly to its luring. "They would cross all of Paris to see an armchair they'd been told was just perfect" (Perec 2011: 31). They gradually find themselves trapped in an illusionary universe of display windows and merchandise:

> From one station to another – antique dealer, bookshops, record shops, restaurant menus, travel agencies, shirt-makers, tailors, cheese-shops, bootmakers, confectioners, delicatessens, stationers – their paths through Paris constituted their real universe: in them lay their ambitions and hopes.
>
> (Perec 2011: 81)

The protagonists develop their consumption habits and preferences within the group or gang of nine or ten people to which they belonged. As such, their preferences are group determined rather than being individualistic. They looked to others with learning in mind. For example, they paid attention to how the others dressed (Perec 1965: 38). They were hence ready for "pecuniary emulation" and the kind of consumption it encouraged among those who commanded some money. The protagonists of the novel enjoy enormously buying cheap, making a good bargain, but also occasionally indulging themselves in "conspicuous consumption"[8] (Perec 1965: 51). They know how to buy, cheap or dear, with or without bargaining. When they buy something, they do it with an eye to how others would see it, without which conspicuous consumption would not make sense. Hence their shopping practices are culturally coded and embedded. They are truly Parisians with their allegedly 'exquisite' taste and purchasing practices. The reverse is also true: when they are out of context, they could not function. During the eight months they spend in Tunisia, the most interesting eight months of their life (Perec 1965: 128), which constitute an exceptional interregnum in their trajectory with a certain therapeutic function, their shopping habit is disrupted. At a time when the profit-motivated Pier 1 Imports or the idealistic Fairtrade International were not yet in sight, the bazaars of Tunisia filled with local crafts would have been expected to exert even a greater attraction for travelers who really had a genuine taste for the different. In sharp contrast with the spell of Parisian display windows, these 'oriental' bazaars with their performance-artist salesmen could not entice them (Perec 1965: 143–144).[9] They are therefore as much carried along with the tide because of the symbolic exchange aspect of buying. The cultural codes within which this activity is embedded make for them an enormous difference. The inability of Jèrôme and Sylvie to function as aspiring consumers in Tunisia casts a light on the way they operated in the usual state of things characteristic of their Parisian phase.

It is not so much the big business–dominated production side that they come face to face with in their daily lives, as with its ancillaries such as the advertisement industry, not to mention *L'Express*, a weekly mouthpiece that trained them in the "art of living' and served as their lodestar, in fact a handy compass without which they could not do in this world of consumption culture (Perec 1965: 45). It was also their accomplice (Perec 1965: 47–48). It is as if the advertisement industry left production industry in its shadow, made it invisible to the bare eye. Jérôme and Sylvie, like most of their friends, worked directly or indirectly for the advertisement industry. It was this industry that made their lives miserable in more than one sense of the term (Perec 1965: 97–98). William Blake, the prophetic poet referred to the factory system of the Industrial Revolution as a "Satanic Mill" grinding men. Karl Polanyi displaced the analogy from factories to the "self-regulating market mechanism", of which he was the eminent theorist. He called the first half of the second part of his book, *The Great Transformation*, "Satanic Mill". Together with the second half, entitled "Self-Protection of Society", this second part explored the "Rise and Fall of Market Economy" (Polanyi 1944: vii). He was particularly appalled by the labor market, "the most potent of all modern institutions" (Polanyi 1944: 83) that ground man into labor. It is Perec who, probably unknowingly, but with great intuition, shifted the metaphor of "grinding" (*broyer*) to the realm of precarious employment in the advertisement industry, thereby squaring it.

One major accomplishment of Polanyi was to draw parallels between the present and the past by recourse to the evidence of anthropology that could serve as a proxy for the historical data that was unavailable. This enhanced the importance of anthropology from the viewpoint of recent economic history and contemporaneous economic theory. Mainstream economic theory uses anthropology in a very restricted sense, to substantiate its assumptions concerning the behaviour of *homo oeconomicus*. In contrast, Polanyi brought anthropology back into the assistance of economic theory to enrich the latter by ridding it of the idea of the inevitability of progress as well as to re-introduce diversity of forms, agents and institutions. To accomplish this objective, he made extensive use of the then-existing anthropological literature as well as concepts such as 'basic human needs', 'human motives' and 'quality of life'. By so doing, he revived a strong side of institutional economics that was already extremely important in the work of Thorstein Veblen, a founding father of the original institutionalism (Özveren 2007).

If Polanyi used anthropological subjects, that is, natives, as a way of casting a new light on historical subjects of a bygone era, Veblen used the lessons of anthropology to investigate modern economic agents. What legitimized the application of anthropology to contemporary phenomena was Veblen's discovery of the survival of ancient traits. In his view, thanks to this 'survival thesis', the contemporary 'leisure class' was the result and inheritor of the barbarian ruling class of remote history, in fact, its remake. Culture survives is disguised forms:

> A distinction is still habitually made between industrial and non-industrial occupations; and this modern distinction is a transmuted form of the barbarian distinction between exploit and drudgery. Such employments as warfare, politics, public worship, and public merrymaking, are felt, in the popular apprehension, to differ intrinsically from the labor that has to do with elaborating the material means of life. The precise line of demarcation is not the same as it was in the early barbarian scheme, but the broad distinction has not fallen into disuse.
>
> (Veblen 1899: 26)

The implication of Veblen's controversial discovery is nevertheless profound. The study of modernity is a legitimate and important task for anthropologists. As of the last quarter of the 20th century, anthropologists running out of unspoiled native tribes to study turned their attention to the observation of ghettos, countercultures, identities and ethnicities. This trend has rejuvenated anthropology at a time when its archrival in this respect, sociology, lost prestige because it could not approach this kind of subject matter as innovatively. Perec's *Les Choses* pays tribute to sociology. There are references to the beginnings of "motivation", "content analysis" and to reputable sociologists like Wright Mills, Paul Lazarsfeld, William Whyte, Hadley Cantril and Herbert Hyman (Perec 1965: 30, 32, 33). There is also an allusion to seeking enlightenment in sociology during the Algerian War (Perec 1965: 82). This kind of 'scholastic' use of and respect for sociology by the protagonists is justified by the traditional strength of sociology in France since the 19th century – further reinforced in the 1960s.

Rereading *Les Choses* differently with 'anthropological' glasses

It is high time we apply some anthropological insight to the otherwise primarily 'economic' reading of this novel. Perec (2011: 14) himself told that among his sources of inspiration for the novel was the *Mythologies* (1972) of Barthes, first published in 1957, where he explored the modern equivalents in consumer culture of ancient myths. Moreover, Perec claimed his characters were mirrors he held onto certain 'myths' of the time (Perec 2011: 22). Prehistoric and modern humans are millennia apart. Yet Baudrillard spoke of the "new savage man" of the modern times as being unable to find his way out amidst the proliferating vegetation and jungle of objects that are neither flora nor fauna and of "hunter-gatherer anthropoids" wandering nowadays in the jungle of cities (Baudrillard 1970: 18, 27).

Both Veblen and Polanyi as institutional economists made extensive use of anthropology. Why should we not do something similar with respect to the interpretation of Perec's novel? Why should we not replace the false anthropology concerning human behaviour of neoclassical economics, which Veblen despised, with a genuine anthropology, and use it as an aid in reinterpreting the motives and behaviour of Jérôme and Sylvie? Why should we thus not part ways with a blind commitment to the assumption of *homo oeconomicus*? We are in fact given a hint by a leading anthropologist about the direction to take:

> The hunter [of the hunter-gatherer society], one is tempted to say, is 'uneconomic man.' At least as concerns nonsubsistence goods, he is the reverse of that standard caricature immortalized in any *General Principles of Economics*, page one. His wants are scarce and his means (in relation) plentiful. Consequently, he is 'comparatively free of material pressures,' has 'no sense of possession,' shows 'an undeveloped sense of property,' is 'completely indifferent to any material pressures,' manifests a 'lack of interest' in developing his technological equipment.
>
> (Sahlins 1974: 13)

Why should we not treat our protagonists not as individuals but as both a household and members of a team that consisted of a consumption-culture gang of some nine or ten people endowed with feelings of mutual support and solidarity? We know that group behaviour was of tantamount importance for the protagonists as it gave them a sense of cohesion (Perec 1965: 92), solidarity and security, just as the case had been with prehistorical hunter-gatherers.

We witness this household is on the move. It moves from Paris to Sfax to Bordeaux but it also moves continuously within Paris and Tunisia. We do not know if this will continue in the Bordeaux episode, but as they aspire to settle for a different life there, we have some reason to assume it will not. This state of continuous movement reminds one of the metaphor of '[Odysseus'] journey' as distinct from '[Abraham's] exile' as differentiated by Emmanuel Levinas. Whereas 'journey' comes with a sense of eventual return, 'exile' is more to do with banishment, that is, the ancient biblical tragic situation of no return (Lambropoulos 1992: 215–216). We are faced in *Les Choses* with a true odyssey with a deferred return. The endpoint is fixed in space as the settlement that comes after a migratory existence. The history of mankind displays one stage that came before the so-called Neolithic, that is, the Agricultural Revolution, the Paleolithic, where the normal state of things was the continuously moving social life of nomadic gangs as clusters of hunter-gatherers. This state of nomadic existence has been characterized unconventionally and therefore polemically as "The Original Affluent Society" after the title of Galbraith's immensely successful book (Sahlins 1974: 1). The affluence was a function not so much of the abundance of goods available as that of limited wants.[10] The abundance was a function of the fact that wants were provided by the gifts of nature, over which no private property existed. The absence of individual property rights over resources was a big bonanza for the hunter-gatherers until the relative depletion of natural resources that encouraged the establishment of exclusive property rights. On the consumption side, there existed a constraint due to the limited carrying capacity of the household that was constantly on the move. Put differently, the impossibility of storage combined with high transportation costs discouraged the consumption of durable goods and channeled consumption to nondurables that were readily available and consumable on the spot such as fruits and prey. It is no surprise that a kind of minimalist and self-satisfactory Zen culture – quite different from the consumption culture underwriting our civilization – went hand in hand with the hunter-gatherer stage of civilization (Sahlins 1974: 1–2).

Compared with prehistorical hunter-gatherers as depicted by economic anthropology, Jérôme and Sylvie face two different constraints and an advantage. They live in a world of private property rights that are by definition exclusive (Perec 1965: 73). Combined with this, they are also faced with a budget constraint. This comes as an intransigent, insurmountable 'pecuniary' constraint (Perec 1965: 76). Perec speaks repeatedly of the central role of money he had in mind as he wrote his novel (Perec 2011: 21). These two disadvantages are less than compensated with our characters' one seeming advantage. Just like the other members of their gang, they have 'storage space', that is their apartment, which is *"encombré"* (cluttered) (Perec 1965: 63). It is overly used in case of Paris and underused in case of Sfax (Perec 1965: 126–128). The more they exploit this advantage, the more it becomes a true constraint (Perec 1965: 20–21). Be that as it may, the fact that they can potentially store launches them on a different path than their prehistorical precursors. This is the path of consumption where their unlimited wants clash with the true limits of their meagre means. They become path-dependent. The more they tend to consume, the more they realize the inherent limitations in this cul-de-sac due to their limited means. Their unhappiness becomes self-expanding. Jérôme and Sylvie behave as if they were hunter-gatherers in a world that is radically different from that of the hunter-gatherer era of human history. Thus, motives, behaviour and context become essentially irreconcilable. Their motives are acquired through learning and because of the indoctrination of the consumption culture. Their behaviour simulates that of hunter-gatherers as if by instinct. The resemblance between the two worlds is illusory. It is a product of the consumption culture that indoctrinates the individual-as-consumer, as if everything was readily available irrespective of the limitations. In the world they lived, it is almost a rule to always desire more than one could acquire. It is not they who decreed it; it was a law of the civilization (Perec 1965: 50).

It is thanks to this pumped-up illusion that Jérôme and Sylvie and their likes can behave as if they were hunter-gatherers coming to terms with their limits only obliquely and working out second-best solutions that serve them to perpetuate their illusions and thereby aggravate their dissatisfaction. A good example of a second-best solution is their discovery of the flea market. When they discover the immense possibilities of the flea market, they reinvigorate their regular 'hunting-gathering' strolls (Perec 1965: 37). Jérôme and Sylvie resemble hunter-gatherers not only because they wander around to gather but also because of the way they behave. Their behaviour when they choose to live from one day to the next by spending in six hours what they have made in three days (Perec 1965: 79) makes perfect sense when related to the behaviour of their Zen-minded hunter-gatherer prehistorical precursors as depicted by the economic anthropologist:

> That, I think, describes the hunters. And it helps explain some of their more curious economic behavior: their 'prodigality' for example – the inclination to consume at once all stocks on hand, as if they had it made. Free from market obsessions of scarcity, hunters' economic propensities may be more consistently predicated on abundance than our own.
>
> (Sahlins 1974: 2)

The above epoch of their lives is described as "*[Le] temps de la vie sans amarres*" (the period of life without root) or "*quelques années de vie vagabonde*" (some years of vagabond life)[11] and is succeeded by "*les temps de la securité*" (the times of security) (Perec 1965: 94, 154). The contrast between the two ways of life is associated with nomadic and settled life respectively. Not surprisingly, security comes at the cost of freedom. It is the group that first disintegrates as members move one by one to settled life with 'roots' and leave Jérôme and Sylvie in a vacuum (Perec 1965: 93–94). The two protagonists follow their predecessors with a prolonged delay when they finally succumb to a new settled way of life in Bordeaux at the end of the novel. This is a final farewell to their previously contradictory lifestyle that against all odds could only be pursued at a high price under artificially simulated circumstances. If at all, only after this transition can they be expected to behave individualistically as true *homo oeconomicus*.

Notes

1 A very recent and excellent example is Thomas Piketty's *Le capital au XXIe siècle* where the author engages himself in a dialogue primarily with Honoré de Balzac and Jane Austin, but also with Henry James, Naguib Mahfouz and Orhan Pamuk, as he explores the inequalities of wealth and income over time and in comparative perspective (Piketty 2013: 179, 184–187, 193, 376–384, 602–603, 642–661, 665–667, 703).

2 By 'neoclassical economics' we refer to the developed form of "marginalist thinking" (Roncaglia 2005: 279–281, 350) as also characterized by Heinz D. Kurz in his *Economic Thought: A Brief History*. The purpose here is not to make a straw-man but to summarize the main characteristics of a widespread economic approach to the benefit of the less specialized reader (Kurz 2016: 57–68). Without such a generalization, it would be impossible to speak intelligibly of any school of thought as it is always possible to observe differences among the members of any school when approached more closely. See also (Screpanti and Zamagni 1993: 177–178) for the importance of "identfying a common denominator, a substantial unity of thought".

3 Whether or not this poses problems from the literary perspective remains to be addressed. Fortunately, as noted above, characters are of lesser significance in the progression of Perec's narrative and they are not to be confused with some 19th-century literary characters whose psychological depth and metamorphoses were all important from the viewpoint of the novel. Perec's characters are more of 'typage' than being proper characters in the above sense. Perec's characters do not conflict with each other and thereby differentiate themselves either. They move linearly in a parallel fashion. This facilitates our task immensely.

162   *Eyüp Özveren*

4 According to Jean Baudrillard, if we admit that the need is never the need for a particular object but a need for a social 'difference', it will be easier to understand that there will never be a full satisfaction of the need concerned. Hence the above picture fits instead with his "generalized competition" corresponding to "an uninterrupted process of differentiation and overdifferentiation" (Baudrillard 1970: 108, 292). However, this is a sneak preview if not actually a part and parcel of an interpretation to which we will return later on.

5 There exists one study that pursues this investigation further along the neoclassical line, only to shift to a slightly different terrain by incorporating some lessons from the work of Amartya Sen (Pignol 2011).

6 There can also result a lasting resentment because "[t]he best alternative according to the preference that a person actually happens to have may not be the best (or even maximal) according to a preference she would prefer to have (and work toward realizing" (Sen 2002: 18).

7 This leads us to the proliferating literature on the economics of happiness, the discussion of which remains beyond the scope of this paper. It suffices here to say that, for Perec, happiness resembles endless accumulation insofar as one could not stop being happy once one is launched on this way (Perec 2011: 12). But this is an entrapment. Perec emphasizes that within the consumer society, there exists space for a specific kind of happiness associated with modernity that is to do with relations to 'objectively beautiful' things and this is quite real in its own sense (Perec 2011: 26). Yet this happiness has nothing to do with Happiness with a capital 'H' that remains impossible within the very same context.

8 Both concepts are cornerstones of Thorstein Veblen's theory of consumer behaviour (Veblen 1899: 33–40, 60–80), which presupposes a social environment and not an isolated Robinson Crusoe assumption as is the case with the neoclassical construct (Kurz 2016: 58–60).

9 They also did not have the know-how necessary for success in these local marketplaces. The anthropologist Clifford Geertz demonstrated how rich in detail are the procedures in such occasions (Geertz 1978). It is not easy to come out successfully from such a negotiated process.

10 Whereas in modern consumer society which Galbraith characterized as affluent, abundance was actually lost for good (Baudrillard 1970: 92).

11 At one point the protagonists consider becoming thieves in order to make a shortcut to wealth with the dream of making a sensational escape encircling the world and only ultimately settling in a remote yet idyllic place with an aggreeable climate in the periphery of Europe (Perec 1965: 103–104). Hence even in their dreams, they roam around as long as possible in mind and the settlement option as a deferred ending.

Bibliography

Barthes, R. (1972), *Mythologies*, New York: Hill and Wang.
Baudrillard, J. (1970), *La société de consummation*, Paris: Éditions Denoël.
Galbraith, J. K. (1958/2000), "The Dependence Effect", in B. Seyoum and R. Abraham (eds.), *Sources: Notable Selections in Economics*, New York: Dushkin and McGraw-Hill, 229–234.
Geertz, C. (1978), "The Bazaar Economy: Information and Search in Peasant Marketing", *The American Economic Review*, 68 (2): 28–32.
Kurz, H. (2016), *Economic Thought: A Brief History*, New York: Columbia University Press.
Lambropoulos, V. (1992), *The Rise of Eurocentrism: Anatomy of Interpretation*, Princeton, NJ: Princeton University Press.

Özveren, E. (2007), "Karl Polanyi and Return of the 'Primitive' in Institutional Economics", *Journal of Economic Issues*, XLI (3): 783–808.

Perec, G. (1965), *Les Choses: une histoire des années soixante*, Paris: René Julliard.

Perec, G. (2011), *En dialogue avec l'époque*, Nantes: Joseph K. English translation by Bellos, D. (2011), *Things: A Story of the Sixties with a Man Asleep*, London: Vintage.

Pignol, C. (2011), "Can Metaranking Express the Misfortunes of Consumption? A Discussion From the Reading of *Things* by G. Perec", in R. Ege and H. Igersheim (eds.), *Freedom and Happiness in Economic Thought and Philosophy: From Clash to Reconciliation*, New York: Routledge, 256–272.

Piketty, T. (2013), *Le capital au XXIe siècle*, Paris: Seuil.

Polanyi, K. (1944), *The Great Transformation: The Political and Economic Origins of Our Time*, Boston, MA: Beacon Press.

Poster, M. (ed.) (1988), *Jean Baudrillard: Selected Writings*, Stanford, CA: Stanford University Press.

Roncaglia, A. (2005), *The Wealth of Ideas*, Cambridge: Cambridge University Press.

Sahlins, M. (1974), *Stone Age Economics*, London: Tavistock Publications.

Schumpeter, J. A. (1942), *Capitalism, Socialism and Democracy*, New York: Harper.

Schumpeter, J. A. (1983), *The Theory of Economic Development*, New Brunswick, NJ: Transaction Publishers.

Screpanti, E. and Zamagni, S. (1993), *An Outline of the History of Economic Thought*, Oxford: Clarendon Press.

Sen, A. (2002), *Rationality and Freedom*, Cambridge, MA: The Belknap Press of Harvard University Press.

Veblen, T. (1899), *The Theory of the Leisure Class: An Economic Study of Institutions*, New York: A Mentor Book.

Part III

Facing change

Reflections of economic development
and crises in historical
and literary texts

11 Transforming economic and social relations

Modern economy in the novels of Uşaklıgil

Reyhan Tutumlu Serdar and Ali Serdar

In this paper, while trying to figure out representations of economic relations in literature by focusing on the novels of Halit Ziya Uşaklıgil, one of the prominent novelists of Ottoman/Turkish literature, first we briefly summarize the Ottoman empire's integration into the capitalist world system. Though dissemination of capitalist relations across empire led changes at the macro level, it also affected the daily economic and social relations of the Ottoman /Turkish community, which can also be considered as a part of a "modernization" process. In this respect examining how these changes in Ottoman/Turkish society were represented in the novels written in that era gives us significant clues to interpret how these transformations were experienced. In this study three novels of Uşaklıgil are going to be examined within the framework of Marxist literary criticism and focusing on concepts such as social class, exploitation, money economy, alienation, reification, competition and fashion. In order to interpret the literary problems posed by the texts we also refer to Lukács' views on reification and Simmel's commentary on the role of money in modern culture.

Economy and literature in late 19th-century Ottoman/Turkish society

The 18th and 19th centuries were the ages of great transformation for the Ottoman state and society. The starting point of this transformation can be traced back to the 16th century, and this historical process, which meant incorporation of Ottoman economy into the world system, has been examined in depth in the works of the economic historians such as Şevket Pamuk, Reşat Kasaba, Huricihan İslamoğlu İnan and Immanuel Wallerstein. In this course of transformation, in which an autonomous empire turns out to be a state dependent on the capitalist world economy, numerous substantial economic, social and cultural changes took place in the Ottoman state and society. It is pointed out that the liberalization process of the Ottoman economy began with the 1838 Free Trade Treaties (Kasaba 1993: 45); however, considering the history of land and agricultural regime of Ottoman Empire, it can be stated that the most dramatic changes took place through the process of the ownership of lands. With the 1858 Land Legislation buying and selling of lands was freed (Pamuk 1988: 218–219) and "private property" was legitimized in Ottoman society; moreover in 1867 right of owner-ship of lands by foreigners was entitled. In 1840, the first paper money was deliv-ered, and soon it became widespread. The first industrial investments intended for the military were made by the state in the 1830s and 1840s (Pamuk 1988: 228), like the production of gunpowder, cannon and uniforms. In 1860–61, the first Ottoman budget was prepared (Kasaba 1993: 48). In 1863 together with English and French capital Osmanlı Devleti Ziraat Bankası (Ottoman State Bank of Agri-culture) was established (Pamuk 1988: 210). The construction of railways was accelerated in the second half of the 19th century, which in advance leads to both the growing of domestic trade and integration of the Ottoman economy with the European markets. Besides those historical incidents were a proliferation of com-modity production in agriculture and an increase in urban population. Because of these, the entire phenomenon summarized above, another significant dramatic change was the gradual growth of the state apparatus and birth of the modern bureaucracy. In 19th century "the mode of organization of the state apparatus" (Wallerstein et al. 2004: 93) had completely changed and the rapid growth of the bureaucracy concluded with "new divisions and groupings among the different fractions of the ruling bloc" (Wallerstein et al. 2004: 93). In other words, the way the politics, culture and economics perceived was also changed.

Those changes mentioned above, which can be summarized as the incorpo-ration of the Ottoman economy by the world economy, a change of commerce rates against the Ottoman state on behalf of European markets, transformation of property relations, the birth of modern bureaucracy, and changes in class structure can be read as transformations that took place at the macro level. Therefore, it is not erroneous to assume that those macro-level transformations had reflections on the micro level, namely daily life and human relations. And this micro level com-prises phenomena like family economies (decline, loss of property, vice versa), relationship with money, desire for moving to the upper class, commerce, alienation, reification, division of labor, exploitation, etc. and all are represented or at least had potential to be represented in literature.

It is not a coincidence that Ottoman/Turkish wo/men of letters first encoun-ter with western novels and publication of first Turkish novels took place in this period of transformation. Indisputably, one can observe economic relations in narratives of Turkish literature. In case of the novel, as a form of modern narra-tive, during the period of Tanzimat literature (1860–96), especially in the works of Ahmet Mithat, one can frequently encounter themes like investment, gaining money, making profit, borrowing and lending money, growth of capital by loan-ing, and prominence given to work.[1] Yet again in the narratives of Fatma Aliye, the first woman novelist of Turkish literature, who was influenced by Ahmet Mithat Efendi, similar themes can be detected. However, established Turkish literary crit-icism generally examines the works of the periods of Tanzimat and Servet-i Fünun on the basis of "Westernization", and by and large limited their interpretation con-cerning economic relations with focusing on the protagonist of novel, stating that generally they are either a member of "upper class", working in government office as a civil servant or "alafranga"[2]/dandy prodigals (Mardin 2000; Moran 1998).

Servet-i Fünun literature (1896–1901) was one of the significant movements in terms of both literary history and political thought, flourished and ended in the period of Abdülhamid II, in which strict control over society either by censorship or sending opponents to exile thrived. Maybe for that reason in Turkish literary history Servet-i Fünun is generally considered a period apathetic to social and political problems. The works of the period are mostly reduced simply to the problem of "Westernization" and scrutinized in terms of East-West dichotomy. Halit Ziya Uşaklıgil (1867–1945) was a major writer of the period and his works are mostly interpreted within the framework of westernization by distinctive Turkish literary critiques such as Berna Moran (1998), Ahmet Hamdi Tanpınar (1988) and Cevdet Kudret (1998). On the other hand, some critiques like Robert P. Finn (1984) and Orhan Koçak (1996) make consequential interpretations of social and economic relations detected in the novels of Uşaklıgil. However, there is a lack of comprehensive study concentrating on Uşaklıgil's works mainly on basis of economic relations in the history of Turkish literature.

In Turkish literary history, besides the theme of "westernization", Uşaklıgil is perceived as the forerunner of the novel genre, mainly in terms of technique. For example, Ahmet Hamdi Tanpınar (1988), a prominent Turkish literary historian, emphasizes the significance of Uşaklıgil and states that "[in our literature] novel writing initiates with Halid Ziya" (275). Robert P. Finn (1984), while agreeing on Uşaklıgil's significance in general, particularly puts forward *Aşk-ı Memnu* (*Forbidden Love*): "*Aşk-ı Memnu* is perhaps the most technically brilliant novel in the Turkish language" (135). Fethi Naci (2000), a well-known literary critic, also emphasizes the importance of *Aşk-ı Memnu* (*Forbidden Love*) and states that in terms of literary criteria it is the first Turkish novel (48). Summarizing the evaluations of critiques, we can commentate that Uşaklıgil can be accepted as the pioneer of modernization in Turkish literature. Moreover, we try to expose that reflections of modernization in Uşaklıgil's works are not limited to form/ technique but can be observed in content also.

Two of the novels, *Aşk-ı Memnu* (*Forbidden Love*, 1900) and *Mai ve Siyah* (*Azure and Black*, 1889), which we are going to examine, were written in the period of Servet-i Fünun. Although the publication date of *Ferdi ve Şürekâsı* (*Ferdi and his Partners*, 1894), which we are going to examine as the third novel, precedes the Servet-i Fünun period, when the literary characteristics of the novel are taken into consideration one can observe the close resemblance with the other works of the Servet-i Fünun period. The distinctive features of *Ferdi ve Şürekâsı* (*Ferdi and his Partners*) from the other two novels gives us notable evidence about the transforming economic and social relations, and gives us an opportunity to interpret those differences.

Reified economic and social relations: *Ferdi ve şürekâsi* (*Ferdi and his Partners*)

Ferdi ve Şürekâsı (*Ferdi and his Partners*) is based on the love relations between İsmail Tayfur, a lower-middle-class accountant and his handmaiden Saniha, who lives in İsmail Tayfur's house, and Hacer, who is the daughter of İsmail Tayfur's boss. İsmail Tayfur's desire to move to the upper class leads him to prefer Hacer, which means money and prosperity, rather than Saniha, with whom İsmail Tayfur is in love. The catastrophes originating from İsmail Tayfur's choice designates the novel's plot.

Ferdi ve Şürekâsı (Ferdi and his Partners) is based on the dichotomy of prosperity and poverty, and this dichotomy is reflected by the characters and their habitation. On the one side, there is İsmail Tayfur, who after the death of his father has to say farewell to his desires, gives up education and begins to work: "[he] has to go to the office where his father had died, knock the door, and ask for bread from the occupation which had killed his father" (22). Saniha, who was brought by his father to his home as a handmaiden after the death of his mother, is another significant figure situated in this dichotomy. On the other side, there is Ferdi Efendi and his daughter Hacer, both of whom rely on the power of money, and think that everything can be bought by that power. This dichotomy is reflected in their habitation by the description of the households of İsmail Tayfur and Ferdi Efendi. The only asset İsmail Tayfur has is the small house left by his father. İsmail Tayfur is living in a small room of this small house. In contrast to İsmail Tayfur's room, decorated with numerous ornaments, furniture, statues and tulles, Hacer's room is sparkling prosperity, gorgeousness and brilliance (33–35). In addition, via the comparison of this highlighted prosperity with the poverty of İsmail Tayfur, the difference between two worlds becomes more striking.

İsmail Tayfur is working in a private company as an accountant, and as a white-collar worker his outstanding problem is his struggle to earn a living. This struggle is reflected through examples in which a sacrifice must be made. For example in order to buy the writing table he wants, which costs 4 liras, İsmail Tayfur has to save money for two years. Alternatively, in order to buy a dress for Seniha, İsmail Tayfur has to reconsider his budget, and only by sacrifices is he able to buy her a dress. With these details in the narrative of the privation of Saniha and İsmail, Tayfur's life is emphasized. Getting married to Hacer, to possess her property, and by that way realizing his desire to move to the upper class seems to be the only solution of İsmail Tayfur against poverty. By and large not only his mind but his mother and Hasan Tahsin, İsmail Tayfur's coworker and his deceased father's friend, are also directing and manipulating him towards this solution, namely to Hacer.

Hasan Tahsin Efendi, who has been working as an accountant in Ferdi Bey's company ever since it was established, namely for 35 years, is a distinctive character; he is a unique character considering not only the novels of Uşaklıgil's but also in terms of Turkish literature. In the very first pages of the novel, Hasan Tahsin Efendi speaks about the establishment and growth of the company at length. In this narration, the growth of company is told analogous with the exploitation of company workers. For example, detailed numbers about the company's capital and wages are comparatively given. When company was established, its capital was 3000 liras, and the wage of a worker was 4 liras. At the end of 18 years, wages were raised to 12 liras, and capital was increased to 60 000 liras (11–12). Now, after 35 years, wages are 25 liras and capital is 100 000 liras. With this comparison, the uneven growth of capital and diminishing wages are displayed. The mechanism of exploitation that lies in the essence of capital is explained by Hasan Tahsin in the following sentence: "He [Ferdi Efendi] forgets that in the money he holds in the safe deposit box, which stays behind him as a steel base for his arrogance and pride, there are pieces from my life, my blood" (9). Hasan Tahsin's comments are not restricted to exploitation. He has keen and deep perceptions about the nature of his work and its effects on his life. But before quoting his words, it must be stated that it is not easy to come across characters like Hasan Tahsin in Turkish literature, who has consequential observations about his own occupation and the division of labor based on specialization in general.

> The real meaning of numbers in an accountant's life should be known! His life is no longer a life; his personality is no longer a personality, do you believe? The numbers, which took 35 years of my life, what they have done to me, do you know? There are some moments that I want to express my ideas with numbers . . . Numbers have much more place in my mind than language! If I proceed in this idea, I could say, "four and four is sixteen" instead of saying "I am hungry". Since numbers made me forget all existing things and made my feelings dull. . . . As a matter of fact I am astonished that I did not give my children's names as numbers. For example, Münir, he is a hammer-like boy; if his name would be 9, it should suit him well! Do not laugh!
>
> (13–14)

It is explicit that because of Hasan Tahsin's occupation, his relationship with numbers diffused into all fields of his life; moreover, numbers dominate his life. In this regard, it can be argued that the destruction of human relations and human nature because of the proliferation of capitalist relations is reflected as alienation and reification. Karl Marx, in the chapter he dedicated to "the fetishism of commodities" in the first volume of *Capital*, clearly describes how the process of commodification affects human relations in detail. The effect of numbers on Hasan Tahsin's life can be interpreted as an outcome of the process of commodification. However, the situation exceeds what Marx has suggested, and Georg Lukács (1988), in his work *History and Class Consciousness* takes commodity fetishism as a departure, and explains the phenomenon by using the term "reification": "Because of this situation [capitalism] a man's own activity, his own labour becomes something objective and independent of him, something that controls him by virtue of an autonomy alien to men" (86–87). Because of capitalist relations, alienation and reification arise. Loss of the meaning of life, the degradation of character nearly to nothingness, the replacement of thought with numbers which belong to the area of work are materialized not only at the level of imagination, but also at the level of reality, befalling real human beings. And this is not limited to a single person, to Hasan Tahsin in our case, but is related to the diffusion of commodity relations, as Georg Lukács (1988) points out: "His [the worker's] fate is typical of society as a whole in that this self-objectification, this transformation of a human function into a commodity reveals in all its starkness the dehumanized and dehumanizing function of commodity relation" (92).

Hasan Tahsin's quoted monologue's order in the narrative is also profound. Hasan Tahsin is speaking in front of his colleagues, who are trying to resolve a calculation error for 12 hours, after Hasan Tahsin has been scolded by his boss Ferdi Efendi, whom he has known ever since his childhood. The traces of alienation are not limited to characters. The narrator also defines the relationship between Hasan Tahsin and İsmail Tayfur as "kinship of calculation", which resembles the discourse of the characters. So to speak, work is exceeding its natural limits, and defines even interpersonal relations; in our case, the definition embraces a strong connection such as kinship.

It must be stated that in the following chapters of the novel the themes of class relations, prosperity and money relations are preserved; however, the theme of alienation and the discourse of Hasan Tahsin, which are displayed strongly, are limited with this section of novel. Orhan Koçak also notices this section of novel. However, Koçak (1996) interprets this scene as a Romanesque instrument resulting from a shift of model in Uşaklıgil's novels, namely the influence of Balzac on Uşaklıgil: "the degrading company atmosphere is not originated from Ottoman society, it is there because of them are in Balzac's novel" (115). Although the absence of the theme of alienation in the other novels of Uşaklıgil seems to support Koçak's assertion, reflections of diverse aspects of modern economic relations in Uşaklıgil's novels and Uşaklıgil's indication that these parts are mainly the manifestations of his own life in his memoirs (Finn 1984: 107) leads us to think that this narration is far from a simple imitation or shift in model.

Ferdi Efendi, who up to here was represented as a boss, is also a father supervising his daughter's welfare and needs, and the narrator summarizes the worldview of Ferdi Efendi as such:

> He is a man; deciding that he is born to be winning, win, win anytime; never ever think that there are other things valuable then money in the world. . . . his ideas are based on the utilization of money as a purpose, and he accepts this as the only wisdom; his horizon has never broadened and his projection is limited with money.
>
> (Uşaklıgil 1984: 17)

Like reification and alienation, which we have mentioned, in the capitalist economy "money" also appears to be a "thing" that takes possession of human life. Georg Simmel (1997) argues that in modern societies "money grows to become an end itself" (235), or at least perceived like that. Simmel (1997) continues to discuss the psychological effects of money precisely:

> In the entire fabric of human purposive action there is perhaps no intermediate link in which this psychological trait of growth of the means to an end appears so purely as with money; never has a value which an object possesses only through its convertibility into others of definitive value been so completely transferred into a value itself.
>
> (235)

As a consequence of this psychological effect, like in Ferdi Efendi's case, everything can be reduced to possession of money: "From the necessity that exists throughout life to focus on the acquisition of money as the immediate goal of one's efforts, there can arise the belief that all happiness and all definitive satisfaction in life are connected with the possession of a certain sum of money" (Simmel 1997: 235).

Within the framework of this worldview Ferdi Efendi has two purposes: "To fill his safe deposit box as much as possible, and adjust his daughter to this fortune" (Uşaklıgil 1984: 41). Believing that he can possess everything, buy anything, Ferdi Efendi is not contented with providing her daughter's material needs such as clothes and finery and decoration, he also "buys" a governess for her education, a female servant for her personal grooming, and a small female child (Melakzat) to make friends with Hacer (Uşaklıgil 1984: 41). It is explicit that conceiving human beings as things once again recalls the tendency of reification. Ferdi Efendi's desire to govern, and possess everything, leads him to deny the frontiers of "private life", as can be seen in his reading of her daughter's diary without permission. Ferdi Efendi learns that his daughter is in love with İsmail Tayfur from her diary; however unexpectedly he meets her daughter's will calmly and considerately. After all, the solution to the problem is obvious for Ferdi Efendi: if his daughter will be happy, there is no objection to purchasing İsmail Tayfur. Giving him a small portion of company stock solves the problem. However, if a value scale is to be prepared for Ferdi Efendi in order to determine whether money or his daughter is more precious for him, the answer arises in the final scene of the novel, in which Ferdi Efendi's house is on fire. While Ferdi Efendi sees his daughter in blazes, he first attempts to rescue his safe deposit box, but is unable to rescue either his daughter or his safe deposit box (Uşaklıgil 1984: 174–175).

Ferdi Efendi's daughter Hacer also embraces her father's ideas, and internalizes his worldview. She also thinks that she can acquire anything she wants, and after her father's approval that she can marry İsmail Tayfur; she never thinks of any other options, including the possibility of İsmail Tayfur's refusal. İsmail Tayfur is unaware of Hacer's love, and does not know he is going to be the son-in-law of Ferdi Efendi; however Hacer does not hesitate to present herself as the fiancé of İsmail Tayfur, as it is told, because she is obsessed with the idea of possession. Of course, this excessive self-confidence, this grandiose self is the outcome of her upbringing. Hacer can possess any object she desires, and her relationship with other persons seems to be the continuum of her object relations; in other words, the object-subject distinction is disappeared at both the reality and imaginary levels. This situation can explicitly be observed in her relationship with Melekzat. Melekzat is "given" to Hacer "as a small girlfriend" (Uşaklıgil 1984: 41). In fact, Melekzat is

> such a girl, bought in order to be placed in a corner of a house like a weird statue, or as an ornament thrown away in a part of car randomly. . . . Hacer needs someone to play with, here it is Melekzat who is given to her . . . Hacer

is fond of Melekzat like a toy for her various ambitions; Melekzat is fond of
Hacer like an owner of cat of which its head is pat, ears are pulled

(Uşaklıgil 1984: 42–43)

It is clear that those verbs chosen in the quotation, "buy", "give", makes
human beings a part of object world, and words "toy", "ornament", "statue"
erase the liveliness of human beings, turns them into objects. The psychody-
namic reasons behind this situation need further attention, however it can be
asserted that behind this worldview there lies the capitalist relations and money
economy which have penetrated human psyche, and resulted as reflections of
alienation and reification.

Assigning significance to money beyond its role as an instrument of
exchange of commodities is directly related with the proliferation of capitalist relations. In this regard, the turning of means to ends, or asking money for
money can be seen in the novel in the form of matching or let us say equalizing
human beings with money. For example, Hasan Tahsin Efendi while describing Hacer, uses human qualities together with material ones: "[She has] Blue
eyes, yellow hair, [she is] white as the spring cloud, thin like water flower;
a hundred thousand liras in the form of fourteen-year-old girl! . . . A hundred thousand liras!" (Uşaklıgil 1984: 31). The same attitude can be observed
in narrator's description of Ferdi Efendi: "As Ferdi Efendi was becoming a
hundred thousand lira man, he wanted to turn his daughter into a hundred
thousand lira girl" (Uşaklıgil 1984: 41). An image of walking, speaking and
loving a hundred thousand liras is the signification of the distortion of human
relations, and this is substantial for displaying the degree of money economy's
penetration of human relations.

The final scene of the novel is also remarkable. One night, Hacer hears İsmail
Tayfur and Saniha's dialogue, and learns that İsmail Tayfur is in love with Saniha.
Realizing that the object she believes she is acquiring (she had bought) does not
belong to her leads to great self-destruction, in a hysterical crisis, Hacer does not
give permission to İsmail Tayfur to leave the home, and sets fire to her room,
and as the fire spreads together with the company bureau the house burn down.
Because of this fire, in which Hacer dies, it is notable that Ferdi Efendi loses all of
his property together with his daughter; however, as a good capitalist Ferdi Efendi
starts from the scratch. İsmail Tayfur goes mad, and continues to live while signing imaginary company documents at his writing desk.

A life deteriorated by competition: *Mai ve Siyah* (*Azure and Black*)

In *Mai ve Siyah* (*Azure and Black*), the story of lower-middle-class Ahmet Cemil,
his love to his friend Hüseyin Nazmi's sister Lamia, his aspiration to marry her,
and his attempts to publish a poetry book in order to become a well-known man
of letters, and his disappointment and failure in terms of being unable to realize
those aspirations is narrated.

His father is an advocate, and after finishing military school, he is enrolled at Mekteb-i Mülkiye (Faculty of Political Science). As İsmail Tayfur, Ahmet Cemil must work after the death of his father; his sole property is a house that his father has left. Another resemblance between the two characters is that Ahmet Cemil is also working in the private sector, not for the state as a civil servant, unlike many protagonists of Ottoman Turkish novels. In addition, his position in relations of productions makes him more prone to the negative effects of capitalism.

A significant attitude of Ahmet Cemil is that he continuously compares himself with Hüseyin Nazmi, his school friend. They are enrolled at the same school, both interested in literature; the sole distinction between the two is prosperity. Ahmet Cemil covertly envies Hüseyin Nazmi's prosperity, admiring his richness, and it can be argued that even he is clandestinely sustaining a competition with him: "Oh! He should be prosperous too. How happy Hüseyin Nazmi at all!" (69); "Oh! He should too have such a room, such a library, such books" (72). Ahmet Cemil, before graduating from school, has to earn his living by doing translations, gaining few wages, and by giving private lessons. Yet his desire to become a man of letters leads him to work in a publishing house, which is also publishing a newspaper. In these circumstances, it can be asserted that he is having an asymmetrical competition with Hüseyin Nazmi, which leads him to feelings of inadequacy. The notion of competition is also seen in *Ferdi ve Şürekâsı* (*Ferdi and His Partners*), between İsmail Tayfur and his school friends, like Ahmet Cemil and Hüseyin Nazmi; however in *Mai ve Siyah* (*Azure and Black*) the notion of competition is diffused throughout the entire narrative in a detailed way. Therefore, it can be asserted that the theme has continuity with that of Halit Ziya Uşaklıgil, and Ahmet Cemil's competitive attitude can be read as an approval of his integration into capitalist relations.

Competition, moving into the upper class and his desires are intermingled, and over-determine Ahmet Cemil's actions. Although he has not had wholehearted feelings about his boss's son Vehbi, he takes no notice of Vehbi and his sister's marriage. Besides after the death of his boss, the publishing house is owned by Vehbi, and Ahmet Cemil is promoted to the position of editor in chief of the newspaper, about to fulfill one of his desires. Afterwards he accepts Vehbi's suggestion to become a partner of publishing house, by mortgaging their "small" house, which is the sole property of his family. The basic motivation behind Ahmet Cemil's acceptance of this suggestion, as a member of the lower middle class, is his desire to move to upper class, by leaving behind the anxiety of losing his sole property. He asks himself: "Why are you afraid of using capital?" (Uşaklıgil 2003: 266). It must be remembered that while acting all the way he is thinking of Hüseyin Nazmi and his prosperity.

Ahmet Cemil, even in his love relations, is surrounded by economic compulsions. He is in love with Hüseyin Nazmi's sister Lamia; his basic motivation behind this relationship is once again his aspirations. He never talks about his feelings with Lamia, but he is dreaming of getting married to her. In his mind, his situation and lack of money hinders him from exposing his feelings. He is waiting to become prosperous in order to talk to Lamia. Lamia's setting in Ahmet Cemil's mind as an object of desire closely related to Ahmet Cemil's intrinsically competitive relationship with Hüseyin Nazmi and his admiration for Hüseyin Nazmi's assets. So once again, his desire to move into the upper class, his competitive feelings and his love are intermingled.

However, Ahmet Cemil does not acquire this result in his investments and his dreams. He loses his share in the publishing house and says farewell to his position, editor in chief, of the newspaper. Lamia marries another man, so he loses his dreams of her. In addition, in sum, he loses his imaginary competition with Hüseyin Nazmi. Robert P. Finn (1984), in his book *The Early Turkish Novel*, also considers Ahmet Cemil's dreams about literature, and interprets Ahmet Cemil's self-destruction as associated with economics:

> Ahmet Cemil is not solely the victim of economics, however, but also the evaporation of the romantic ideas which have sustained him. There are economic forces which aid in the disenchantment, to be sure, as when he is unable to sue for Lamia's hand in marriage because of penury. . . . The economic impingement on the world of the artist has been made, however, and it becomes harder and harder to ignore the new order in which Ottoman society found itself. Halid Ziya's hero signals the advent of a new system in which increasing involvement in the world of commerce and the functioning of a money-based society is to be the role of the hero.
>
> (134)

The sections related to the publishing sector are significant for displaying the "money-based society" which Finn emphasizes. While trying to gain money Ahmet Cemil is exploited by publishers: he makes translations in return for low wages, he does not get paid what he deserves, and mostly he is not paid completely and on time. He has to run after the publishers to be paid (Uşaklıgil 2003: 83). On the other hand, after his sister's husband is in charge of the publishing house Ahmet Cemil is promoted, but some of his colleagues are discharged, and Ahmet Cemil keeps silent about these releases.

> Contrasted with Ahmet Cemil's romantic world of the mind is the real one of the milieu of publishing and urban life in Istanbul at the turn of the century. The newspaper office is the arena in which the main developments of the novel occur, placed within the context of economic competition and personal rivalries.
>
> (Finn 1984: 130)

Those scenes related to the publishing sector reflect Ottoman society's incorporation into the capitalist world system as well as the level of diffusion of capitalist relations in daily life.

Vehbi represents the capitalist boss in this novel and his depictions are completely negative: Vehbi at the economic level abuses individuals, exploits them and discharges them cold-bloodedly, and in terms of personal relations, he is cruel, insensitive and malignant. İdentified as a tippler, he cheats on his wife İkbal, first with the maid Seher, then with his father's second wife, namely his stepmom, who is 16 years old. He continuously beats İkbal, she has a miscarriage, and at the end, İkbal dies because of him. Behind the loss of Ahmet Cemil's share also lies Vehbi, because he is aware that without working as editor in chief Ahmet Cemil is unable to pay his redemptions, so he discharges Ahmet Cemil on purpose, and Ahmet Cemil has to leave publishing house. In this regard, it can be asserted that Vehbi in terms of moral and social relations is more malignant and cruel than Ferdi Bey, who is also self-seeking and keen on money. The negative depictions of capital holders are striking; it can be inferred that although Uşaklıgil did not explicitly criticize capitalism, it seems that he covertly and unconsciously has taken a side in terms of social classes.

At the end of the novel, while Ahmet Cemil says farewell to his dreams of moving into the upper class, being a prosperous and well-known man of letters and marrying Lamia, he accepts becoming a civil servant, which he keeps away up to day. On the one hand being a civil servant means renouncing his dreams; on the other hand, it is a more secure life when compared to the cruel and competitive working life he left behind. In fact, when his education is taken into consideration the occupation he should naturally do seems to him as a 'recession'. However, what makes his situation more dramatic is the scene in which he encounters Hüseyin Nazmi at port when leaving Istanbul for his new duty. Hüseyin Nazmi is also beginning his new duty and leaves Istanbul. The two friends boarding ship on the same day go to different directions for their duties. While Hüseyin Nazmi is going west "to a beautiful place he is longing for", Ahmet Cemil is going to a "far" place he is assigned to, east, by a ship going to Süveyş (Suez) (Uşaklıgil 2003: 394). This encounter indicates that Ahmet Cemil also loses his imaginary competition.

Well-defined social boundaries: *Aşk-ı Memnu* (*Forbidden Love*)

In *Aşk-ı Memnu* (*Forbidden Love*), Bihter is getting married to Adnan Bey, a rich widower quite older than she is, for money. Bihter's mother Firdevs Hanım and Adnan Bey's daughter Nihal are against this marriage. Bihter does not find the happiness in her marriage, and begins to live a forbidden love relationship with Adnan's Bey young and handsome nephew Behlül. Nihal is also in love with Behlül, and soon they are engaged, which makes everything more complicated.

As it has been mentioned, critiques read *Aşk-ı Memnu* (*Forbidden Love*) in terms of westernization, and designate it as a novel narrating the lives of the upper classes of the era (Tanpınar 1988; Moran 1998; Finn 1984). Unlike these critiques, Ahmet Evin (1983) in his book titled *Origins and Development of The Turkish Novel*, asserts that the novel represents the lives of more than one class: "*Aşk-ı Memnu* is not so much a novel of a single class, as it has consistently been viewed by variety of critics, as it is of class relationships manifested in the cosmopolitan milieu of a post-Tanzimat mansion" (220). In other words, the upper-class lives of

Adnan Bey and his family, the desire of Melih Bey's family (Firdevs Hanım and her daughters) to move into the upper class, the servants working in Adnan Bey's mansion as the representatives of lower classes, and the relationship among these classes are reflected in *Aşk-ı Memnu* (*Forbidden Love*).

Firdevs Hanım and her daughters were previously rich, but after the loss of Melih Bey, because of the expenses they have incurred while not working, their wealth has ceased to exist. Through the marriage of Bihter and Adnan Bey, they find a chance to become once again members of the upper class. The meaning of this marriage can be grasped in Bihter's thoughts, reflected by narrator's indirect speech:

> Marriage with Adnan Bey meant one of the largest *yalıs* on the Bosporus. It meant the yalı which distinguished itself, as you passed in front of it, by the chandeliers, heavy curtains, inlaid Louis XV walnut chairs, lamps with huge shades and gilt tables and chairs visible from the window and by the white punts and mahogany boat drawn up in its boathouse, each with its neat cover over it.
>
> (Uşaklıgil 2001: 44)[3]

As it can be inferred from the paragraph, Bihter's attitude towards marriage is closely related with "things". Başak Deniz Özdoğan (2012) in her article titled, "Tracing the Monsters in Ottoman Turkish Novels: Reification in Halid Ziya Uşaklıgil's Novels" interprets Bihter's situation in terms of commodification and reification: "Abstracting the marriage into objects Bihter's eyes commodify the real persons, her dreams and even her body" (100). So the state of reification has a continuity in the novels of Uşaklıgil. Moreover this attitude is not limited to members of the working class; capitalist relations embrace every person from any class, which again recalls Lukács' (1988) assessment: "The fate of the worker becomes the fate of society as a whole" (91).

Although Bihter seemed to move into the upper class, by the way she behaves, in the eyes of her personnel she never ever becomes a member of upper class. She uses the power she has acquired to bring employees into line, sending them away from home, and dismissing them. She is portrayed as a nouveau riche whose eyes are dazzled by the power she has gained. In addition, as her role turns to being a "boss", she becomes a member of Uşaklıgil's negatively depicted upper classes.

On the other hand, unlike the other two novels which we are examining, there is little evidence of the working life of protagonists. The sources of Adnan Bey's wealth or where he works or in which sector he deals are unspecified; rather his hobby of wood carving is mentioned. However, even if in a line, it is mentioned that his brother (Behlül's father) is working in a village as a civil servant (Uşaklıgil 2001: 111). Therefore, Adnan Bey's wealth should not be derived from his family; however the labor or investments behind this prosperity are invisible. Additionally there is also no comment on Bihter's deceased father Melih Bey's occupation, and sources of his wealth. This silence about work and capital differentiates *Aşk-ı Memnu* (*Forbidden Love*) from *Ferdi ve Şürekâsı* (*Ferdi and his Partners*). When it comes to work or maintenance, only employees of the mansion and Kette, a chanter whom Behlül meets in his nightlife, are on the scene. The singer, cook and other employees find a place in the novel mostly through their moral judgements and attitudes towards Firdevs Hanım and Bihter and Behlül's relationship.

Since the main setting of the novel is a mansion, economic relations mostly related to the private sphere and household are represented in *Aşk-ı Memnu* (*Forbidden Love*). Compared to the other two novels, more emphasis is given to signifiers such as fashion, decoration and clothes and finery. The narrative attitude seen in the description of Hacer's room in *Ferdi ve Şürekâsı* (*Ferdi and his Partners*) (33–34) or Ahmet Cemil's aspirations about his sister İkbal's wedding in *Mai ve Siyah* (*Azure and Black*) (189–190) are diffused through the whole novel. The emphasis given to fashion, and thus to commodities, once again recalls the concept of commodity fetishism. Fashion has played a significant role in the development of capitalism and the diffusion of capitalism in daily life. Walter Benjamin (1999) pointed out the relationship between fashion and commodity fetishism as such: "Fashion prescribes the ritual according to which the commodity fetish demands to be worshipped" (8). Through fashion the relationship between commodities and individuals is regulated and manipulated; in that sense fashion can easily be related to the socio-politics of capitalism. Following these lines, it can be asserted that the predominance of fashion in Uşaklıgil's novels cannot be interpreted without considering the development and diffusion of capitalism in Ottoman society.

Conclusion

Economic transformation significantly affected Ottoman society and the consequences of the diffusion of capitalist relations in the novels can first be observed in class relations. The characters of the novels are mainly from the working class or bourgeoisie. The acceptance of 'private property' by Ottoman state is reflected as private companies in which characters ought to work in order to earn a living. The acceleration of the money economy in Ottoman society by the delivering of paper money in 1840 is also reflected in the novels. Possessing, investing, using the money is one side of this monetary relation. On the other hand, money also motivates characters at the symbolic level. As an outcome of the money economy and capitalist relations, characters' relations with other individuals and objects are disturbed, and even members of the upper classes could not escape this degradation, and are subjected to reification and fetishism of commodities. Thus, the sources of unhappiness of the characters are closely related to the consequences of capitalist relations. In that sense, Uşaklıgil's characters demonstrate that Ottoman society has been integrated into the capitalist system.

A more comprehensive and holistic study about Halit Ziya Uşaklıgil's novels, moreover, about the Servet-i Fünun period based on economic relations, is yet needed. However, in this study, though we deal only with three novels of Uşaklıgil, at least we observe some of the basic phenomena related to the modern economy. It can be asserted that exploitation, moving to the upper class, alienation and reification, the money economy, competition and fashion are the consequences of the modern economy which have negative effects on the human psyche; these are handled and reflected by Uşaklıgil in a modern genre, namely the novel. Uşaklıgil's comprehension and reflection of these phenomena requires a revision of assumptions about Uşaklıgil in particular, and Servet-i Fünun in general, that literature of this era is apolitical and far from social.

Notes

1 By considering those basic concepts one can presume that Ahmet Mithat's way of understanding 'economics' connotes Weberian Protestant ethics. See Deniz T. Kılınçoğlu. "Weber, Veblen ve Ahmet Mithat Efendi'nin Kahramanları" (Weber, Veblen and the Characters of Ahmet Mithat Efendi). Eyüp Özveren (ed.) *Kurumsal İktisat* (Institutional Economics). İstanbul: İmge Yayınevi, 2006, pp. 441–472.
2 "Alafranga" is a term designating upper-class persons who were extremely westernized, used widely by many writers and critiques.
3 Translation of the paragraph is taken from Robert P. Finn (1984: 136–137).

Bibliography

Benjamin, W. (1999), "Paris, the Capital of the Nineteenth Century", in W. Benjamin (ed.), *The Arcades Project*, Cambridge, MA: Harvard University Press, 3–13.
Evin, A. Ö. (1983), *Origins and Development of the Turkish Novel*, Minneapolis, MN: Bibliotheca Islamica.
Finn, R. P. (1984), *The Early Turkish Novel 1872–1900*, İstanbul: Isis Press.
Kasaba, R. (1993), *Osmanlı İmparatorluğu ve Dünya Ekonomisi: On Dokuzuncu Yüzyıl*, K. Emiroğlu (trans.), İstanbul: Belge Yayınları.
Koçak, O. (1996, Autumn), "Kaptırılmış İdeal: Mai ve Siyah Üzerine Psikanalitik Bir Deneme", *Toplum ve Bilim*, 70: 94–152.
Kudret, C. (1998), *Türk Edebiyatında Hikâye ve Roman*, İstanbul: İnkılap Kitabevi.
Lukács, G. (1988), *History and Class Consciousness*, R. Livingstone (trans.), Cambridge, MA: The MIT Press.
Mardin, Ş. (2000), "Tanzimat'tan Sonra Aşırı Batılılaşma", in *Türk Modernleşmesi*, İstanbul: İletişim Yayınları, 21–79.
Marx, K., (1977 [1867]), *Capital, a Critique of Political Economy*, vol. 1, New York: Vintage Books.
Moran, B. (1998), "Alafranga Züppeden Alafranga Haine", in *Türk Romanına Eleştirel Bir Bakış 1*, İstanbul: İletişim Yayınları, 196–202.
Naci, F. (2000), "Aşk-ı Memnu", in *Yüzyılın 100 Romanı*, İstanbul: Adam Yayınları, 47–53.
Özdoğan, B. D. (2012), "Tracing the Monsters in Ottoman Turkish Novels: Reification in Halid Ziya Uşaklıgil's Novels", in S. Alcorn and S. Nardi (eds.), *Twisted Mirrors: Monstrous Reflections of Humanity*, Inter-Disciplinary Press, 95–102.
Pamuk, Ş. (1988), *100 Soruda Osmanlı-Türkiye İktisadî Tarihi 1500–1914*, İstanbul: Gerçek Yayınevi.
Simmel, G. (1997), "On the Psychology of Money", in D. Frisby and M. Featherstone (eds.), *Simmel on Culture: Selected Writings*, London: Sage Publications, 233–243.
Tanpınar, A. H. (1988), "Hâlid Ziya Uşaklıgil", in Z. Kerman (ed.), *Edebiyat Üzerine Makaleler*, İstanbul: Dergâh Yayınları, 275–278.

Uşaklıgil, H. Z. (1984), *Ferdi ve Şürekâsı*, İstanbul: İnkılâp ve Aka.
Uşaklıgil, H. Z. (1987), *Kırk Yıl*, İstanbul: İnkılâp Kitabevi.
Uşaklıgil, H. Z. (2001), *Aşk-ı Memnu*, İstanbul: Özgür Yayınları.
Uşaklıgil, H. Z. (2003), *Mai ve Siyah*, İstanbul: Özgür Yayınları.
Wallerstein, I., Decdeli, H. and Kasaba, R. (2004), "The Incorporation of the Ottoman Empire Into the World Economy", in Huri İslamoğlu-İnan (ed.), *The Ottoman Empire and the World Economy*, Cambridge: Cambridge University Press, 88–97.

12 Mechanization experience in agriculture in Turkey

The Pomegranate on the Knoll[1]

Selin Seçil Akin[2] and Işil Şirin Selçuk[3]

Yaşar Kemal, who usually focuses on the problems of the people who live and work in Çukurova, a little city in the Mediterranean region of Turkey, tells the story of a group of peasants dealing with the side effects of the mechanization of agriculture in *The Pomegranate on the Knoll* (2006). Examination of economics and literature together is a known approach. For instance, Stephen Ziliak assigns *The Grapes of Wrath* (2009) by John Steinbeck as a microeconomic course book. A. Atik (2008) analyzes machine metaphors in popular culture including cinema, computer games and literature. P.A. Cantor's paper (1994) "Hyperinflation and Hyper reality: Thomas Mann in Light of Austrian Economics" uses Thomas Mann's short story (1925), "Disorder and Sorrow", to analyze Ludwig von Mises' theory of inflation. C. Chavagneux (2012) uses Charles Dickens' *Hard Times* (1854) to understand the behaviour of individuals, particularly based on utilitarianism in the period of industrial revolution. In this paper, we plan to contribute to this approach with the example of *The Pomegranate on the Knoll*. We aim to interpret that both economics and literature are complements of each other to understand the mechanization process of agriculture in Turkey during 1950s.[4] We do so by showing the similarities between the theory of mechanization and the plot as well as the parallelism between economic history and the storyline in the novel. The novel discusses the obstacles of seasonal work in cotton production, and the unemployment problem caused by mechanization. It also gives historical context about tractor use in agriculture in Turkey, and reflects Marx's view on mechanization.

In the first part, we present a literature review of mechanization and machine breakers. The story in the novel can be related to the Marxist theory of mechanization, which makes a connection between the use of machines in the production and dismissal of workers. It is also necessary to examine the mechanization in the work of David Ricardo, to whom Karl Marx refers, and Adam Smith, to whom Ricardo refers. Therefore, we analyze the evolution of economic theory regarding the subject of mechanization from Adam Smith to Karl Marx.

We then investigate the mechanization process of agriculture in the economic history of Turkey. We can see that mechanization was a priority in agriculture in Turkey during the early 1950s. The symbol of agricultural development was the tractor. Turkey imported tractors, which were sent as the first goods within the scope of the Marshall Plan with the help of foreign resources in 1949. There was a big increase in the number of tractors between the years 1948–52 because loans were used for buying imported machines. As a result, there was a rise in acres of land that were planted and harvested in those years. While this situation caused an increase in the income of "big farmers", it created an unemployment problem for seasonal workers. Afterwards, this resulted in migration from rural to urban areas.

Finally, we make a connection between economic theory, the process of mechanization in agriculture, and the novel. The significance of this novel is that it emphasizes the problem of unemployment caused by mechanization in Turkish agriculture during the early 1950s. The spread of tractors had a negative impact on the lives of seasonal workers. Their only hope for solving their problems was the mystical pomegranate tree that was mentioned by an old peasant.

Mechanization and machine breaking

Mechanization has been an important issue for the history of economic literature. Out of his contemporaries, Marx was the most concerned with the effect of mechanization on employment. To understand Marx's view on mechanization we should review classical economic thought as well.

According to Smith, the division of labor increases the quantity of work, which has three reasons. Firstly, it leads to a rise in the ability of workers. Secondly, it saves the time which is lost by passing work from one to another. Finally, it results in the invention of machines which enables one laborer to do the work done by more than one person earlier. If the proper machine is used, the required labor decreases, and the work becomes easy. The root of machine use is division of labor (Smith 1776: 21–24).

He mentions that capital can yield profit or revenue in two ways, as fixed capital and circulating capital. Buying machines can be considered as an example of fixed capital. Smith examines the sort of capital in agriculture as follows: "That part of the capital of the farmer which is employed in the instruments of agriculture is fixed, that which is employed in the wages and maintenance of his laboring servants is a circulating capital" (Smith 1776: 364–365).

To understand Smith's view on mechanization, we should examine his classification of general stock. The general stock of any country or society is divided into three parts. The first part is used only for immediate consumption, and it yields no revenue. The second part is fixed capital, which does not circulate but yields revenue. It includes four objects: "all useful machines and instruments of trade which facilitate and abridge labor", "all those profitable buildings which are the means of procuring revenue", "the improvements of land", and "the acquired and useful abilities of all the inhabitants or members of the society". The last part of general stock is circulating capital, which both circulates and yields revenue. It consists of four articles: money, provisions, materials and finished work (Smith 1776: 367–369).

Beside the point that Smith gives importance to machines, he also emphasizes that fixed capital cannot make profit without circulating capital:

> Every fixed capital is both originally derived from, and requires to be continually supported by a circulating capital. All useful machines and instruments of trade are originally derived from a circulating capital, which furnishes the materials of which they are made, and the maintenance of the workmen who make them. They require, too, a capital of the same kind to keep them in constant repair.
>
> No fixed capital can yield any revenue but by means of a circulating capital. The most useful machines and instruments of trade will produce nothing without the circulating capital, which affords the materials they are employed upon, and the maintenance of the workmen who employ them. Land, however improved, will yield no revenue without a circulating capital, which maintains the laborers who cultivate and collect its produce.
>
> (Smith 1776: 370)

In 1817 Ricardo published the first edition of his work *On the Principles of Political Economy and Taxation* (1817), arguing that mechanization would lead to be a benefit of the laborers by lowering prices. He had claimed that mechanization would lower production costs by increasing productivity so that this process would lower the prices of commodities. This would lead to an increase on the real income. Therefore, machinery was beneficial to all the different classes including laborers.

> The class of laborers also, I thought, was equally benefited by the use of machinery, as they would have the means of buying more commodities with the same money wages, and I thought that no reduction of wages would take place, because the capitalist would have the power of demanding and employing the same quantity of labor as before, although he might be under the necessity of employing it in the production of a new, or at any rate of a different commodity.
>
> (Ricardo 1817: 392)

However, there is an important change on his opinions in edition 3 of the book with a new chapter called "On Machinery". In this chapter, David Ricardo changes his view that machines are advantageous to all societies.

> My mistake arose from the supposition, that whenever the net income of a society increased, its gross income would also increase; I now, however, see reason to be satisfied that the one fund, from which landlords and capitalists derive their revenue, may increase, while the other, that upon which the laboring class mainly depend, may diminish, and therefore it follows, if I am right, that the same cause which may increase the net revenue of the country,

may at the same time render the population redundant, and deteriorate the condition of the laborer.

(Ricardo 1817: 388)

Therefore, an increase in the net income of a society does not necessarily mean that its gross income would increase as well. Moreover, by using machines, the laborer class becomes unemployed. According to Ricardo, the reasons that capitalists tend to use machines can be harmful for laborers. Capitalists need to increase the rate of profit by using less labor and substituting for machines. In this respect, an increase in the price of labor would lead to an increase in the use of machinery.

> With every increase of capital and population, food will generally rise, on account of its being more difficult to produce. The consequence of a rise of food will be a rise of wages, and every rise of wages will have a tendency to determine the saved capital in a greater proportion than before to the employ-ment of machinery. Machinery and labor are in constant competition, and the former can frequently not be employed until labor rises.
>
> (Ricardo 1817: 395)

Marx describes a machine as a "mechanism that, after being set in motion, per-forms with its tools the same operations as the worker formerly did with similar tools" (Marx 2001: 535). However, he opposed the idea that the machine is the sophisticated version of tools. He also disagrees with the classification of these two forms according to which mode of power (human power or natural power or machine power) they use:

> Mathematicians and mechanicians, and in this they are followed by a few English economists, call a tool a simple machine, and a machine a complex tool. They see no essential difference between them, and even give the name of machine to the simple mechanical powers, the lever, the inclined plane, the screw, the wedge, &c. As a matter of fact, every machine is a combina-tion of those simple powers, no matter how they may be disguised. From the economic standpoint this explanation is worth nothing, because the histori-cal element is wanting. Another explanation of the difference between tool and machine is that in the case of a tool, man is the motive power, while the motive power of a machine is something different from man, as, for instance, an animal, water, wind, and so on. According to this, a plough drawn by oxen, which is a contrivance common to the most different epochs, would be a machine, while Claussen's circular loom, which, worked by a single laborer, weaves 96,000 picks per minute, would be a mere tool. Nay, this very loom, though a tool when worked by hand, would, if worked by steam, be a machine.
>
> (Marx 2001: 532)

The development and improvement of machinery led not to increasing exchange value but to raising the quantity of production. Using more machines in the production process increases the productivity of the labor force. Therefore, all the capitalists want to increase the use of machines in order to raise profits, which provokes a competition between them. This competition leads to more use of machines, and more division of labor. This continuing increase in the division of labor forces laborers to compete because now one laborer can do the work that can be done by more laborers previously. At the same time, work becomes simpler and uniform and wages decrease. Eventually, the art of the work becomes valueless. Therefore, the labor force becomes unskilled (Marx 1992: 42–50).

According to the Marxist view, machinery is not different from other constant capital. It only adds its own value to the product, and it does not create surplus value. Even if the cost of machine is equal to the labor power substituted by machine, labor materialized in it is less than the living labor it replaces (Marx 2001).

Machine use profoundly transforms the structure of the production process and increases exploitation in different ways. Firstly, capitalists employ children and women instead of men because machines reduce the need for muscular power (Marx 2001). By using the cheaper labor power of children and women, they intensify the exploitation. Secondly, machines enable the increase of labor productivity and shorten the required labor time, so at the same time it allows capitalists to enjoy profit by prolonging the working day (Marx 2001). Machines can increase surplus value by decreasing the number of laborers employed by a capitalist. Capitalists will also increase the length of the working day in addition to the use of machines to raise surplus value (Marx 2001). However, society will react to this, and as a result, they will return to the old working-day hours. Then, we face the other effect of mechanization, the intensification of labor (Marx 2001).

As Marx (2001) claimed, with the use of the machine, the competition, and the fight between machine and labor has started. The reason behind this is that machines are the material basis of the capitalist mode of production. Mechanization extends the use of capital while it causes dismissal of workers in the same proportion or decrease in the price of labor power.

These effects of mechanization can result in a movement called machine wrecking. Throughout history, the examples of machine-wrecking activities can be observed. Machine wrecking, which is sometimes called Luddite, is a reactionary attitude against the machines. Eric Hobsbawm's article "The Machine Breakers" (1952) characterizes Luddite as an effective collective bargaining by riot and describes wrecking as a simply a technique of trade unionism in the period before, and during the early phases of, the industrial revolution. He defines two types of machine breaking. In the first one, they are not hostile to machines but they are against employers. On the other hand, the second sort of wrecking implies hostility to new machines, especially labor-saving ones (Hobsbawm 1952).

> I think [it is] fair to claim that collective bargaining by riot was at least as effective as any other means of bringing trade union pressure, and probably

more effective than any other means available before the era of national trade unions to such groups as weavers, seamen and coal-miners.

(Hobsbawm 1952: 66)

Laborers thought that some machines posed a threat to their livelihoods. In the 17th century in Europe laborers revolted against the ribbon loom. In 1758 the workers who were dismissed because of this machine set a wool-shearing machine on fire. In the very beginning of the 19th century, a Luddite movement occurred against the power-loom and these machines were destroyed (Marx 2001). However, these struggles should not be against machines but against the capitalist use of them. It took a long time for this to be understood by the workers:

It took both time and experience before the workpeople learnt to distinguish between machinery and its employment by capital and to direct their attacks, not against the material instruments of production, but against the mode in which they are used.

(Marx 2001)

The problem is not directly related to the machine but to the capitalist use of it. Marx identified the problem with the private ownership of machines by capitalists. Therefore, it is the capitalist, not the machine, who shortens employment. Although machines are "the victory of man over the forces of Nature", capitalist use of them can hurt labor (Marx 2001).

There are two consolations in the process of mechanization. Firstly, the fact that laborers consider this situation as temporary seems as a consolation. Nevertheless, it can be a permanent problem. The other consolation is that machines acquire the whole production area systematically. That limits their destructive effects. However, these two consolations constitute a contradiction because the slow 'step by step occupation of mechanization makes this situation a chronic problem. In addition, the temporary influence of mechanization becomes permanent since machines continuously enter new production areas. As a result, laborers revolt against the instrument of labor (Marx 2001).

In this section, we discussed classical economic thought on the process of mechanization. Now, we will examine how Turkey experienced this process in agriculture during the early 1950s.

Agricultural mechanization in Turkey

After the Second World War, in the second half of the 20th century, the world experienced profound changes in the organization of economic activity. As Eric Hobsbawm mentions in *Age of Extremes*, "The Social Revolution 1945–1990, portrays the most dramatic and far-reaching social change of the second half of this [20th] century as the 'death of the peasantry' which cuts us off forever from the world of the past" (Hobsbawm 1994: 289). Turkey also faced shifts in politics, economic policies, culture and socio-economic classes in this period.

The first use of machines (steam engines) in Turkey was during the Balkan War and the following years. After World War I, around 60 motor ploughs were imported to increase grain production. In the early stage of the Republic, the Ministry of Agriculture gave subsidies to farmers to buy tractors. The number of tractors increased between 1950 and 1953 because of liberalization of international trade and foreign aid like the Marshall Plan (SPO 1962: 7–8). The tractor, which saves animal and human power, was the symbol of agricultural mechanization.

Although Turkey had reserves more than twice its import volume and a 100 million dollar international trade surplus in 1946, the country received foreign aid, first under the Truman Doctrine and then under the Marshall Plan (Boratav 2009: 99). At the root of foreign aid, there is an 'intervention', which is done for 'underdeveloped countries' to make them reach the level of 'developed countries' within the framework of 'modernization theory' (Tören 2008: 182–183). The Marshall Plan had an important role in the deepening of capitalist relations in Turkey. It was implemented with activities such as the import of agricultural machinery, the modernization of agriculture, irrigation construction and road construction activities. Policies were stated by the Democrat Party to the advantage of big landowners against small farmers (Boratav 2009: 105). Although big landowners could easily buy tractors, small farmers could also buy tractors with the aid of loans given by Ziraat Bank (Oktar and Varlı 2010: 12). However, we speculate that our story was before those small farmers could buy tractors due to two reasons. Firstly, the protagonists just meet with tractors so this period should be the beginning of this progress. Small farmers were able to acquire tractors in the following stages of mechanization. Secondly, we do not have any example of small peasants who take loans to buy tractors in the novel.

The transformation of the capitalist process of accumulation after the Second World War included both private sectors' industrialization strategy and was a part of Truman Doctrine and Marshall Plan (Tören 2008: 190). The aim of foreign aid as part of the Marshall Plan was to increase the capacity of agricultural production in Turkey (Oktar and Varlı 2010: 11 transferred from Çavdar). This aim was appropriate to the Democrat Party's targets and policies. As shown in Figure 12.1, the number of tractors increased especially between the years 1948–1953.

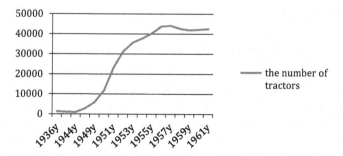

Figure 12.1 The number of tractors

The figures below are derived from the data of a 1952 survey.[5] The average number of houses and the average population are shown in Table 12.1.

Regarding this issue, the Çukurova area is an important area to observe and research these facts. Çukurova plain covers the cities of Adana, Mersin, Osmaniye and Hatay with the rivers of Seyhan and Ceyhan. This region is one of the most important and productive agricultural areas, especially in cotton production, of modern Turkey as well as in the former periods. Therefore, when examining the socio-economic impacts of agricultural mechanization, the area of Çukurova must be taken into account.

In the Mediterranean region, where Çukurova is located, agriculture has been the main industry in the regional economy. In the region, high economic value agricultural products are grown and for this reason it becomes desirable to invest in the region. Thus, the Mediterranean region is a good example of the rise in tractors between 1948 and 1951. According to survey data, approximately 200 tractors were added between those years in the Mediterranean region (Figure 12.2).

In the 1950s, landowners could get cheap loans. Tractors were sold not under simple market conditions but they were purchased by loans (Keyder 1983: 142). Besides this, with the aid of machine imports, mechanization in agriculture gained speed in Çukurova. Robinson, in his study in 1952, summarizes this situation as follows:

> The Chukurova thrives on cotton. It was to increase the production of this foreign exchange-yielding crop that the Marshall Plan turned the Chukurova

Table 12.1 Sample of 1952 survey

Region	Number of average houses	Average population
Central Anatolia	145	852
Mediterranean	145	837
Aegean	287	1,257
Marmara	198	1,016
Southeastern Anatolia	83	465
Black Sea	161	1,412

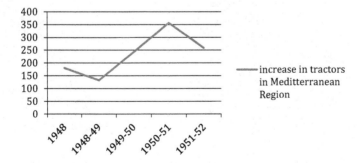

Figure 12.2 Increase of tractors in Mediterranean region

into the most heavily mechanized area of comparable size in Turkey, perhaps of the Middle East. Of the 6,500 tractors imported into the country since 1948 under ECA auspices, between 1,200 and 1,500 have found their way to the Chukurova. Latest tally indicates that 3,720 machines are now at work on Chukurova farms. This total represents a 460 per cent increase over the 1948–1952 period.

(Robinson 1952: 451)

This led the landowners to dismiss the sharecroppers from the terrain. This situation can be seen in the results of the above-mentioned survey (Figure 12.3). Migrant agricultural laborers who came from surrounding mountains or plains were employed in the cotton work. In those years cotton producers took the advantage of price recovery caused by the Korean War and raised their profit (Zürcher 2000: 331).

The 1946–1953 period could be described as agricultural development years. It is obvious that tractor use in agriculture led to a rise in cultivated land. According to a 1952 survey, this ratio was 66% and as decares it was 308,835 in Mediterranean region where Çukurova is. The fields in which cotton was planted in Mediterranean region increased approximately 200,000 decares from 1948 to 1951 (Figure 12.4).

However, the other side of mechanization was a decrease in employment. The number of laborers who were employed by farmers fell sharply between 1948 and 1952 in the Mediterranean region (Figure 12.5). Instead of permanent workers, temporary workers were preferred because tractor use is a kind of labor-saving machine. The next section considers the unemployment problem during the process of mechanization in Turkish agriculture, which is discussed in this section, by telling the storyline of the novel.

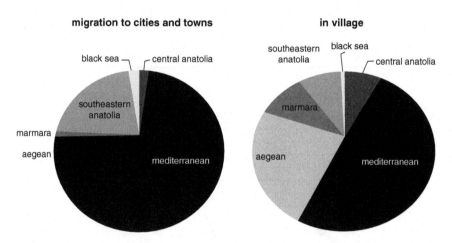

Figure 12.3 The number and the region of sharecroppers' unemployment as a result of tractor use

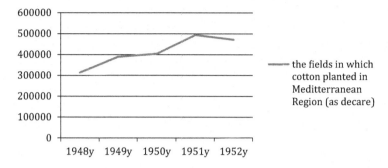

Figure 12.4 Cotton-planted fields in the Mediterranean region

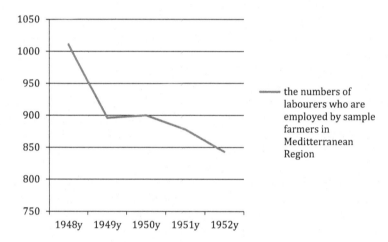

Figure 12.5 The number of laborers employed by sample farmers in the Mediterranean region

Yaşar Kemal and *The Pomegranate on the Knoll*

Yasar Kemal usually writes about the people that live in Çukurova and their economic and social problems. He explains the reason as "the one who doesn't write his/her own Çukurova cannot become an important writer".[6] We believe that he says so because he knows the social life and the problems of this area, which is close to his hometown, very well. He is best known for a series of novels named *Ince Memed* (*Mehmet, My Hawk*), which tells the peasants' struggle against landlordism. In this paper, we focus on his lesser-known novel *The Pomegranate on the Knoll*. He describes the novel as "one of my best works in which nature and human relationship is described" (Kemal 2006).[7]

The Pomegranate on the Knoll (2006), which is written by Yaşar Kemal, is the story of five people – one of them is a child – who went to Çukurova to find work. The novel emphasizes the problem of unemployment, which resulted from mechanization in the agriculture sector. It is the story of peasants from a mountain village that decide to go to Çukurova to work because the seeds in their land are decayed. They sell the only goat they have in the hope of buying more than one goat after coming from Çukurova. They do not believe that they will not find work because the previous year's landowners needed a lot of laborers. Despite the threat of malaria, they go to Çukurova. One of their companions is a child, a sheep man, who suffered from a landowner.

When they reach a farm in Çukurova they see several tractors, harvesters, ploughs, carriages and lorries. We can understand from the brand names Massey-Harris and Ferguson that they are imported within the frame of the Marshall Plan. They learn that the woman landowner, who employed Memet two years ago, fired almost all laborers. A labourer exaggerates the effect of machines on the landowner by saying that 'she falls in love with the machines' (Kemal 2006:17–18). We also witness an example of machine breaking. Lame Dursun breaks the head of a Massey-Harris machine. After this, he is put in jail. The only employed laborer is a driver who operates those machines. Landowners dismiss sharecroppers from their lands. They also learn that another landowner has sold all oxen when he bought a harvester. They curse and spit on a machine they see on the road by saying "Damn Çukurova, damn the machines" (Kemal 2006: 25).

Economic relations are not always regulated under market conditions but sometimes they are regulated according to the principle of reciprocity. In this novel, protagonists help a peasant who is thrashing and this peasant gives food to the protagonists. Polanyi gives information about reciprocity as follows:

> Reciprocity and redistribution are able to ensure the working of an economic system without the help of written records and elaborate administration only because the organization of the societies in question meets the requirements of such a solution with the help of patterns such as symmetry and centricity. Reciprocity is enormously facilitated by the institutional pattern of symmetry, a frequent feature of social organization among nonliterate peoples. The striking "duality" which we find in tribal subdivisions lends itself to the pairing out of individual relations and thereby assists the give-and-take of goods and services in the absence of permanent records.
>
> (Polanyi 2001: 51)

When they meet an old man, he offers some small work for them because machines cannot harvest leaning crops. They begin to hope again, and they believe that they can find work and earn money. They meet with many laborers like them who look for work. All the laborers are hungry, poor and they are all surprised by the new situation. Everywhere is full of tractors, harvesters, ploughs, carriages and lorries. They see dead people who could not stand these conditions since working conditions in Çukurova are bad. The weather is too hot, and there is a high risk of catching malaria. However, they do not want to give up hope. They visit almost all villages in Çukurova to find work. Unfortunately, they returned from almost everywhere empty-handed. Another side of this story is that there is a child who faces unfairness in his village. He hopes that he would never face unfairness again in Çukurova. To be sure, he asks the farmer whether he can get his money from work.

They realize that after these tractors come, people are changed at once and they become completely different. Even they are not looking the faces of the other people; they only adore these machines. All these examples show that working conditions and unemployment affected people psychologically.

They face reality when they see one of the big landowners who insults them. In this point, it is understood that the problem is not machines themselves but the capitalist use of them. The landowner says, "long live [Marshal] Marshall" during his speech. This is another indication that the tractors are imported within the frame of the Marshall Plan.

When they see a village with trees, their hope is kindled again. In this village, an old peasant mentions a pomegranate tree that will solve their problems of unemployment, malaria and bad living conditions. Their only hope is finding this tree, which is mystical and powerful, they believe. Now they had one more purpose besides finding a job: to find the pomegranate tree. They believe that if they can find the pomegranate tree, they would both find work and fight Yusuf's malaria. It reflects the Anatolian people's superstitions and mystical beliefs as intensively used in literature.

While searching for the tree, they meet a truck farmer who accompanies them. They learn at the truck farm that such a tree does not exist. A guest who comes to the truck farm tells them all the trees are removed. He says in mentioning Çukurova, "There is nothing sacred in this plain anymore, and neither is the pomegranate tree" (Kemal 2006: 86).

They are disappointed when they hear that the pomegranate tree does not really exist. However, they still want to believe it exists and they keep going to find it. Finally, they find the roots of a pomegranate tree. They pray at the roots of it. On the other hand, the child worker is so frustrated that he does not participate. His expectations are wasted. The next morning the others cannot find the child. He escapes with the dagger. Finally, they return to their village disappointed and without hope.

The connection between the novel and economic context

The Pomegranate on the Knoll offers examples of several problems linked with employment relations, provides highlights about the context of economic history of Turkey, and reflects Marx's view on mechanization. Kemal (2006) discusses both the unemployment problem because of mechanization and the obstacles of seasonal work. In addition, we witness capitalist use of machines, child labor and bad working conditions including illnesses while the protagonists search for work.

The novel focuses on the labor in cotton production, setting the social dynamics in Çukurova area. In this area, seasonal work is very common. Seasonal agricultural workers go to Çukurova at a specific time of the year, saving the money that they earn during this period, and using it for their consumption for the rest of the year. Hence, job security was a problem for them even before the process of mechanization. We understand that there is an unemployment problem in this mountain village because the main characters know that their only chance of being employed is through the seasonal job in Çukurova.

Kemal (2006) focuses on the way Turkey experiences mechanization in the 1950s. Turkey received tractors from abroad as a part of the Marshall Plan. Landowners in Çukurova also take advantage of using tractors instead of manpower because it increases the labor productivity in cotton production. However, it also leaves seasonal workers without a job.

The novel reflects how social relations of production change with the mechanization of the agricultural system. With the high use of tractors in agriculture, employers need less labor power in the production of cotton. This is the main problem that peasants face in addition to the regular problems of seasonal work, such as lower wages, bad working conditions and long work hours. We can see the examples of Marx's argument about the competition between machines and laborers through the competition between tractors and seasonal workers. The problem is related to the private ownership of tractors by the landowners. After the use of tractors, landowners need fewer laborers, which is also parallel to Marx's argument. In the novel, we can also observe the example of machine breaking, which is discussed above. Peasants blame tractors for being unemployed, and one of them, Lame Dursun, breaks the property owner's tractor.

Conclusion

Economic phenomena are not only treated by economic theories but they are also the subjects of literature and art pieces. In this paper, we analyze how economics and literature explain the social and economic aspects of the mechanization process in different ways with the help of *The Pomegranate on the Knoll*. This novel strongly reflects the economic transformation in Turkey in the first half of 1950s via the laborers who try to find a job in Çukurova. Despite its positive effects on productivity, the tractor has also been the cause of unemployment problem in the agriculture sector.

Kemal's (2006) words underline the unemployment problem in this area, and how this influences the peasant's life throughout the novel. The readers can imagine the social consequences of unemployment because literature can dramatize the social dimensions of economic problems. The protagonists cannot find jobs, they face bad conditions in Çukurova, and their families need money. Economic theory can emphasize these problems; however, it does not include the social interaction between people, and the feelings of people as a response to the economic problems.

These parts can be complemented with the help of other social sciences such as history, political science, sociology, anthropology and psychology. Literature, art and cinema also contribute to the understanding of economics. In these cases, literature can be more useful compared to economics in focusing on social aspects of economic problems.

On the other hand, economic theory can bring explanations that are more useful to the problem. In the literature, we know that with the high use of tractors, peasants cannot find a job that easily. Nevertheless, we do not have the direct causal relation in the novel. Economic theory can provide a theoretical explanation to this relation. Moreover, economic theory can offer real-life examples from that historical period.

Our study shows that economics can collaborate with other social sciences, and take cultural and social aspects of that period into account in order to explain economic facts in history. Therefore, this paper explains how the process of mechanization in Turkish agriculture led to an unemployment problem in Çukurova during early 1950s by following an approach that uses the collaboration of literature and economics.

Notes

1 We are grateful to Altug Yalcintas, Murat Baskici and Burcu Yilmaz for their comments and suggestions. The usual disclaimers apply: the authors are solely responsible for any remaining errors and omissions.
2 Ankara University, UMass Amherst
3 Abant Izzet Baysal University
4 Although time is not given in the novel, we understand that the event was taking place in the very beginning of 1950s.
5 *Türkiye'de Zirai Makinalasma* (results of a survey conducted by the Ankara University, Faculty of Political Science), Ankara.
6 Milliyet – 03.10.2012: http://gundem.milliyet.com.tr/-cukurova-sini-yazmayan-hicbir-yazar-buyuk-romanci-olamaz-/gundem/gundemdetay/03.10.2012/1605890/default.htm
7 It is a quotation received from the Turkish edition of the novel.

Bibliography

Atik, A. (2008), "Marx'da Makine Metaforu (Machine Metaphor in Marx's Theory)", (Yüksek Lisans Tezi-Master's Degree Thesis), Ankara Üniversitesi Sosyal Bilimler Enstitüsü, Ankara.

Boratav, K. (2009), *Türkiye İktisat Tarihi (Turkish Economic History)*, Ankara: İmge.

Cantor, P. A. (1994), "Hyperinflation and Hyperreality: Thomas Mann in Light of Austrian Economics", *The Review of Austrian Economics*, 7 (1): 3–29, http://EconPapers.repec.org/RePEc:kap:revaec:v:7:y:1994:i:1:p:3-29 (accessed July 23, 2014)

Chavagneux, C. (2012), "Pour l'Economie Politique", http://alternatives-economiques.fr/blogs/chavagneux/2012/02/08/dickens-et-les- economistes/ (accessed July 23, 2014)

Devlet Planlama Teskilati (State Planning Organization) (SPO) (1962), "Tarım Makinaları İmalatı Sanayii Birinci Beş Yıllık Kalkınma Planı (Agriculture Machinery Manufacture First Five-Year Development Plan) (1963–1967)", Yardımcı Çalışmaları, 22 Ekim, 1962, Ankara.

Hobsbawm, E. J. (1952), "The Machine Breakers", *Past and Present*, 1 (1): 57–70.

Hobsbawm, E. J. (1994), *Age of Extremes: The Short Twentieth Century, 1914–1991*, London: Abacus.

Kemal, Y. (2006), *Hüyükteki Nar Ağacı (The Pomegranate on the Knoll)*, İstanbul: Yapı Kredi Yayınları.

Keyder, Ç. (1983), "The Cycle of Sharecropping and Consolidation of Small Peasant Ownership in Turkey", *Journal of Peasant Studies*, 10 (2–3): 130–145.

Marx, K. (1992), *Ücretli Emek ve Sermaye (Wage Labor and Capital)*, S. Belli (trans.), Ankara: Sol Yayınları.

Marx, K. (2001), *Capital*, vol. I, London: Electronic Book Company, http://site.ebrary.com/lib/ankarauniv/docDetail.action?docID=2001687 (accessed July 23, 2014).

Milliyet (2012, October 3), "Çukurova'sını yazmayan hiçbir yazar büyük romancı olamaz" (The One Who Doesn't Write His/Her Own Çukurova Cannot Become an Important Writer), http://gundem.milliyet.com.tr/-cukurova-sini-yazmayan-hicbir-yazar-buyuk-romanci-olamaz/gundem/gundemdetay/03.10.2012/1605890/default.htm (accessed July 23, 2014).

Oktar, S. and Varlı, A. (2010), "Türkiye'de 1950–54 Döneminde Demokrat Parti'nin Tarım Politikası" (Agricultural Policy of Democrat Party in 1950–54 Period in Turkey), *Marmara Üniversitesi İ.İ.B.F. Dergisi*, XXVIII (1): 1–22.

Polanyi, K. (2001), *Great Transformation: The Political & Economic Origins of Our Time*, Boston, MA: Beacon Press, http://site.ebrary.com/lib/ankarauniv/docDetail.action?docID=10014733 (accessed July 23, 2014).

Ricardo, D. (1817), *On the Principles of Political Economy and Taxation*, 3rd edition, London: Electric Book Company, http://site.ebrary.com/lib/ankarauniv/docDetail.action?docID=2001615 (accessed July 23, 2014).

Robinson, R. D. (1952), "Tractors in the Village: A Study in Turkey", *Journal of Farm Economics*, 34 (4): 451–462.

Smith, A. (1776), *Wealth of Nations*, London: Electric Book Company, Available at: http://site.ebrary.com/lib/ankarauniv/Doc?id=2001574&ppg=369 (accessed July 23, 2014).

Tören, T. (2008), "Dış Yardım (Foreign Aid)", in F. Başkaya and A. Ördek (eds.), *Ekonomik Kurumlar ve Kavramlar Sözlüğü: Eleştirel Bir Giriş*, Ankara: Maki Basın Yayın.

Türkiye'de *Zirai Makinalasma (Agricultural Mechanization in Turkey)* (1954) (results of a survey conducted by the Ankara University, Faculty of Political Science), Ankara: A.U.S.B.F Yayını, 39–21.

Ziliak, S. (2009), "Introduction to Microeconomics Syllabus", http://sites.roosevelt.edu/sziliak/files/2011/11/Ziliak-The-Grapes-of-Wrath-course-Econ-102-syllabus-Fall-2009.pdf (accessed July 23, 2014).

Zürcher, E. J. (2000), *Modernleşen Türkiye'nin Tarihi (Turkey: A Modern History)*, İstanbul: İletişim.

13 An intertextual analysis of the village novels by Village Institute graduates

Socio-economic scenes of the Turkish village between 1950 and 1980

Esra Elif Nartok*

> "The peasants . . . came to see the world no longer as something infinitely vast like the universe and as circumscribed and small as the village bell-tower, but as a concrete reality consisting of states and peoples, social strengths and weaknesses, armies and machines, wealth and poverty. . . . [Herefrom] a spiritual world emerged."
>
> Antonio Gramsci (2000: 115)

When Mahmut Makal wrote his first book *Bizim Köy*[1] in 1950, it attracted the attention not only of Turkey's literary authorities, but of its politicians as well.[2] Makal was a graduate of one of the Village Institutes in Anatolia and a teacher who was working in an Anatolian village at the time. In that period, after the Democrat Party (DP) had come to power and began the process of closing the Village Institutes, the words and testimony of an Institute graduate, and a village teacher, highlighting the socio-economic problems of the village, had important repercussions.

The Village Institutes were an educational project in Turkey between the late 1930s and the mid-1950s, seeking to transform the Turkish countryside by training village children who would be sent to village schools as teachers.[3] The idea behind the Institutes was, "the regeneration of the village from inside in a meaningful and conscious way" (Tonguç cited in Timur 2008: 212). The idea of regeneration of the village from inside needed mobilizing the village's own resources and discussed the two main problems, poverty and illiteracy, that the new Republic had faced since its foundation in 1923 under the leadership of Mustafa Kemal Atatürk. It inherited a rural problem from the Ottoman Empire wherein peasants formed most the population but the lowest strata of the society, suffering under primitive methods of agricultural production as well as from illiteracy (Tütengil 1975). Through the process of establishing a modern nation out of its rural population (Karpat 1963: 65), economic development and cultural development were perceived as intrinsically linked and the Village Institutes was one of the projects of the new Republic carried out by the Republican People's Party (RPP), which aimed to achieve both. Unfortunately, a few years after their foundation, the

Institutes were closed by the DP, which criticized it as an education in line with communist aims and therefore did not serve society. The closure of the Institutes created a political polarization between those supporting the Institutes (generally the RPP and the left) and the conservatives (the DP). The Institutes were closed but the country's rural question was still to be solved.

In a period where 'the village' was a big issue in Turkey's economic, social and political agenda, *Bizim Köy* discussed the actual conditions of Turkey's villages and peasants, which were far from those targeted by the Turkish Republic nearly 30 years after its establishment. Therefore, as Yaşar Nabi Nayır, a Turkish author argued, it needed to be read not only as a literary work, but also as "a report written for the sake of the development of the Turkish village, and the Turkish villager's attainment of his human rights" (quoted in Rathbun 1972: 17). In this context, it also constituted a warning for the state authorities about the poor social and economic conditions that the peasants were suffering.

Later Fakir Baykurt and Talip Apaydın, also Institute graduates, published their books, which paralleled *Bizim Köy* in content and motivation. However, their books took the form of novels. Although *Bizim Köy* and the other authors' village novels were not enough to compensate for the social neglect Turkey's villages suffered, they succeeded in drawing the attention of literary and political authorities, as well as a broader readership, to village issues. These novels gained significant popularity between 1950 and 1980, a period in which literature and the social sciences were closely connected and in which the novel, the village and the social and economic development of the country were being discussed in conjunction (Naci 1976; Kayalı 2010; Timur 2002).

The tendency to confine literature to a definite theoretical area constitutes a prominent issue in literary discussions. Belge (1997: 51) describes this tendency as "making literature academic" It results in literature being treated as though it is separate from the socio-economic and socio-political problems of history. However, as Williams (1977: 53) states, literature is "decisive evidence of a form of social development of language", which is extremely sensitive to the socio-economic and socio-economic developments as well as power relations. For that reason, "such 'pure' literary theory is an academic myth" (Eagleton 1996: 170).

The village novels written by Institute graduates[4] are representative examples of what is retrospectively called "the village literature tradition" in Turkish history. They are one of the best examples of literature in close relationship with socio-economic problems and power relations. They are products of the Village Institutes, one of the projects of the early Republic in the framework of rural development, and shed light on the socio-economic and socio-political problems of the country during the 1950–1980 period. These novels tell village stories written by "three peasants"[5] trained in the Institutes as teachers and organic intellectuals[6] of the country in Gramscian terms, i.e. trying to be the intellectuals of the subaltern social groups and opposing the existing social order and transform it by way of literature.

This chapter aims to reveal the socio-economic network behind the village novels by employing the logic of "intertextuality", developed by Julia Kristeva

(1986) depending on the Bakhtin Circle's theory. In this sense the novels are taken into consideration with other texts dealing with the socio-economic problems of the period.[7] This chapter argues that the village novels of Institute graduates heavily feature and respond to the socio-economic problems that marked the political debates in the period between 1950 and 1980, such as land reform, rural poverty, the mechanization of agriculture and the capitalist transformation of agricultural production in a critical way.

The first section of the chapter summarizes the content and organization of the village novels to make clear general patterns about the characters and plots. In the next section the early village novels are discussed, particularly in the context of their criticism of the absence of enough land reform and primitive methods of agricultural production. After that, the last section concentrates on the late village novels, which focus mainly on the process of mechanization and capitalist transformation of agriculture as well as the novel's convergence to the Turkish Left's discourse of the time.

Content and organization of the village novels

The village novels focus on a specific village and examine it economically and sociologically. The themes of these novels vary by agricultural sectors (rice growing, tobacco farming or shepherding) or incidents that arise in village life (struggles for land, water conflicts or grape harvests). The novels take central Anatolian villages as their subject and present the actual conditions of the peasants and the social hierarchy in the village with respect to general production and distribution relations in the country. In this sense, the main starting point of the novels is the social stratification and hierarchy of the country and the village is presented as a sample of this stratification and hierarchy.

The novels have a trilateral organization in which the social environment reflected in the village is typically divided into three groups which encounter each other in various circumstances. The first group consists of the state authorities, big landowners, national and comprador bourgeoisie, men of religion and intellectuals. All of them can be collected under the title of 'dominant bloc' as they share their oppressive attitudes towards the peasants. This bloc represents the ruling class and the mechanism creating social stratification and hierarchies. The second group is the peasants. Most of the time they are seen as passive and helpless agents against the dominant bloc but sometimes they engage in opposition activities. The main antagonism in these novels is established between the dominant bloc and peasants, between the oppressors and the oppressed. Therefore, the trilateral organization is structured around an antagonistic social polarization. However, it is necessary to note that this antagonism is not absolute. Some members of one antagonistic camp can be seen siding with the members of the other. Thus, the third group seen in the village novels can be classed as good people in corrupt institutions. Those who are linked with the dominant bloc by occupation but decide to stand by the peasants – populist state officials and village teachers – can be found in this category.

The narratives of the village novels are situated in the times in which they were written. These novels were written and published between 1950 and 1980 and their plots centre on the significant socio-economic and political developments of this period. This includes the closure of the Village Institutes, the transition from a single-party to a multi-party regime, the proliferation of mechanization in agriculture, the big landowners' rise to high positions in bureaucratic cadres and the crystallization of social polarization. It also saw the rise of the leftist opposition and the development of production relations in agriculture within a capitalist framework. The stories in these novels are situated in central Anatolia, where petty commodity production was the prevailing economic form associated with agricultural production through sharecropping. In addition, peasants in this region were politically passive, having difficulty in acting collectively and being historically conservative with religious rituals and beliefs dominating their lives (Frey 1966: 17). Keeping these conditions in mind, these novels shed light on a definite social evolution under the influence of capitalist relations of agricultural production and the changing lives of the peasants in this process (Timur 2002: 92).

However, it is necessary to note that these novels should be taken into consideration with respect to a periodization since the novels of the 1950s considerably differ from those of the 1960s and 1970s. For instance, the early village novels bear the traces of Kemalist populist peasantist ideology[8] while those written after the mid-1960s cross over into the impact of the Turkish Left. Therefore, without such a periodization, what these novels tell and advocate stays blurred or seems contradictory or one could draw incorrect generalizations. In other words, looking at the social, political and economic developments of the periods seriously and thinking about the novels in accordance with these developments is the very condition of an intertextual reading. From this perspective, although it is possible to see the three social layers established around an antagonistic relationship in the village novels, the features and functions of these layers multiply and become clear in the late village novels.

The early village novels: primitive methods of agricultural production, the irrelevancy of the state and the helpless peasant

The early village novels attempted to identify social problems and demonstrate them to society. This willingness to write about such issues can be traced back to the authors' education in the Village Institutes, which encouraged students to write about everything related to life in their villages (Bayrak 2000: 62). The students' works were published regularly in *Köy Enstitüleri Dergisi* (the *Journal of the Village Institutes*). Their early works reflected the education they received in the Institutes and the Kemalist peasantist ideology that marked that education. In that context, the goal of literature was to fulfil the duty of being a mirror, reflecting social realities.

In the early period of the village novels, the main difficulty in the peasants' lives is the harsh natural conditions, with the state being criticized for not taking reasonable measures against such conditions. In this period, the peasants are portrayed as stuck between hard natural conditions and primitive agricultural production methods. They are passive agents deprived of the economic, social and cultural means to improve their conditions. The state, therefore, is needed to provide them with assistance. However, the state produces no reasonable solution to peasants' problems due to its irrelevance in their lives, inevitably resulting in poverty and oppression for the villagers. The typical examples of this kind of narrative are Makal's *Bizim Köy* (1970[1950]), Apaydın's *Sarıtraktör*[9] (1972[1958]) and *Yarbükü*[10] (1962[1959]) and Baykurt's *Yılanların Öcü*[11] (1959).

Makal's book *Bizim Köy* is built on a relationship devoid of contact, between the peasants and the state, in which the latter's negligence is responsible for the oppression of the former. It portrays a village in which the peasants suffer from hot, burning summers and harsh winters that damage the productivity of the land. Villagers are deprived of practical tools for coping with the vagaries of nature, working with their two hands and perhaps a few oxen – in many cases they cannot afford to buy oxen and use their own hands to plow instead, and, in the end, perish (Makal 1970: 36). To overcome their plight, they look to the state to engage with their problems and produce solutions, but they are disappointed. Makal (1970: 51–52) mentions that the government is supposed to be a "father" to the peasants; however, it does not see the harsh material conditions the peasants are in.

The state's relationship with the peasantry was problematic from the very early years of the Republic. Whereas the founder of the Republic, Atatürk, exalted the peasantry as "masters of the people" and several institutions were established ostensibly for the well-being of the peasants, their economic conditions never changed for the better.[12] Therefore, the state's irrelevance to the peasants' lives can also be seen in this book in the depiction of state institutions whose economic and social policies are rarely compatible with the peasants' actual demands. The following passage reviews the functioning of the agricultural cooperatives:

> In seven or eight of the villages in our Province there are Agricultural Co-operatives. These Co-operatives were originally established with the best intentions, having in mind the benefit of the villager. But to-day they have brought him to an impasse, because, while the villager, acting from the motives of economy, has had the money from them, he has not always spent it to the best advantage. By simply paying off his debts with the borrowed money he has had temporarily relief. . . . The majority are unable to pay off their debts. They must pay interest on what they still owe; and when that is doubled, they get to a point when they are quite unable to meet them. Thus, the villager is prosecuted, and then it is that the demon of want appears. In the villages of this neighbourhood more than half the villagers who associated with the Co-operative have been prosecuted.
>
> (Makal 1965: 39–40)

In such a situation, in addition to natural difficulties such as aridity, infertility of the land and crop shortages, the state's institutions turn peasants into debtors.

In this sense, the institutions established to promote agricultural production are deprived of solving peasants' economic problems; instead, they in a sense putting them in a more difficult situation.

In that period, one reason the natural conditions posed a challenge for peasants' lives is presented as the infrastructural insufficiency of the villages. Apaydın's *Yarbükü* focuses on water scarcity, a common problem in central Anatolia, the location of many village novels. In this novel peasants suffer from a lack of water for irrigation, which causes conflicts in the village. It is suggested that although this scarcity comes from nature, the state could still take measures to assist the peasants but fails to do so. In the novel, it is said, "Once the government had this area examined with the idea of building a dam, but later somehow they changed their minds. So, this place here, Yarbükü, was left on its own" (Apaydın 1959: 10). This is the novelist's voice, and it argues that, like all villages, Yarbükü has been abandoned to its fate. In cases where the peasants appeal to the government for help to solve their problems, they are not listened to and must continue to face their hard lives on their own (Apaydın 1959: 88).

Undoubtedly, one of the most important issues of the period was the acceleration of mechanization in agriculture. It is necessary to recall that the new Republic targeted agricultural development; however, the number of agricultural machinery as well as agricultural production was limited until the Marshall Plan was extended to Turkey in the post-1945 period. Within the scope of Marshall Plan, Turkey undertook development strategies like other less developed countries in that world conjuncture. In this period, Turkey's imports increased significantly thanks to American funds and a significant part of imports consisted of agricultural machinery (Keyder 1987: 119). Furthermore, this period also coincides with the country's transition to a parliamentary regime in which the DP came to the power. The DP stood for "an autonomous economy . . . without the interference of bureaucratic control" (Keyder 1987: 118). One of this party's main arguments was that the new state under the leadership of the RPP had not penetrated rural society and that it had taken a domineering approach in its policies (Yalman 2002: 33). For this reason, the DP is known for its policies supporting the rural development in that period, i.e. increased imports of tractors and spreading them to the villages (Keyder 1987: 119).

The first use of the tractor in the village is central to Apaydın's *Sarı Traktör*. This novel is based on an intergenerational story telling of the young Arif's love of tractors and his struggle to persuade his father to buy one. The tractor symbolizes modern production techniques against the traditional means of agricultural production. It centres on the conflict between the traditional and the modern, symbolically between the father and the son, around an intergenerational element because the changes in the means of production, i.e. transition from non-technical manual labor to tractors, are narrated by comparing the production conditions under which the father works with those of the son. Although the DP's policies were always criticized by the authors because of the Party's responsibility for the closure of the Institutes, Apaydın's narrative of the tractor coincided with the DP's discourse (Türkeş 2001: 217). However, it can be understood from the novel that as the hardships of nature on the peasants marked the village novel in the 1950s, the tractor was presented as a solution to the struggle between nature and the peasants more than constituting support for the DP's policies.

As well as the old production means, the old relations of production is one of the most important issues in the novels of the period. Since the pre-capitalist relations of production had yet to be resolved in the country, its most important participant, big landowners, were very important for that period. Although the necessity of land reform was on the agenda of political elites of the country in late 1940s, adequate land reform was not accomplished due to political reasons, essentially the organic relations of the bureaucratic elite and big landowners (Karaömerlioğlu 2000: 119). Thus, "despite the distribution of some state lands, nothing of such historic significance as dissolving 'backward' agricultural relations or reducing severe inequities came from the land reform of 1945" (Karaömerlioğlu 2000: 133). Thus, the peasants remained oppressed and exploited by local notables and big landowners.

Apaydın mentions this issue first in his novel of *Yarbükü* in 1959 by telling the story of a poor peasant who worked for an *ağa*[13] in the past. This peasant focuses on how the *ağa* oppresses the peasants holding smaller lands, exploits their labor and how the government remains unresponsive to the situation (Apaydın 1959: 87–88). This point is brought to the fore in Baykurt's *Yılanların Öcü*, written in the same year. This novel starts by focusing on the unequal distribution of land resulting from the failure of the RPP to implement adequate land reform. In the past, land was sold to the peasants rather than being distributed equally, so that the social order in which the big landowners derived power from their property was protected in the village of Karataş, the setting of the novel. The *muhtar*[14] of the village is one of the big landowners in the village because he could afford to buy a large amount of land when it was being distributed during the period of the RPP. Due to the success of the DP in bringing big landowners into its ranks, the *muhtar* is an important representative of the DP in the novel. Throughout the novel, the DP is having captured the state apparatus and implementing its negative policies through the peasants who give it their support (Tatarlı and Mollof 1969: 221). Deriving his strength from the DP, the *muhtar* oppresses the poor peasants and uses violence against them. Therefore, in this novel Baykurt hints at patronage relations, which constituted one of the characteristic features of the DP period. Regarding its treatment of land reform, patronage relations and criticism of the RPP and the DP, *Yılanların Öcü* can be read as a transition novel, serving as a bridge between the early and late village novels.

The late village novels: the clientelistic relations, the agrarian bourgeoisie and the exploited peasant

In the early 1960s, the authors moved from the idea of "identifying social problems" to "leading society to address social problems" (Bayrak 2000: 65). In this period literature was not only a "mirror" reflecting social realities but also a "tool" in the struggle to confront the "corrupt order" (Apaydın et al. 1971: 13). This shift in the authors' literary attitudes should be read in the light of the socio-political and socio-economic developments of the country in the 1960s.

The most important economic change in the 1960s was the country's adoption of import-substitution industrialization as its economic developmental strategy, which favoured industry over agriculture whilst the capitalist transformation of agriculture continued. Politically, it faced military intervention on May 27, 1960, paving the way for the reconstruction of state-civil society relations. The 1961 Constitution, implemented following the military intervention, allowed those who remained outside the power bloc in the country to be organized under economic and political organizations (Yalman 2002: 35–36). From that time on, the authors of the village novels consistently sided with the left. They supported and took important roles within the Workers' Party of Turkey (TİP) and the Teachers' Trade Union of Turkey (TÖS). This shaped their perception of socio-political and socio-economic issues and their reflection of these issues in the novels.

Their adoption of the leftist ideas and ways of organizing coincided with their adoption of socialist realism, creating significant shifts in the narratives of the village novels. In this period, they thought of themselves as "fighters" in a "social struggle" against the corrupt order (Bayrak 2000: 232). Baykurt states that, "Although we do not expect a large-scale progressive leap from literature, literature has duty and responsibility to help this progressive leap a reality. We want to fulfil this responsibility as authors" (Bayrak 2000: 232). The authors thought of literature in terms of its responsibility to the laboring classes of society (i.e. workers and peasants) who produced life and had the ability to change it. They called this kind of literature "guided literature" (Bayrak 2000). In this context, bringing the peasants' stories from the perspective of the peasants themselves formed a part of their responsibility to the laboring classes as peasant intellectuals.

Taking a leftist stance in their political struggle and a socialist-realist perspective in literature, the issues already pointed out in the novels of the 1950s – i.e. absence of land reform, the mechanization in agriculture, the capitalist transformation in agricultural production – are considered in a broader perspective, confronting social relations of production and distribution as well as property relations. Considering these points, one of the striking shifts marking this period is that the state, which had been 'neutral' in the sense of 'being the father' of every citizen despite being criticized in the 1950s, consisted of class relations in the late village novels. The state in this period sides with big landowners and the bourgeoisie, which makes it a part of the dominant bloc, responsible for peasants' economic and social oppression and exploitation.

The hard natural conditions lose their importance in the village novel in this period because the authors focus on the relations between bourgeois class fractions and laboring classes of the country, instead of the relations between nature and peasants in the village. For instance, Baykurt's *Kaplumbağalar*,[15] written in the second half of the 1960s, shows the shift in the narrative of the state and hints at a criticism of distribution and property relations. This novel tells the story of peasants who turn a steppe in their village into a vineyard. Working together, they succeed against natural obstacles thanks to the assistance of the village teacher.[16] The harvest time for the grapes grown in the village's common vineyard resembles a Bakhtinian carnival[17] in which the peasants entertain each other and practice a money-free economy, not selling their products but distributing them to their neighbors. After the peasants build the vineyard, state personnel working under the General Directorate of Land Registry and Cadastre come to the village and dispossess the peasants of the vineyard. The peasants can only have the vineyard again if they pay rent for it to the state. But the peasants are too poor to pay this rent and the vineyard is abandoned. Afterwards, the peasant remark: "We have the state keeping a tight rein on us. It has its iron nails in us" (Baykurt 2008: 318). Against the money-free economy the peasants establish, the state tries to make peasants pay rent for useless land – i.e. a steppe before the peasants' effort – without considering the peasants' poor economic conditions. In this way, the state is portrayed as a malevolent force, described as digging its "iron nails" into the peasants.

Another characteristic feature of this period is the criticism of clientelistic relations directed towards populist political parties such as the DP and the Justice Party (JP). The DP, known for utilizing patronage relations in which political power rewards its supporters in return for their support or services (Sunar 1985: 2077), was not in power in this period; however, a comprehensive criticism of this party was made by the 1960s thanks to the relatively free environment that the 1961 Constitution created and the authors' engagement with the Turkish Left. It can be argued that the authors saw the JP as a continuation of the DP in terms of its conservative ideology and populism based on clientelist relations so that the narrative of the DP also connoted that of the JP.

The novels focus on the exchange of goods and services for political support. One of the critical examples of this is in Baykurt's *Irazca'nın Dirliği*,[18] the continuation of *Yılanların Öcü*, the transition novel discussed earlier in the previous section. In *Yılanların Öcü*, the connection between the *muhtar* and the DP is portrayed as a one-sided relationship; what the DP gives the *muhtar* in return for his support is not clear. That the relationship is in fact reciprocal is revealed in *Irazca'nın Dirliği*. Specifically, the *muhtar* is to remove opponents of the DP from the local voter rolls in exchange for a certain amount of credit and a tractor. In the following passage, he explains his mission and its reward to his wife:

Wife, they promoted me at the bank for the elections! Take notice, wife, I will take the tractor and turn the fields upside down. This government is going to put us in order. I will belong to the Turkish government, as its own farmer. This is called smarts, wife! As soon as I give them the voter list, they will discard all the pimps. First, they will discard Kara Bayram, then Irazca, and then her daughter-in-law. Ağali and his family and Kosa too! You all will watch me succeed! What do those scoundrels have to do with the election while they don't support the government? Our president is very intelligent, as he wants to avoid the possible opposition. What would they vote for anyway? Those ignorant pimps! If you tell me that I am ignorant as well, wife, I say you might have a point. However, what I have is smarts, so I support the government. I am being a democrat. They are not, those deviants! That's the reason why I have the tractor, wife! I got promoted at the government's bank. . . .

(Baykurt 1961: 55)

Those whom the *muhtar* removes from the voter list are engaged in a struggle over land with him. Therefore, they oppose the *muhtar* – and the DP, as a source of his power. This is an important passage that shows the poor peasants on one side and the powerful factions, aligned per their economic interests, on the other. Moreover, this passage criticizes that economic institutions (agricultural cooperatives and banks) and policies (credits and machinery to support peasants) are not conducted with respect to a comprehensive rural development program; rather, they were enmeshed with clientelistic relations. Therefore, the credits and tractors are given not to the peasants but to the big landowners in exchange for their political support for the DP.

In the village novels of this period, the big landowners are generally represented by the characters the *bey*[19] or the *ağa* apart from the *muhtar*s. These figures controlling large land holdings and means of production are portrayed as parts of the dominant classes oppressing ordinary villagers and exploiting their labor as well as having strong ties to the government. These characters also denote the nascent agrarian bourgeoisie in the period of the development of capitalist relations in agriculture. Unlike the novels of the previous period, the novels of this period take the characters of the *ağa* and the *bey* in the context of the relations of production and distribution as well as the property relations. In this point, it is necessary to understand that in "dominated-dependent countries", the class of big landowners representing another mode of production is present in the capitalist social formation, together with the other bourgeois factions organized by the state, based on the common economic interests (Poulantzas 2000: 127).

Since these novels illustrate the conditions in central Anatolia, where petty commodity production was common, the *bey* employs workers as sharecroppers or shepherds on his farms.[20] In Apaydın's *Ortakçılar*,[21] Hilmi Bey is a figure with strong ties to "Ankara", which refers to the government. He lives in a modern farmhouse in the village in the rice-growing season and in Ankara for the rest of the year. The novel starts with the arrival of Sefer, an Institute student, at Hilmi Bey's farm. A sharecropper tells Sefer of their working conditions on this farm:

> "Sefer, how do you think we are doing? Don't you know that we are crawling? . . . [W]e have been working hard on that pimp's field. We work day and night without a break. Soon, our Hilmi Bey will show up and divide the product. He is going to take everything from us, offering several excuses . . . After working so relentlessly for six months, we will be just left with a bagful of rice. Can you call this living? Do you know anyone more outrageous than a sharecropper?"
>
> (Apaydın 2007: 26)

In this passage, the story he tells goes beyond Hilmi Bey's farm and describes the working conditions of all sharecroppers, in which they suffer under unequal relations of distribution. Hilmi Bey and his fellow big landowners maintain a high standard of living by exploiting the villagers' labor capacity and their connections with the state forces enables this exploitation. Thus, while the villagers seem to be freed from feudal exploitation and oppression, they nevertheless suffer under the exploitation and oppression of the nascent agrarian bourgeoisie (Tatarlı and Mollof 1969: 218).

The authors do not limit their criticism to exploitative forces such as the agrarian bourgeoisie. They also direct their criticisms at other factions of the bourgeoisie, such as local and foreign capitalists, Turkish and American businessmen. In the village novels, they are allowed to enter the villages and take part in exploitation and oppression of peasants thanks to Turkish-American cooperation. It is important to note that this cooperation started about a decade before it was reflected in the novels. This can be explained by the acceleration of the anti-imperialist struggle in the Turkish left and the authors' engagement in leftist politics.

In this period, the novels clearly refer to specific economic programs within the scope of Marshall Plan. One of the main features of this period is its criticism of the country's dependence on foreign sources, especially the US. Baykurt's *American Sargısı*[22] offers a detailed narrative of American capital and its relation to domestic capital and the state. The novel introduces a Turkish businessman, the owner of a mining company who participates in the meetings of the "Aid Mission to the Government of Turkey" working together with American officials. His business is in the mining sector and he wants to expand to other sectors, including petroleum. However, the existing legislation on natural assets is very restrictive, so he supports the DP for being critical of bureaucratic control on the economy.[23] At a meeting of the aid commission, he says: "Elections are approaching. If we work hard . . . we can get the Ball resolution passed. I mean the petroleum resolution". These words evoke a real situation in Turkish history, during the DP government. An American expert, Max Ball, prepared a bill, known as the "Ball draft", which would offer petroleum assets up to the control of foreign companies (Uluğbay 2009).

The Marshall Plan was pointed to in the early village novels without being enunciated directly and without an anti-imperialist framework. As discussed in the previous section, the policies based on this Plan were affirmed in a sense, with the need for agricultural machinery for peasants suffering from pre-modern agricultural production methods. As for this period, the authors still focus on the need for the implementation of modern agricultural production methods and agricultural machinery in order to achieve rural economic development for the country; however, they advocate that this should not be achieved through external sources as it makes the country dependent on foreign funds.

An early, albeit brief, example of this issue can be found in Baykurt's *Onuncu Köy*.[24] In this novel, a peasant complains about the financial difficulties Turkey faces despite the state's rhetoric of development:

> " 'We have progressed, we have developed! We have done a lot of things in a short time!' We are about to burst from boasting, God forbid! Fine, [referring to the government], you have progressed; we got it, stop shouting it out! Who is going to hear it? Progressed! You even import your needles! Progressed! You cannot even produce a pill for fixing a stomach-ache! Half of you are

ruled by *ağa*s; you can only serve imported milk powder in your schools . . .
Is that how you progressed?"

(Baykurt 2013: 192)

This peasant recognizes the country's dependence on foreign resources by looking at the imported tractors whose numbers are increasing in the village and the
powdered milk distributed in the village schools with the help of American aid.
Thus, he disputes the government's discourse on the country's development. He
suggests that if the country's development strategies depend on foreign resources,
economic development will not be achieved. His discourse reflects the idea of
"non-capitalist economic development" of the Turkish Left, which the authors
supported during the 1960s and 1970s.[25]

Conclusion

This chapter has examined the village novels written by Village Institute graduates Talip Apaydın, Fakir Baykurt and Mahmut Makal between 1950 and 1980 in
an intertextual framework. It has attempted to reveal how the novels interacted
with and responded to the socio-economic changes in the country at the time. The
first section of the chapter concentrated on explaining the context and organization of the novels around which the stories of peasants are told, the characters are
formed. The second section examined the early village novels written in the 1950s
focusing on their criticism of insufficient land reform and primitive methods of
agricultural production. The third section focused on the late village novels written between 1960 and 1980, centred on the process of mechanization in agriculture and capitalist transformation of agricultural production.

In terms of their socio-economic and socio-political connotations, the village
novels by Institute graduates always tended to overstep their literary boundaries.
In the late 1950s, one of authors whose novels were examined in this chapter,
Baykurt (quoted in Apaydın et al. 1960: 11), claimed that their novels would
become "essential documents" over the next 30 years for those interested in socio-
political and socio-economic issues and those who felt themselves responsible for
the country's problems.

The village novels touch upon several socio-economic problems. The novels
of the 1950s particularly try to depict the reasons behind the backwardness of
peasants' economic conditions and rural economy. In the novels, the reasons are
presented as the lack of sufficient land reform and the primitive methods of agricultural production as well as the state's irrelevancy. In parallel to the Kemalist
populist peasantist ideology inherited from the Village Institutes, a passive and
helpless peasant image marks the novels of this period, in the meantime, it is
emphasized that they do not deserve to be the lowest strata in Turkish society.
Rather, they deserve comprehensive social and economic reforms, as they are
most of this society. However, the novels claim that the economic institutions and
agricultural banks as well as the state's policies for rural economy are not enough
to address peasants' economic problems.

By the 1960s, and with the rising impact of the left and anti-imperialist struggle in Turkish politics, the authors adopted a socialist-realist point of view in their literary works. This resulted in significant shifts in the narrative of socio-economic issues in the novels. Within the realm of socialist realism, they highlighted the class character of literature and argued for the necessity of telling the stories of the laboring classes, who constituted the poor majority of the county. In that sense, in addition to their goal of transforming the political field by supporting leftist parties and organizations, their goal was to transform the literary field for the sake of this majority. In line with these aspirations, they saw their novels as a means for struggle. With this impact in mind, the social relations of production and distribution as well as property relations are questioned when discussing the major socio-economic developments of the period such as the rise of clientelistic relations, the acceleration of the capitalist transformation of agricultural production, and the mechanization in agriculture. Therefore, the novels of this period present the reason for the peasants' backwardness as the exploitative and oppressive classes organized under the dominant bloc – big landowners, domestic and foreign bourgeoisie and the state that generally supports these classes, not the exploited and oppressed peasants.

As Eagleton (1996: 11) argues, to read any literary work is also to rewrite it in a different context. In his words, "There is no reading of a work which is not also a 're-writing'". In this sense, this chapter has attempted to read the village novels with other political, historical and economic texts as far as they permit and to rewrite them in an intertextual context. Hence, it has not made any pretense of presenting the most true or accurate reading of these novels; rather, it has proposed an alternative reading of them.

Notes

* The author wishes to thank Dr. Çınla Akdere, whose recommendations enriched this chapter, as well as Ben Sessions for doing the final reading and Sinem Barut for translating the novel passages from Turkish to English.
1 The direct translation of the book's title is *Our Village*; however, it was translated to English under the name of *A Village in Anatolia*. For the translated version of the book, see Makal (1965).
2 In the 1970 edition of the book, the last section presents the first comments of notable figures, from famous writers such as Nâzım Hikmet, Vâlâ Nureddin and Sabahattin Eyüboğlu to prominent journalists such as Nadir Nadi, Abdi İpekçi and Çetin Altan and from politicians such as Samet Ağaoğlu and Nihat Erim to well-known foreign press such as *The Times* and *Le Monde*. This diversity reflects the novel's reception in different fields. For further detail, see Makal (1970: 180–191).
3 Whilst experimental attempts at the Village Institutes started in 1937 onwards, the original phase of the institutes was operational between 1940 and 1946 when Hasan Ali Yücel was the minister of National Education and İsmail Hakkı Tonguç was the administrator for elementary education. For further detail, see Nartok (1990) and Karaömerlioğlu (2006).
4 The village novels cannot be boiled down to the novels of Village Institute graduates, because there were many famous authors, such as Yaşar Kemal, Kemal Tahir and Orhan Kemal, who have been retroactively included in the village literature tradition for their works focusing on village themes.

5 The authors Makal, Baykurt and Apaydın gained a reputation as "three peasants" of the Turkish literature (Bayrak 2000).

6 See Gramsci (2000: 300) for further detail about his explanation of the organic intellectual.

7 Other texts can be any text dealing with the same problem such as scholarly publications, the documents of political parties, historical texts interested in the period between 1950 and 1980.

8 Kemalist populist peasantist ideology regards the peasants as primitive, needing to be modernized, but wise, bearing the essence of the nation. For further detail, see Karaömerlioğlu (2006).

9 *The Yellow Tractor* in English

10 *The Waterside Thicket by the Cliff*

11 *The Revenge of Snakes*

12 For further detail, see Karaömerlioğlu (2000).

13 *Ağa* refers to a landowner in Turkish, having feudal connotations. As these novels were written during the process of capitalization of agriculture in which feudal relations started being resolved, it refers to a feudal residue more than a feudal element completely in the village novels. Therefore, it refers to the big landowner as a form of respect.

14 *Muhtar* means the headman of a village or quarter in Turkish.

15 *The Turtles*

16 The village teacher represents the authors in the novels. The village teacher is a revolutionary figure who is originally a villager and devotes himself to the peasants' emancipation. The main duty of this figure is to awaken and mobilize the peasants. As this chapter focuses on the village novel's responses to the socio-economic developments of the period, the village teachers are not the focus of this chapter. However, to understand the ideological dimensions of the novels, it is crucial to understand the role of these characters.

17 In Bakhtin's theory, carnival is the system of popular joyful images. It is a world of "topsy-turvy, of heteroglot exurbance, of ceaseless overrunning, and excess where all is mixed, hybrid, ritually degraded and defiled" (Stallybrass and White 1986: 8). The people gather in the marketplace at carnival time, which is generally the time of labor and productive growth. A money-free economy marks carnival practices based on collective labor with the consciousness of freedom (Bakhtin 1984: 95, 206–207).

18 *Irazca's Livelihood*

19 *Bey* refers to a big landowner who employs waged workers on his farms. This character differs from the *ağa* because the *ağa* usually forces the peasants to work on his farm without pay. Therefore, the *bey* is part of new capitalist relations of production in agriculture whereas the *ağa* evokes the older feudal relations.

20 He is depicted as more modern than the *ağa* because he has strong relations with urban areas – sometimes even residing in the city – and his only relation to the village is that his economic activity depends on his farm there.

21 *The Sharecroppers*

22 *The American Bandage*

23 For the DP's idea of the autonomous economy without bureaucratic control, see Keyder (1987: 118).

24 *The Tenth Village*

25 This was a prominent issue in Turkish leftist circles, which were marked by their anti-imperialist stance. In the documents of the trade union, TÖS, which the authors were members of, it is proposed that the non-capitalist mode of development is the most suitable route for Turkey's developmental path (Koç 2012: 108). Non-capitalist mode of development was an idea prominently defended by the *Yön* movement, a leftist movement in Turkey, which combined Kemalism, nationalism and socialism.

Bibliography

Apaydın, T. (1959), *Yarbükü*, İstanbul: Varlık.

Apaydın, T. (1972), *Sarı traktör*, İstanbul: Başak.

Apaydın, T. (2007 [1964]), *Ortakçılar*, İstanbul: Literatür.

Apaydın, T., Binyazar, A., Cihangir, M., Kanar, H. and Kudret, C. (1971), *Devrim için edebiyat*, Ankara: TÖS.

Apaydın, T., Baykurt, F., Kemal, O., Makal, M. and Tahir, K. (1960), *Beş romancı köy romanı üzerine tartışıyor*, İstanbul: Düşün.

Bakhtin, M. M. (1984), *Rabelais and His World*, H. Iswolsky (trans.), Bloomington, IN: Indiana University Press.

Baykurt, F. ([1959] 1962), *Yılanların öcü*, İstanbul: Remzi.

Baykurt, F. (1961), *Irazcanın dirliği*, İstanbul: Remzi.

Baykurt, F. ([1961] 2013), *Onuncu köy*, İstanbul: Literatür.

Baykurt, F. (1967), *Amerikan sargısı*, Ankara: Bilgi.

Baykurt, F. ([1967] 2008), *Kaplumbağlar*, İstanbul: Literatür.

Bayrak, B. (2000), *Köy enstitüleri ve köy edebiyatı*, Ankara: Özge.

Belge, M. (1997), 'Üçüncü dünya ülkeleri açısından Türk romanına bir bakış', in B. Aksoy and N. Aksoy (eds.), *Türk edebiyatına eleştirel bir bakış: Berna Moran'a armağan*, İstanbul: İletişim.

Eagleton, T. (1996), *Literature Theory*, Minneapolis, MN: Blackwell.

Frey, F. W. (1966), *Regional Variations in Rural Turkey*, Cambridge, MA: Center for International Studies, Massachusetts Institute of Technology.

Gramsci, A. (2000), *The Gramsci Reader*, New York: New York University Press.

Karaömerlioğlu, A. (2000), 'Elite Perceptions of Land Reform in Early Republican Turkey', *The Journal of Peasant Studies*, 27 (3): 115–141.

Karaömerlioğlu, A. (2006), *Orada bir köy var uzakta: erken Cumhuriyet döneminde köycü söylem*, İstanbul: İletişim.

Karpat, K. H. (1963), 'The People's Houses in Turkey, Establishment and Growth', *Middle East Journal*, 17 (1/2): 55–67.

Kayalı, K. (ed.) (2010), 'Bizim kuşağın Kemal Tahir okuma serüveni', in *Bir Kemal Tahir kitabı: Türkiye'nin ruhunu aramak*, İstanbul: İthaki, 41–60.

Keyder, Ç. (1987), *State and Class in Turkey: A Study in Capitalist Development*, London: Verso.

Koç, Y. (2012), *TÖS: antiemperyalist bir öğretmen örgütü*, İstanbul: Kaynak.

Kristeva, J. (1986), *The Kristeva Reader*, New York: Columbia University Press.

Makal, M. ([1950] 1970), *Bizim köy*, Ankara: Bizim Köy Yayınları.

Makal, M. (1965), *A Village in Anatolia*, P. Stirling (ed.) and W. Deedes (trans.), London: Vallentine, Mitchell.

Naci, F. (1976), *Edebiyat yazıları*, İstanbul: Gerçek.

Nartok, B. (1990), "Köy enstitülerinin yönetim çözümlemesi ve günümüz açısından değerlendirilmesi", (Unpublished master's thesis), TODAIE, Ankara.

Poulantzas, N. (2000), *State, Power, Socialism*, London: Verso.

Rathbun, C. (1972), *The Village in the Turkish Novel and Short Story 1920 to 1955*, Paris: Mouton.

Stallybrass, P. and White, A. (1986), *The Politics and the Poetics of Transgression*, New York: Cornell University Press.

Sunar, İ. (1985), 'Demokrat parti ve popülizm', in F. Aral and M. Belge (eds.), *Cumhuriyet dönemi Türkiye ansiklopedisi: cilt 8*, İstanbul: İletişim.

Tatarlı, İ. and Mollof, R. (1969), *Marksist açıdan Türk romanı*, İstanbul: Habora.
Timur, T. (2002), *Osmanlı-Türk romanında tarih ve kimlik*, Ankara: İmge.
Timur, T. (2008), *Türk devrimi ve sonrası*, Ankara: İmge.
Türkeş, A. Ö. (2001), 'Taşra iktidarı!', *Toplum ve Bilim*, 88: 201–234.
Tütengil, C. O. (1975), *100 soruda kırsal Türkiye'nin yapısı ve sorunları*, İstanbul: Gerçek.
Uluğbay, H. (2009, November 20), "Cumhuriyet döneminde petrol politikaları", www.ulugbay.com/blog_hikmet/?p=109 (accessed June 20, 2014).
Williams, R. (1977), *Marxism and Literature*, New York: Oxford University Press.
Yalman, G. L. (2002), "The Turkish State and Bourgeoisie in Historical Perspective: A Relativist Paradigm or a Panoply of Hegemonic Strategies", in N. Balkan and S. Savran (eds.), *The Politics of Permanent Crisis: Class, Ideology and State in Turkey*, New York: Nova, 21–54.

14 Theatre in crisis, theatre of crisis

Economics and contemporary dramatic writing and shows

Martial Poirson

Whereas discretionary affinities between "the theatre and the prince" long conferred an air of extravagance to the performing arts, the former is now a victim of both the current economic crisis as well as a reduction in subsidies prescribed by a political culture obsessed with demonstrating that it no longer has the means to finance its ambitions. In this new economic configuration, the theatre, partially emancipated from the age-old supervision of public authorities, is paradoxically given new liberties and thus new rules by which to reinvent itself. A resource-poor target of a free-market offensive, the theatre, an experimental terrain for the crisis, is also a privileged witness to the deterioration of artists' working conditions, the bursting of the speculative bubble, and the emergence of new forms of marginalization resulting from the post-industrial transition. The exposure and condemnation of these new forms of marginalization have not, however, resulted in a form of theatre that is predominantly veristic or realist: on the contrary, symbolization has allowed for a detached observation of the socio-economic situation by means of the epic story, the chorale or stage directions, all of which remain exterior to the story. Theatre fully exploits the "crisis of economic rhetoric" (Méchoulan 2011), a manifestation of the animus between the competing demands of pragmatism and economic modeling, the consequences of which are particularly prejudicial as they are perceived as unavoidable necessities dictated by circumstance and imposed by fact.

It is no accident that Michel Vinaver, an important figure in the business world turned playwright on the forefront of economic questions, titled his most recent play *Bettencourt Boulevard ou Une Histoire de France* (2014), claiming to have been "enthralled by this story" and to have "been lured into working on it" (Vinaver 2014). Despite its idiosyncratic title and obvious allusion to current events, Vinaver uses a style of fable to transpose a well-known political and financial scandal into a play in which "comedy may surface but in which tragedy prevails during a captivating sequence of episodes" (Vinaver 2015). This type of theatrical extrapolation, born from a metaphorical relationship with the economy, is notably perceptible in author and stage director Joël Pommerat's work. Starting with *Au monde* in 2004, in which "for the first time politics and economics take the stage" in the sentimental sphere, and including *Les Marchands* (2006), *Je Tremble* (2007–2008), *Cercles/Fictions* (2010), *Ma Chambre Froide* (2011) and finally *La Grande et Fabuleuse Histoire du commerce* in 2012, Pommerat's plays are largely influenced by economic themes. Per the founder of the Louis Brouillard company, playwrights must fully accept the economy's omnipresence in the public and private spheres:

> I think that the economy is now part of everyone's life. It is abundantly clear that deciphering human existence means understanding this reality that is part of every person's conscious. For the past fifteen years, a change in the world and in its citizens has been underway. In principle, the word "social" does not interest me so much, no more than the word "political". I was fascinated with the economy at one point but in the end let it drop. Then I realized that if I wanted to talk about emotions I had to rethink these dimensions.
>
> (Pommerat 2013: 79)

For Pommerat, as for many playwrights, an awareness of the economy's inescapable and omnipresent dimension goes hand in hand with a denial of the socio-political impact of his artistic creation. The latter is most noticeable in a crisis-era theatre that has shaped dramatic writing since the 1970s, especially over the last 15 years. Denying any ideological dimension to dramatic writing is symptomatic of the ambivalence in contemporary theatre, in which critical posture refuses to recognize itself as such and relies on the spectator's opinion to be the final judge.

This *theatre in crisis*, conducive to the emergence of new forms of political posturing, is also incontestably a *theatre of crisis* seeking to link an artistic creation to the historical content that engenders it, at the risk of deconstructing its own aesthetic and ideological devices. Resolutely meta-theatrical and self-referential, it further shows that a *theatre in crisis* cannot afford to ignore a *crisis of the theatre* in the sense that modes of production, distribution and reception are intricately linked to systems of representation. A vast dramatic repertoire, distinguishing itself not only from the militant writings and poetic experimentations which nonetheless inspired it (Dario Fo, Vinaver, Koltès, Lagarce, Jouet, Novarina), but especially from Brecht's theatre, takes hold of the crisis to prolong the symbolic clash in other ways. It seeks to experiment with an appropriate form of *economic dramaturgy* that does not limit itself to a simple dramatization of the economy.

Having sought responses, primarily in the annals of theatre, to questions that contemporary French playwrights were unwilling to ask, today's artistic milieu has undergone a curious, axiological reversal because of the global crisis. This new type of stage writing (e.g. Pommerat or Garcia), focuses, and sometimes obsessively so, on crisis-era theatre at a time when unorthodox economists (e.g. Lordon, Moulier-Bouting) delighted in appropriating theatrical performance to sway the public opinion that, at least in theoretical terms, seemed unmoved. It is this antagonistic theatre that will be the subject of the present article. Mindful of the artistic and ideological interests of a largely oneiric, poetic and indirectly only political repertory, it will seek to demonstrate a dramaturgical renewal made possible by a form of economic plot construction. Seizing upon salient current events, this theatrical form seeks to reconnect with non-mainstream forms of dramatic writing to examine them and positions itself, in aesthetic terms, to challenge them and thus reveal their aporetic nature. Using a dramatic protocol that relies on metaphorical device, parable, myth, symbolism, fable and fairytale, the playwrights who will be cited later in this text bring to light the process of symbolizing the economy through allegory and, consequently, quirkily shed light on the obscure pillars, the hidden fantasy and the buried, cultural subconscious of a political economy that is too often forgetful of its philosophical and anthropological origins, if not of its purely fictional dimension.

Axiological reversal

After centuries of being considered by classical, then neoclassical political economists as foes, theatre and economics are now expected to cohabitate peacefully if not have their destinies inextricably linked. Just as the performing arts are an experimental playground for the new economy, the contemporary repertoire is paradoxically, yet frequently cited by politicians and the media as a potential solution to the endemic, global crisis impacting our globalized societies. If not a solution to the problem this repertoire, lacking in critical substance and subversive tone, is at the very least a gateway to understanding the inadequacies of today's economic doctrine. The theatre is thus erected at times as a heuristic agent able to facilitate an understanding of complex, socio-economic mechanisms (Lordon 2011) while at others as a panacea for re-humanizing a world (Lipovetsky 2013) facing imminent economic "horror" (Forrester 1996).

The consensus on the structural deficits to be expected in the performing arts and the legitimacy of the public service's support of the theatre, absent an expectation of a return on investment, is threatened by a populist and an individualistic shift toward an economy of recreational theatre as well as by the rising power of neoliberalism's obsession with cognitive capitalism's predictable delusions (Moulier-Bouting 2007, 2010). Thus, in a France whose cultural hegemony and influence have supposedly been weakened by globalization, a new, political rhetoric is emerging that describes culture as being a "catalyst for growth", an "economic indicator" and a "comparative advantage" all while the problematic model of "creative industries" and "artistic capitalism" are maturing globally. After long being relegated to the margins of the economic market, culture is now at the epicentre of the market's transformation. Certain official declarations, such as François Hollande's July 15, 2012 speech at the Festival of Avignon, in which he affirms that "the Festival of Avignon is an asset to France" and that "culture is an investment that creates jobs and economic activity. That's why culture is part of our economic development plan!" are indicative of this trend.

Political doctrine about culture, oscillating between policy statement and economic reasoning, has thus stalled, foreshadowing a dismantling of the public service infrastructure and an expectation that culture becomes an integral and active component of sustainable growth, especially in times of crisis.

Contradictory injunctions

It is thus unsurprising, as part of this "late capitalism" (Jameson 2011), to witness the emergence of self-declared artist-entrepreneurs (Toma 2011), who seek to commercialize unique, value-added "cultural services" as marketable products, brands or labels. The ambivalence of their position is clear: it not only opens the door to a neoliberal affront that seeks either to scrutinize artistic value by reframing it in a production cycle, or even to capture the rents generated by artistic creation (Citton 2014), all while sabotaging its operational and assessment mechanisms. In clearly paradoxical fashion the economics of the performing arts, an atypical if not archaic sector of market activity (Baumol and Bowen 1966), is suddenly thrust into the limelight of economic theory as the new, potential vanguard of cognitive capitalism (Barbéris and Poirson 2013) at the very moment that threats to the artistic professions, especially those in theatre, result in a fresh alienation of creative work (Menger 2003 or Citton in this volume).

And yet, now that management techniques have replaced 'artistic criticism', and the support for artists' welfare benefits has been debased because of a reorientation of cultural politics unfavorable to the artists' cause, the theatre is under pressure to stage the crisis without consistently limiting itself to its usual, placatory, descriptive mechanisms. Playwrights and men of theatre are under pressure to respond to this expectation by analyzing the economy with their own aesthetic and ideological tools all while the "unexplored territories of an economy" that is "normalizing the exceptional" are mobilizing intellectuals from various disciplines (*Esprit* 2010: 31). Meanwhile economists such as Frederic Lordon pride themselves on using the theatre as a heuristic, or even a hermeneutic mechanism. By way of his "serious comedy about the financial crisis", Lordon, an unorthodox and dismayed economist, candidly proposes to "render the crisis surreal". In other words, he endeavors to approach the euphemizing or denial strategies of its sociopolitical consequences from a different angle:

> It is not enough to call it a capitalist crisis. We must stage it, or at least make it heard. . . . A necessary political reaction, the theatre of crisis over-stages the crisis in a context in which the behavioral world tends to under-emphasize it and in which dominant rhetoric focuses its efforts on de-emphasizing it.
>
> (Lordon 2011: 132–133)

A new form of economic theatre that uses a lexicon infused with real and immediate stage experience to express itself seeks to expose the "theatrical anthropology of the speculator" by summoning finance to the stage (*Esprit* 2012: 79).

Beyond opportunistic or contextual effects, this theatre of crisis implicitly reveals the basic truth of all "theatrical representation", which consists of purchasing, for a given time and in each space, the actor's voice, gesture and even his moving body. The theatre, a consensual mechanism of debts, based on arbitrary signs and remuneration for a symbolic exchange, appears to be a fitting space for deconstructing the processes and mechanisms of economic transactions. Koltès masterfully demonstrates this deconstruction by way of the "deal" that underlies the dramatic structure of *Dans la solitude des champs de coton* in 1985; or, in a wholly different approach, the transaction that inspired Claudel's *L'échange* as early as 1894 and more clearly so in the second version in 1951. When the theatre takes hold of the economy and transforms it into a literary or artistic object, it concurrently designates its own economic modes of operation in a perspective that is no longer simply analogical but structurally homological.

Structural homology

Since the decline of the productivist model of the "Trente Glorieuses" and the onset of the current crisis that is seemingly increasingly structural, more so since the 2008 subprime crisis, a new theatrical sequence has emerged in the contemporary repertoire. It is characterized by an unprecedented rise in stage writing rightfully qualified as economic dramaturgy rather than dramaturgy of the economy given that theatre and economy are linked by a mutual implication in the genre. This relationship goes beyond a simple thematic or topical allusion to the financial crisis and constitutes an economic fiction that reveals economics' own fictional dimension. Thus, the objective is no longer to allow the spectator, listener or reader to imagine a world that seeks to remain obscure, or to personify virtual and intangible speculative operations: these important figures of industry, finance and negotiation are now incarnated, in frequent though non-exclusively satirical form, on stage. It is of no more concern than the personification of the virtual and intangible speculative operations exemplified by François Hollande during his presidential campaign in January 2012, when identifying his "real adversary" whose "foothold had become an empire": "It is without name, without face, without party and will never run for office, never be elected. And yet it governs. This adversary is the financial sector" (Hollande 2012).

On the contrary the theatre of crisis does seek to oppose one abstract notion – that of the political economy – with another – that of fictional theatre – by adapting its dramatic devices. Thus, for a non-negligible portion of the current repertoire, seeking out a lucid form of a *dramaturgy of economics* consists of experimenting with the economics of dramaturgy. The financial economy, supplanting questions that permeate modern and contemporary theatre, is thus a matrix for the theatre that henceforth dedicates a considerable share of its attention to the conflict and the violence of the world to which its spectators bear witness. Even if the relationship between art and money today is not novel, it is worth noting that it has reached an unprecedented intensity: it profits from the endemic and recurrent crises that are shaking our fragile economies to the detriment of the theatre's modes of operation. Consequently, the economic crisis is feeding the "crisis of drama" in the same way in which the crisis of drama provides economics with a fitting, dramatic framework. In many cases the *theatres of economics* provide a platform for the *economics of theatre* to play out. It is for this reason that this economic dramaturgy is gaining increasing traction from poetic, if not mystical experimentation, finding its meaning in theatrical gesture: more so from choreographic movements and choral structure favorable to the emergence of a voice of stage directions, than from heuristic, pedagogical, didactical or militant examinations of the mechanisms and strategies at work within the market.

Presages of monetary dramatization can be traced back to late 17th- and 18th-century theatre, characterized by the dramatization of trade and interest inspired by a strengthening form of possessive individualism (Poirson 2011) as well as its attempts at symbolizing the economy. Even 19th-century (Fix and Fougère 2012) political theatre staged power struggles and acts of domination that were at the very heart of the system of industrial production. Contrary to its late 17th- and 18th-century predecessors, today's theatre is preoccupied with speculation and can be characterized by a scission central to our historic bifurcation: the moment when theatre no longer saved face by being partisan to an illusory game. In dramaturgical terms this scission is staged by portraying the monetary system's gridlocked mechanisms as well as the failure of contractual relationships at the heart of economic dogma. Breaking this aesthetic and ideological barrier requires a strategy for undermining the liberal fiction that is based on the following logic: on the one hand a process of staging its own shortcomings, its inability to respect the promises made under its illusory pact; on the other hand, more subtly so, a mechanism for weakening its fictional regimes by overwhelming its system of credibility.

Even more so since the beginning of the 21st century this dramaturgy of economic crisis has been structured around a philosophy of divergence common to numerous playwrights despite the varying postures they may adopt. Contrary to popular belief, monetary dramaturgies have not largely inspired an objectivist or materialistic theatre but rather a theatre of fabling that seeks inspiration in the parable, the supernatural and the fantastical to encapsulate "economic fiction's" anthropological character and function in contemporary societies by way of symbolism and ritual. These dramaturgies have not confined the dramatization of the economy to the most directly or explicitly militant forms of this struggle. To the contrary they have nourished an oblique dramaturgy that finds within the well of imagination the motivation of a fantasy strategy inherent to the theatrical fable, but which is understood to be congruent with the economic fable. A significant number of playwrights frequently and meaningfully rely on salient current events as inspiration for appropriating the theatrical cannon of centuries past and rewriting them to provide a new, poetic perspective on them. New dramaturgies and new theatrical performances closely examine the dominant political economy using identifiable mechanisms from performance theatre, on a theoretical and practical level, by taking into consideration its contradictions as well as its omissions.

Active dramaturgy

For the past 30 years, and especially over the last 15 years, French-language plays, in addition to peer-reviewed manuscripts submitted to French theatres and French publishing houses, have provided a basis for inventorying the number of plays that are directly or tangentially related to the crisis. Such a large neoliberal repertory provides insight into today's postmodern societies all while re-examining the use of a political theatre that rarely describes itself as such but that recognizes its own commensurate skill in diversion, thus roping in the spectator. It successfully highlights the tendency of a specific type of contemporary theatre to stage the mechanisms of economic activity and thought that are assumed to be an authentic part of the fictional production despite somewhat successful attempts by its partisans to characterize it as being unquestionably both positivist and objectivist.

Contemporary productions, using the tested techniques of a repertory theatre that has abandoned its satirical approach to worlds dominated by money or by the mythological imprint of a political economy, constitute the basis for a *dramaturgy of the economy* that seeks to flush out the predominant cultural subconscious at the heart of today's economic rhetoric. This theatre of crisis, on the margins of a documentary theatre that stages the crisis to illustrate its internal mechanisms and to depict its causalities and consequences, employs one-upmanship and euphemism to analyze a non-mainstream perception of current events. This strategy is comparable to that of "Perseus and the Gorgon", in which "vanquishing the medusa requires an indirect approach: the use of a mirror" (Lescot 2012: 74). Michel Vinaver stages the "Bettencourt affair", a political and financial scandal, using identifiable on-stage characters using their real and thus recognizable names. In the "most scorching of current events" he seeks out "the eternal mechanisms of legends and myths" without hesitating to compare "the justice system" or "medical expertise" to Antiquity's *deus ex machina*. Nor does he seek to examine the present by using the measuring rod of "its past, its roots in the past 100 years of French history" to summon "its modern manifestations in which the intimate, the political and the economic are inseparable" (Vinaver 2014). Several trends appear, illustrating a cultural subconscious about the economy, that are present within statistical modeling and theorization. These tendencies unveil concerns that are distinct even if they must be considered in rapport with one another. Three predominate dramatic structures can be identified within this framework: detour, overflow and countercurrent all structure the aesthetic and ideological mechanisms of this theatre of crisis.

Dramaturgical detour uses a symbolic process of mediation, by way of metaphoric expansion, to illustrate the indissociably dramaturgical and economic authority of market mechanisms that are considered through the lens of an intentional allegorization that seeks to bring to the limelight economic dogma's relationship to the foundations of nominal illusion, monetary convention or contractual systems. Such is the case in David Lescot's *Homme en faillite* (2007): a liquidator is authorized to seize the belongings of a man who is literally and figuratively stripped of his belongings. This play aims to illustrate the materialization of an "acute, philosophical awareness between man and property" (Lescot *L'Homme*). The dystopic and uchronic method of opposing two distinct eras is one of the preferred forms of this type of dramatic structure which allows for metaphoric amplification. This is also the case in Emmanuelle Pireyre's *Laissez-nous juste le temps de vous détruire*, staged by Myriam Marzouki at the Maison de la Poésie in 2012: at a time when "living has become a full-time job" (Sequence 4, Table 14.1)

(Pireyre manuscript) the "satellite dish wielding property owner" who "triumphs in the glories of his barbecue grill" is an opportunity to evoke the gentrification of postwar households, a prelude to the impending ecological apocalypse.

In the same vein Joël Pommerat evokes in his research notes for *La Grande et Fabuleuse Histoire du commerce* (2012) a diptych of the 1960s and the first decade of the 21st century: the singular destinies of traveling salesmen, "brave soldiers who are nonetheless committed and steadfast in their convictions" but who are also "ordinary citizens in a world of hollow words and misguided values". He is destined to call to the stage "the great and fabled story of commerce", a conduit for examining a fiduciary society based on "trust: a word that has lost its meaning":

> For me this play is a conduit for staging the ideologies that orient and drive human behavior in today's world. It is a way to demonstrate the way in which commerce – buying and selling – is an activity at the very heart of today's world and how it influences the way in which we perceive ourselves, the way in which we define that which is human as well as our relationships. I want to show how market logic is a source of instability and confusion in our minds and how it breaks down the relationship we have with others, if not with a group, as well as the trust we can have in them.
>
> (Pommerat, *La Grande*)

Informal discussions between colleagues about clearly trivial marketing or sales strategies are evidence of a flawless, professional *ethos* in which the principles of macroeconomics and trade systems take on the allure of a modern Odyssey:

> People generally distrust sales and commerce . . . whereas without these two life cannot exist . . . Do you realize that? . . . In the absence of salespeople, and good ones at that, people will stop buying and if they stop buying factories will close and if factories close nobody can earn a wage, leaving only unemployment and misery.
>
> (Pommerat 2012: 6)

Whereas dramaturgical detour embraces a non-mainstream and accessory approach to the economy, perceived in its systemic if not eco-systemic dimension, what I qualify as *dramaturgical overflow* opts for a frontal and transitive approach: the writing focuses on real economic variables, the perverse interworking of business, on production externalities, the industrial impact on ecology, social systems, morals and aesthetics, the spread of consumerism and its contaminating or reifying effect. This approach relies on extending the liberal paradigm by saturation and defending its own principles especially those related to the excesses of rational behaviour. It frames itself within the vicious cycle of enterprise, of the factory and its means of production and organization. Under the elective pretext of industrial organization and production (Hamidi-Kim 2010), these plays criticize recent methods of disaffection due to work and consumption, as well as of the destabilization or pauperization of employment; find fault in the efficiency of a new-age process of unequal distribution of wealth; annihilate the ethical framework of utilitarianism supported by emphatic images of humanitarian crises as well as personal tragedies. Magnus Dahlström's *L'Usine* uses dialogue between a team of metalworkers in the basement of a factory whose memory is tainted by the recollection of an accident whose victim is the impetus for an announced restructuring. The discourse relative to production imperatives ("never turn your back on the machine, should anything go wrong . . ., never turn your back, should things get out of control . . .") converges with the survival instinct in a cannibalistic factory that becomes the personification of alienated labor and duplication: "Death in your fingers . . . it is not I who is here, it is someone else who has taken over my life . . ." (Dahlström 2003). A similar example can be found in Philippe Malone's *L'Entretien* in which three women, each with a different job (a managing director, a union representative and her daughter, who are interviewed) in the service industry reconcile one another against the backdrop of an employees' chorus. The career strategy provides the basis for questioning the value of work as well as the challenges of existing and becoming part of a group (Malone 2006: 34).

Dramaturgical backhand, contrary to dramaturgical overflow, uses economics' nominal variables as fuel for criticizing the destructive impact of economic dogma and the performativity of its rhetoric. Criticism is aimed primarily at speculative activities, the self-fulfilling outcomes of its fictive creations, and the abusive usage of art to narrate the histories of a "mythocratic" scheme, which form mostly around speculation, and the virtual or immaterial values of the economy. These plays stage the economies of affect as the foundation of new management and marketing practices which use and abuse the mechanisms of storytelling to "brainwash us". In *Les Marchands* Joël Pommerat's female protagonist is an employee at the Norscilor factory who is literally and figuratively constrained in both her professional and personal life. Pommerat attacks the labor theory of value, "the decaying myth of our modernity", by employing an innovative theatrical technique that is a new mode of production. To this end, he uses an epic dramatic device that relies on a constant contradiction between a supposedly authentic voice-over ("The voice you hear now is mine") and a twitchy, mute pantomime of crepuscular characters who continually contradict it, breaking the narrative unity and the necessary fictional coherence.

In *Le Système de Ponzi*, dedicated to the famous late 19th-century Italian-American crook from whom Bernard Madoff would draw inspiration (Lescot 2012), David Lescot returns to the origins of the financial system, understood as a widely accepted mechanism of debts in which plot construction acts as a generator of economic value underwritten by the socio-political structure. This epic and choral theatre unveils the omnipresence of the economy: "the century to come would be defined by Ponzi, not by utopias, nor by political regimes or wars, but by money" (*Le Monde* 2012). At the heart of a dramaturgy characterized by the free flow and the incessant transformation of monetary symbols, at the mercy of the voluntary illusions that it stockpiles, the play gives centre stage to "speculative folly".

At times these various structures converge into a *hybrid dramatic proposition*. Starting with *Lamineurs* (2003) and continuing until *Expansion du vide sous un ciel d'ardoises* (2013), Christophe Tostain evokes the consequences of the postindustrial shift on the labor worker to highlight the man's subjugation to economic considerations. The first play is set in a factory whose machinery serves as a consistent metaphor for the oppression of the masses in a world that is falling apart because of a "physical and psychological depression" and in which man becomes "the very executioner of his own humanity" (Tostain 2005). The second takes place in a shopping centre on the edge of Paris whose transformation from a supermarket into a hypermarket changes the organization of labor as well as management techniques. It portrays management as a "steamroller obsessed with optimizing productivity that dehumanizes both its workers and itself" (Tostain 2013). The disconnect that defines the foundations of these new forms of exploitation is revealed by a discourse that is itself interrupted, choppy, and that tends to disintegrate due to a kind of imitative harmony between industrial gesture and dramatic language:

> I am looking to work on a fractious, charged text that, contrary to its predecessors, is not composed of frames that would allow for temporal omission. A single word can change a text's context, place, and temporality. Thus, despite the false impression of continuity, action is discontinuous, rhythmical. To illustrate the varying managerial models that labor to exert increasing and harassing pressure to optimize return and productivity, the breaks will become increasingly clear and violent.
>
> (Tostain note of intent)

Linguistic burnout, plot disintegration, physical collapse, dilution of sociability, question of the fictional pact . . . What exactly does this theatre of crisis, with its various meanings and devices, advise in terms of a future rapport with the economy? Clearly it has placed in the background, alongside the long-used annals of theatre's archetypes, the secondary role played by the crisis and its presumed authors to the benefit of the theatre of trial and judgement. It thus engenders an eye-opening system of ostentation of both the dramatic possibilities inherent to the economy as well as its eminently performative vocation: as a descriptive discipline (economic fact), normative discipline (economic models), predictive discipline (economic forecasts) or even prescriptive discipline (expectations or recommendations). Economics is founded upon both the stylization of *realia* in which it selects meaningful variables, and on the ability to mobilize stakeholders by means of a powerful mechanism of debts with potentially directive outcomes.

As performance art, theatre is favorably suited to exploit the jurisdictions of dramaturgy and stagecraft of such ambivalence. By taking hold of the language and substance of the crisis, theatre is able to adopt two opposing political postures: the first of which tends to extend the metaphor of economic rhetoric throughout a structure of meaningful analogies in order to reveal and raise awareness about the metaphoric subconscious of the seemingly objective and pragmatic presentation of proven outcomes of economic activity; the second of which, to the contrary, focuses on the system's hidden realities that are obscured by the discipline of economics, which models itself on a purely abstract framework absent any empirical possibilities. By staging the correlations and consequences that economics adamantly seeks to euphemize, blur or obscure, going as far to qualify them as "externalities", the theatre obstructs attempts at economic modeling through application. By shedding light on the system's hidden realities, the theatre gives form and substance to the abstraction of economic imaginaries and to its reckless structure.

Political posture

Visibility is central to the visual arts that seek to expose populations relegated to the marginalized domains of political representation by pushing to the forefront the link between democracy and the market. When it is all said and done the theatre of crisis proposes to remedy to this "under-representation" by actively contributing to the establishment of a "narrative democracy" (Rosanvallon 2014: 14, 26) as well as by bringing face to face, within the public sphere, two competing representation devices: visibility, which is characteristic of artist-capitalism, founded on the creation of market-oriented exhibition devices[1] and dogmatic entrapment, is thus placed in opposition with visuality (Brighenti 2010), which is characteristic of a critical stance that seeks to expose subaltern minorities hitherto relegated to the margins of political representation. Manuel Pereira does just this with his "figures of the world" in *Permafrost*, dedicated to the "frozen" or "immutable life" of factory workers, or in other words to industrial reification, in which he stages the laborer's sort by disassociating the voice and the bodies of the actors: "On the stage, the actors work independently of the voices that they adopt. An entire people gravitate around Man and Woman. These figures are able to evolve, act, and speak naturally amongst themselves although the audience cannot distinctly make out what they are saying" (Pereira 2010: 8).

Claudine Galea has a similar objective in *Les Invisibles*, which portrays a family, victim of the industrial crisis, who begins distributing advertising leaflets: a retired mother, a physically fragile father broken by his former job on a production line, a daughter who works as a secretary and a son who is an unemployed automobile mechanic. The family members are reunited and melded into a single chorus as they distribute the advertising leaflets. As such they are simultaneously omnipresent and yet nonexistent in society's eyes. The family's solidarity, however, is not a safety net. It is rather a way to pool their handicaps, combine their solitude and accumulate their helplessness: "We do everything together/ Everything that is inexpensive/If we were not together we would not make it/ We are the fingers of a single hand/The four of us bonded/We are not getting by" (Galea 2012: 13–14). The organic metaphor of the fingers, fundamental to holistic politics, thus becomes the very symbol of the disaffiliation and the relegation of the laborer's mutilated body, thrown on the scrapheap to make way for the postindustrial transition.

Nasser Djemaï's *Les Invisibles* seeks similar outcomes in a play dedicated to those forgotten by the history of France's industrial reconstruction following the Second World War: she traces the "tragedy of the Chibanis", the poor, retired workers of France's economic immigration whose days consisted of working in the factory, the Sonacotra foyers and sentimental isolation due to geographical distances. Thrice disowned as laborers, immigrants and retirees, this demographic is the specter of failure in France's Republican integration model. Stigmatized, they are the manifestation of France's shameful conscious, having forgotten the people who rebuilt the country and who were yet still excluded from society: "France became their country, they brought their dreams with them, but they became phantoms. They paved the roads, built the HLMs, and produced quantities of spare parts from production lines and machine tools". Reduced to a simple equation of labor supply, these immigrant workers are generics, perfectly replaceable and, put bluntly, "without a history", straight from a mathematical equation: "But in the collective subconscious these foreign workers are immortal because they are replaceable. They are not born, they are not raised, they do not age, they have a single purpose: TO WORK". When they become too inept to work, they are cast aside and relegated to the collective conscious's limbo, or in other words, to society's blind spot: "Thrown overboard right along with the working class and its struggle. They had no purchasing power, they became invisible" (Djemaï 2011: 5–7).

Giving voice and body to economic modeling's forgotten beings, to those excluded from public and symbolic space, dually relegated to the outskirts of an economic system (as an adjustment variable) and to the margins of a democratic model (voiceless), means engaging in active awareness building by establishing a theatrical scene in the "oppositional public space" alongside the structured public space that belongs to the bourgeois voice (Negt 2007); it also means opposing the "hidden texts" belonging to the culture of resistance in opposition to the dominant "public texts" (Scott 2008: 32–33) through empowerment.

At stake is an effort to leave the reader or spectator with a sense of unfulfillment by way of a repertoire which dares seek a remedy for evil by condemning market-driven exhibition via theatrical mockery:

> I am looking for something behind the action, the words, the situation. Something that is not easily identified, something that must perform, something that must meddle in, slip between the lines of the gestures and the spoken words like a hyper-present phantom reality that is stronger as an embodiment than if it were designated by the text or by the cast of actors, by their spoken, highlighted intentions. A phantom reality like these phantom appendages that were amputated but whose presence continues to be felt.

Admitting that "nothing is more political than style, above all the actor's style, his way of acting" to clarify the organic link between writing and the stage, Joël Pommerat shows us the way to a true gestural philosophy, the source of renewed political agency. If "money is the sublime value" and if it "gives value to all that exists, to a gesture, to a discourse", the theatre of money is likely one of the most capable artistic forms, given adequate performance protocols, for challenging systems of social construction and economic appraisal of value. This is what gives it, even more so than its social engagement: a sense of responsibility in the politics of representation.

Martial Poirson
Full Professor of Paris 8 University

Note

1 Goods, as well as people, such as those in reality shows, who are distant descendants of the "human zoo" and its ethnic shows.

Bibliography

Barbéris, I. and Poirson, M. (2013), *Economie du spectacle vivant*, Paris: Puf.

Baumol, W. and Bowen, W. (1966), *Performing Arts: The Economic Dilemma*, Boston, MA: MIT Press.

Brighenti, A. M. (2010), *Visibility in Social Theory and Social Research*, New York, Basingstoke: Palgrave, McMillan.

Citton, Y. (ed.) (2014), *L'économie de l'attention, nouvel horizon du capitalisme?* Paris: La Découverte.

Dahlström, M. (2003), *L'Usine*, Paris: Les Solitaires intempestifs.

Esprit n°361 (2010, January), "Les Impensés de l'économie".

Esprit n°385 (2012, June), "La crise, comment la raconter?".

Fix, F. and Fougère, M.-A. (eds.) (2012), *L'Argent et le rire de Balzac à Mirabeau*, Presses Universitaires de Rennes.

Forrester, V. (1996), *L'horreur économique*, Paris: Fayard.

Galea, C. (2012), *Les invisibles*, Montpellier: Espaces 34, 13–14.

Hilaire, N. (2008), *L'artiste et l'entrepreneur*, Paris: Cité du Design éditions.

Jameson, F. (2011), *Le postmodernism ou la logique culturelle du capitalism tardif*, Paris: Ecole nationale supérieure des Beaux-Arts de Paris.

Le Monde (2012, January 23).

Lescot, D. (2012), "La Finance sur les planches", *Esprit*, 385: 74–81.

Lescot, D. (2012), *Le Système de Ponzi*, Arles: Actes Sud.

Lescot, D. Note of intent to stage in *L'Homme ne faillite*.

Lipovetsky, G. (2013), *L'esthétisation du Monde. Vivre à l'âge du capitalisme artiste*, Paris: Editions Gallimard.

Lordon, F. (2011), *D'un Retournement l'autre, comédie sérieuse sur la crise financière en quatre actes, et en alexandrins*, Paris: Seuil.

Malone, P. (2006), *L'Entretien*, Montpellier: Espaces 34, www.editions-espaces34.fr/

Méchoulan, E. (2011), *La crise du discours économique. Travail immatériel et émancipation*, Québec: Editions Nota Bene.

Menger, P.-M. (2003), *Portrait de l'artiste en travailleur: métamorphoses du capitalisme*, Paris: Seuil.

Menger, P.-M. (2009), *Le travail créateur: s'accomplir dans l'incertain*, Paris: Gallimard-Seuil-EHESS.

Moulier-Bouting, Y. (2007), *Le capitalisme: la nouvelle grande transformation*, Paris: Editions Amsterdam.

Moulier-Bouting, Y. (2010), *L'Abeille et l'Economiste*, Paris: Carnets Nord.

Mutitudes n°39 (2009, April).

Negt, O. (2007), *L'Espace public oppositionnel*, Paris: Payot.

Pereira, M. (2010), *Permafrost*, Montpellier: Espaces 34, www.editions-espaces34.fr/

Pireyre, E., *Laissez-nous juste le temps de vous détruire*, Author's manuscript.

Poirson, M. (2011), *Spectacle et économie à l'âge classique*, Paris: Classiques Garnier.

Pommerat, J. (2007), *Théâtres en présence*, Arles: Actes Sud Papiers.

Pommerat, J. (2012), *La Grande et Fabuleuse Histoire du commerce*, Arles: Actes Sud Papier, Scene 1, p. 6.

Pommerat, J. (2013), "Je pense que l'économie est rentrée dans la vie de l'homme de la rue", *UBU, scenes d'Europe*, 54/55, "Thêatre et argent", 2nd semester.

Pommerat, J., Note of intent to stage in *La Grande et Fabuleuse Histoire du commerce*.

Rosanvallon, P. (2014), *Le Parlement des invisibles: Raconter la vie*, Paris: Seuil.

Scott, J. C. (2008), *La domination et les arts de la résistance: Fragments du discours subalterne*, Paris: Editions Amsterdam. Speech given at Bourget on January 21, 2012: www.parti-socialiste.fr/articles/retrouvez-le-discours-de-francois-hollande-au-bourget

Tarkos, C. (2012), "L'Argent", in *Ecrits poétiques*, Paris: P.O.L. Editions.

Toma, Y., Jamet-Chavigny, S. and Devèze, L. (dir.) (2011), *Artistes et entreprises*, Besançon: D'Ailleurs.

Tostain, C. (2005), *Lamineurs*, Montpellier: Espaces 34, www.editions-espaces34.fr/

Tostain, C. (2013), *Ciel étoilé au-dessus du vide*, Montpellier: Espaces 34, www.editions-espaces34.fr/

Vinaver, M. (2014, March 9), "L'affaire Bettencourt est un crash", *Le Monde*.

Vinaver, M. (2015), *Bettencourt Boulevard ou une histoire de France*, Paris: L'Arche.

Vinaver, M. *Bettencourt Boulevard ou une histoire de France*, Paris: L'Arche.

15 Restructuring the attention economy

Literary interpretation as an antidote to mass media distraction

Yves Citton

A considerable amount of articles, conferences, monographs or collective publications have been devoted over the past 20 years to the relations between economics and literature. Most of them have focused on the economic content of literary works, answering the general question: *how do authors X or novel Y represent economic relations?* While this remains a stimulating way to have economics and literature cross each other's path, I will suggest another approach to set them into dialogue, by taking stock of the new developments of what is increasingly called "the attention economy".

Poets, playwrights, novelists and artists did not wait for economists to realize that attention was a scarce resource. As Richard Lanham eloquently stressed, what is rhetoric, but attention economy practiced and taught more than 2,000 years before Herbert Simon, Dallas Smythe or Richard Serra explicitly theorized it in the 1970s? Even before modern art competed for mass audiences, the notion of "style" has often been elaborated as an attention-catching device (Lanham 2006). But if it is accurate to say literature preceded economics in paying attention to attention, this article hopes to suggest that literature may still be ahead of the game, now that attention has been widely recognized as being our most scarce and most precious resource. Were we to conceive of the literary experience primarily as an attentional practice, we might find in it a possibility to overcome some of the dead ends in which our commercially driven mass media have trapped our collective attention.

The attention economy and the upsetting of old economics

Discussions about the attention economy took off around 1996–97 with a series of interventions and debates launched around Michael Goldhaber, who claimed a "new economy" was emerging: "like any economy the new one is based on what is both most desirable and ultimately most scarce, and now this is the attention that comes from other people" (Goldhaber 1996). The main argument could be summarized as follows.

In the "old" economy, which lasted from the Neolithic period until the end of the 20th century, scarcity would concern mostly material resources and goods. The production of material goods required human attention, but economies were organized around the trading of the things which embodied productive labor. These goods were used in the (re)production of human life, but the economic sphere dealt with the *indirect* (re)production of human life through material goods.

In the "new" economy, which is only emerging at the beginning of the third millennium, an increasing amount of resources are devoted to the *direct* (re)production of human life, as witnessed by the expansion of services (to the expense of agriculture and industry) in the distribution of the workforce. Humans always took "direct" care of other humans, but it was usually done outside of the economic sphere (by mothers, grandparents, children, priests, etc.). As the service economy takes an ever-expanding share of our GDP, producing human capacity and human relations is increasingly important.[1]

As the digital economy unfolds, the production of cultural goods, which also dramatically expanded throughout the 20th century, provides cultural services not only on a new scale, but within a new configuration: digital cultural goods (text, music or video files), even if they still require material resources to be invented and produced in their prototype, can now be reproduced, communicated and broadcasted at a marginal cost close to zero—at least as far as the individual emitter and the receiver are concerned, since apart from the purchase of the computer and from the monthly connection cost accruing to the individual subscriber, the collectivity still needs to mobilize a lot of material resources and energy to produce, operate and cool the servers spread throughout the world.

The ability offered to individuals to share or download a book, an image, a song, a film on the Internet "for free" (once equipment, connection and electricity cost are taken care of) has led many to focus their definition of "the new economy" on the *non-rival* nature of cultural goods in a digital environment: I can give you my music file without losing it, whereas I lose my car or my pen if I give them to you. The attention economy is here to remind us that cultural goods are non-rival in their communication, but *not* in their reception—where another form of rivalry counterbalances the superabundance of available goods: the opportunity cost of devoting one's attention to *this* rather than *that* cultural product.

In the "new" economy, therefore, the main scarcity—and hence the new source of value—is no longer in the material goods traded among economic agents, but in the *human attention* needed to "consume" them. Since it is still necessary to produce computers, servers and power plants (and food, medicine, houses and clothing) for people to sustain their life and for cultural goods to circulate, the new economy did not so much *replace* the old one, as it *adds another layer* which is rapidly taking a hegemonic role over the whole economic sphere, reconfiguring the lower layers in line with its new logic.[2]

Talks about the "information overload" or about the need to "(re)design organizations for an information-rich world" (Toffler 1970; Simon 1971) predates the late 1990s, but it is only at this moment that "the attention economy" has become a household name (among Internet futurologists and marketers, if not among economists), as the following Ngram Viewer charts, based on occurrences compiled from the Google Books database show (see Figure 15.1 for English and Figure 15.2 for French).

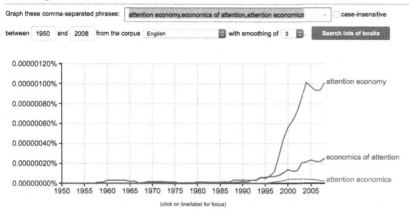

Figure 15.1 Search with "attention economy", "economics of attention", "attention economics" (1950–2008)

Source: Google Books Ngram Viever

Link: https://books.google.com/ngrams/graph?content=attention+economy%2Ceconomics+of+attention%2Cattention+economics&year_start=1950&year_end=2008&corpus=15&smoothing=3&share=&direct_url=t1%3B%2Cattention%20economy%3B%2Cc0%3B.t1%3B%2Ceconomics%20of%20attention%3B%2Cc0%3B.t1%3B%2Cattention%20economics%3B%2Cc0

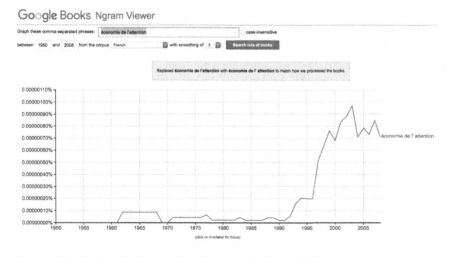

Figure 15.2 Search with "économie de l'attention" (1950–2008)

Source: Google Books Ngram Viever

Link: https://books.google.com/ngrams/graph?content=économie+de+l%27attention&year_start=1950&year_end=2008&corpus=19&smoothing=3&share=&direct_url=t1%3B%2Céconomie%20de%20l%27%20attention%3B%2Cc0

Apart from the debates generated around Michael Goldhaber's claims in close interaction with the discussions about a new digital economy, Georg Franck published his book *Ökonomie der Aufmerksamkeit: Ein Entwurf* in 1998, which sketched a broader sociological approach for the attention economy, with an emphasis on issues of visibility, celebrity, reputation and prominence (Franck 1998, 1999). In 2001, John C. Beck and Thomas H. Davenport released for Harvard Business School the most widely known book adapting these issues for managers and marketers, helping them build strategies more finely tuned to the "attention-scape" specific to each situation (Beck and Davenport 2001). While advertisers, spin doctors and PR experts were more and more explicitly referring to the attention economy, cultural critics like Jonathan Beller were putting it at the core of their denunciation of the capitalist society of the spectacle (Beller 2006).

From one side of the ideological spectrum to the other, there seemed to be an agreement on the revolution about to happen: "In the past, attention was taken for granted, and goods and services were valuable. In the future, many goods and services will be given away for free in exchange for a few seconds or minutes of the user's attention" (Beck and Davenport 2001: 213). The attention economy upsets our oldest economic habits: instead of having to pay to gain books, we will soon be paid to read them. Since a book, a film or a commercial ad exists only where it is viewed by human subjects, the consumer is now holding the most precious currency in her head (rather than in her purse). In this new economy, "to look is to labor": "mass media, taken as a whole, is the deterritorialized factory, in which spectators do the work of making themselves over to meet the libidinal, political, temporal, corporeal and ideological protocols of an ever-intensifying capitalism" (Beller 2006: 112, 181; see Smythe 1977 for an earlier version of this argument).

While economics as we knew it still rules the industrial production of the paper, films, computers, trucks and container ships which bring us the means to connect to the Internet, the attention economy is setting a whole new set of rules, turning all of our models upside down, since the main form of scarcity is now owned by the receiver rather than by the producer. In our societies ever more devoted to services, to the direct production of human relations and to the communication of cultural goods, economics has to be updated and re-invented, by taking attention as its new form of capital.

Towards a literary management of attention?

While literary scholars will welcome being paid to read, they may think the theoretical debates about the new currency of the new economy concern mostly economists. They would be wrong. What is happening with the upsetting of the traditional economic models is no less than *economics becoming literature* – we literary scholars are *already* paid to read, aren't we? (So are most economists and most researchers.) The attention economy provides us with a most exciting example of the intimate relation between economics and literature since attention economists are merely re-discovering what literary writers and critics have been practicing and theorizing for decades and centuries.

If we bring a new phrase into the search engine provided by Google Books Ngram Viewer (the "economy of attention"), and if we expand its historical scope further back, all the way to 1850 instead of 1950, a new picture emerges, different from the supposed "revolution" of the late 1990s (see Figure 15.3 for the English and 15.4 for the French).

While expanding the historical scope merely reveals that people already wrote about the "économie de l'attention" in French before the Internet, since the use of the phrase had a first peak around 1900, the addition of "economy of attention" to the search in English tells us a much more interesting story. That the peak of paying attention to attention appears to be in the first quarter of the 20th century, rather than in the first decade of the 21st century, may be due to a statistical fluke (since today's publishers of new books may not want their latest release to be made available on Google Books). What we can learn from going back to the data charted on these curves, however, is that the phrase "economy of attention" was not so much used by economists, or marketers, but rather – for more than a century before Michael Goldhaber and Georg Franck – by rhetoricians, literary critics, psychologists and theorists of aesthetics.

Two books devoted to the attention economy help us understand this displacement of the lexicographic curve, towards the beginning of the 20th century and towards the arts. Art historian Jonathan Crary produced the most fascinating and

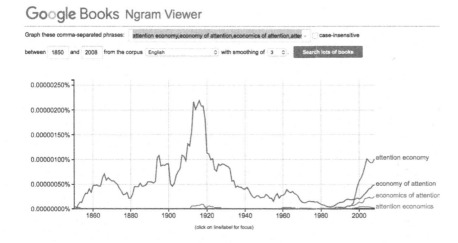

Figure 15.3 Search with "attention economy", "economy of attention", "economics of attention", "attention economics" (1850–2008)

Source: Google Books Ngram Viever

Link: https://books.google.com/ngrams/graph?content=attention+economy%2C+economics+of+atten tion%2C+attention+economics%2C+economics+of+attention+&year_start=1850&year_end=2008& corpus=15&smoothing=3&share=&direct_url=t1%3B%2Cattention%20economy%3B%2Cc0%3B. t1%3B%2Ceconomics%20of%20attention%3B%2Cc0%3B.t1%3B%2Cattention%20econo mics%3B%2Cc0%3B.t1%3B%2Ceconomics%20of%20attention%3B%2Cc0

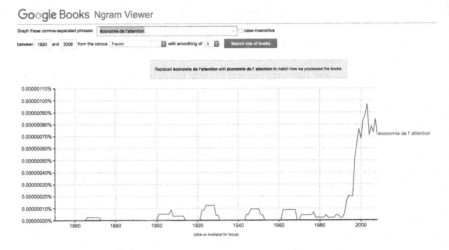

Figure 15.4 Search with "économie de l'attention" (1850–2008)

Source: Google Books Ngram Viever

https://books.google.com/ngrams/graph?content=économie+de+l%27attention+&year_start=1850
&year_end=2008&corpus=19&smoothing=3&share=&direct_url=t1%3B%2Céconomie%20de%20l
%27%20attention%3B%2Cc0

stimulating study to date on the history of the modern management of attention. He shows that the last decades of the 19th century witnessed a striking rise in the study of human attention as four parallel trends converged towards making it a crucial problem of the time: experimental psychologists developed new devices to measure it; managers needed new tricks to keep the workers attentive to the boring repetitive actions demanded by the assembly line; the emerging consumer society needed new baits to lure shoppers into freshly designed modern stores; new media technologies emerged to capture the spectators' gaze into ever more amazing visual experiences (from the Kaiserpanorama to cinema and beyond). The current rediscovery of the crucial issues of the attention economy – including its pedagogical/pharmaceutical form of Attention Deficit Disorder – merely rehashes a fundamental problem that is at least 150 years old:

> Since the late 19th century, and increasingly during the last two decades, capitalist modernity has generated a constant re-creation of the conditions of sensory experience, in what could be called a revolutionizing of the means of perception. . . . Inattention, especially within the context of new forms of large scale industrialized production, was treated as a danger and a serious problem, even though it was often the very modernized arrangements of labor that produced inattention. It is possible to see one crucial aspect of modernity as an ongoing crisis of attentiveness, in which the changing configurations of capitalism continually push attention and distraction to new limits and

thresholds, with an endless sequence of new products, sources of stimulation and streams of information, and then respond with new methods of managing and regulating perception.

(Crary 1999: 13–14)

Rhetorician Richard Lanham suggests we should broaden our historical horizon even further: attention economists have been around for more than 2,000 years, since rhetoric, while "usually defined as 'the art of persuasion', might as well have been called 'the economics of attention'" (Lanham 2006: xii). Whether the orator grabs our interest in his initial *captatio benevolentiae*, whether he sustains it by inserting stories in his argument, or whether he fuels it by appealing to our effects of compassion or indignation, his specialized skills consists in the management of his audience's attention. Well before the assembly line, the Galeries Lafayette or cinema was invented, rhetoricians, literary writers and critics were already developing an economy (and an economics) of attention in their speeches, poems, tales, novels and treatises. Foresight or wishful thinking, Richard Lanham wants us to believe these literary skills – practiced for 2,000 years and abundantly discussed as "economy of attention" by scholars in stylistics one century before the current rise of the "attention economy" – will soon be viewed as central to the current reconfiguration of our modes of production:

> The devices that regulate attention are stylistic devices. Attracting attention is all about style. If attention is now at the center of the economy rather than stuff, so then is style. It moves from the periphery to the center. Style and substance trade places. And so do real property and intellectual property. . . . The arts and letters now stand at the center. They are the disciplines that study how attention is divided, how cultural capital is created and traded. When our children come home and tell us they have majored in English or art history, no longer need we tremble for their economic future.
>
> (Lanham 2006: xi–xii)

Hopeful (or humourous) as this may sound, a good point is made. Most of what we (in the rich Western world) produce and consume depends crucially on questions of design, i.e. style (looks, brands, fashion, etc.). Hundreds and thousands of workers are hired, displaced, laid off when a certain style (Apple, GM, Tommy Hilfiger) starts or stops being trendy. The countless bubbles on which our economic growth relies (before they burst) always rest on matters of persuasion and belief; even in our age of automated trading, machines may be driven by numbers, but bulls and bears still feed on elaborate forms of discourse, rather than on raw data. As for the more mundane realities of the attention economy, what are cultural goods but stylistic devices?

Hence it is not so irrational to advise young generations to turn to literary masters like Shakespeare and Goethe, Gracián and Proust, Pavese and Rushdie, to understand, absorb and master the fine art of attention management. The relation between literature and economics would thus develop on an entirely new ground.

We would no longer look for economic realities (trade, debt, exploitation) in the plots of famous novels to understand how literature "represents" the economy. Instead, we would analyze how stylistic devices govern the reader's attention within the limited space of the book, to understand how comparable stylistic devices govern our individual and collective attention within the open space of our societies.[3] We would no longer try merely to recognize economic mechanisms at work in fictional worlds. Instead, models of storytelling, of analogical thinking, of navigating within a complex web of information, of staging and performing communication would be developed in close reading of literary texts, to be projected onto our economic reality. Such a reversal is already practiced in literary courses designed for business schools all around the world, with "Shakespeare for Managers" as a classic of the genre. Perhaps the theoretical frame provided by the attention economy can help us go beyond this application of literary tricks to business practices.

Four regimes of attention

Attention comes in many forms. Psychologists and neuroscientists show that a lot of what our attention catches, sorts out, registers or brushes aside is done without our being aware of it at all: our brain attends to many complex tasks before we can even think about paying attention to them.[4] Apart from this first difference between *back-of-mind* and *front-of-mind* attention, Beck and Davenport make two other helpful distinctions. "You pay *voluntary* attention to things you find innately interesting, things you'd focus on even if doing so were explicitly forbidden. *Captive* attention is thrust upon you", as when you have to suffer through commercial ads before the main feature in a movie theatre. "We pay attention to some things because we wish to avoid negative experiences (*aversive* attention)", for instance when we notice a danger sign, whereas "we pay attention to other things because we think they may bring us positive experiences (*attractive* attention)", for instance when we see the feature film after the commercials (Beck and Davenport 2001: 23).

Such categories do not seem to help much for accounting for the literary experience: don't we all read books voluntarily, with the best of our front-of-mind abilities, because we find them attractive? Maybe not: for several children – and probably for *all* of us initially – reading literature in school is motivated by aversive attention (we want to avoid a bad grade), developed in a captive setting (we can't wait for the school day to end), with a good help from our back-of-mind (as we desperately try to recollect what the teacher was talking about while we drifted off, daydreaming). Even in our adult age, the quality and intensity of the attention we devote to any book or page are very much mixed and fluctuating.

Over the last 200 years, however, literary studies have progressively developed a specific, and rather odd, economy of attention, which we may now take for granted, but which deserves closer consideration. I will attempt to describe its originality by contrasting it with the four "regimes of attention" French sociologist Dominique Boullier has identified in a series of suggestive articles not yet translated into English (Boullier 2009; Boullier 2012: 41–57).

The first regime relies on the sudden stimulation provided by an *alarm* (in French: *alerte*): a threat, a warning sign, an opportunity pops out and makes me notice it. Alarms are characterized by their saliency: they jump at us, from unexpected places, even if we were not particularly looking for them. The regime of alarm is dominant in the way the media constantly attempt to draw our attention in terms of scandals, crises and scoops. Countless Hollywood movies and TV series also rely on a steady diet of (back-of-mind) alarms as they speed up their editing, knowing that our brain is wired to suspect a potential threat in each significant alteration of our sensory field.

In direct symmetry to this state of exposure to constantly renewed forms of saliency, the regime of *loyalty* (in French: *fidélisation*) relies on the identification of trusted channels which we consider as safe and reliable sources of goods and data. Style is precisely what helps us identify such trusted channels, through the names of brands or authors, through artistic currents and schools characterized by specific aesthetic features, through certain manners of acting or speaking which inspire our confidence or diffidence.

The third regime of attention identified by Dominique Boullier is *projection*: wherever we go, we carry with us a certain sensitivity; we filter the stimuli through a certain number of criteria which we constantly tend to "project" around us, to orient ourselves within old and new environments. Our attention – and our identity – is defined by what we are sensitive or insensitive to: certain smells, certain views, certain tolerances and allergies, patterns, *gestalts* and *imagos*, which trigger pleasure or pain in us. Projective attention allows me to feel at ease everywhere, to negate, so to speak, the diversity of the environments through which I travel, since it pushes me to "attend" to the same things wherever I am. Boullier explicitly plays with the military connotations of "projection of power": the extreme model of projective attention is that of a colonizing mission, which deletes local features to impose the colonizer's standards.

Finally, the last regime of attention, which stands in symmetrical opposition to projection, is that of *immersion*: instead of recognizing the same familiar things in all the environments I cross, I am led to dive into immersive worlds which are originally alien. Apart from what we can experience in movie theatres or video games, the most emblematic experience of immersive attention is provided by my first arrival in an exotic city where I don't speak the language, don't know the customs or standards, and where I have to find my way on my own. Since I neither master nor even know the rules of the games played by the locals, my attention consists in an attitude of multidirectional and open-minded vigilance: as dangers and rewards may come from all sides, in any shape and size, my awareness of my environment needs to be as intense, yet wide and unfocused.

These four regimes of attention are not to be seen as exclusive of each other: Dominique Boullier presents them rather as four polarities which help us analyze and map the specific mixed attention we mobilize in any situation. I took time to summarize them because I believe they can help us better understand the specificity and importance of what has been developing over the last 200 years in literary studies. If we use these four poles to map various experiences in terms of attentional regimes, we could first oppose the ideal of *classical art*, based on the projection of rules, norms and expectations, and on the loyalty to certain pre-existing styles, to the practice of *modern art*, keen to shock us with alarms and eager to immerse us in unfamiliar situations. But we would also be in a position to sharpen the fundamental distinction which makes literary interpretation a perfect "antidote" (counterbalance if not counter-poison) to our mass media regime of collective distraction.

These four "polar" regimes allow Dominique Boullier to show the pernicious effects of a *mass media* configuration riding merely on *alarms*: the political agenda is subjected to a constant state of distraction, due to the reliance on alarms (scandals, shocks, disasters, crises) to draw audience (along with advertisement money). This regime structurally keeps us from collectively addressing the long-term issues which loom at the horizon, and which we can only discuss after they explode in our face – i.e. when it is too late for anyone to devise satisfactory and non-catastrophic solutions. In the economy and in politics, not to mention the most obvious case of environmental issues, our mass media collectively fail us because of their structural mix of ceaseless alarm, preventing any anticipatory reflection, and of rigidly formatted *projection*: whatever news may come from around the world, it will be "processed" (like processed cheese) within a maximum of 90 seconds of images and two minutes of expert comments on the evening TV broadcast. The crucial function of "agenda setting", which commands the orientation and focusing of our collective attention, is not so much conditioned by content as by formal constraints: even the most intelligent and benevolent journalists are bound to "project" this formatting on the reality they attempt to "cover" (a suggestive expression!), just in the same way as an army projects its power on the land it attempts to occupy. Mental occupation is what attention is all about, uncomfortably surfing on the thin line between oppressive alienation and purposeful absorption.

Literary interpretation as attentional regime

In contrast with the mix of alarm and projection which seems to characterize our current mass media regime, *literary interpretation* could be between the poles of loyalty and immersion. It pushes *loyalty* to its limits insofar as – with the development of hermeneutics since the late 19th century, of psychoanalysis after the 1930s, of the *nouvelle critique* in the 1960s, and of deconstruction at the end of the 20th century – it attempts to be loyal to the text even against or beyond its author's self-conscious intentions. In spite of the return to neo-historicism and *critique génétique* after the 1990s, most current practices of literary interpretation are founded upon the premise of the quasi-sacredness of the text: changing a word or even a comma in a page written by Mallarmé, Thomas Mann or Ezra Pound would be sacrilege – just as altering the word of the Prophet or the letters of the Torah. Where the interpretive activity consists in looking as attentively as possible at something which preexists (here: the text), it is founded upon a necessary (even if evolving) loyalty to this preexisting "letter" (for which a new "spirit" has to be ceaselessly reinvented).

As it has been practiced over the last 200 years, literary interpretation can also be considered as an experience in *immersion* – a point which can be illustrated on at least two levels. First, as Italian critic Arturo Mazzarella has shown, the experience of reading modern literary fictions enacted, illustrated, explored and mapped the experience of immersing oneself in "virtual reality", which our current video games merely brought to a more absorbing form of sensory achievement (Mazzarella 2004, 2008).[5] If it is common for a reader to be immersed in a fictional (possible) world, one could think the interpreter should, on the contrary, do whatever is possible to extract him- or herself from this immersive delusion, to analyze and study the text with a maximum of critical distance. It seems however, that the interpretive stance – in spite of, or rather *because* of, its critical dimension – represents an emblematic form of immersion, as defined in terms of attentional regime by Dominique Boullier.

As a polar opposite to projection, the specificity of the regime of immersion consists in diving into an unfamiliar, or even alien, environment, an environment where one can no longer project one's customary habits, standards, criteria and expectations. This is the real challenge of the interpretive adventure as it has taken its current shape over the last decades: its goal is not so much to achieve a position of mastery, in light of which the text could finally be explained (away), made transparent, brought to its ultimate truth, but rather to confront our preexisting forms of knowledge and certainty with a radical textual alien, which will help us refine and improve our fatally reductive and oversimplified worldview.[6] We may think we "understand" a page by Cervantes, Laurence Sterne or Denis Diderot when we first read it, in which case there is no need for literary interpretation. This form of practice is premised upon opacities or problems perceived as blurring the meaning of the text. Moreover, *literary interpretation is an attentional regime which construes problems in the (apparently transparent) messages which circulate around and through us*: it "projects" on the texts (even the most familiar ones) the attitude of multidirectional and open-minded vigilance required by situations of immersion in an alien environment.

Hence the constitutive paradox and tensions of this peculiar regime of attention: it uses its loyalty to the letter of text as a leverage to suspend its familiarity with the apparently transparent message of the text; it projects us into the work under conditions of immersion which make it impossible for us to project our preexisting standards. As Figure 12.5 attempts to show, literary interpretation is located half-way between two aesthetical regimes. It shares with classical art a common attitude of loyalty, attentive to stylization and to the transmission of formal norms through time and space, even though it is as suspicious as possible towards our tendency to project standards which neuter the problems raised by the encounter with alien forms of life. It shares with modern art this desire to immerse oneself in a radically de-stabilizing situation, even though it is suspicious towards a regime where alarms pop out by themselves, by their own saliency: instead, it favors the

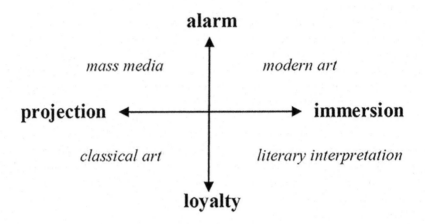

Figure 15.5 Regimes of attention (adapted from Boullier 2012)

patient uncovering of problems construed from within our relation with the alien (rather than in reaction to it).

The attentional regime of literary interpretation appears as a polar opposite to the attention induced by our current mass media configurations. Instead of mobilizing pre-parametered reactions to endlessly renewed alarms, imposed upon us from an outside which almost totally escapes from our control, crushing our agency and condemning us to feelings of powerlessness, literary interpretation nurtures new sensibilities and new forms of agency, by construing highly focused problems patiently elaborated in dialogue with the exterior letter of the texts. We could thus consider the procedures of focused re-orientation constructed by interpretive attention as an antidote to the weapons of mass distraction showered upon us by the dominant media.

Rather than as enemies, however, it may be more fruitful to consider them as complementary. If it is to survive in not-always-friendly environments, any organism needs to rely upon alarms and projections of familiar standards, helping it react to previously identified threats and opportunities. Apart from this short-term processing of urgent information, it also needs a more reflexive system to devise new patterns in unforeseeable data, to re-orient itself in the constant flow of information by construing new meanings in it. A sound ecology of attention needs to rely both on the projective processing of alarms and on the interpretive elaboration of meaning. The main threat to our collective survival may come from the current imbalance between the overpowering dominance of the media apparatuses and the dramatic weakening of the institutions which traditionally nurtured and fostered our interpretive skills.

From economy to ecology, from literary studies to media archaeology

Let me summarize my overall argument before concluding it. Theorists of the attention economy tell us that an old process of valorization (based on visibility, reputation, celebrity, fame, prominence) is gaining new ground, thanks to the evolution of our modes of production, social relations and means of communication. Even if it is likely to remain an exacerbated cause of conflicts and wars, as global and local environmental threats put our collective survival at risk, issues relative to the scarcity of material resources are dominated by issues relative to the scarcity of individual and collective attention. In an intensely mediated world largely run by the procedures of formal democracy, the superabundance of cultural goods, made possible by their digitalization, puts the attentional filtering (of what matters more or less for us as social agents) in the hottest of spots. Even a summary glance at our current attention economy suggests we are experiencing a crucial moment in what Jonathan Crary described as the "ongoing crisis of attentiveness" associated with modernity.

Economists are summoned to develop new models and to devise a whole new set of principles to understand the dynamics of this emerging attention economy. Scholars in rhetoric, aesthetics and literary studies can bring a significant contribution to this necessary re-deployment of the economic discipline, since the analysis of "the economy of attention" can draw from a rich toolkit developed by generations and generations of research on issues of styles, design, semiotics, suspense, verisimilitude, balance, variation, modulation, perceptive saliency or formal consistency. The mapping of four regimes of attention helps us see more precisely what could be the contribution of literary studies to the restructuring of our collective attention ecology: the mix of loyalty and immersion nurtured by the interpretive attitude provides an essential counterweight to the mix of alarm and projection fostered by the current configuration of our mass media.

No less than economists, however, literary scholars are summoned to rethink and reshape their modes of research and teaching. If the attention economy upsets and reconfigures economics as a provider of models explaining social interactions, it also dissolves literary studies as an autonomous field of inquiry. Interpretive attention – conceived simultaneously as a reflection on our interpretive practices and as a reflective practice of interpretation – is less specific to literary studies than to the humanities at large (including philosophy, semiology, history, the history of techniques, arts and sciences, but also anthropology, sociology and maybe even economics). Similarly, it would be highly reductive to limit the object of interpretation merely to texts (even if texts have their semiotic specificity): the reflective practice of interpretation needs to bear on the mixed bag identified as "media objects". If traditional economics needs to reconfigure itself under the emerging dominance of the attention economy, literary studies need to reconfigure themselves within the emerging field of study identified as *media archaeology*.[7]

The attention economy cannot be studied independently from the technical devices which mediate our relations to our environments. From this point of view, the economic paradigm may be an obstacle to the proper accounting of our collective attentional ecosystems. Its most basic notions (production, exchange, trade, price, profit) are toothless, inappropriate or to be reconfigured drastically to explain and measure what happens with and around human attention. More damagingly even, the fundamental tenets of methodological individualism, which continue to dominate economics, would be a terrible obstacle to a proper understanding of human attentiveness, where any attentional move is always over-determined by phenomena of "joint" (i.e. transindividual) attention: in virtually all situations, I end up paying attention to *this* rather than *that* because others (before or around me) are or have been paying attention to it. If human attention can be better understood, it will be in terms of technically mediated *collective ecosystems*. Hence this worrying conclusion for economists: there can be no satisfactory economic study of the attention economy, only an ecosystemic approach to the attention *ecology*.

The conclusion is equally demanding on literary scholars: if interpretive practices need to be rethought within the technically mediated collective ecosystems, which structure and over-determine human attention, their work needs to be redeployed on a different conceptual and historical scale – the scale provided by media archaeology. Within the broader context of an ecological approach to perception and media,[8] this enlarged scale of operation expands in three directions which disrupt the traditional boundaries of the literary field (still strongly divided into centuries and methodologies). First, media archaeology revisits past cultural mediations (usually pre-1900) to show that our most current interrogations about our newest media were already discussed and played out in very different historical contexts, giving us more critical distance towards a fascination with novelty, which blinds us to what may be actually unheard of in our new situation. Second, media archaeology uncovers unsuspected dimensions in the cultural configurations of the past, helping us gain a fuller and more vivid view of yesterday's problems reconsidered in light of today's issues. Third, media archaeology blurs the boundaries between academic research and artistic experimentation, mixing theoretical approaches geared towards the acquisition of knowledge with practical experiments relying on sensory experience to question and alter our worldviews.

In profound continuity with the conception of literary interpretation delineated earlier as a necessary counterbalance to the hegemony of media distraction, media archaeology invites us to pay attention to the long term, to practice loyalty by construing unsuspected proximities between distant periods, to focus our view on the media itself (rather than on its content), to elaborate on its effects in terms of deeper meaning (rather than superficial information), to immerse ourselves in unfamiliar territories to estrange ourselves from our immediate surroundings. Even defined along these sketchy lines, media archaeology provides literary scholars with the opportunity to join historians, film theorists, mediologists, anthropologists, artists and – why not? – economists, to devise common exercises and manoeuvers in attention ecology.

Notes

1 An important critique of the many delusions generated by this "great transformation" of our economies has been written by Méchoulan 2011.
2 For a broader view on this evolution, see Moulier-Boutang and Yann (2012).
3 For a summary attempt to view the novel as shaping our relational gestures over the last 300 years, see Citton 2013.
4 For a good synthesis on the current research by neuroscientists, see Lachaux 2011.
5 On issues of immersion, see also Citton 2014b.
6 For more development on this point, see Citton 2012, chapters 6–8.
7 For good introductions to this field, see Parikka 2012; Huhtamo and Parikka 2011; Zielinski 2006; Gitelman 2006.
8 See Strate 2006, Casey Man Kong (ed.) 2006, along with the foundational study by James Gibson (Gibson 1996).

Bibliography

Beck, J. and Davenport, T. (2001), *The Attention Economy: Understanding the New Currency of Business*, Cambridge, MA: Harvard Business School.

Beller, J. (2006), *The Cinematic Mode of Production: Attention Economy and the Society of the Spectacle*, Hanover: Dartmouth University Press.

Boullier, D. (2009), "Les industries de l'attention: fidélisation, alerte ou immersion", *Réseaux*, 154: 233–246.

Boullier, D. (2012), "Composition médiatique d'un monde commun à partir du pluralisme des régimes d'attention", in C. Pierre-André (ed.), *Conflit des interprétations dans la société de l'information*, Paris: Hermès, 41–57.

Citton, Y. (2012), *Gestes d'Humanités: Anthropologie sauvage de nos expériences esthétiques*, Paris: Armand Colin.

Citton, Y. (2013), "Reading Literature and the Political Ecology of Gestures in the Age of Semiocapitalism", *New Literary History*, 44 (2).

Citton, Y. (2014a), *Pour une écologie de l'attention*, Paris: Seuil, translated in English as *The Ecology of Attention*, Cambridge: Polity Press, 2016.

Citton, Y. (2014b), "Histoire de l'illusion immersive et archéologie des media", in A. Braito et al. (eds.), *Technologies de l'enchantement: Pour une histoire multidisciplinaire de l'illusion*, Grenoble: ELLUG.

Crary, J. (1999), *Suspensions of Perception: Attention, Spectacle and the Modern Culture*, Cambridge, MA: MIT Press, 13–14.

Franck, G. (1998), *Ökonomie der Aufmerksamkeit: Ein Entwurf*, Munich: Carl Hanser.

Franck, G. (1999), "The Economy of Attention", *Telepolis*, www.heise.de/tp/artikel/5/5567/1.html.

Gibson, J. J. (1996), *An Ecological Approach to Visual Perception*, New York: Psychology Press.

Gitelman, L. (2006), *Always Already New: Media, History, and the Data of Culture*, Cambridge, MA: MIT Press. Google Books, Ngram Viever.

Goldhaber, M. (1996), "Principles of a New Economy", www.well.com/user/mgoldh/principles.html

Huhtamo, E. and Parikka, J. (2011), *Media Archaeology: Approaches, Applications, Implications*, Berkeley, CA: University of California Press.

Lachaux, J.-P. (2011), *Le Cerveau attentif: Contrôle, maîtrise, lâcher-prise*, Paris: Odile Jacob.

Lanham, R. (2006), *The Economics of Attention: Style and Substance in the Age of Information*, Chicago: University of Chicago Press.

Lum, C. M. K. (ed.) (2006), *Perspectives on Culture, Technology and Communication: The Media Ecology Tradition*, Cresskill: Hampton Press.

Mazzarella, A. (2004), *La Potenza del falso: Illusione, favola e sogno nella modernità letteraria*, Roma: Donzelli.

Mazzarella, A. (2008), *La grande rete della scrittura: La letteratura dopo la rivoluzione digitale*, Torino: Bollati Boringhieri,

Méchoulan, É. (2011), *La crise du discours économique: Travail immatériel et émancipation*, Montréal: Éditions Nota Bene.

Moulier-Boutang, Y. (2012), *Cognitive Capitalism*, Cambridge: Polity, translated from French, *Le capitalisme cognitif*, Paris: Éditions Amsterdam, 2007.

Parikka, J. (2012), *What Is Media Archaeology?* Cambridge: Polity.

Simon, H. (1971), "Designing Organizations for an Information-Rich World", in M. Greenberger (ed.), *Computers, Communication, and the Public Interest*, Baltimore, MD: Johns Hopkins Press.

Smythe, D. W. (1977), "Communications: Blindspot of Western Marxism", *Canadian Journal of Political and Social Theory*, 1 (3): 1–27.

Strate, L. (2006), *Echoes and Reflections: On Media Ecology as a Field of Study*, New York: Hampton Press.

Toffler, A. (1970), *Future Shock*, New York: Random House.

Zielinski, S. ([2002] 2006), *Deep Time of the Media*, Cambridge, MA: MIT Press.

Index of Names

Index of Economics and Literary Terms

Printed in the United States
by Baker & Taylor Publisher Services